Changing God's Law

This volume identifies and elaborates on the significance and functions of the various actors involved in the development of family law in the Middle East. Besides the importance of family law regulations for each individual, family law has become the battleground of political and social contestation. Divided into four parts, the collection presents a general overview and analysis of the development of family law in the region and provides insights into the broader context of family law reform, before offering examples of legal development realised by codification drawn from a selection of Gulf states, Iran, and Egypt. It then goes on to present a thorough analysis of the role of the judiciary in the process of lawmaking, before discussing ways the parties themselves may have shaped and do shape the law.

Including contributions from leading authors of Middle Eastern law, this timely volume brings together many isolated aspects of legal development and offers a comprehensive picture on this topical subject. It will be of interest to scholars and academics of family law and religion.

Nadjma Yassari is a senior research fellow at the Max Planck Institute for Comparative and International Private Law in Hamburg where she heads the Department for the Laws of Islamic Countries. In April 2009, Nadjma Yassari established the Max Planck Research Group 'Changes in God's Law: An Inner Islamic Comparison of Family and Succession Laws', which she has been leading since. Her main fields of research are national and private international law of Islamic countries, in particular the Arab Middle East, Iran, Afghanistan, and Pakistan with a special focus on family and successions law.

Islamic Law in Context

Series Editor:

Javaid Rehman, Brunel University, UK

The Islamic Law in Context series addresses key contemporary issues and theoretical debates related to the Sharia and Islamic law. The series focuses on research into the theory and practice of the law, and draws attention to the ways in which the law is operational within modern State practices. The volumes in this series are written for an international academic audience and are sensitive to the diversity of contexts in which Islamic law is taught and researched across various jurisdictions as well as to the ways it is perceived and applied within general international law.

Woman's Identity and Rethinking the Hadith

Nimat Hafez Barazangi

Changing God's Law

The dynamics of Middle Eastern family law

Edited by Nadjma Yassari

Changing God's Law

The dynamics of Middle Eastern family law

Edited by Nadjma Yassari

Routledge
Taylor & Francis Group
LONDON AND NEW YORK

First published 2016
by Routledge
2 Park Square, Milton Park, Abingdon, Oxon OX14 4RN

and by Routledge
711 Third Avenue, New York, NY 10017

First issued in paperback 2018

Routledge is an imprint of the Taylor & Francis Group, an informa business

British Library Cataloguing in Publication Data
A catalogue record for this book is available from the British Library

Library of Congress Cataloging in Publication Data
Names: Yassari, Nadjma, 1971- author.
Title: Changing God's law : the dynamics of Middle Eastern family law / by Nadjma Yassari.
Description: Farnham, Surrey, UK England ; Burlington, VT, USA : Ashgate, 2016. | Series: Islamic law in context | Includes bibliographical references and index. | Description based on print version record and CIP data provided by publisher; resource not viewed.
Subjects: LCSH: Domestic relations—Middle East. | Law—Middle East—Islamic influences.
Classification: LCC KMC156 (print) | LCC KMC156 .C473 2016 (ebook) | DDC 346.5601/5—dc23
LC record available at http://lccn.loc.gov/2015043628

ISBN 13: 978-1-138-60570-1 (pbk)
ISBN 13: 978-1-472-46495-8 (hbk)

Typeset in Times New Roman
by Swales & Willis Ltd, Exeter, Devon, UK

Contents

Notes on contributors vii
Preface xi

Introduction: new family law codes in Middle Eastern countries: reforms that are faithful to Islamic tradition? 1
MARIE-CLAIRE FOBLETS

PART I
Breaks and continuities in Middle Eastern law 15

1 **Breaks and continuities in Middle Eastern law: women after the 2011 revolutions** 17
CHIBLI MALLAT

2 **Contextualizing family law reform and plural legalities in postcolonial Pakistan** 34
SHAHEEN SARDAR ALI

3 **Family law, fundamental human rights, and political transition in Tunisia** 68
MONIA BEN JÉMIA

PART II
Legislation 81

4 **Struggling for a modern family law: a Khaleeji perspective** 83
LENA-MARIA MÖLLER

5 Between procedure and substance: a review of law making in Egypt 113
NORA ALIM AND NADJMA YASSARI

6 The financial relationship between spouses under Iranian law: a never-ending story of guilt and atonement? 131
NADJMA YASSARI

PART III
Judiciary 151

7 Les pouvoirs du juge tunisien en droit de la famille 153
SALMA ABIDA

8 Divorce in Egypt: between law in the books and law in action 181
NATHALIE BERNARD-MAUGIRON

9 Personal status law in Israel: disputes between religious and secular courts 204
IMEN GALLALA-ARNDT

PART IV
Party autonomy 223

10 Marriage contracts in Islamic history 225
AMIRA SONBOL

11 Our marriage, your property? Renegotiating Islamic matrimonial property regimes 245
M. SIRAJ SAIT

Index 287

Contributors

Salma Abida served as a judge at the court of first instance in Tunis from 2001–2009. In 2009, she joined the Center of Legal and Judicial Studies where she conducts studies on the development of current legislation in force and its adaption to changing socioeconomic circumstances. In April 2015, she joined the Minister of Justice's office as an advisor to the Minister. Salma Abida's work focuses on the possibilities of transforming national law to meet relevant international standards. She is a member of different ministerial commissions for law reform, has presented at international conferences, and has published numerous articles in different legal fields.

Shaheen Sardar Ali is Professor of Law at the University of Warwick, UK and former Vice-Chair of the United Nations Working Group on Arbitrary Detention (2008–2014) as well as a former member of the International Strategic Advisory Board, Oslo University (2012–2014). She has served as Professor II, University of Oslo, Norway, Professor of Law, University of Peshawar, Pakistan, as well as Director of the Women's Study Centre at the same university. She has served as Cabinet Minister for Health, Population Welfare, and Women Development, Government of the Khyber Pukhtunkhwa (formerly North West Frontier Province of Pakistan), and Chair of Pakistan's first National Commission on the Status of Women. She served on the Prime Minister's Consultative Committee for Women (Pakistan), and the Senate National Commission of Enquiry on the Status of Women (Pakistan). Professor Ali has published extensively on human rights; in particular, women and children's rights, Islamic law and jurisprudence, international law, and gender studies.

Nora Alim is an independent researcher based in Cairo, Egypt. She is a doctoral candidate at the University of Hamburg and a former research associate at the Max Planck Institute for Comparative and International Private Law (2009–2013). She holds the Legal State Examination from Germany and a LLM. in International and Comparative Law from the American University in Cairo, Egypt. Nora Alim wrote her LLM. thesis on the future of the International Criminal Court in the Arab world. In 2009, she joined the Max Planck Research Group on Family and Succession Law in Islamic Countries. Her PhD dissertation discusses informal marriages in Egypt, Tunisia, and Jordan and examines the question of how state law is to respond when individuals decide to establish family law relationships outside the formal state framework. Currently, Nora Alim is working as a legal consultant on the project 'Supporting women as economic actors during the transition period', launched in 2013 by the MENA-OECD Investment Programme. The project examines to what extent legal frameworks may negatively impact women's involvement in the economy in Algeria, Egypt, Jordan, Libya, Morocco, and Tunisia.

Monia Ben Jémia is Professor of Law at University of Carthage, Tunis. She holds a PhD from the University of Tunisia and wrote her thesis on public policy and family international private law relationships. She teaches law at the Faculty of Legal Sciences in Tunis, especially private international law, intellectual property law, and criminal law. She also served as a visiting professor and has taught at numerous universities such as Aix-en-Provence, Sorbonne/Paris, and Lyon. Professor Ben Jémia has published on personal status law in Tunisia, gender violence, and immigration issues. Her recent research is focusing on the impact of the so-called Arab Spring on women's rights.

Nathalie Bernard-Maugiron is a senior researcher at the French Institute of Research for Development (IRD) in Paris. She holds a PhD in Public Law from Paris University and wrote her thesis on the Egyptian Supreme Constitutional Court and the protection of human rights (published in 2003). Dr. Bernard-Maugiron works on personal status law, the judiciary, and the transition processes in Egypt and in the Arab World. She was a part-time faculty member at the Political Science Department of the American University in Cairo from 2001 to 2005 where she taught Egyptian constitutional law and human rights courses. She was co-director of the Institut d'études de l'Islam et des sociétés du monde musulman (IISMM) at the École des hautes études en sciences sociales (EHESS) in Paris from 2010 to 2014. Since 2009, she has taught a seminar on Contemporary Law in the Arab world at IISMM/EHESS.

Marie-Claire Foblets is Director at the Max Planck Institute for Social Anthropology. She was trained in law at the universities of Antwerp (1977–1979) and Leuven (1979–1982) in Belgium and received an education in Thomist philosophy. For a decade, she practised law with a law firm that specialized in matters affecting migration and minority issues while simultaneously receiving her PhD in social and cultural anthropology. For more than 20 years Professor Foblets has taught social and cultural anthropology at the universities of Antwerp and Brussels. Before joining the Max Planck Society in March 2012, she was Ordinary Professor at the Catholic University of Leuven, where she headed the Institute for Migration Law and Legal Anthropology. She is a member of various networks of researchers, focusing either on the study of the application of Islamic law in Europe, or on law and migration in Europe, including the Association Française d'Anthropologie du droit, for which she served as co-president for several years. In 2012, Professor Foblets accepted a position with the Max Planck Society, where she established a new Department of 'Law & Anthropology' at the Max Planck Institute for Social Anthropology in Halle a.d. Saale (Sachsen-Anhalt).

Imen Gallala-Arndt is a senior research fellow at the Max Planck Institute for Comparative and International Private Law. She holds a DEA in Public Law from the University of Tunis Carthage as well as an LLM and PhD in Law from the University of Heidelberg. After having worked for the peace process projects at the Max Planck Institute for Comparative and International Public Law in Heidelberg, Imen Gallala-Arndt joined the Max Planck Institute in Hamburg in 2006. Since April 2009, she has been a member of the Max Planck Research Group on Family and Succession Law in Islamic Countries. In this framework, she is currently writing a post-doctoral monograph on interfaith marriages in Tunisia, Lebanon, and Israel. Imen Gallala-Arndt has published on various legal issues relating to Islamic countries, especially constitutional law as well as comparative and international family law.

Chibli Mallat is Presidential Professor of Middle Eastern Law and Politics, University of Utah and EU Jean Monnet Professor of European Law, Saint Joseph's University, Lebanon. He has held research and teaching positions at Princeton, Yale, Harvard, the School of Oriental and African Studies, the École des hautes études en sciences sociales, and the Islamic University of Lebanon. Amongst his publications are *The Renewal of Islamic Law* (1993), *Introduction to Middle Eastern Law* (2007), and *Philosophy of Nonviolence: Revolution, Constitutionalism and Justice beyond the Middle East* (2015).

Lena-Maria Möller is a senior research fellow at the Max Planck Institute for Comparative and International Private Law. She holds an MA in Middle East Studies and a PhD in Law. Her recently published doctoral dissertation examines the processes of family law codification in Bahrain, Qatar, and the UAE, their outcomes as well as the judicial application of the new family codes (*Die Golfstaaten auf dem Weg zu einem modernen Recht für die Familie?*, published 2015). Lena-Maria Möller's research and teaching experience is in Muslim family law as well as in comparative and private international law and she has held teaching positions at the University of Hamburg and the University of Augsburg. Currently, Lena-Maria Möller is preparing a post-doctoral research project which explores how contemporary Muslim jurisdictions engage with and frame vague and still undefined legal concepts.

M. Siraj Sait is Professor of Law and Finance at the University of East London and Director of the Centre of Islamic Finance, Law and Communities (CIFLAC). He is a graduate of the Universities of Madras, Harvard, and London and formerly worked with the United Nations and the Government of Tamil Nadu, India as a public prosecutor. He has headed the UN Iraq Evaluation Commission and chaired the Benadir Somalia legal drafting committee, and is a member of the UN Advisory Group on Gender Issues. Sait's publications on gender, development, and Islamic law were ranked highly for research in the UK Research Excellence Framework 2014.

Amira Sonbol is Professor of Islamic History, Law, and Society at Georgetown University, Qatar. Amira Sonbol specializes in the history of modern Egypt, Islamic history and law, women, gender, and Islam and is the author of several books including *The New Mamluks: Egyptian Society and Modern Feudalism*; *Women, the Family and Divorce Laws in Islamic History*; *The Creation of a Medical Profession in Egypt: 1800–1922*; *The Memoirs of Abbas Hilmi II: Sovereign of Egypt*; *Women of the Jordan: Islam, Labor and Law*; and *Beyond the Exotic: Muslim Women's Histories*. Professor Sonbol is Editor-in-Chief of HAWWA – *Journal of Women of the Middle East and the Islamic World* – and Co-Editor of *Islam and Christian-Muslim Relations*. She teaches courses on the history of modern Egypt, women and law, and Islamic civilization.

Nadjma Yassari is a senior research fellow at the Max Planck Institute for Comparative and International Private Law in Hamburg where she heads the Department for the Laws of Islamic Countries. In April 2009, Nadjma Yassari established the Max-Planck Research Group 'Changes in God's Law – An Inner Islamic Comparison of Family and Succession Laws' which she has been leading since. Her main fields of research are national and private international law of Islamic countries, in particular the Arab Middle East, Iran, Afghanistan, and Pakistan with a special focus on family and successions law. In her recently released monograph *Die Brautgabe im Familienvermögensrecht – Innerislamischer Rechtsvergleich und Integration in das deutsche Recht* (2014), she considers the function of the dower within the marital property law regimes of pre-modern Islamic law, contemporary Muslim jurisdictions, and German law. Nadjma Yassari studied law in Vienna, Paris, and London. She holds an LLM degree from the University of London, School of Oriental and African Studies and an LLD from the University of Innsbruck.

Preface

This volume is the outcome of the three-day international conference 'The Dynamics of Legal Development in Islamic Countries – Family and Succession Law', held on 17–19 October 2013 at the Max Planck Institute for Comparative and International Private Law in Hamburg, Germany. The conference marked the completion of the first project phase of the Max Planck Research Group 'Changes in God's Law – An Inner Islamic Comparison of Family and Succession Law', which was established in 2009 and has since promoted an in-depth interdisciplinary and comparative analysis of family law regimes in the Muslim Middle East and North Africa.

The Max Planck Institute for Comparative and International Private Law is one of 80 research institutes of the Max Planck Society for the Advancement of Science. The Institute is dedicated to performing foundational research and promoting the transfer of knowledge in the fields of comparative and international private law and business law. By analysing similarities and differences in the legal regimes of Europe as well as other parts of the world, we study the interaction of private rule making, national legal systems, supranational law, and interstate treaties. Our research also serves to lay the groundwork for an international understanding of law and to help develop rules and legal instruments with which the application of national law can be better coordinated in cross-border matters.

The Max Planck Research Group 'Changes in God's Law' was established with the mandate to research and analyse contemporary family and succession laws in Muslim jurisdictions. Its research paradigm is built on three pillars: first, an interdisciplinary approach and a consideration of the law in practice; second, a comparative examination of the law within the Islamic world; and, third, an assessment of the influence procedural rules have on the shaping of the law.

Against this background, the overarching goal of the October 2013 conference was to identify and further elaborate on the significance and functions of the different actors involved in the development of family law in Muslim jurisdictions. Our event saw 70 scholars and practitioners from 20 countries travel to the Institute to explore both the various approaches to legal developments in family and succession law in Islamic countries and the actors who influence this process. The dynamics of this process were, in part, examined via country reports presented on selected Islamic countries. Serving to complement this perspective, three parallel workshops took an in-depth look at the primary actors involved in these developments: law makers, private individuals (through their expressions of party autonomy), and the judiciary. Each workshop began with a short set of introductory remarks, which served to prompt the subsequent roundtable discussion. This format promoted an exchange of ideas and experiences between the conference speakers and the participants hailing from both practice and academia.

The workshop on legislation illuminated, among other topics, legislative goals, the law-making process, the reform of law through codification, the actors influencing the formulation of new laws, and the various associated problems which emerge. The workshop on the shaping of law by means of party autonomy primarily considered the degree to which spouses could abrogate dispositive marital law through marital agreements and thus reach tailored contractual agreements. The legal aspects to be covered by such contracts include rights in respect of property, marital assets, and divorce agreements. Finally, the workshop on the judiciary provided insight into the current efforts of family law judges. Matters of particular focus included judicial training, judicial discretion in the interpretation of indefinite legal terms, and the difficulties posed by the latter task.

This volume comprises selected contributions presented at the conference, which have been revised and updated to accommodate the recent legal and political developments, as well as additional articles by experts in the field of Muslim family law. It is hoped that this volume will enrich and foster the current scholarly discourse on Middle Eastern law by not only discussing the substance of the law, but by looking back at why, how, and by whom the law has been shaped. The vast diversity of legal interpretations that can be found in contemporary Muslim jurisdictions – all claiming for themselves to enact and apply what is believed to be a divine set of rules – illustrates the changing and dynamic nature of Muslim family law. By looking at the very actors changing the law, the contributions to this volume, despite their historically and regionally diverse focuses, all demonstrate the degree of human agency that shapes God's law.

Nadjma Yassari

Introduction

New family law codes in Middle Eastern countries: reforms that are faithful to Islamic tradition?

Marie-Claire Foblets

Introduction

The originality of this volume lies in the richness of the perspectives presented on the vast and highly dynamic topic of the way in which Islamic countries seek to align their family law with the new realities of male-female and parent-child relationships. No fewer than ten countries are analysed in detail with a view to understanding not only the complexity but also the many pitfalls faced by such research: Iran (Nadjma Yassari), Qatar, the United Arab Emirates, and Bahrain (Lena-Maria Möller), Tunisia (Monia Ben Jémia; Salma Abida), Pakistan (Shaheen Sardar Ali), Jordan (Amira Sonbol), Egypt (Amira Sonbol; Nathalie Bernard-Maugiron; Nora Alim and Nadjma Yassari; Chibli Mallat), Israel (Imen Gallala-Arndt) and, albeit without being the subject of a separate report, Morocco (M. Siraj Sait). Most of the contributions focus on the study of Islamic law in particular; an exception is the chapter on Israel, for example, which looks at the Jewish faith and its specific legal system (*Halakha*). The volume's main subject is, however, the developments in Islamic family law in the Middle East. This brief introduction will thus also refer principally to this aspect.

One characteristic shared by all the contributions to this volume and which, to my mind, makes this collection particularly valuable, is that the authors do not simply offer an interpretation of the legislative texts and the case law and departs from them, but also include the wider context in their analyses – both historical (often linked directly or indirectly to the colonial legacy) and contemporary – which serve as the backdrop to the astonishingly rapid changes which family law has undergone in recent years in the countries of the Middle East. That context helps us better understand the current legal developments in those countries, which are both profoundly revolutionary and yet relatively stable. Stable in the sense that, unlike other areas of law in Middle Eastern countries that have seen many foreign borrowings (such as contract law and criminal law), Islamic family law, on the whole, has remained relatively free of the phenomenon known in the literature as 'legal transplants'. This is true in spite of several decades of Western colonization. But it is also true that, more recently, the legislatures of several Middle Eastern countries have opted for an impressive series of legislative reforms – some of which certainly deserve to be called 'revolutionary' – introduced in order to adapt family law in Islamic countries to new social realities. They do so in more or less radical fashion.

Back in the early 1990s, a comparative study, published by Bernard Botiveau, assessed the risks of a legislative shift in the area of family law in various countries in the Arab world. He wrote in a highly nuanced way, in this regard: 'The "right to speak the law" includes not only the capacity to establish a norm and to get people to accept it as binding. It also includes the capacity to offer an interpretation that is not to be called into question.'[1] Many contributions to this volume reveal, by means of concrete illustrations, how relevant this observation remains, showing that the effective application of the reforms introduced by the state institutions of the countries studied here is no easy task and does not necessarily produce the desired effects.

It is not my intention to go into detail here of the various illustrations provided in this rich collective volume. By way of introduction, I wish to shed light on the (principal) social challenges that underlie each contribution, by offering two perspectives that may be particularly helpful to an English-speaking audience, which is less familiar with the subject. A first perspective is one that emerges from several contributions to this volume, namely, that what we are seeing in several countries of the Middle East is something that can be called a new family law. The latter certainly continues to be based on the classical *fiqh*, but that *fiqh* is one that has been amended both by various legislative acts and by case law.

A second perspective has to do with the role assigned to the judicial authorities and to judges in particular. A theme that runs through the entire volume – illustrated in each case within the context of one particular society, sometimes crossing the borders of several countries as in the analysis offered by Siraj Sait – is the way the courts have, on some occasions, been taking a conservative position, that is, drawing on traditional sources, while on other occasions adopting a more liberal approach, which takes greater account of fundamental rights as enshrined in certain international conventions. Salma Abida, who has been following developments in Tunisian case law since 1956 in the area of personal status, concluded: 'The judges' oscillation between tradition and modernity ultimately reflects a more general oscillation, that of Tunisian society between the traditional model of the patriarchal family and the liberal model of the family based on the principles of equality and liberty.' The same applies to the nine Muslim countries studied in this volume, even though it is true that the change is not as marked everywhere as in Tunisia, where Abida has observed an about-face taking place since the end of the 1980s.

These two perspectives are respectively the focus of the first and the second parts of this brief introduction. Being personally more familiar with the legislative policy of Morocco, and since there is no separate study devoted to that country in this volume, I have taken the liberty of illustrating my comments from time to time with examples of Moroccan domestic law seeking to achieve that fine balance between a reform of family law that is suited to life in a modern, dynamic society and the requirement that it remain sufficiently firmly rooted in its own religious normativity ('le référentiel religieux).

Codification of family law in Middle Eastern countries: a wave of recent legislative reforms

In what follows, I pay particular attention – albeit very succinctly – to some major legislative reforms discussed in this volume, with a focus on their impact (real or potential) on the lives of families when it comes to balancing (at best) the rights and obligations of each household member, while bearing in mind the specific circumstances and individual needs in each situation. At the risk of oversimplifying some of the findings presented here, the contributions point to several realities – in comparative law one may speak of characteristics – that are more or less common to the ten countries studied.

Family relations in all ten countries are currently governed by family codes, some of them having been recently amended. Amendments usually give rise to a number of criticisms, both before and since they entered into force. In nine of the ten cases under scrutiny here,[2] the rules that apply in the field of family law – whether recently amended or not – have the same source: Islamic legal doctrine, known as *fiqh*. The main differences between the old and the new legal texts, as far as the amended texts are concerned, lie primarily in the form, as well as in some more detailed substantive rules; however, the latter do not in themselves constitute an exception to the fundamental principles of Islamic law. Some (new) codes, like the new *Mudawwana* in Morocco, also contain a number of provisions that are addressed more particularly to nationals residing abroad or engaged in mixed marriages and that seek to regulate a number of specific aspects of their family life. These provisions reveal a particular type of legal arrangement of family life at the international level that draws as much on private international law as on the domestic legal system.

From the outset, it is probably fair to say that – except perhaps for some provisions of the 1956 Tunisian Family Code – the legislation in even the newest Codes – the ones in Qatar, the United Arab Emirates, and Bahrain - does *not* break with the traditions of Muslim family law. In all countries under investigation, the majority of the rules are inspired by one of the main rites (also called schools) in Islam, a few being the outcome of comparison among them. Where written law is silent or insufficiently specific, the legislatures call upon judges to turn to the rite most commonly practised in their country and to *ijtihad* (the effort of jurisprudence) to find a solution.

This does not mean, however, that the new Codes are devoid of any element of substantial reform. Most legislative reforms that were introduced during the period under scrutiny concern the position of women and children. They express the desire on the part of the legislatures to improve women's position within the framework of the family by placing them on an equal footing with men as regards both marriage and its dissolution, as well as in their relationships with their children. This is new.[3] The same can be said of the protection of the child, who is the subject of several provisions in various Codes. Some provisions on child protection are now formulated in identical terms to those of the International Convention on the Rights of the Child. 'The Family Code is, in our view, a piece of legislation intended to protect the weakest members of society (women, in this case) and to guarantee the rights of children', wrote the authors of the first annual report on the implementation of the amended Moroccan Family Code (2004). 'Therefore, the Code's objective is to safeguard the family against all forms of injustice and discrimination. To this end, the Moroccan legislatures have reinforced the Code with several provisions and mechanisms. In comparison with the previous situation, the new Code constitutes a qualitative advance in family matters, making it possible to promote women's rights and their social status by reducing the social inequalities that continue to exist.'[4]

On the whole, however, it may be said that in countries that have amended their family law code(s), there is continuity between the new laws adopted and the former ones, as the new codes continue to draw inspiration from the same sources. Middle Eastern family law, which is the title chosen for this volume, remains clearly in line with religious – here Islamic – tradition governing that area of the law, notwithstanding numerous legislative amendments and, at times, surprisingly liberal positions taken by judges in individual disputes. There's no lack of evidence to this effect.

First, it may even be said that in some instances, codification elevates the principles of Islam into mandatory rules, whether as regards marriage and its dissolution, descent, legal capacity, or wills and successions. In some countries, such as Morocco or Iran, the law mandates the intervention of the Public Prosecutor's Office in all these matters.

Second, there is the legal terminology that the legislatures in various countries have opted to use. The terms used in the legislation are most often the same as those found in the well-known books of the majority doctrine that applies in that country.

Third, as I will explain below, in most countries the Code requires judges to follow the lead of the Islamic rite (or school) whenever there is no written legal rule available, or if the latter is incomplete or imprecise. Such a provision confirms, in a sense, the prohibition against judges relying on sources other than Islamic ones in the area of family relations. Yet, as we know, classical Islamic law has its own distinctive conception of the status of women and children within the family, which is not the same as the one that currently prevails in a growing number of modern Western legal systems around the world: in the former, the husband is the sole head of the family and it is he alone who has the privilege of dissolving or preserving the marriage bond; the wife is not the legal guardian of her children, even if she has custody – which in certain cases can be taken away from her. Similarly, a child born out of wedlock does not enjoy the same legal protection as a legitimate child, and descent from the father generally exists only within the framework of marriage.

As a result, the following question arises: did the legislatures who drafted the new Codes that now apply in the various countries studied here follow a different path from the one delineated by classical Islam? In order to appreciate the importance of the various reforms under scrutiny, one must review in greater depth the changes that have been made, particularly with regard to the status of women and of children.

In what follows, I review briefly the main legal amendments made in several Middle Eastern countries, distinguishing between provisions that primarily affect women and those that regulate the position of minors.

Reforms concerning the status of women

The principal subjects of the new provisions adopted in the countries that have amended their legislation and that concern women are marriage and its dissolution. The rules regarding inheritance have not undergone any substantial change and are therefore addressed only cursorily in the contributions. I will therefore not address them here.

Marriage

Some legislatures have begun to place women and men on an equal footing as regards the age of nubility, requiring that both sexes have reached a minimum age of 18. This is the case for example in Morocco (Art 19), or in Tunisia (Art 5). Women who have reached the age of majority are now authorized in some countries to marry without the intermediary of a marriage tutor.[5] By contrast, all countries have retained the prohibition against a Muslim woman marrying a non-Muslim man. Similarly, in most countries a woman will not be permitted to marry a foreigner, even if he is Muslim, without prior authorization by a State representative. Except for the Tunisian Family Code, new legislation has not abolished polygamy; rather, some countries subject it to prior court authorization (usually by a judge) in order to safeguard the rights of the first wife and her children, if any, and to permit a wife who does not accept bigamy to petition for divorce, Egyptian law being one example of this last rule. The court can, if necessary, order her husband to divorce her should she be unwilling to be the spouse of a polygamous man. As regards the Islamic matrimonial property regimes and their (re)negotiation, Siraj Sait's very detailed comparative analysis shows that in most Middle Eastern countries the principle of separate estates continues to prevail, even if some legislatures – including those of Tunisia, Algeria, and Morocco – have started allowing spouses to agree on joint management of assets acquired during the marriage.[6] In practice however, it appears that women are unable to take advantage of their marriage to negotiate their property rights. Remarkably, in Indonesian law the statutory regime is that of the community of property. There, as opposed to all other Muslim jurisdictions, property acquired during the marriage becomes the joint property of the spouses.

In several countries the provisions concerning marriage now mean that the family of Muslim spouses will henceforth be headed by both spouses and that the spouses have to work together in taking decisions concerning the management of family affairs. Nevertheless, the husband remains the legal guardian of the children, as was the case under the former regimes, while the wife is their legal guardian only if the husband has died or has been determined to lack the necessary legal capacity. On the other hand, if the marriage is dissolved, custody of the child is ever more frequently awarded first to the mother. However, a mother who remarries loses her right to custody; in some countries she loses it immediately, whereas in others she keeps it provisionally but will lose it once the child has reached a certain age[7] or if she remarries.[8] A divorced non-Muslim mother also loses custody of her child.[9] A mother who has custody can be forbidden to travel with the child outside the country without prior authorization by the legal guardian.[10]

The dissolution of marriage

Traditionally, in Islamic family law, there are several ways of dissolving a marriage. Some newly amended Codes add a few further ones not available under the former regimes.

The form of marriage dissolution that is the object of the most vivid debates, not just within Islam but also among women's rights scholars and spokespersons worldwide, is the form known as *talaq*, i.e. the unilateral repudiation of the wife by the husband without cause. The Moroccan legislature decided in 2004 to *retain* this mode of dissolving a marriage, but has clearly specified that the exercise of this right is henceforth dependent on obtaining a court authorization (the French translation reads: 'divorce sous contrôle judiciaire' which means divorce by court authority), in order to allow the wife to be heard and to guarantee her rights as well as those of the couple's children (Art 79 and following).[11] The court gives authorization to draw up a *talaq* only if the husband has submitted a sum of money to the Court Clerk's office, the amount of which is determined by the court and is intended to cover the rights of the spouse.[12] In the case of a revocable *talaq*, the husband may take back his wife only with her express consent (Art 124).[13] A woman does not have a comparable right to end a marriage by her sole will, except in cases of a *talaq* by mutual consent,[14] a *tamlik*,[15] or a *khul*ᶜ.[16] But even in such cases, it is the will of the man that is taken into consideration in the first instance. The only country that has equalized divorce between man and wife is Tunisia, where the legislature has extended the right to *talaq* to the wife.

The situation for the wife is more advantageous in cases where the legislation allows for divorce on grounds of irrevocable breakdown. Some legislatures have indeed started authorizing a woman who wishes to end the marriage to file a petition for divorce on grounds of *shiqaq*, or irrevocable breakdown. The court is *obliged* in such cases to grant and issue the divorce, 'taking into account each spouse's responsibility for the cause of the separation when considering measures it will order the responsible party to take in favour of the other spouse'.[17] In practice, however, whether divorce on grounds of irrevocable breakdown makes the dissolution of the marriage more easily accessible to women depends to a great – if not decisive – extent on the judge's approach. Some judges consider this form of divorce to be a variant of divorce for fault, in which case the court keeps its discretionary power to evaluate the admissibility of the petition and to set an amount as compensation for the damages suffered by the husband.

From this perspective, the wife is considered responsible for the break-up of the marriage. According to this interpretation, *shiqaq* comes close to a legal separation with compensation whenever the wife fails to convince the court of the sincerity of her request.

Reforms concerning the status of the child

Since the mid-1990s, most legislatures in Middle Eastern countries have also started taking into consideration the protection of children as defined in human rights treaties, something that previous legislatures had largely ignored. The new Codes are now more explicit on the rights of minors and the obligations of parents vis-à-vis their offspring. This is particularly visible by the adoption of the principle of the best interest of the child by most countries, either as a rule in custody law or in child law generally. However, on certain matters relating to children, legislation retains the more traditional vision and still grants priority to the father, in particular as regards legal representation and guardianship (*wilayah*). The status of children is not, however, the central topic of the analyses brought together in this volume, it is a subject that would deserve more detailed study as well.[18]

In matters of paternity, for example, traditional Islamic law recognizes only legitimate descent, i.e. the child must be conceived within marriage. Establishing natural (out of wedlock) paternity is generally prohibited, even though legal devices have been conceived to overcome doubt on the existence or the validity of a marriage, such as the theory of the sleeping embryo (*rāqid*) or the acknowledgement of filiation (*iqrār*). Also, the topic of adoption is a difficult one, as traditional Islamic doctrine prohibits adoption (*tabannī*).[19]

However, the most recent Tunisian case law, as Monia Ben Jémia's contribution explains, as well as the new Moroccan Family Code, now allows for a broad understanding of marriage when it comes to determining the legitimacy of paternity. This enlarged notion allows the inclusion, in addition to a valid marriage,[20] of certain categories of marriage that have been declared null, vitiated marriage, and betrothal (in the latter case provided that the conditions established by the Code have been fulfilled). In 2004 the Tunisian legislature went so far as to admit illegitimate relationships, albeit on a temporary basis only, provided, however, that these are subsequently legitimated by a judgement recognizing the marriage (Art 156 & Art 16). The legal action had to be launched within five years of the entry into force of the Code. The Code also relied on traditional Islamic law to allow for the acknowledgement of descent in cases of sexual relations said to have been entered into in error; it provides, so to speak, for the benefit of the doubt (*shubha*), and, finally, it also permits the recognition of paternity (*iqrār*). These rules also apply in Iran, in Egypt, and in the Gulf states. Finally, in the case of Judaism as well, as we see in Imen Gallala-Arndt's contribution, there is a status of 'reputed spouses', a term used to designate two persons cohabiting as husband and wife without being formally married. She mentions that the Supreme Court has significantly extended the rights of such spouses: they now have not only maintenance and succession rights, but also child adoption rights.

Traditionally in Islam the (legitimate) paternity of a child could not be challenged except on the basis of an oath of anathema (*li'an*). The Moroccan legislatures accept that paternity can henceforth be challenged also by means of expert witnesses commissioned by the court (Art 153).[21] This innovation in a Code that draws inspiration from Islamic law may be surprising: the testimony of experts commissioned by the court may in fact prove to be contrary to the interests of a child, insofar as it makes it possible to challenge the legitimacy of a child at any time, whereas in classical Islamic law the challenge to paternity by an oath of anathema is very difficult. These brief reflections on the rights of children are intended to complete the picture of the principal reforms introduced in recent years into Islamic family law in Middle Eastern countries.

What the contributions brought together in this volume show is that the various reforms that over the years have been put into place both by legislatures and by the judiciary in the countries studied should not be underestimated. What is also evidenced through a number of carefully selected illustrations of reforms presented in these contributions is that the reforms, across national borders, have remained faithful to the religious tradition(s) in which they are rooted, the case of Iran being a very striking one, as shown by Nadjma Yassari's contribution on the financial relationship of the spouse. It is precisely because of this fidelity that one sees certain problems of incompatibility between Middle Eastern family law systems and the requirements of international human rights treaties. Given the latter's characteristic standards of measurement – in particular their various non-discrimination clauses in combination with the protection of the principle of individual autonomy – such problems will, to some extent, continue to arise. And as Imen Gallala-Arndt's contribution shows, the observation applies not only to Islamic family law. The gap that separates a religiously based, prescriptive grammar of family relations and the setting of a standard grounded in (secular) human rights will continue to lead to clashes of views, not just among legal scholars but also in the daily search for justice in individual cases. The result is that some families will continue to be 'caught' in so-called limping situations: their situation is granted recognition in Islamic family law but rejected under human rights criteria of protection (mainly of women and children). There are two possible attitudes in the face of this situation. Either one sees these problems of incompatibility as inevitable ones that cannot be overcome, since God's laws cannot be changed. 'The religious order extracts its legitimacy from God and his law', writes Imen Gallala-Arndt. Or one seeks alternatives that make it possible to resolve these incompatibilities. The contributions included in this volume offer illustrations of legislative measures as well as of legal reasoning contained in court decisions or in publications by creative legal scholars, who devise solutions suited to the lives of believers who do not wish to feel torn between their loyalty to their faith and the needs of daily life. Such scholars welcome more pragmatic veins of thinking that are in line with their religious law but still leave room for individual agency. The use of contractual clauses in the Islamic legal tradition, so well illustrated in Siraj Sait's paper, offers one such alternative: it permits parties to accommodate their situation *within* Islamic law. Contractual clauses and their negotiation – conditioned there as balance of power among the protagonists – make it possible, to a certain extent, to overcome incompatibilities between the requirements of Islamic law and the search for suitable solutions, including in the management of family relations.

The role of judges: between religion and positive law

The choice between these two alternatives is not, however, left entirely to the discretion of the parties involved. One must take into account one of the distinctive features of Islamic law which, in the area of family law in particular, does not make it possible to predict precisely what direction legal reasoning will take in a given case. This feature is the very wide discretionary competence that the majority of countries studied here give to judges who deal with conflicts between spouses and with regard to their children. I have already made reference to this above.

This competence must be understood in its own particular context, that which judges in contemporary Middle Eastern societies face: on the one hand, the imposition of a positivist legal model (the Family Code) and, on the other, the challenge of thinking in a new way about a law that is religiously inspired (Islamic law). The task of a judge in these societies is therefore very distinctive, and must be understood from that particular angle if we are to avoid hasty judgements that would most likely be severely criticized.

Seen from an outsider's perspective, judges in Middle Eastern countries that are competent for settling disputes in family affairs enjoy extensive power to apply the rules in those areas. Their intervention may take a variety of forms. Courts have a competence that is mostly judicial in nature, but it may also be administrative (for example, when tasked with presiding at a marriage, the judge performs a role that is purely administrative, and the same is true for the judge-notary) or discretionary; against some judgements, appeal may not be available (for example, when authorizing repudiation or polygamy, or when designating the sum of money to cover the rights of the wife and child that the husband must deposit with the court before the repudiation is registered).[22] In practice, however, the fact that a judge in any given Middle Eastern country combines multiple functions does not in any way mean that his work is random or arbitrary. The importance of his responsibility resides precisely in his wide-ranging power to decide specific cases in strict compliance with rules that have been laid down in a Code, that is, in a positivist manner, and to dispense justice in a way that, ultimately, draws its inspiration primarily from the divine law.

Jurisprudence in Middle Eastern countries in the area of family law must be understood against the backdrop of this huge responsibility on the part of the judge, which is very different from the task entrusted to a judge in a secular legal context. As well, the risks of misunderstanding are real. Translated into terms that are more easily understandable to an outsider, one could compare the responsibility of judges in applying the reforms in family law with the notion of a hierarchy of norms. The judge is bound by the rules of the Code that applies in his country, but this Code leaves space for interpretation and gives him broad discretionary powers, precisely with a view to allowing him to align his decision with the requirements of Islamic law. One particular question in this regard concerns situations where the Code is silent or incomplete. Is the judge free to choose the norm to apply in these areas? In such a situation, a judge trained in a secular legal system would probably refer directly to the treaties and conventions on human rights that bind his country in order to find a solution that is in line with the principles of justice, equality and equity. But for a judge in a Middle Eastern country, the mandate is different. His decision in such a case should abide by the requirements of Islam and Islamic law, even if those happen to be in contradiction with the principle of equality of the sexes and discriminate between persons on grounds of their sex, religion or descent. Reconciling the two is not always possible.

One ought to understand that judges in the countries under scrutiny carry out their function within a social and cultural environment that is permeated by religion. The guarantees of the exercise of the judicial profession, in the sense that jurists understand these in secular legal systems, are interpreted differently. One should not, therefore, expect a judge to enforce a rule taken from outside the rite that applies in his country when it comes to family matters, unless he is an 'innovator', as Salma Abida qualifies the position taken by judges in Tunisia since 2000 ('Le mouvement innovateur au niveau des juges du fond a basculé le conservatisme du juge de droit'). In her view, the Tunisian Constitution gives support to judges who take a more liberal position, her main argument being that the text of the Constitution clearly distinguishes between the protection of civil rights and the freedom of religion and belief (Art 5 and 18 of the Tunisian Constitution). From a secular (non-Muslim) perspective this sounds self-evident, but it is not. As already mentioned above, in most Middle Eastern family law systems there is a clause in the Family Code or elsewhere according to which any case that cannot be resolved by a strict application of the Code must be judged by reference to the Islamic rite and the effort of jurisprudence (*ijtihad*),[23] which strive to fulfil and enhance Islamic values, notably justice, equality, and amicable social relations. In other words, legislatures do not claim that the Codes cover the entire civil law of persons; they contain a number of provisions, a few of which are indeed quite detailed, but on many points they leave it to the judges to specify the scope with reference to traditional Islamic law. Let there be no mistake, although the new Codes are, *in their extensive scope*, related to 'western' codes, this does not mean that traditional law has been abolished. It remains in force, in particular in the interstices of the law: the latter have to be filled in by reference to the rite and jurisprudence, taking into consideration the precepts of Islam.

The legislatures in a number of the countries studied in this volume were careful to reformulate Islamic law on certain points, in view of making it more responsive to the need of families in the context of a contemporary society, but they did not intend to declare it to be inapplicable. As a general rule, judges base their decisions on the provisions of the Code and on the jurisprudence of the country's Supreme Court. But there is nothing to prevent a judge from also justifying his decision either by reference to a general principle of the Sharia, or to a provision accepted by the rite that applies in his country. In so doing, he confirms the current application of a rule by invoking a whole range of precedents accumulated over a longstanding tradition, which enjoy consensus within the rite that applies in his country or indeed in one of the schools of Islamic law. It is therefore perfectly conceivable that in certain cases, a judge may combine in a single decree or judgement several different available Islamic sources: the Quran, *sunna*, the consensus of the *ulama*, the jurisprudence of ancient Islamic courts, and positive law. This has been a constant principle of the *fiqh*, which was upheld by the legislatures in the domestic legal order.

One way to explicate the position taken by the vast majority of national legislatures in Middle Eastern countries is the concern that prevailed at the moment they adopted the reforms to their family law code: they were very much concerned to introduce changes that would have a positive impact for families as well as for their individual members (spouses, parents, and children), but they also assessed the risks of an upheaval against excessive reformism. From this perspective, both the broad discretionary power of the judge and the insertion into the Code of a clause that enables the court to prioritize religious norms over positive law, whenever deemed necessary, serve to guarantee a certain degree of continuity. In light of this compromise, one can better understand why certain judicial decisions taken by judges in the countries under study, even recent ones, fail to respect international conventions, on the grounds that they are contrary to the rules of Islamic law.

Conclusion

It is difficult to predict how the case law in the countries studied in this volume will further develop in the years to come: in an ever more lenient, liberal direction or, on the contrary, towards an increasing concern by judges to remain in alignment with traditional interpretations of the Sharia. Both developments are perfectly conceivable and they do not exclude one another. The first hypothesis is more confident in the potential of legislative reforms, from a positivistic standpoint, to ensure over the medium term the most appropriate application possible of the new rules, in a way that is also respectful of the requirements of Islamic law. Judges who adopt the latter position are more keen to limit the application of legislative reforms whenever, in their view, these reforms are not sufficiently respectful of the Islamic conceptions of justice and equity. This limitation is linked to an attitude on the part of the judges that reflects a distrust of the content of reforms that are presumed to be inspired by foreign law, and of the way they are interpreted.

There is no quick path to dispelling this distrust. One possible way is to ensure that reforms provide for solutions that are perceived by the majority of those to whom they apply as faithful and sustainable interpretations of Islam, while at the same time adequately addressing their most urgent needs. All that is more easily said than done.

What volumes like this are not meant to do is to show the way forward; their potential contribution is of a different nature. All in all, there is surprisingly little reliable and accessible information published in English to date that allows for comparison, both between recently developed national legislative policies in Middle Eastern in the field of family affairs and between developments in the jurisprudence in these areas. Here is a volume that can help fill the gap. This is all the more useful given the numerous misunderstandings outside Muslim countries about Islamic family law and its capacity to develop solutions that are adapted to the new societal conditions within which families live today. The information contained in the contributions brought together in this book will aid a non-Muslim audience to gain a clearer overview of recent legislative reforms in the domain of the family in Middle Eastern countries and, by the same token, to contextualize the reasoning contained in some judicial decisions, including more recent ones. To properly understand both the reforms and their application, one needs to understand the extent to which the Codes are in fact innovative and how judges are applying them. This is the only way to see *in concreto* the solutions provided by courts in Middle Eastern countries and their jurisprudence, as well as the sometimes significant disparities between the different jurisdictions. This requires taking into consideration the cultural and religious *ambiente* of each of the ten societies under study, while also recognizing the possibilities that these offer.

Notes

1 Bernard Botiveau, *Loi islamique et droit dans les sociétés arabes: mutations des systèmes juridiques du Moyen-Orient* (Karthala 1993), 326.
2 With the exception of Israel, which is the subject of the contribution by Imen Gallala-Arndt.
3 To give more teeth to this aim, the judges competent for family affairs were given increased powers of discretion and oversight over certain controversial institutions, such as polygamy and repudiation, as I explain below.
4 *Rapport annuel sur l'application du Code de la famille* [Annual report on the implementation of the Family Code] (La Ligue démocratique pour les droits des femmes, Centre d'information et d'observation des femmes marocaines, 2005), 3.
5 As has been the case in Morocco since 2004 (Art 24).
6 As has been the case in Morocco since 2004 (Art 49). In case of conflict over property between spouses, it is up to the judge to decide on the division of property between them 'while taking into consideration the work of each spouse, the efforts made as well as the responsibilities assumed in the development of the family assets' (Art 49). This provision presupposes that the judge plays a more active role in the area of proof, a condition that so far has rarely been applied in practice in Moroccan family law. Under the former Code, numerous judgements rejected women's petitions on the grounds that they had not proved their participation in acquiring the assets.
7 As has been the case in Morocco since 2004 (Art 175).
8 The Moroccan Code specifies: with a man who does not fall within the category of relatives whom the child may not marry.

9 This scenario is not necessarily explicitly provided for in a Code, but case law shows that in practice it may be expected that the judge will separate the child from its mother if there is a fear that the child might be reared in a religion other than Islam.

10 As has been the case in Morocco since 2004 (Art 179).

11 This rule also applies in Iran under Article 1133 Iran CC.

12 Article 83. The rights of the wife are specified in Article 84: balance of the *sadaq*, if any, maintenance owing for the legal waiting period and a 'Consolation Gift'. Article 85 provides that the husband must also give an amount to cover child support payments.

13 Contrary to what was the case under the former regime.

14 Translated into French officially as 'divorce par consentement mutuel', and into English unofficially as 'divorce by mutual consent'.

15 *Tamlik* is repudiation granted to the wife by a clause inserted into the marriage contract, or potentially with the consent of the husband after dispute has begun.

16 See esp Salma Abida and Nathalie Bernard-Maugiron's contributions in this volume. *Khul*ᶜ is to be understood as the repudiation by the husband at the wife's request and in return for compensation (official French translation: 'divorce par khol' and unofficial English translation: 'divorce in exchange for compensation by the wife' (*khul*ᶜ may be translated as 'compensation').

17 As has been the case in Morocco, since 2004 (Art 97).

18 On child law in Muslim countries and in particular on parental care and the principle of the best interest of the child, see Nadjma Yassari, Lena-Maria Möller, and Imen Gallala-Arndt (eds), *Parental Care and the Best Interests of the Child in Muslim Countries*, T.M.C. Asser Press (forthcoming 2016)

19 On adoption in Muslim jurisdictions see Nadjma Yassari, *Adding by Choice: Adoption and Functional Equivalents in Islamic and Middle Eastern Law*, 63 AM. J. COMP. L. 927–962 (2015).

20 Presumption of *al-firash*: irrefutable proof of the legitimacy of a child born within marriage or within a year of the separation of the spouses, provided there is (or was) the possibility of sexual relations between the father and the mother.

21 The adoption of this new form of proof (order by the court) is new and has taken many commentators by surprise, the more so since in no instance – except for the *shubha* (doubt) in the case of betrothal – does the Code allow for descent to be established outside marriage. It probably explains why the Moroccan Supreme Court decided differently in a ruling issued on 30 December 2004: the Court declared that the child is legally bound to its father if it was born within a year of a divorce decree, even if the expert testimony, based on DNA tests, concluded that the child was not the biological child of the ex-husband. It regarded an *exequatur* to be granted in Morocco of a decision rendered by a French judicial authority. The Court applied the provisions of the former Code in this leading case, although the new Code had already entered into force. In other cases involving the dissolution of marriage, by contrast, the Court gave the new Code immediate effect, even when the cases in question had been decided at an earlier date, when the former Code was still in force. (October 2005) 7 Revue Al-Milef, éditée par le barreau d'Aljadida 232–236; 63 Revue Jurisprudence de la Cour Suprême 384–389.

22 This complexity of functions assigned to both judge-notaries and family judges responsible for marriage, as well as judges responsible for custody, often confuses legal practitioners who are unfamiliar with judicial practices under Islamic family law systems, and raises concern. That is particularly true for decisions made without any possibility

for the parties to appeal. This is perceived as a violation of one of the core principles of fair trial.

23 *Ijtihad* is the creative effort on the part of the Muslim scholar to reach a solution to a legal problem by interpretations of the relevant texts.

Part I

Breaks and continuities in Middle Eastern law

1 Breaks and continuities in Middle Eastern law

Women after the 2011 revolutions[1]

Chibli Mallat

The Middle East is our bread and butter. We deal with it mostly academically, but sometimes more practically as lawyers, judges, legislators, or human rights advocates. We have all been trying to understand what has been happening since 2011. Some of us have participated in the revolution actively, and many continue to live its hopes and setbacks day and night, while suffering earthquakes of planetary import, including the establishment of an 'Islamic caliphate' over large swathes of territory in Iraq and Syria in the summer of 2014. While we are continuously shaken by momentous events in a still unfolding convulsion of global proportions, there are privileged occasions to stand back and focus on what changed, or did not change, in the lives of Middle Easterners. This is such an occasion.

The topic of the book at hand is family law. Family is an essential part of daily life. Family law tends to be restricted, from an academic perspective, to private law, in particular to marital life, separation, succession, and the rights of the child. This is an area under considerable pressure since the logic of the late-eighteenth-century Atlantic Revolution launched a centenarian call for equality between genders, which until that time Western and Eastern legal regimes had considered formally unequal. The Middle East after the revolution will not fundamentally affect this drive towards gender equality in the strict family sphere. The future is *rebus sic stantibus*, with two steps forward and one step backward in the legal minutiae of family life regulation. Part of the chapter focuses on the absence of radical legislative or judicial change in family law in the wake of the revolution.

Another focus of the chapter will show, in contrast, the immense break that society is confronted with by the irruption of nonviolence as the feminine *anima* of the revolution. That the revolution of women in public life will impact family law is doubtless. How it will is harder to predict.

I come to this reflection with a dual scholarly perspective that directly impacts the present contribution. The first perspective stems from a long-term thesis formulated in a book published in 2007 on the emergence of a coherent field of 'Middle Eastern law': *Introduction to Middle Eastern Law* sought to span the deep legal history of the region, from Hammurabi to the most recent constitutional and legislative reforms.[2] Rather than Islamic law, it put forward the reality of a Middle Eastern law. Rather than a legislative focus, it put an emphasis on the decisions of the courts, a far more telling index of rights lived and disputed between litigants every day. The chapter on family law in *Introduction to Middle Eastern Law* shows how an egalitarian prism has set the pace since the turn of the twentieth century, always advancing gender equality as the parameter of change. This ever-present concern with gender equality, and its occasional setbacks, underlines family law reform and its judicial applications to date.[3]

The second perspective comes from another book just completed, this time on the Middle East revolution which has weighed on Arab lives relentlessly since 2011, and in the case of Iran since the Green Revolution in 2009.[4] The book finds its inspiration in women as the veritable spirit of the revolution, a feminine nonviolent *anima*. The combined weight of the two books colours the present chapter heavily.

The analysis and conclusions reached in my previous research form, therefore, the departing point for appreciating family law and, more generally, the position of women in the wake of a massive revolution still underway. Let me sum up these conclusions as departing points for the present contribution: the search for gender equality in family law proceeds at a steady but slow pace. In contrast, the revolution marks a fundamental moment for women in public life, with the impact of nonviolence as the *anima* of the revolution redefining the philosophy of history. This represents a radical break in the gendered fashioning of society modulated by advances and retreats of women under a philosophy of nonviolence.

Drawing first on conclusions reached in my *Introduction to Middle Eastern Law*, the 200 years of law in what we consider the modern Middle East have been dominated, in the sphere of the family, by a focus on gender equality. It is a universal call, articulated by de Tocqueville in the most eloquent terms in the 1830s.[5] Equality has decisively affected the relations between husband and wife, mother and father, and brother and sister in Middle Eastern family law. Against a solid past of classical Islamic and other Middle Eastern religious laws, where gender equality was not even a question on the horizon of the discussion, the search for equality has moved every single piece of legislation since the first recorded codification of family law in Khartoum in 1916.[6] That year, Sudan introduced a brief legislative act allowing a woman to seek judicial divorce in the event of the prolonged absence of her husband. This represented a significant break based on the Maliki law concept of harm, *darar*, which developed over the twentieth century into a ground for divorce, evidently a fundamental change in the position of a wife subject to the husband's unilateral three-time repudiation (*talaq ba'en*). The legislative process also entailed a methodological innovation described from within the Islamic tradition as *takhayyur* (eclecticism), a bricolage that draws from the four Sunni schools irrespective of what the dominant school of law decrees in a given country. While outright repudiation remained untouched, the aggrieved wife could initiate a divorce procedure based on deep unhappiness in her marital life, in terms that evolved worldwide as the 'incompatibility of character' leading to 'the irremediable breakdown of the marital relation'. The early Sudan break was re-enacted shortly afterwards in the Ottoman Family Code of 1917.[7] Since then, the main reforms have been taking place by governmental fiat in an area where any legislation was considered until then an inappropriate interference with the practice of the courts under a non-codified *fiqh*.[8] From then on, the whole legislative and judicial set of developments in family law has been primarily moved by a clash between conservative advocates of the status quo, where women are legally subordinate to men, and the feminist movement and its supporters seeking to remedy gender inequality by a string of reforms which continue, piecemeal or in a comprehensive family code (*qanun al-ahwal al-shakhsiyya*). After the wide-ranging legislative reforms of the Moroccan Mudawwana in 2004,[9] the most recent developments have taken place in the comprehensive codification passed in the Arab Gulf States.[10] These laws confirm by-and-large the *acquis* of the twentieth century.

The Middle East revolution has not affected this long-term drive in any innovative way. Gender equality remains the defining horizon of legal reform: litigants, legislators, and judges stand for or against making women and men strictly equal in their rights and duties under the laws affecting the family. Had there been a particular earthquake in the field, we would have known. More gravely, there are no harbingers for such demands. The women's movement in the Middle East, despite its importance in matters such as the mobilization carried out in Morocco to enact the reforms of 2004, has chosen in the 2011 revolution not to focus on family issues.

This is due to two main factors. The first – negative – factor is the quick irruption of Islamic and Islamic law discourse in the revolution. This discourse was muted during the initial phase of standing up massively to the dictator, as the Islamist participants rightly perceived that any narrower religious call would undermine the universality of the protests and their chance of success. Instead, the movement rallied openly behind the call for the so-called civil state, *dawla madaniyya*. In Arabic the term *madani* is polysemic enough to encompass the yearning of civil society (*mujtama' madani*) for a place in the sun, as compared to the constrained space it is allowed during dictatorship. More significantly for the ambiguity of the term, *madani* is also opposed to *'askari*, meaning military. *Madani* serves the purpose of Islamists to underline the revolt in countries dominated by the army and police, including former generals and colonels Mubarak, Qaddafi, Ben Ali, and Saleh; all authoritarian leaders who rose from the armed forces, all using the Islamic scarecrow to remain in power. The Islamic movements were therefore content to join the unifying call against their main victimizer: the armed apparatus of the state, comprising secret and not-so-secret services (*mukhabarat*), the police or the army.

As Islamists could easily identify with its anti-military meaning, the unified call for a civil-*madani* state was supported by Islamists and proved capable of assuaging the common front during the revolution. For the non-Islamist wing of the revolution, by contrast, *madani* was a rallying concept in opposition to *dini*, meaning religious. The non-Islamist revolutionaries' 'civil state' served two purposes: 'civil' was an alternative to the military in power; it was also civil as opposed to religious. For Islamists, conversely, *madani* was far more an anti-military slogan than an anti-religious one. The calls overlapped in the early days of the revolution and were not always consistent. The discrepancy rapidly fuelled disagreements after the dictator was toppled, as in Egypt and Tunisia, but it also was evident when the revolution continued without removing the dictator, as in Syria and Bahrain. In all cases, the family law claims remained, on the whole, irrelevant to the revolutionary discourse.

The second factor behind the lack of centrality of family law reform in the 2011 revolution is more positive. Distinct from the ambiguity resulting from the convergence of the revolutionaries on a civil state understood in two inapposite ways, the objective of the revolution was more ambitious than gender equality within the family. With a large participation of women in the revolution across the Middle East, especially in its first, massively nonviolent phases, the demand was one of equal citizenship in the public sphere: the woman as citizen rather than as wife, mother, sister, or daughter.

Unlike its place in family law, where the movement of legislation and court decisions proceeds at a glacial pace, the role of women in society is a defining trait of the Middle East revolution's quick unfolding. If anything, it has exacerbated women's claim to the public sphere and pushed the call higher on the agenda, straight into the constitutional moment that marked the second phase of the revolution after it removed its dictator from power.

This materialized soon after the deposition of the Egyptian dictator. When the first committee for the amendment of the constitution in Egypt was formed under the leadership of former judge Tareq al-Bishri a few days after the flight of President Husni Mubarak from Cairo to his palace on the Red Sea, it recommended the passing of a small set of changes. To Egypt's misfortune, the first amended article prevented candidates from running for the presidency if their spouse was foreign.[11] The Bishri committee changed Article 75 of the Constitution, which had until then merely stated that candidates to the presidency must be over 40 and be the child of two Egyptian nationals – the latter condition a mildly constraining, albeit excessive disposition. The Bishri amendment, which was approved by a national referendum to become fleetingly the new constitution of Egypt,[12] added the requirement that the presidential candidate is 'not to be married to a non-Egyptian'.[13]

This was bad luck because the rest of the constitutional amendments were good and would have probably enthused all Egyptians and non-Egyptians alike. Instead the foreign marital bar became the central focus of a controversy that undermined the rest of the amendments. Local and international human rights advocates were chilled by this very first legal expression of constitutional change, one focusing openly on the marital state of a candidate who was married to a non-Egyptian, understood in this context as a foreign woman. Once the bizarre and unwarranted discrimination appeared in the text, it reminded the world that there was not a single woman in the Bishri committee and that the committee had ignored an important gender equality advance in constitutional law carried out by the Egyptian judiciary itself two decades earlier. In 1995, the Supreme Constitutional Court had invalidated as unconstitutional a similar article, which disqualified judges of the *Conseil d'Etat* (*majlis al-dawla*) who married non-Egyptian women.[14]

Instead of the otherwise reasonable and effective course of Bishri's recommendations, which were, we should remember, carried through as amendments in a referendum at a privileged time of hope and unity, the original dynamism of the Egyptian revolution as one of dignity, equality, and freedom was stifled. Sensing the divisions in society over this article and the atmosphere that accompanied the amendment process, the Egyptian military intervened increasingly forcefully. The 'Bishri constitution' was sidelined overnight by the army, which dictated a self-centred piece of legislation known as the Constitutional Declaration of 30 March 2011. The Supreme Council of the Armed Forces (SCAF) put itself front and centre at the head of legislative and executive power. The whole transitional programme that had started as the amended Bishri constitution, and which was enacted after its wide approval by referendum, was simply bypassed.[15]

What the first Bishri amendment episode also meant was that family law was no longer the main carrier of the gender issue, but that gender had become an iconic dimension of the public sphere. What the 2011 revolution achieved was to put women at the centre of constitutional *citizenship*. The fight is joined and is continuing every day.

So this is how the scene was set in the Middle East revolution: for 200 years, the family law paradigm was inscribed in a long, evolutionary mode of reform seeking to replace the former, unequal, paradigm which had prevailed since Hammurabi. The old paradigm did not even contemplate the question of gender equality, for it stood beyond its intellectual horizon. Kasani (d 1191), one of the Middle East's greatest jurists, wrote it plainly in his famous treatise, *Bada'e' al-Sana'e'*. There are seven categories of women, he explained: 'Those married, those owned, those forbidden because of blood kinship, those forbidden for other reasons (suckling or *musahara*, in-law kinship), those owned by others, those foreign and free, and those who are related (to the man) but whose marriage (with him) is not forbidden.'[16] After all, Kasani said with the confidence of an evident truth for his time, women 'do not have a complete mind, and are usually known for their mental shortcomings.'[17] We are a long way from this worldview.

By the time the 2011 Middle Eastern tsunami struck, and the revolution set the people up against the ruling dictators across one of the most politically backward regions on earth, gender equality in family law had advanced significantly on paper, and to a real extent in practice. The advances (and occasional retreats) are well known in their general traits: marriage was better regulated to protect women; divorce and custody were no longer an absolute fiat of the husband/father; and maintenance was introduced to support women brusquely abandoned by their husbands. A few amendments had even been introduced in the field of succession, allowing for instance a female grandchild whose parents had died to inherit from a grandparent by stepping into her parents' shoes.[18] In the law of marriage, and divorce in particular, a set of substantive and procedural reforms had been adopted, from the prevention of polygamy in Tunisia to the difficult procedural hurdles imposed on husbands marrying second wives in those countries which did not want to go as far as an outright ban on polygamy. In matters of divorce, the Maliki concept of harm was bolstered to raise the status of the unhappy wife almost to the level of repudiating her husband.[19]

In succession law, only one significant taboo had remained across the board for gender equality: the principle of two shares for the female against one share to the male. This remains true even in Shiite law, which had long recognized a daughter as a 'Stur', and who, as per Zoroastrian legacy, had precedence in the succession over a more distant male side of the family, in contradistinction with the *'asaba*-dominated Sunni system.[20] Other than Turkey, where Mustafa Kemal's policy had been relentlessly egalitarian even on that score, the only country in the Middle East where gender equality had been briefly established between sisters and brothers inheriting from their deceased parent was Iraq, between 1958 and 1963. The first measure taken by the new Iraqi government in 1963, however, was the repeal of that disposition in the inheritance law.[21]

Except for these two taboo areas, namely polygamy and the two share/one share rule in male versus female succession, gender equality has progressed steadily on the legislative books and in judicial practice. Regime change anywhere, and in any direction, has not affected this course significantly. Even in Iran, where Islamization was the unconditional ideology after the 1978–79 revolution, the main texts adopted under the Pahlavi dynasty remained, on the whole, undisturbed. Where a retreat had taken place, it was corrected by practice and new regulations were adopted in 1992 to restore the gains made previous to the Islamic revolution.[22] In Iraq, the discussion of amendments to the laws was also shelved promptly in 2003–04.[23]

The problem in Iraq was typical of the dominant sectarian atmosphere, which we now have to take into account more than at any time in the last 200 years. Confronted with the risk of competing and irreconcilable Sunni versus Shiite interpretations, the political upshot has been so radioactive that the old unified family code remains exactly in the shape left by Saddam Hussein. The rigidifying sectarian law also affected the reform process in a divided Bahrain.[24]

Unease with any further reform was palpable when the articles relevant to personal status were discussed for the revision of the Iraqi Constitution. When the Constitutional Review Committee took up the revision of the 2005 Constitution in 2009, it was aware of the extra-sensitive impact of reform in the personal status field. Any change would collapse the whole revision process. Article 41 of the Iraqi 2005 Constitution, which stipulates that 'Iraqis are free in their commitment to their personal status according to their religions, sects, beliefs, or choices', was generally left undisturbed. The amendment agreed in the Constitutional Review Committee changed the language slightly, to emphasize this 'freedom': 'An Iraqi has the right to obligate himself to the rules of his religion and sect in personal status, and the organization of the Personal Status Law shall guarantee that.'[25] In practice there was no change. It is clear that the Shiite-Sunni divergence turned into a central difficulty as soon as one tinkered with family law or any related matter where the two Muslim communities were at risk of divergence. Any change threatened to rekindle the traditional differences, which had been left behind in previous legislation. It was impossible to raise family law issues in public without incurring the risk of a sectarian backlash.

This, therefore, presents both continuity and a break in our field. Family law reform continues to be subject to the 200 year-long evolving paradigm. The political upheaval of recent years has not brought a revolution in either direction on that particular level, but there is an unexpected nuance in the pattern, which is a strong sectarian overtone in countries with mixed Sunni-Shiite populations. Paradoxically, the sectarian fear makes any change far more difficult. In these countries, *takhayyur* and *talfiq*, the centenary-old tools for eclecticism and 'law-shopping', are no longer as flexible. Sunnis and Shiites are more conscious of the political difficulty in jumping over to the other side for legislative inspiration than ever in modern history.

In any case, as in all matters of private law, family legislation does not change easily. To be more precise: the search for equality remains the norm, with a general trend towards more formal and substantive equality. The major reforms of the twentieth century remain on the books, with occasional retreats when a particular brand of extreme Islamism is let loose. In mixed Sunni-Shiite societies, sectarianism is enhanced, with the unintended consequence of leaving the texts untouched for fear of passions being immediately raised. On the whole, family law has been barely affected by the Middle East 2011 revolution, whether or not societies that had risen against their dictators succeeded in removing him from power.

Not so the gender issue in the public law sphere. The debate was 'elevated' to the constitutional level, where the controversy is less about the rights of a woman in the scheme of marriage and succession laws than her place in public life; no longer therefore as wife, daughter, or mother, but as citizen, political leader, or holder of a remunerated job.

In newly freed societies where elections are at last meaningful, the first issue of the citizen woman is about quotas in public position. It is no longer the case that women are prevented from voting. This battle has long been won in most Middle Eastern countries. It is also a planet-wide truism that few women are in a position of leadership, because voting is invariably skewed to the advantage of male candidates. The twenty-first-century public sphere also includes sensitive leadership positions in the private sector, alongside the more traditional 'parity' quotas included in parliaments and cabinets.

To see more clearly into the thicket of woman's equality in the public law sphere, one must keep in mind the constitutional context in which her fight is taking place. The Middle East was a bloc of countries dominated by dictatorships until 2011. So there the vote did not count anyway. The battle for gender equality has been confined to family law, or in an unusually backward looking country like Saudi Arabia, to such 'acid tests' as women being banned from driving or prohibited from walking in the street without some imposed form of dress.[26]

When voting starts to count after the dictator is deposed, the issue becomes one of representation. In the worldwide debate over increased women's participation and representation in the public sphere, the spectrum of answers across society is well known. There are those, including some women, who reject the focus on gender, as opposed to citizenship, by adhering to a formal egalitarian view of the woman as citizen.[27] They want the constitution to be totally gender-neutral irrespective of how inegalitarian the practical reality is: 'This is a recognition that our feminist movement works on confirming in the constitution – in the more general Lebanese social contract, and in all the laws upholding this contract.'[28] In the Middle East, some oppose gender equality for radically different reasons stemming from a gynophobia usually steeped in religious discourse. Most people, I guess, stand on a middle, practical ground and accept arrangements to correct the historical discrimination against women. I belong to this school, which makes the argument in the constitutional field and derives from the unease at seeing half of the population not represented naturally at all three levels of government. A judiciary without women prevents an essential point of view from finding its place on the bench, but so does the lack of leadership in executive positions. With the executive branch remaining at the top of the decision-making ladder in Middle Eastern societies (and elsewhere), cabinets should naturally reflect the natural parity division in society. One is rightly suspicious of a twenty-first century where long-established democratic countries have so few women as prime ministers or presidents. The Middle East revolution is part of that trend, and revolution in its societies offers a significant break with a past that confines its women to a position of subordinate, 'inexistent' political actors. But the road to change at the top is steep. Even in Tunisia, where parliamentary results indicate a tangible progress as detailed below, only one woman was a candidate in a slate of 28 contenders in the presidential elections of 2014.[29]

Despite the importance of the two other branches of government, the focus of attention has been the legislative branch as the most intensive interface of citizenship, where people vote nationally for a large assembly in charge of making laws. A parliament with a small number of women MPs looks immediately suspicious. As a result, the question of quota or *numerus clausus* as corrector of inequalities has everywhere turned into a central issue of the Middle East revolution. In 2005, a 'temporary' quota of 25 per cent of women was introduced in the Iraqi constitution (Art 49.4), which remains operative to date. When the revolution broke out across the region in 2011, the need for quotas was also raised in the countries where the vote became suddenly meaningful: Egypt, Libya, Yemen, and Tunisia. The ongoing battle has elicited uneven results. All four post-dictator countries have seen an active debate, and sometimes change, in women's place in public life as citizen.

This translates legally in quota-based electoral laws for parliament and constitution-making assemblies. Thanks to a formidable mobilization in Libya, the first electoral law adopted for the General National Council (GNC, *al-mu'tamar al-watani al-'amm*, parliament) was a *numerus clausus* system following a so-called zipper list, which also prevents women candidates from being left at 'the bottom' of the list. Lists must alternate women across the board, in a repeat of the device used in Iraqi elections post-Saddam. The Libyan Women's Platform for Peace (LWPP) 'successfully lobbied for a GNC electoral law that would ensure women's participation in the elections by requiring alternating female and male candidates on "zippered" party lists. Of the 33 women elected in the first post-Ghaddafi elections held in July 2012, 32 were elected through party lists and 1 as an individual candidate. Representing 16.5% of the total of 200, women's representation in the GNC in Libya is similar to that of the United States and France.'[30]

Order in Libya has slowly and steadily collapsed since that hopeful moment, which followed the fall of Tripoli and the end of Qaddafi on 20 October 2011. By 2014, chaos prevailed. It is expressed institutionally with the emergence of two parliaments and two governments. The militia atmosphere, which dominated the country after the dictator's comeuppance, pushed the gender issue into the background. In 2012–13, the dispute over the national elections to establish the 60-member Constitutional Drafting Assembly (CDA, *al-hay'a al-ta'sisiyya li-siyaghat mashru' al-dustur*) saw a retreat of female participation in favour of regional representation. The 60-member assembly comprises three sets of delegates, 20 for each of the three regions, Tripolitana, Cyrenaica, and the South (Fezzan). This was partly adopted in recognition of the punishment of Cyrenaica by Qaddafi for half a century. The good will towards Cyrenaica, where the people of Benghazi are rightly clamouring for a voice which they were systematically deprived of, led however to a clear abnormality. The South of the country was considered one electoral district and saw a third in seat allocation on the CDA despite comprising 7 per cent or less of the overall Libyan population. Meanwhile, the formidable work of women to establish themselves at the heart of the constitutional debate was undermined by an electoral law reducing their CDA number to six, a quota of 10 per cent. This loss from the first parliamentary elections was further reduced in practice. Only five women sit on the CDA.[31]

In Yemen, a more positive story briefly emerged until the collapse of order with the Huthi occupation of Sanaa in 2014. Here also, the descent into militia rule in 2014 bodes ill for the country at large, where the voice of weapons became increasingly dominant despite a remarkably nonviolent revolution achieved through the painful removal from presidency of 'Ali 'Abdallah Saleh in 2011. Before the Huthi militias took over the capital in the summer of 2014, a National Dialogue (*hiwar watani*) was conducted under the auspices of the UN from March 2013 to January 2014. The National Dialogue endeavoured to pay particular attention to the participation of women and youth (with the bar for youth put rather high at the age of 40). Delegates to the National Dialogue comprised 20 per cent youth and 30 per cent women, and the choice of the 565 delegates discussing the future of the country has respected this threshold. This underlined also the remarkable success in the quality of the Dialogue, especially since the one-year long process carried the voices of both women and youth to the heart of the constitutional discussions. This was also true beyond the corridors of the National Dialogue. The circles of free discussion opened in Sanaa by the deposition of 'Ali 'Abdallah Saleh include several fora where women are active and vocal.[32] The central question surrounding the constitutionalization of the revolution, the step planned next at the end of the National Dialogue, was whether the UN representation quota would be maintained. That in itself would have created a major precedent in the Middle East. But as in Libya, the collapse of order stifled the movement. In 2014, the Huthi takeover of the capital froze the whole process, while the secessionist movement in South Yemen was steadily developing.

Of all four countries that succeeded in deposing their president-for-life in 2011, Tunisia has fared best, as is generally acknowledged after the success of the second parliamentary elections in October 2014. The 2011 electoral law following the Jasmine Revolution established parity with an alternative listing of men and women: 'Candidates shall file their candidacy applications on the basis of parity between men and women.'[33] Out of 217 seats, women received 58, a proportion of 27 per cent.[34] The 2014 Constitution anchored the yearning for gender parity in Article 46: 'The state seeks to achieve equal representation for women and men in elected councils'. In the parliamentary elections held on 26 October 2014, the trend was confirmed. Women received 31 per cent of the votes, securing 68 seats, and confirming the early revolutionary gains.[35]

The positive result correlates with the sense of a stabilization into constitutional rule as achieved with the free conduct of national elections: parliamentary elections were held for a second time in three years in October 2014; and, for the first time in the country's history, a presidential election was held shortly thereafter in November 2014. Tunisia also benefited from the attention of the main Islamist party, the Nahda, to an enhanced position of women in its discourse and appointments within the party.

Only Egypt seems to have ignored the need for a women's quota. The representative system in Egypt suffers from a deep imbalance originally created by a vision of a corporatist constitution, one which considered success to be contingent on half the members of parliament being 'workers or peasants'.[36] This antiquated system survived the Nile Revolution, leaving little or no room for gender-attentive constitutionalism. 'In the Nov 2011-Jan 2012 elections to the new Egyptian parliament [508 members], only 8 women (1.8%) were elected. The supreme council of the military forces [sic] (SCAF) appointed additional 10 MPs, whereof 2 are women, bringing women's overall share to 2.2%.'[37] Female representation was faring worse than under Mubarak, a reflection of the ascendancy of the Muslim Brotherhood, which proved far less savvy and attentive to this major symbol of progress than their Nahda colleagues in Tunisia. The marginalization of women continued in the 100-member-strong Constituent Assembly (CA), which the elected Parliament originally appointed, with only six women in the initial make-up of the CA in 2012.[38] Marginalization was also honed by the military. The final Constituent Assembly, which passed the 'Sisi Constitution' of 2014, was 50 members strong and had only five women on it. This is reflected in the text of the Constitution, where there is only a faint trace of gender-corrective representation.[39]

Egypt's case is particularly tragic in view not only of the importance of the country in the Middle East, but also because of the particularly disturbing practices that have developed into a unique characteristic of the counter-revolution: the targeting of women and their deliberate humiliation in the public sphere. A counter-revolution per se is not surprising. There is no revolution without counter-revolution. But the troubling characteristic of the Middle East counter-revolution lies in its deliberate choice of targeting women. 2011 featured women in the streets in unprecedented numbers[40] and iconized women's participation into a hallmark of the revolution.[41] The counter-revolution chose women as a privileged target to roll back the spirit claimed at Tahrir Square, a spirit which, in the words of historian Khaled Fahmy, had not been encountered since the dawn of recorded Egyptian history: 'But we did something in Tahrir that has never been done in the history of Egypt, going all the way back to the pyramids.'[42]

The salience of a repressive gender-specific policy was particularly troubling as Egypt's counter-revolution, spearheaded by the military, steadily developed. A gendered perspective of the revolution underlines the setbacks since those hopeful, early days of January–February 2011. Soon after Mubarak was deposed in the mass movement that included hundreds of thousands of female participants, the objective of the military and the police was to take women off the streets altogether. Harassment of women rose to unprecedented levels, turning into massive and systematic sexual violence, including the infamous 'virginity tests'.

One notable instance during this period in which the Egyptian state perpetrated sexual violence against women happened in March 2011, when the military detained 17 women at a protest and subjected them to forced 'virginity testing'. Abdel Fattah Al-Sisi, the head of military intelligence at the time, defended this action by the army on the ground that 'proving' the women were virgins would protect the army against 'false' accusations of rape (operating on the faulty logic that only virgins can be raped, an idea bound up with patriarchal conceptions of female 'purity'). Protests in public spaces intensified and fractured during the build up to the first post-revolutionary Presidential elections, and were frequently accompanied by sexual violence including gang rapes.[43]

It may not be a coincidence that the new ruler of Egypt was the initiator of that policy. Violence against women, which has plagued the 'private' sphere in laws and practices since time immemorial, has become a feature of the counter-revolution across the region. In Lebanon's Cedar Revolution of 2005–06, a harbinger of the Middle East-wide 2011 revolution, the counter-revolutionary tide was clearly on the offensive when journalist May Chidiac was targeted by a bomb on 25 September 2005. She was maimed, losing her arm and leg, before bravely recovering and continuing the struggle.[44] Targeting women activists is a consistent policy of Iran's rulers. It became an icon of the counter-revolution, where a young woman bled to death in the street, and government-supported or incited violence against women in the public sphere remains palpable. From systematically repressing women's freedom to dress to acid attacks in the city of Isfahan in October 2014, gender-based incitement against women who do not conform with a subordinate position in society has increasingly given way to their violent punishment as the hallmark of government policy. Similar to the Shi'i religious rulers of Iran hardening their position, extreme religious militancy focusing on the subordination of women was also resurgent in the Sunni world. Both use female subordination as a deliberate brand of their policy. The counter-revolution came to be defined in both the ruling class and the rising Islamist movements as a women-focused suppression. Syria is a prime example. On 16 March 2011, one of the first organized demonstrations took place in Marja Square, the heart of Damascus, consciously reproducing the precedent traced by the Argentinian women of the Plaza de Mayo. The silent occasion featured leading activist women alongside those whose male parents were languishing in prison.[45] The demonstration was ruthlessly repressed. The women of Marja Square were beaten up and/or arrested, after which the government unleashed its full might against nonviolent demonstrators, spreading all over Syria for five straight months. As the revolution militarized, it started losing ground to Islamist-led violence. On 9 December 2013, one of the main participants in the Marja demonstration, Razan Zeituneh (Zaytuna), was kidnapped in the 'liberated' outskirts of Damascus, which she had refused to leave, under the watch of a self-portrayed 'moderate' group led by a local Islamist warlord. In both instances, women have been the prime target of violent subjugation. This cannot be a coincidence.

Libya saw a similar development, at a different tempo. Qaddafi had been particularly brutal in trying to subdue the revolt against him, which included fear mongering against women demonstrating against him.[46] On 25 June 2014, the killing of Salwa Bugaighis in Libya represented a significant low point of the post-Qaddafi era, epitomizing the rise of violence at the hands of the Islamist militia.

In Bahrain, on 4 December 2014, human rights advocate Zainab al-Khawaja was sentenced to three years in prison for *lèse-majesté*.[47] A few days earlier, her sister Maryam had been sentenced to one year in prison 'for assaulting a police officer'.[48] News of women defying the ban on driving, being arrested, and driving again has become cyclical in the Kingdom of Saudi Arabia.[49] Everywhere in the Middle East nonviolent actions led by women are countered by the repression of sitting despots or, as in Egypt, by their like-minded successors, or by Islamic militants who cannot brook the logic of nonviolence competing with their destructive and brutal bent. The State of the Islamic Caliphate (*dawlat al-khilafa al-islamiyya*, aka ISIS or *da'esh*) is its ultimate expression. For women it is the pushback against a thousand years of progress into a violence not seen since the pre-modern age: the physical subjugation of women as war booty and slaves, and their physical elimination by lapidation and other gruesome methods of torture and murder.[50] This grotesque, criminal victimization openly expressed by SIC/ISIS, appears as the extreme form of an all too evident pattern of subjugation common to modern Middle Eastern authoritarianism. Whether in Sisi's Egypt, Salman's Saudi Arabia, Asad's Syria, Khamene'i's Iran, or the local variations put forward by various self-professed Islamic groups of which Baghdadi's SIC/ISIS is the most extreme, nonviolent, revolutionary women are the prime target of the long-established or newly arrived ruler. SIC/ISIS is only the most glaring advocate of women's subjugation by formal enslavement under a long defunct reading of Islamic/Middle Eastern law and the allegedly 'divine' order of things. Such a reading of God's law goes against the grain of 200 years of enlightened thinking animated by gender equality and is consciously expressed as a tool of fear and domination. SIC/ISIS's main difference with the language of the dictators in place across the region is that the SIC/ISIS advocacy of gender repression is open and deliberate.[51] When Bashar al-Asad had the women demonstrating in Marja dragged by their hair, imprisoned, and tortured, he didn't trumpet his violence and take open pride for it. ISIS does.

Examples of renewed structural gender oppression can be multiplied, which underline a decree of reality introduced to history through the Middle Eastern door in 2011. As they participate in a massive revolt, women are generally nonviolent. So long as the *anima* of the revolution is nonviolent, women are at its forefront. When nonviolence recedes before violence, women are pushed back brutally and deliberately. Their voices are made far less effective as young men in military garb take over the street and dictate their wills upon the population. Violence kills the revolution by silencing the nonviolent *anima* carried out symbolically and effectively by women. In a philosophy of history defined by nonviolence as its *anima* in 2011, the Middle Eastern revolution can only be understood through a prism, which is heavily gendered. Women stand, in reality and potentiality, at the centre of the public sphere. In that context, family law comes second to citizenship as the heart of a millennial fight.

Notes

1 This chapter is based on the keynote address the author held at the conference 'The Dynamics of Legal Development in Islamic Countries - Family and Succession Law' in October 2013 at the Max Planck Institute for Comparative and International Private Law in Hamburg, Germany.

2 Chibli Mallat, *Introduction to Middle Eastern Law* (OUP 2007).

3 Ibid. ch 9 'Family Law: the Search for Equality' 355–402.

4 Chibli Mallat, *Philosophy of Nonviolence: Revolution, constitutionalism, and justice beyond the Middle East* (OUP 2015).

5 Mallat, *Introduction to Middle Eastern Law* (n 1) 355–56, 402.

6 Sudanese circular no 17 of 1916 (Arts 14 and 15), cited e.g. in Yvon Linant de Bellefonds, *Traité de droit musulman comparé*, vol 2 (Mouton 1965) 478; see also Mallat, *Introduction to Middle Eastern Law* (n 1) 363, fn 2 and accompanying text.

7 For a recent overview, Saime Belkiz Akgunduz, 'Reforms Concerning Women Rights in the Family Act of 1917 in the Ottoman Empire' (2011) 2 Journal of Rotterdam Islamic and Social Sciences 1–25 <http://dx.doi.org/10.2478/jriss-2013-0020> accessed 22 May 2015; on judicial divorce allowed by the Code (Art 131), see s 6.12.3 'Divorce due to discord'.

8 On codification generally, Mallat, *Introduction to Middle Eastern Law* (n 1) ch 7 'Introduction: From the Age of Codification to the Age of Case-Law' 239–43; on family law codification, ibid. 363–64.

9 Ibid. 398–402.

10 See the comprehensive Möller chapter in the present book.

11 For context and developments, Mallat, *Philosophy of Nonviolence* (n 3) 142–44.

12 Ibid. 142. The Bishri Amendments were made public on 16 February 2011, and the referendum that enacted them passed on 20 March.

13 '*wa alla yakuna mutazawwijan min ghayr misriyya*'. For a comparative chart of the changes, see Chibli Mallat and others, 'Al-dustur al-masri fi mir'at thawrat al-nil, muqarana fil-ta'dilat al-muqtaraha' [The Egyptian constitution in the mirror of the Nile revolution, a comparison of the suggested amendments] (*Right to Nonviolence*, 8 March 2011) <www.righttononviolence.org/wp-content/uploads/2011/03/20110308_egypt-constitutional-amendments-_ar2.pdf2.pdf> accessed 22 May 2015. The other troubling amendment was that the candidate should not have 'either himself, or one of his parents, acquired another nationality' (*wa alla yakuna qad hasala aw ayy min*

walidayh 'ala jinsiyya ukhra). It is not clear to me against whom amongst the potential presidential candidates the combination of these troublesome requests was targeted, but the net was cast wide.

14 Details and references in Mallat, *Philosophy of Nonviolence* (n 3) 142–43, fn 22 and accompanying text. The decision of the Supreme Constitutional Court No 23/16 invalidating the provision of Law 73 forbidding the appointment of a judge to the *Conseil d'Etat* (*majlis al-dawla*) married to a non-Egyptian was issued on 18 March 1995, available at <www1.umn.edu/humanrts/arabic/Egypt-SCC-SC/Egypt-SCC-23-Y16.html>.

15 Mallat, *Philosophy of Nonviolence* (n 3) 143, fn 23 and accompanying text; see also Nathalie Bernard-Maugiron, 'Egypt's Path to Transition: Democratic Challenges behind the Constitution Reform Process' (2011) 3 Middle East Law and Governance 43; Karen Stilt, 'The End of "One Hand": The Egyptian Constitutional Declaration and the Rift between the "People" and the Supreme Council of the Armed Forces' (2013) 16 YIMEL 43–52.

16 'Ala' al-Din al-Kasani, *Bada'e' al-sana'e' fi tartib al-shara'e'*, vol 5 (Cairo edn, Matba'at Sharikat al-Matbu'at al-'Ilmiyya 1910) book on *istihsan* [preference], 118–19.

17 Ibid. 155: *'lakin laysa laha kamal al-ra'i li-qusur 'aql al-nisa' 'adatan'*. I argue in *Introduction to Middle Eastern Law* (n 1) that this is a classical world view in which equality between men and women was simply not part of the collective mentality. This is true both in the Eastern and Western better tradition, including leaders of the European Enlightenment. No better Kasani-like illustration than Spinoza (d 1677), in the very last paragraph of his posthumous (and unfinished) *Political Treatise*: 'But if by nature women were equal to men, and were equally distinguished by force of character and ability, in which human power and therefore human right chiefly consist; surely among nations so many and different some would be found, where both sexes rule alike, and others, where men are ruled by women, and so brought up, that they can make less use of their abilities. And since this is nowhere the case, one may assert with perfect propriety, that women have not by nature equal right with men: but that they necessarily give way to men, and that thus it cannot happen, that both sexes should rule alike, much less that men should be ruled by women. But if we further reflect upon human passions, how men, in fact, generally love women merely from the passion of lust, and esteem their cleverness and wisdom in proportion to the excellence of their beauty, and also how very ill-disposed men are to suffer the women they love to show any sort of favour to others, and other facts of this kind, we shall easily see that men and women cannot rule alike without great hurt to peace. But of this enough.' Benedict de Spinoza, *Political Treatise* (R Elwes tr, 1883) <www.constitution.org/bs/poltreat.txt> accessed 13 September 2015.

18 Mallat, *Introduction to Middle Eastern Law* (n 1) 399.

19 Ibid. 373–77 (on the adoption of the concept by the Iraqi scholar Bint al-Huda and the Egyptian lawyer Fathiyya Shalabi).

20 Mallat, *Introduction to Middle Eastern Law* (n 1) 24–32 (on the concept of '*asaba* in Middle Eastern law), 26 (on Zoroastrian *stur* and the Shiite system), 359–60 (on the prevalence of '*asaba* in modern Sunni codes).

21 See Chibli Mallat, 'Sunnism and Shi'ism in Iraq: Revisiting the Codes' in Chibli Mallat and Jane Connors (eds), *Islamic Family Law* (Graham and Trotman 1992) 72–73, 88–90.

22 Mallat, *Introduction to Middle Eastern Law* (n 1) 390–91 and references cited; see also Nadjma Yassari, *Die Brautgabe im Familienvermögensrecht* (Mohr Siebeck 2014) 98–99 and her update on Iranian family legislation, Nadjma Yassari, 'Iran: Das neue Gesetz zum Schutze der Familie 2013' [2014] Das Standesamt 125–27.

23 The Governing Council had issued Decree 137 on 29 December 2003, which was perceived as an attempt to transfer jurisdiction away from national courts in matters of personal status. Text of decree in English available at <www.casi.org.uk/analysis/2004/msg00067.html>. The decree was not signed by Paul Bremer, at the time the head of the Coalition Provisional Authority, and was therefore not enacted into law. While the idea resurfaced in the 2005 Constitution, see below, the attempt to deprive national courts of personal status competence in favor of local sectarian courts or quasi-judicial authorities did not go anywhere even after the occupation had formally come to an end.

24 See Möller (n 9) in Part II of this volume.

25 CRC amendments on file with author, who attended the deliberations of the Committee in 2009.

26 The driving ban for women in Saudi Arabia is a typically trivial issue transformed into a major national and international crisis as an 'acid test'. The ban imposed on Saudi women was challenged publically for the first time in 1990, and the movement has not abated since, see below, *in fine*. For the 'acid test' concept generally, see Mallat, *Philosophy of Nonviolence* (n 3) 179–81, and its illustration in the dress imposed on women or banned from them, at 181–88.

27 See the argument e.g. of 'Izzat Sharara Baydun, *Muwatina la untha* [Citizen not female] (Saqi 2015), especially at 34: 'It remains for our society . . . to remove from its sight the received beliefs and thoughts which see women as dependent (*ittikaliyyat*) because they are female, and must remain so, bereft of the benefits and the equality they are entitled to.' While the position of the author in practice is more nuanced, as she focuses in the book on laws also in the way they affect the position of women in practice, the formal argument of women as equal citizens can be found in the final rejection of the quota requested by several Libyan women advocates and their supporters, see below nn 29–30 and accompanying text.

28 Ibid. 34.

29 See Nedra Cherif, 'Tunisian Women in Politics: From Constitution Makers to Electoral Contenders' (2014) FRIDE Policy Brief no 189 (November 2014) <http://fride.org/download/PB_189_Tunisian_women_in_politics.pdf>.

30 See reference and more details in 'RN Support for LWPP Call for Inclusive Constitutional Process' (*Right to Nonviolence*, 1 June 2013) <www.righttononviolence.org/press-release-rn-support-for-lwpp-call-for-inclusive-constitutional-process> accessed 22 May 2015.

31 This is recorded in detail in the early constitutional discussions on who will participate in the drafting of the Libyan constitution: 'The debate [over women's representation in the projected constitutional committee/assembly] was heated over the degree of participation of women in the council.' While the head of the provisional committee advocated 12 women out of 60, the women's lobby argued for a minimum of 15. The opponents, which had their way eventually, rejected the principle on the basis of the Constitutional Declaration (3 August 2011). They argued that the Constitutional Declaration consecrated formal and gender-neutral citizenship equality. See *Mashru' qanun bi-sha'n intikhab al-hay'a al-ta'sisiyya li-siyaghat al-dustur* [Draft law on the election of the founding committee for the writing of the constitution] (20 May 2013), addendum entitled '*mudhakkara shariha*' [explanatory memorandum], s 3 on '*al-mar'a*' [women]. This particular section takes up a good half of the nine-page memorandum (on file with author, from a visit to Libya in late June 2013).

32 I briefly participated as advisor to the UN mission to Yemen led by Jamal Benomar in summer 2013 and witnessed in Sanaa some sessions where women were articulate and

influential speakers, despite many of them speaking from behind a – rather stern – full veil/*niqab*.

33 See Quota Project, Tunisia, al-Majlis al-Watani al-Taasisi (2011) <www.quotaproject.org/uid/countryview.cfm?CountryCode=TN> accessed 22 May 2015.

34 Ibid.

35 See Cherif (n 28).

36 Mallat, *Philosophy of Nonviolence* (n 3) 153–54.

37 See Quota Project, Egypt, Majlis al-Chaab (2012) <www.quotaproject.org/uid/countryview.cfm?CountryCode=EG> accessed 22 May 2015.

38 Maria Caspani, 'Infographic: Egypt's constituent assembly' (*Thomas Reuters Foundation*, 3 September 2013) <www.trust.org/item/20130903155620-wae6d> accessed 22 May 2015.

39 The Egyptian Constitution of 2014 mentions that 'the state guarantees the achievement of equality between men and women in all civil, political, economic, social, and cultural rights' (Art 11), but in electoral terms this is restricted to the local councils: 'Every local unit shall elect a local council by direct and secret ballot for a term of four years. A candidate shall be at least twenty-one (21) Gregorian years of age. The law shall regulate the other conditions for candidacy and procedures of election, provided that one quarter of the seats shall be allocated to youth under thirty-five (35) years of age and *one quarter shall be allocated to women*, and that workers and farmers shall be represented by no less than 50 percent of the total number of seats, and these percentages shall include an appropriate representation of Christians and people with disability.' (Art 180, emphasis added).

40 Numbers are difficult to gauge, both in absolute and relative terms, but the early weeks of the nonviolent revolution saw a 30 per cent ratio of women to men in the demonstrations in Egypt, more women than men in the lead in Syria, and while segregated, large squares taken over by women in Sanaa. For numbers see Mayla Bakhache, 'Women in the Arab Revolutions' in Hassan Krayyem (ed), *The Arab Spring: Revolutions for Deliverance from Authoritarianism, Case Studies* (L'Orient des Livres 2013) 223–39.

41 Tawakkul Karman in Yemen being the most famous following her Nobel Peace Prize in 2011.

42 See Charlotte Alfred, 'Mubarak's Case is a "trial of Egypt's revolution"' *The Huffington Post* (12 June 2014) <www.huffingtonpost.com/2014/12/06/mubarak-trial_n_6277740.html> accessed 22 May 2015.

43 Heather McRobie, 'The common factor: sexual violence and the Egyptian state, 2011–2014' (*OpenDemocracy*, 6 October 2014) <www.opendemocracy.net/5050/heather-mcrobie/common-factor-sexual-violence-and-egyptian-state-20112014> accessed 22 May 2015.

44 See her autobiography, May Chidiac and Amal Moghaizel, *Le Ciel m'attendra* (Florent Massot 2007).

45 For details of the early upheaval in Syria, of which the Marja Square demonstration was one of the most powerful expressions, see Mallat, *Philosophy of Nonviolence* (n 3) 40, 57, 63 and literature cited.

46 Illustrated in the case of Eman al-Obeidi, see e.g. 'Thorough investigation urged over Libya rape case' (*Amnesty International*, 28 March 2011) <www.amnesty.org/en/press-releases/2011/03/thorough-investigation-urged-over-libya-rape-case> accessed 22 May 2015. Amnesty International and Human Rights Watch did not, however, find evidence of mass rape in Libya during the revolution.

47 'Bahrain: Jail sentence for "insulting the king"' (*Amnesty International*, 5 December 2014) <www.amnesty.org/en/documents/mde11/048/2014/en> accessed 22 May 2015.

48 'Bahrain: Maryam Al-Khawaja remains defiant after in absentia prison sentence' (*Amnesty International*, 1 December 2014) < www.amnesty.org/en/articles/news/2014/12/bahrain-maryam-al-khawaja-remains-defiant-after-absentia-prison-sentence> accessed 22 May 2015.

49 See e.g. 'Saudi Arabia: the authorities continue to punish activists for speaking up' (*Amnesty International*, 4 December 2014) <www.amnesty.org/en/documents/document/?indexNumber=mde23%2F036%2F2014&language=en> accessed 22 May 2015.

50 SIC seems the more appropriate acronym, since the caliphate is the distinguishing feature of the movement, it being the first self-established caliph since the fall of the Ottoman Empire. For the SIC acronym in English, see Max Rodenbeck, 'Iraq: The Outlaw State' *The New York Review of Books* (25 September 2014) <www.nybooks.com/articles/archives/2014/sep/25/iraq-outlaw-state> accessed 22 May 2015.

51 There is a cottage industry on ISIS, which is summarized in two good book reviews published in the summer of 2015, Anonymous, 'The Mystery of ISIS' *The New York Review of Books* (13 August 2015) <www.nybooks.com/articles/archives/2015/aug/13/mystery-isis> accessed 13 September 2015; Edward Mortimer, 'Caliph country: the rise of ISIS' *Financial Times* (4 September 2015). My point about SIC/ISIS's characteristic flouting of its brutality is made in Chibli Mallat, 'The path towards defeating ISIS' *The Daily Star* (Lebanon, 4 August 2015).

2 Contextualizing family law reform and plural legalities in postcolonial Pakistan

Shaheen Sardar Ali

Introduction

Family law reforms in the Muslim world represent a fascinating yet challenging example of the ongoing contestations between contemporary notions of justice, equality, and human rights on the one hand and established understandings of Islamic jurisprudence (*fiqh*) on the other.[1] They also represent a critical shift in Muslim thinking globally, in that family law is now being discussed as a multi-layered and complex subject straddling religion, politics, economics, gender equality, and women's rights. New interlocutors in this discussion include Muslim women, NGOs, print and electronic media, national, regional, and international human-rights bodies, and national parliaments.[2]

Historically, family law reform projects in the Muslim world, including Pakistan, have been conceptualized within a framework of patriarchal norms and an understanding of a contractual nature of marriage and divorce supported by religious texts (mainly the Quran and the *sunna*, or teachings and practices of the prophet). Though religious texts ensured women a legal status and distinct (if not equal) rights in all spheres of life, Muslim women have continually confronted 'a moral and anthropological context that privileged male authority and the male voice'.[3] Family law reform in the Muslim world, often referred to as 'woman-friendly reform',[4] is an attempt at 'neutralizing' some of the unfettered male power within the institutions of marriage and divorce without displacing or challenging what are perceived as immutable religious texts. Simultaneously however, where 'Islamist' parties or individuals have come into power (for instance Nimeiri in the Sudan, Imam Khomeini in Iran, and Zia-ul-Haq in Pakistan), they have engaged in law reform based on different readings of those same texts, leading to changes in the law adversely affecting women in these jurisdictions.[5]

The general premise underlying Islamic family law is that society consists of male-headed households where men hold authority and provide and protect vulnerable, weak, and dependent females in their charge. In other words, family law reform implicitly assumes the supremacy of a *wilāya-qiwāma* ('guardian-provider') nexus, that is, the connection between men's authority over women and their obligation to protect and maintain them. The main dynamic of law reform is the challenge mounted to this nexus by some societal constituencies. 'Complementarity' rather than 'equality' informs measures for law reform, in the belief that such distinctions between the positions of men and women (e.g. polygamy, unequal inheritance rights, males as guardians, and females as wards) are defined by the Quran and *sunna* and are therefore unquestionable. Although diversity in interpretation of the primary sources of Islamic law allow for differing juristic opinions, resulting in laws that are woman-friendly, the opposite trend also continues, particularly at the societal level. This chapter advances the argument that the state and her people, government officials of various departments, judicial officers etc, all subscribe to this framework to a greater or lesser degree; and that law reform and family law development are constrained within these parameters.

A distinctive feature of family law reform in Pakistan is its embeddedness within the common-law colonial legacy of 'Anglo-Muhammadan' as well as Islamic law. This legacy manifests itself in codification projects at state level as well as through the case law of the High Courts and Supreme Court. Whilst both arenas of legal development are informed by Islamic law, they do not always reinforce one another, resulting in less coherence and continuity between the two than is desirable. One of the hallmarks of *sharia* is its plurality of opinion, which is responsible for legal change as well as flexibility in the application of the law. Codification, on the other hand, removes the possibility of change and leaves little room for judicial flexibility. Contemporary codified law reform in the Muslim world is thus a double-edged sword, shutting down the flexible interpretative space of the Islamic legal traditions. In other words, the evolutionary potential and dynamic streak inherent within Islamic law has been and is being 'fossilized' by Western-inspired codification.

The historical development of 'modern' Pakistani family law and its reform is an intricate canvas, which brings into relief features that are specific to the Pakistani legal landscape. These include the influence of her colonial legacy and common law, the powers and place of the courts, the 'myth' of the 'Islamic' character of the state, and the influence of all of these on the development and the dynamics of family law in Pakistan today.[6] The present chapter contextualizes family law reform within these plural legalities operating in postcolonial Pakistan. It demonstrates that, in the zealously guarded domain of the 'Muslim' family, law reform is a 'subtle, almost imperceptible process of filtration through a maze of cultural norms and prevailing political . . . compulsions',[7] but one which ultimately has limited impact. The result has been half-hearted, piecemeal, and incoherent reform in a top-down legislative process with minimal implementation on the ground.

The chapter is presented in six sections. Following the introduction (section one), section two contextualizes family law within the Islamic legal traditions. Section three presents a historical overview of Pakistan's colonial legacy and the influence of common law with section four analysing features of inherited 'Anglo-Muhammadan' law in postcolonial Pakistan. Section five then proceeds to analyse the dynamics of law reform engaging with the contestations arising out of the interpretative plurality of the Islamic legal traditions at the level of state, legislature, judiciary and society. Section six presents some concluding reflections.

The *wilāya-qiwāma* nexus and the 'paradox of equality'[8]

There exists a complex body of literature framing the ongoing disputes over Muslim women's rights within the family, their wider linkages to women's status, and the interpretative space offered by Islamic legal traditions within which to analyse these plural legalities.[9] In attempting to understand the dynamics of Muslim family law, writers have tended to use a theoretical framework that explains gender hierarchies and inequalities from an Islamic law as well as from an international human rights perspective.[10] Hevener's[11] classification of international human rights as evolving from the corrective to the protective and finally to the non-discriminatory legal state where women have equal rights in all spheres is one I have employed in earlier work.[12] An example of a 'corrective' right is the Muslim woman's right to inherit, albeit half the share assigned to a male relative in the same position. This 'correction' came in seventh-century Arabia, where women were not *sui juris* and capable of inheriting. That this half share was a *minimum*, with potential for increasing as and when society evolved, was not taken forward; the minimum became the maximum, fixed and unchangeable. Examples of 'protective' rights in Islamic law are many, but include the right not to be forced into a contract of marriage; the right to initiate dissolution of marriage by '*khul*ᶜ'; and the right to decide the time period for breastfeeding.[13] In the area of family law, most of the rights of women have been placed within the 'corrective' and 'protective' categories despite marriage in Islam being a civil contract between two consenting parties. The particular nature of Muslim marriage prevents the female party from acquiring equality, since the husband is conceptualized as the 'provider', and the wife as the one provided for (through *mahr* (dower) and maintenance).[14] This inherent contradiction of what may be termed 'the paradox of equality' drives the dynamics of family law and reform in the Muslim world.

Esposito presents a compelling analysis of the unequal family law rights and responsibilities accorded to Muslim women and men, based on the distinction between *muᶜāmalāt* (socioeconomic relationships, necessarily evolving and mutable) and *ᶜibadāt* (immutable religious duties to God).[15] Esposito believes that these categories result in a 'hierarchisation of *Quranic* values', with women and men being full equals in the spiritual and moral domain of *ᶜibadāt* but unequal in the socioeconomic and family law field of *muᶜāmalāt*; but that, since such inequality in the sphere of socioeconomics and the family is subject to change with changing societal perceptions, there remains the potential for complete equality between women and men.[16] A word of caution needs to be raised here. As I have stated elsewhere:

> Although Esposito's attempt at hierarchisation of rights within the Islamic tradition is an important step in his endeavour to develop a modern framework

> for achieving equality for the sexes and within family law, we must not lose sight of the fact that, in his attempt to realise the legislative value of *Qur'anic* verses, he places emphasis on exegesis (*tafsir*).[17]

This, Esposito argues, is due to the necessity of uncovering the motive, intent, or purpose behind Quranic passages. This approach reasserts the original influence of Quranic values in the early development of law and, as such, seeks to renew the process by which Quranic values were applied to newly encountered social situations in the first centuries of Islamic legal history.[18] But it needs to be recognized that it was the very process of exegesis itself which resulted in restrictive interpretations of Quranic verses regarding the status of women; *tafsīr* can work in both directions and is subjective.[19]

The principle of 'gradualism', too, offers a thoughtful approach to understanding the religious text in Islam, arguing that by sowing the seeds of (albeit unequal) rights in seventh-century Arabia, the ground was prepared for such rights to gradually evolve into complete equality between women and men in all spheres of life.[20] Proponents of equal inheritance rights for women use this gradualist argument, suggesting that moving from no inheritance rights to rights which were half those of men was a promising departure point for women over 1,300 years ago. After all, no Quranic text or *sunna* prohibits giving *more* than a half share.[21]

Approaching the position of women within Islamic family law through an interpretative discourse over 'text and context' is also a well-trodden path, and one that offers hope to scholars arguing for equal rights within the Islamic legal traditions.[22] The practice of polygamy and the supposed right of a husband to beat his wife if she is disobedient[23] are often flagged up as examples of where a contextual analysis of the Quranic text can be advocated to present a woman-friendly interpretation.[24]

From a theoretical perspective, and in order to appreciate the dynamics of family law reform in Pakistan and other Muslim jurisdictions, I propose that a persuasive analysis can be arrived at by deconstructing how a Muslim woman as an autonomous legal person is transformed into an inherently *dependent* legal person under the perpetual guardianship (*wilāya*) of a male 'protector and provider' (*qawwām*). In classical *fiqh* (jurisprudence), the edifice of the patriarchal model of Muslim family law is wholly constructed upon the concept of *qiwāma*, with the man as the woman's 'protector and provider' (whether fathers and daughters, husbands and wives, or so on). This '*qiwāma* postulate', as Mir-Hosseini terms it,[25] transformed what had been a socio-cultural norm into a legal norm, and thereafter crept into both non-codified principles and codified family law in Muslim jurisdictions globally. Related to and serving to perpetuate gender hierarchies and the '*qiwāma* postulate' is the concept of *tamkīn* ('submission/obedience'). Making *qiwāma* contingent upon *tamkīn* means that wifely obedience becomes a material fact in family law cases, the husband being able to refuse maintenance if his wife has disobeyed him (in this context we find the word *nushūz* or 'rebellious disobedience' being used). The relationship between *qiwāma* and *tamkīn* has far-reaching consequences, as the absence of *tamkīn* justifies the denial of maintenance and protection.[26]

'Guardianship' (*wilāya*) is another important concept within the Islamic legal traditions, which is subject to a diverse range of scholarly interpretations regarding its meaning, scope, and application. Generally, Islamic legal conceptions (informed by classical *fiqh* and social perceptions) understand *wilāya* to be the blanket rights of a male over (i) a minor, incapacitated, or disabled ward in all major decisions relating to person and property, and over (ii) a female relative regarding consent to marriage.[27] A major focus of discussion over *wilāya* has been the right of an *adult* woman to conclude a marriage without the consent of her guardian (her *walī*). Schools of juristic thought differ as to the reach and remit of this right, i.e. whether the consent and presence of the *walī* is mandatory to the point that his absence would make a marriage void (we see this in the term *wilāyat al-ijbār*, 'marriage guardianship with power of coercion') or whether consent is simply recommended as desirable and important to protect the female's interests. Views on the subject over the centuries suggest that every school of juristic thought has held its own unique position but has faithfully reported those of other schools.[28] This classical doctrine, known as *ikhtilāf al-fuqahā'* ('diversity of opinions'), offered interpretative plurality as and when circumstances required. The colonial thrust towards codification and a black-letter approach to law weakened this egalitarian approach within the classical Islamic legal traditions. Masud has suggested that every rule of law within the Islamic traditions has gone through a three-stage process: (i) interpretation (of the source text); (ii) construction (of a rule); and (iii) reconstruction (as and when required, due to changing situations and demands).[29] Using examples from the writings of classical jurists, he illustrates 'the shifting framework of reasoning' employed to arrive at rulings based upon *maqāṣid al-sharīʿa* ('objectives of the law') rather than upon a specific text.[30] Applying this process to the doctrine of *wilāya*, Masud concludes that the concept of *wilāya* guardianship is one of social preference and not one of basic legal requirement.[31] For implementation within a pluralistic Muslim society, social preferences trump any law reform *even if* it finds legitimation in religious texts.

I would like to propose some further development in this framework, by suggesting that the *wilāya-qiwāma* nexus was thus interpreted, constructed, and re-constructed by jurists, and informed by prevalent social norms, in an attempt to control the resources, and the distribution thereof, that underpin the institution of marriage and its dissolution. Deconstruction of the linkage between *wilāya* and *qiwāma* requires an ends-oriented analysis of resource allocation and control within the institution of marriage, rather than a 'gender and equal rights' framework. The paradox of equality is seen at play in the dynamics of family law reform where two conflicting norms are pulling reform in opposing directions: if the contractual element of the Muslim marriage is taken as a basis, then two consenting parties who have capacity ought to be entering into an equal partnership of marriage. But this is not possible looking at the marriage from the opposing position, where the husband assumes the role of protector and provider.

From 'Islamic' to 'Anglo-Muhammadan' family law? A historical overview of Pakistan's colonial legacy and the influence of common law

Haider Ala Hamoudi's 'The Death of Islamic Law'[32] presents us with a challenging idea: the presence of a comprehensive 'Islamic law' is a myth, exemplified by the selectivity of Muslim states in choosing which aspects of *sharia* to incorporate into their state law. Hamoudi is of the view that 'law-making in many modern Muslim states gives rather short shrift to *sharia*, seemingly ignoring it in all areas save the law of the family and replacing it elsewhere with European-transplanted law'.[33] Even 'Islamists', he points out, engage in this selectivity:

> The Islamist does not want God's law to reign supreme in areas such as corporate law and the law of business entities where economic consequences may be dire . . . On the other hand lies the law of the family, where God's law is deemed a vital necessity, and any development, any evolution, any alteration of the rules established centuries ago . . . will not be countenanced.[34]

Hamoudi's analysis flags up the contested and porous nature of Islamic law and its receptivity to extrinsic influences, including local customary norms and European legal systems. It also lends support to the argument advanced in this chapter, that successive regimes[35] have, as a socioeconomic and political strategy, colluded to ring-fence a certain form of 'Islamic' family law as *the* signifier of Muslim identity to be preserved at all costs.

Centuries of Muslim rule and of legal institutions applying Islamic law preceded the British colonization of the Indian subcontinent.[36] In their pursuit of a colonial system of legal dispensation, the British shed aspects of (Indian and Mughal) legal governance but retained the 'family laws' of native communities, including Muslims. Siddique reiterates the generally held view that the colonial policy of retaining Islamic family law resulted from a convergence of economic interests between colonial legal systems (whose aim was to extract economic surplus) and the indigenous Muslim elite (whose aim was to reinforce their economic and socio-political dominance).[37] Anderson notes:

> Where the landed gentry and certain merchant groups were organized according to the dynastic principles of family and clan, the administration of family law played a role in broking wealth and power at the local level, ultimately underpinning the very intermediaries whose cooperation was essential to effective colonial rule.[38]

In other words, the political economy inherently at play due to the contractual nature of Muslim marriage, whilst lending support to existing patriarchal structures, also favoured colonial policies of governance.

The British colonial state initially adjusted existing structural features into new institutional forums, including the establishment of the colonial court. An hierarchy of civil and criminal courts was established by the Hastings Plan of 1772 tasked with applying indigenous legal norms. This meant, in respect of Muslims, 'the laws of the Koran . . . in all suits regarding inheritance, marriage, caste, and other religious usages or institutions'.[39] The birth of 'Anglo-Muhammadan law' thus came about by the application of British models of procedure and adjudication to a literalist, scripturalist 'Islamic law' explained by *maulvis*, religious scholars who acted as advisers to the courts. Derrett[40] states that starting with the 1772 doctrine (the Hastings Plan) that, in cases where indigenous laws seemed to provide no rule, the matter should be decided according to the Roman-law formula of 'justice, equity and good conscience', by 1887 was held 'to mean the rules of English law if found applicable to society and circumstances'.[41] By 1875, 'Anglo-Muhammadan Law' had been displaced by new colonial codes in all subjects except family law and certain property transactions.[42]

Alongside this procedural Anglicization of Islamic law, its substantive content, too, became coloured by the British rulers' insistence on a black-letter approach to law.[43] The interpretative plurality within Islamic law that had allowed it to remain cognitively open to changing societal needs and contexts was now frozen in its tracks by colonial judges' demands for simplistic responses that constituted *'the'* law. Two contemporaneous developments fed into this process: because of the need for knowledge of indigenous legal arrangements, the translation of works on *sharia* and *fiqh* from Arabic and Persian into English and the collection of local customary 'laws' was undertaken, leading to an impressive body of scholarship. But in trying to pin down 'Islamic law' its flexibility was lost; some texts and perspectives became privileged, while others were ignored. In this regard, Charles Hamilton's 1791 translation of *Hedaya*,[44] Baillie's rendering of *Fatawa Alamgiri*,[45] Sir William Jones's 1792 translation of *Al-Sirajiyya*, the translation of *Mishkat-ul-Masabith* (extracts from *Fatawa Kazee Khan*), and of *Principles and Precedents of Muhammadan Law* by Macnaghten became the textual bases of Anglo-Muhammadan law. Local Muslim elites also contributed to the development of Anglo-Muhammadan law through their writings, including the Tagore Law Lectures of 1891–92, Abdur Rahim's *Muhammadan Jurisprudence*, and Mulla's *Principles of Muhammadan Law*. These 'textbooks' of Anglo-Muhammadan law became part of a definitive, textual Islamic law as inherited by postcolonial Pakistan. As Kugle notes: 'The effects of British rewriting have created a lens of texts, terms and experiences which continue to distort the view of Shariah today.'[46] Siddique has stated that it merits further probing whether or not Muslims themselves, for instance, played a prominent subsequent role in the political contestations around, and eventual definition and development of, what came to be called Anglo-Muhammadan law.[47]

Confronted with (often inadequately) translated legal information and with native *maulvis* whose inputs reflected the complexity of pluralist legal traditions, a state of persistent distrust by colonial rulers of indigenous *maulvis* led to the collection and compilation of a corpus of local 'customary law'. In the late nineteenth century, following the adoption of the Punjab Laws Act of 1872, revenue collectors were tasked with ascertaining customary practices in every village. Yet this project was initiated with a preconceived notion that 'custom' was stable within a fairly static society and that, once ascertained, 'customary law' could be codified and dispensed within a British-inspired, colonial legal system. I have elsewhere challenged this perception by suggesting that:

> culture is an evolutionary process of our 'beings' and 'doings'. It is an intricate tapestry that both reflects and detracts from collusions and resistances (individual/collective), to dominant behavioural norms in society at various points in our histories . . . [I]t is important to remind ourselves of the highly political nature of this project: Who has the power to define culture determines whose voices are being heard and represented in this undertaking.[48]

Certain examples of the codification of custom arrived at by a 'useful' collusion of the colonial power and landed Muslim gentry, such as the exclusion of Muslim women as heirs in respect of land and other immovable property, were subsequently contested politically. Whilst such colonial understandings of the nature of 'customary law' were not strictly *inaccurate*, they nevertheless 'were arrested, frozen forms of representation'. The dynamics of family law reform in postcolonial Pakistan reflect the struggle between these frozen forms of representations at the formal, official, and elitist levels of state and society and at the grassroots.

Features of inherited 'Anglo-Muhammadan' family law in postcolonial Pakistan

What then were the features of this 'Anglo-Muhammadan' law that was inherited in 1947, and which Pakistan took forward as a state established in the name of the Islamic religion? How painlessly did this colonial, socio-legal construct find acceptability in the newly independent Pakistan? To what extent did Anglo-Muhammadan law form the basis for law reform and subsequent legal developments? These questions go to the heart of the dynamics of family law reform in Pakistan and will be addressed in the sections below.

The most prominent feature of Anglo-Muhammadan law was the hybridity and plurality of the norms informing it. Ironically, it was through the very effort for achieving a necessarily artificial uniformity that the reverse effect came about. Principles of Islamic law, English secular legal principles, and customary norms interacted to provide an 'amoebic, boundary-less set of regulatory norms'.[49] Anglo-Muhammadan law also accorded continued privilege to autonomous legal orderings away from the capital in peripheral regions where *panchayats* (village councils), *jirgas* (decision-making assemblies), and other local dispute-resolution forums were left untouched; hence the continued and thriving position of local customary law and 'cultural Islam' well into post-independence Pakistan with her pluralist legal and judicial system.[50]

Whilst the pluralist legal system passed on to Pakistan was substantively fraught with contradictions, duality, and (colonial) compromise, it was the rules of procedure that created what was for the vast majority of the population an alien legal system. The widespread and mandatory use of documentation in matters of law and evidence, together with the amplified role of the scribe, led to the alienation of a largely non-literate people, making legal institutions inaccessible to most of the population. But the most unforeseen consequence of Anglo-Muhammadan law and legal scholarship was perhaps its contribution to an environment in which a new politics of Muslim identity could flourish; a number of Islamicized laws were adopted in the area of family law between the eighteenth and twentieth centuries. The administration of Muslim law by a non-Muslim colonial power transformed personal law into grounds for organized political struggle, and in the late nineteenth and early twentieth centuries the Islamic identity thus engendered became a basis for colonial resistance.[51] Colonial vocabularies of identity such as 'Hindu' and 'Muslim', accompanied by artificial and monolithic concepts of 'Hindu personal law' and 'Muslim personal law' became part of the popular imagination of the postcolonial state and the dynamics of law reform. Ironically, it was Anglo-Muhammadan law, this inflexible, scripturalist, and colonially generated version of Islamic law that became the enduring legacy Pakistan inherited at the time of partition in 1947.

Muslim Personal Law (Shariat) Application Act 1937

The culmination of this influence of religious identity on law came with the Muslim Personal Law (Shariat) Application Act 1937 (the MPL),[52] as prior to its adoption Islamic personal law in India varied by region and community, often informed by customary practices.[53] The act originated in efforts, primarily among some religious scholars (*ulama*), to secure statutory enforcement of *sharia*. Their successful lobbying resulted in the 1937 Act, which abrogated what were seen as 'non-Islamic' customs. Anderson sums this up thus:

> The Act affirmed, in the political arena, the equivalence of Muslim identity and a certain form of *sharia*. It was a statute of indigenous instigation, but its form and purpose reflected a view of *sharia* that had been reshaped under the British administration.[54]

It also highlighted the limits of law reform in the sphere of Islamic family law, especially where the empowerment of women was concerned. Its preamble, acknowledging Muslim women's organizations as new interlocutors in family law reform alongside religious scholars, is self-explanatory:

> For several years past it has been the cherished desire of the Muslims of British India that Customary Law should in no case take the place of Muslim Personal Law. The matter has been repeatedly agitated in the press as well as on the platform. The Jamiat-ul-Ulema-i-Hind, the greatest Moslem religious body has supported the demand and invited the attention of all concerned to the urgent necessity of introducing a measure to this effect. Customary Law is a misnomer in as much as it has not any sound basis to stand upon

> and is very much liable to frequent changes and cannot be expected to attain at any time in the future that certainty and definiteness which must be the characteristic of all laws. *The status of Muslim women under the so-called Customary Law is simply disgraceful. All the Muslim Women Organisations have therefore condemned the Customary Law as it adversely affects their rights.*[55] They demand that the Muslim Personal Law (*Shariat*) should be made applicable to them. The introduction of Muslim Personal Law will automatically raise them to the position to which they are naturally entitled. In addition to this [the] present measure, if enacted, would have very salutary effect on society because it would ensure certainty and definiteness in the mutual rights and obligations of the public. Muslim Personal Law (*Shariat*) exists in the form of a veritable code and is too well known to admit of any doubt or to entail any great labour in the shape of research, which is the chief feature of Customary Law.[56]

Having expressed dissatisfaction with customary laws and their adverse impact on Muslim women, Section 2 of the Act, however, rolls back on what it aspired to in the preamble by stating that:

> Notwithstanding any customs or usage to the contrary, in all questions (save questions relating to agricultural land) . . . the rule of decision in cases where the parties are Muslims shall be the Muslim Personal Law (*Shariat*).[57]

The 'collusion' of colonial rulers with India's Muslim landed gentry is evident here when 'questions relating to agricultural land' are excluded from the remit of the 1937 Act. This trend of excluding women from inheritance continued well into the post-independence era, and it was only in 1962 that amendments to the 1937 Act conceded this right to women.[58] Also, in the interest of political expediency, un-Islamic customary practices denying Muslim women their rights were ignored when 'Islamizing' other laws.[59]

The Dissolution of Muslim Marriages Act 1939

Another response to the rising demands of Indian Muslims for Islamic family law during the colonial era was the Dissolution of Muslim Marriages Act 1939 (DMMA).[60] The Act's preamble states that its purpose was to 'consolidate and clarify the provisions of Muslim law relating to suits for dissolution of marriage by women married under Muslim law and to remove doubts as to the effect of the renunciation of Islam by a married Muslim woman on her marriage tie'.

The 1939 Act codifies and regulates the grounds on which a woman married under Muslim law may obtain a judicial decree of dissolution of marriage from the courts. Section 2 of the Act enumerates these grounds, which include, *inter alia*: the husband's whereabouts being unknown for four years, failure by a husband to maintain his wife for two years, failure to perform marital obligations for three years, the husband's impotence, insanity, or his suffering from leprosy or VD. Cruelty and abuse, whether physical or mental, and emotional distress inflicted by the husband are also grounds for dissolution. The wife may also seek divorce if the husband interferes in how she manages her property or obstructs her in the performance of her religious profession or practice. One subsection extends the 'option of puberty' (*khyar-ul-bulugh*), by which a girl can repudiate a marriage entered into while she was a minor (including a marriage contracted on her behalf by her father or grandfather). Another important provision is Section 5, which states that dissolution of the marriage contract under the Act will not affect the wife's right to dower.[61]

The dynamics of family law reform in postcolonial Pakistan

In its present formulation, modern Pakistani family law is by and large a colonial construct derived from the Quran, *sunna*, *ijmā*ᶜ, and *qiyās*, all of which is seen through the prism of Anglo-Muhammadan law.[62] Simultaneously, this law has over the centuries been influenced by the writings of scholars, *ulama*, *muftis*, and *maulvis*. Customary practices, too, have significantly informed and influenced popular as well as 'formal' understandings and applications of family law by the courts and population. Family law has found expression and articulation in reports and recommendations of various Law Commissions[63] and codified laws.[64] The socioeconomic and political environment of the postcolonial state, too, has played a tangible role in family law developments, as we will see later. A complex and intricately inter-woven canvas of regulatory norms has thus evolved under the overarching umbrella of Islam and *sharia*. Pearl and Menski make the apt observation that:

> Islamic law has always been a matter of religion as much as law, so that formal legal changes through state law were never quite able to override the sphere of *shari'a*, even if it may appear so.[65]

The existence of contesting narratives in family law implied by Pearl and Menski finds support in a number of Islamic-law scholars, including An-Na'im, who is of the view that family law remains 'a highly symbolic location of the struggle between the forces of traditionalism and modernism'.[66] The conflict is at multiple levels: within Islamic law itself there is the contest between 'traditionalist' and 'modern' interpretations; another contest exists between 'Islamic law as an entity and the secularists of Western liberal thought'.[67] It is to this unrelenting and ongoing tension underpinning family law reform that we now turn our attention.

The past's simultaneous absence and presence in family law reform

Family law reform in Pakistan adopts as a given starting point the 'received' versions of Anglo-Muhammadan laws and legal institutions left behind by the colonial rulers. To this extent, the past is present in the family law dispensation of Pakistan in that it is common-law based, precedent-bound, adversarial, structured, and hierarchical.[68] Simultaneously, however, survivals from the precolonial Islamic-law model of governance are also discernible in such local dispute-resolution forums as *jirgas, panchayats*, and courts led by *qadis* (judges), drawing upon an 'eclectic body of rulings'[69] of Islamic law, inquisitorial and responsive to their immediate social context. This duality has led to contested narratives of what constitutes 'Islamic' family law both at the formal and informal levels. Which aspects of this 'received' family law reflect 'authentic' Islamic law, it might be asked, and from where did non-Muslim colonial law makers derive the legitimacy to legislate on Islamic law? As the successor state to colonial Britain, what are the 'Islamic' or 'Muslim' credentials of Pakistan's law makers? Who are the controllers and custodians of family law reform in Pakistan? Which school(s) of juristic thought do they represent, if at all, and on what basis are *reforms* within family law 'Islamic' and applicable to all Pakistani Muslims?[70]

Minimal discussion on these difficult questions has set the trend for an uncritical, ahistorical, and de-contextualized discourse of family law reform.[71] Rather than undertaking a critical review of the inherited, colonial legal system in order to establish a dispensation of justice representative of the post-partition population, the elitist colonial project continued. This approach towards law reform encouraged a piecemeal 'fix what appears wrong and everything will be fine' strategy.[72] Siddique argues that there is an 'absence of the past in Pakistan's reform narratives'[73] and a reluctance to probe into the precolonial period to draw comparisons and lessons and to ascertain the extent to which the colonial legal system was an 'alien' imposition.

The central 'official' narrative in 1947, at the birth of the state of Pakistan, was that of a cohesive polity of Muslims who had struggled for an independent state in order to live in accordance with Islamic principles and laws. Beneath the surface, though, existed the parallel narratives of the multiple identities of the various communities inhabiting the new state of Pakistan. Imbued with rich and deeply entrenched cultures, customs, and traditions, these communities paid little deference to formal laws legislated by the state. Law reform within the sphere of the family only served to highlight opposing perceptions of what Islamic law stated and of how it might apply to various communities on the ground. Here the dynamics of family law reform in Pakistan entered contested terrain, with both the past and present being mapped in different ways to provide different signposts to the future. No narrative of the past is immutable, and the narrator often reads from a self-interested script. In the colonial past, it had been impossible for the British to approach Islamic law on its own terms due to their ignorance of *fiqh*, as well as the imperative to undermine the legitimacy of Mughal rule and Islamic jurisprudence.[74] The British attempted to appropriate Islamic law through translation and codification, but both proved to be flawed processes.[75] In postcolonial Pakistan, too, law reform which was acceptable to all sections of the population – to all those different narrators of the past and present and signposters to the future – was virtually impossible to achieve. The outcome has proved to be similar to the colonial past, in that law and its reform remain only partially acceptable as 'Islamic'. Proponents of 'Islamized' law reform post-1947 continued with the same fundamental misconception as the colonial rulers: that 'Islamic' law could be completely codified and located in an authoritative text that could be readily implemented, and that one comprehensive text would apply to all Pakistani Muslims as a single, homogenous community.[76] But rather than recognize the need to pass legislation informed by principles of Islamic law, reform was instead undertaken in a cautious and half-hearted manner. Fearful of being castigated for *not* passing legislation that was in consonance with Islamic law, those charged with reforming family law tried to please all constituencies but ended up pleasing none. Conservatives denounced reforms as too liberal and un-Islamic, while women's rights activists and NGOs felt that they had not gone far enough. There remains today a disconnect between, on the one hand, family law reform that has the potential to alleviate social, economic, and political disempowerments and alienations and, on the other, Pakistan's official law-reform discourse.[77]

The Muslim Family Laws Ordinance 1961: 'Western' liberal imposition or return to 'original' Islamic law?

Another dynamic of Islamic family law reform in Pakistan is the polarization of perspectives and subsequent lack of unanimity on the form and content of Islamic family law. There is a continual state of tension between those who wish to hark back to a 'pristine' and 'just' Islamic legal system implemented in seventh-century Arabia and those who believe modernization through the codification and formalization of the judicial system is the only way forward. A further dynamic within this is the selective use within that 'pristine' Islamic law of forms by which women's rights to property, education, marrying a person of their choice, and so on, are absent. When challenged, this denial of women's rights is either skirted around or justified in the name of 'cultural Islam'.[78] The legal system of Pakistan and its reform processes do not engage with communities on the ground in an attempt to seek their inclusion and allay fears regarding the 'Islamic' legitimacy of laws adopted. Neither do they capture practices on the ground, thus failing to reflect peoples' understandings of which legal norms ought to apply to them. This disconnect leads one to pose the question: who sets the agenda for family law reform? Are they representative of the common Pakistani, or are they simply voicing the interests of elites? To what extent do people share ownership of the law-reform project, and how can it be made more inclusive?

After Independence, consistent pressure from women's groups led to the setting up of a Commission on Marriage and Family Laws (the 'Rashid Commission')[79] in 1955, briefed with exploring ways of restricting polygamy and giving women more rights of divorce than had been granted under the Dissolution of Muslim Marriages Act, 1939. The Rashid Commission reported in 1958, and three years later some of its recommendations were enacted in the form of the Muslim Family Laws Ordinance (Ordinance VIII of 1961).

As an example of the 'Islamization' of laws, Pearl and Menski hailed the provisions of the 1961 Ordinance as being 'as impressive as the reforms for instance introduced by Ataturk in Turkey in the opposite direction so many years ago. It may well be that Pakistan's "Islamisation" will provide the inspiration for other

Muslim countries over the next 20 years.'[80] Ironically, although it was undertaken in a spirit of 'Islamization' with a view to codify, hitherto uncodified principles of Hanafi Sunni Islamic law, some provisions of the 1961 Ordinance have been contested within communities and before the courts, which have handed down varying pronouncements as to precisely how 'Islamic' or 'un-Islamic' it is.[81]

The Commission's major recommendations had included the abolition of polygamy, but, as has consistently been the case in Pakistan, elected governments find themselves unable to legislate and to implement meaningful reforms because of popular pressure. It took an army general, Mohammad Ayub Khan, to promulgate the Muslim Family Laws Ordinance 1961 (MFLO), but even then polygamy was only limited (and even that half-heartedly) rather than abolished outright.

Yet the 1961 Ordinance did contain some very important provisions advantageous to women. Under the Sunni Hanafi understanding of Islamic law the unilateral right to terminate the marriage contract belongs to the husband, and he must pay the wife dower on his third pronouncement of the word *ṭalāq*, 'I divorce you'.[82] In 1961, for the first time in the history of the subcontinent, the right to this instantaneous and irrevocable triple *ṭalāq*[83] was curtailed, and the principles of two other forms of divorce (*talaq-i-ahsan* and *talaq-i-hasan*) which offer time and scope for reconciliation were incorporated into statute, thus regulating and formalizing the divorce process.[84] For women, the right to divorce by *khulᶜ*[85] and a right to divorce that has been delegated to her by the husband (*talaq-i-tafwid*), recognized under traditional Islamic law, were also recognized in statute, the latter being incorporated as an option in the standard marriage contract (the *nikah-nama*). Polygamy was restricted, in that a husband desirous of a subsequent marriage had to submit an application to the Arbitration Council besides seeking the permission of his existing wives.[86] The chairman of the Arbitration Council would then need to satisfy himself that the proposed marriage was 'necessary'.[87] However, these provisions were neutered by the fact that an existing wife's refusal to grant consent would not prevent the husband from remarrying, while failure to obtain permission from the Arbitration Council would not invalidate a subsequent marriage. The only reprisal for non-compliance is that, in the event of failure to obtain permission, the husband is liable to:

> pay immediately the entire amount of the dower, whether prompt or deferred, due to the existing wife/wives, which amount, if not so paid, shall be recoverable as arrears of land revenue; and on conviction upon complaint be punishable with simple imprisonment which may extend to one year, or with fine which may extend to Rs. 5000, or with both.[88]

A review of post-1961 cases, however, reveals that very few cases have been filed invoking failure to seek prior permission or to register a marriage. In the few reported cases, a plea was advanced to declare the subsequent marriage void and illegal,[89] but courts held these marriages valid as provided by the MFLO.

The Ordinance also provided security for children of any predeceased issue of a deceased person under section 4 of the MFLO by providing that the child steps into the shoes of their deceased parent as regards inheritance.[90] An-Na'im describes section 4 of the MFLO as 'a significant reform to the classical law of inheritance by allowing for orphaned grandchildren by predeceased sons or daughters, to inherit.'[91] This provision of the law presents a departure from traditional Hanafi understandings and interpretation of Quranic injunctions on the subject which is informed by the principle that 'the nearer excludes the further'. The table of heirs in Hanafi Sunni law of inheritance are divided into 'sharers', 'residuaries', and 'distant kindred'. This implies that where sons and daughters (sharers) predecease their parent(s), their children slip from the category of sharers and are liable to be excluded from inheritance.[92]

Proponents of section 4 of the MFLO allowing children of predeceased children to step into the shoes of their deceased parents to receive their share of inheritance argue that nowhere in the Quran are grandchild/ren prohibited from inheriting from their grandparents. This change in traditional Hanafi law of inheritance was justified on the basis that:

> The Ordinance aims at alleviating the sufferings of the children whose unfortunate lot it is to lose their father or mother during the lifetime of their grandfather, or grandmother as the case may be. The construction of such statutes should be just sensible and liberal, so as to give effect to the purpose for which they are passed.[93]

To date, the most consistent attack on family law reform has been mounted against section 4 of the MFLO (i.e. placing sons and daughters of predeceased children in the shoes of their parents as regards inheritance rights.). One of the earliest cases was *Mst Farishta v The Federation of Pakistan*,[94] where the Shariat Bench of the High Court of Peshawar accepted the argument that section 4 of the MFLO was contrary to the injunctions of Islam and therefore invalid. The Government appealed the decision[95] and the Shariat Bench of the Supreme Court reversed the earlier decision holding that: 'section 4 of the Muslim Family Laws Ordinance VIII of 1961 is a special statutory provision which is intended to be applied only to Muslims of Pakistan as a class by itself, and from that point of view, constitutes a personal law for the Muslims . . . with the result, that its scrutiny was outside the jurisdiction of the High Court . . .'[96] Likewise, in the case of *Allah Rakha v Federation of Pakistan*, the Federal Shariat Court declared that:

> The inclusion of the grandchildren in the inheritance from the grandfather in the presence of the sons and daughters at the time the succession opens and to have per stripes a share equivalent to the share which such predeceased son or daughter would have received if alive is, therefore, nugatory to the scheme of inheritance envisaged by Qur'an.[97]

The swing of the judicial pendulum continues from section 4 MFLO being declared a positive development[98] in accordance with the spirit of Islam to being contrary to the injunctions of Islam.

The 'text and context' discourse and its implications for the development of Islamic family law

A major dynamic of family law reform in Pakistan is the ongoing 'text and context' debate in Islamic law, which is evident at all levels of state, government, and society. The diversity in interpretation of Islamic legal texts vis-à-vis the contexts in which these have been received, understood, and applied has resulted in piecemeal reform that has not received universal acceptance on the ground. This is evident from reports of all law commissions constituted to date, as well as from the judgements of the Pakistani courts.[99] Recommendations relating to laws on polygamy highlight this conundrum. All law-reform commissions and committees so tasked have devoted much time and attention to the subject but have never recommended its complete prohibition, simply because the debate has resulted in multiple interpretations of the Quranic text relating to polygamy. Expressing dissatisfaction with the recommendations of the Family Law Commission 1956, the report of the 1997 Commission of Inquiry on the Status of Women stated:

> In Pakistan, polygamy escaped decisive censure of the Muslim Family laws Ordinance, 1961. The Ordinance neither banned polygamy nor did it effectively restrict the practice. Even though the law requires the husband to secure permission from the Arbitration Council prior to entering into a second marriage, the valid grounds for such a permission are wide enough to give the Arbitration Council total discretion.[100]

Islamic family law permits a man to be lawfully married to up to four wives at the same time. Polygamy thus stands permitted in Islam, although the Quranic verse on the subject includes clear provisos:

> And if you fear that you cannot act equitably towards orphans, then marry such women as seem good to you, two, three or four, but if you fear that you shall not be able to deal justly [with them] then only one.[101]

This raises a number of questions. Does, for instance, the Quran create an *obligation* to be polygamous, or is it a qualified option to be exercised under those circumstances set out in that verse?[102] Al-Hibri is of the opinion that the mere fact that the Prophet Mohammed was polygamous in his later life is no evidence of a 'right' of all men to be polygamous. She argues that Quranic verses state clearly that neither the Prophet nor his wives are like other men and women and employing it as a pretext for polygamy, is not appropriate.[103] Secondly, the verse that has been used to justify polygamy also attaches a condition for such action, i.e. a requirement to deal justly with all one's wives. Reinforcing this is the Quranic statement (verse 4:129) that 'Ye are never able to be fair and just among women even if you tried hard'. 'Modernist' Muslim scholars are of the opinion that for evolving a rule of law relating to polygamy these two verses must be read and interpreted together.[104] In response to the above argument, some Muslim thinkers assert that the word *taᶜdilū* has a different meaning in verse 4:129 (to 'deal justly') to that in verse 4:3 (to 'do justice'); hence the view that these verses *cannot* be combined to draw an inference.[105] Abdur Rahman Doi also challenges the view of modernists who consider verse 4:129 as a legal condition attached to polygamous unions.[106] Citing Shaikh Mohammed bin Sirin and Shaikh Abubakr bin al-Arabi, he makes the point that the inability of a man to do justice between women referred to in the Quran is in respect of love and sexual intercourse only. The justice required of a man is, in the opinion of these scholars, confined to matters of providing equality in residence, food, and clothes to his wives. By this argument, so long as a man can provide these he is seen as being 'just' between women.[107]

So, given such contestation over the Quranic basis for polygamy, how had the Rashid Commission reached its recommendations? The Commission had drawn on 'reformist' textual interpretations and sought inspiration from other Muslim states where polygamy had been abolished.[108] But the strong dissenting note of Maulana Ihtesham-ul-haq Thanvi, a member of the Commission, and a fear of adverse public opinion, had led to a 'watered down' version which regulated rather than abolished polygamy altogether.

Judicial Ijtihād: the 'silent Islamization' of the Pakistani judiciary as a vehicle for law reform

In his book *The Role of Islam in the Legal System of Pakistan*,[109] Martin Lau emphasizes the role of the judges in 'appropriating' Islam and Islamic law and 'its integration into the vocabulary of the courts'.[110] This has been a 'conscious process aimed at fulfilment of the general desire to indigenise and Islamize the legal system at the end of colonisation.'[111] This judge-led process used the language of Islamic law to enhance the powers of the judiciary and widen the scope of constitutional guarantees of rights. At the same time, judicial attitudes are inevitably reflective of societal perceptions as well as wider cultural perceptions, and are not always in consonance with 'official' law. As demonstrated in *Farishta* and other cases, judges have not been shy in declaring a statute as 'un-Islamic' and therefore invalid, laying bare the fragility of any law-reform process, even if undertaken in the name of Islam.[112]

Postcolonial Pakistan inherited a common-law system, including her court system, which continues to date. During the 1980s, Zia-ul-Haq amended the constitution to create Shariat Courts with the remit to entertain cases in the realm of Islamic law. Even he, however, was conscious of the limits of his 'Islamization' process, and hence a 'saving' clause was inserted declaring personal laws to be outside the remit of these Shariat Courts, and it was this that became the basis for the appellate judgement in *Farishta*.

Despite attempts at 'Islamization' of the legal and judicial system through case law and law reform, it is obvious that within the judiciary itself there are opposing perspectives at play. Even the Federal Shariat Court had to reconcile the common-law legacy with the Islamic legacy by stating:

> . . . the Court maintains a balance between the Judges trained in the common law tradition and the Ulama' Judges, who are experts in the Islamic legal tradition, with the result that each issue presented before the Court is shaped and refined in a unique way by the two traditions before a final decision is rendered. Silently, swiftly, but surely *ijtihād* is being undertaken in a new way.[113]

The 'Islamization' of law and law reform by the judiciary is being undertaken within the framework of the Constitution of Pakistan and is reminiscent of the judicial *ijtihād* of the colonial period, where Muslim judges took on the role of using Islamic law in its context rather than in its classical renderings. By (judicial) '*ijtihād*' is meant the deduction of legal principle through *a priori* reasoning, without recourse to the teachings of a school of jurisprudence. An example of judicial *ijtihād* is the interpretation of *khul*ᶜ developed by the Pakistani judiciary and the meaning placed upon the concept in their decisions as described below.

In Islamic family law, the dissolution of marriage may take any one of the following routes: (i) at the instance and initiative of the husband (*ṭalāq*); (ii) at the instance and initiative of the wife (*khul*ᶜ); (iii) by mutual consent (*mubāra'a*). Contrary to popular perceptions, the Quranic injunctions on the subject, outlined in Sura 4, 'Women' (*Al-Nisā'*), fall short of according men a unilateral right to dissolve the marriage tie without assigning any cause. In a landmark Pakistani case, *Mst Khurshid Bibi v Mohammed Amin*,[114] their Lordships were of the view that *ṭalāq* is not an unfettered right, as verse 4:35 of the Quran provides for the appointment of arbiters to curtail its unbridled exercise. These fetters, however, also have their limits, and if the husband is determined to go ahead with the pronouncement of divorce then no court is competent to stop him from doing so (the 1961 Ordinance has, however, attempted to regulate and provide a role for judicial forums to restrain the husband).

But Islamic law also confers on a woman the right to seek dissolution of the marriage tie. In cases cited from the time of the Prophet Muhammad, the only question asked of the woman would be whether she was willing to forego her dower. If she agreed, the marriage stood dissolved.[115] It was only later that this right became qualified, the woman having to convince a court of her fixed aversion and of the irretrievable breakdown of the marriage in order to obtain *khul*ᶜ.[116] Although some leading judgements from Pakistan's superior courts have tried to equate a man's right to pronounce *ṭalāq* with the woman's right of *khul*ᶜ,[117] there are major differences between these two modes: no matter what obstacles one places in the way of a husband's right to *ṭalāq*, at the end of the day *ṭalāq* may be pronounced with or without the intervention of a court; but if a woman fails to convince a judge of the genuineness of her case, she cannot unilaterally terminate the marriage.[118] Social construction of the content of a woman's right to *khul*ᶜ overrides her rights under Islamic law.

Under a 2002 amendment to the Family Court Act 1964, where the wife seeks dissolution on the basis of *khul*ᶜ the court is simply required to pass an order to that effect on return of the dower to the husband without going into their previously held position that full repayment of dower is not automatic in all *khul*ᶜ cases. In *M Saqlain Zaheer v Zaibun Nisa*,[119] for instance, the court refined and clarified the concept of *zar-i-khula* (the sum which needs to be repaid by the wife) in a manner that has benefited women by insisting that reciprocal benefits received by the husband should be taken into account: continuously living together, bearing and rearing children, housekeeping, and so on can be counted as benefits offsetting the sum that the wife has to repay.

This particular amendment has been criticized due to the fact that it does not require the court to go into the details of whether the wife should repay *mahr* to the husband in lieu of *khul*ᶜ or whether is she entitled to keep some of it (as stated in *M Saqlain Zaheer v Zaibun Nisa*). Under the 2002 amendments, courts simply have to rubber-stamp the *khul*ᶜ so long as the dower is returned, without developing the argument that taking back from the wife what the husband gave at the time of the marriage is against the spirit of Islam and an injustice to the wife. Amendment of the law relating to *khul*ᶜ appears to have overturned gains obtained through case law, in what amounts to a 'two steps forward, one step back' situation.

Conflicting 'Islamization'(s) or plural Islam? The incoherence of law reform

That Islamic law is plural in its interpretation, adoption, and practice is an oft-repeated position for most writers on Islamic law and one that has been advanced in the present chapter. Competing interest groups play out their preferred understandings of Islamic law, and family law is the most common battleground for the opinions reflecting this plurality. As outlined in preceding sections, family law in Pakistan is based on principles of Islamic law; the judiciary has consistently developed its jurisprudence within an Islamic legal framework. However, some constituencies within Pakistan have always challenged the 'Islamic-ness' of the legal and judicial system, demanding 'wholesale replacement of the inherited colonial system'.[120] Whilst the judiciary has discretely led the 'Islamization' process through judicial decisions by invoking Islamic law as central to its decisions, this has not always been perceived as sufficient or, in some cases, the 'right type' of 'Islamization'. The late 1970s and 1980s saw an aggressive form of overt 'Islamization' as government policy, when Zia-ul-haq declared this to be his legitimating factor for overthrowing a democratically elected government. A number of laws were adopted in the name of Islam, the most controversial and damaging of these being collectively known as the 'Hudood Ordinances'[121] (from Arabic '*ḥudūd*' meaning 'the bounds of acceptable behaviour').

Two parallel approaches to 'Islamization' thus emerged in Pakistan, coexisting in an uneasy relationship and with unintended adverse effects on women in particular. The Muslim Family Laws Ordinance exemplified a progressive interpretation by casting traditional Islamic law into a modern legal framework; the Hudood ordinances, on the other hand, represented a version of Islam and Islamic law that was based upon a literal and often misplaced interpretation of the sources.[122] For example, section 7 of the MFLO attempted to institute a divorce procedure by requiring the husband to send a written notice of divorce to the chairman of the Arbitration Council set up under the Act. The purpose of this provision was to ensure that the authorities were aware of the change of marital status and that both parties were free to remarry should they choose to do so, and it was therefore an attempt to protect women from being the subject of ex-husbands who, having pronounced divorce, could later question their own divorce were their ex-wives to remarry.

The most explosive provision of the MFLO, however, is section 7(1), which seeks to ensure that a copy of the written notice of *ṭalāq* provided to the chairman of the Arbitration Council is also given to the wife, making the fact of the divorce clear and unequivocal. Contravention of this procedure makes the husband liable to simple imprisonment of one year and/or a fine. This seemingly straightforward procedural requirement since 1979 (until the passage of the Women Protection Act 2006), became the cause of grave miscarriages of justice as the MFLO interacted dynamically with the provisions regarding *zinā'* (fornication and adultery) in the Hudood ordinances and has given rise to a large body of case law.

Prior to the Prohibition of *Zina* (Enforcement of *Hudood*) Ordinance 1979, in most legal cases relating to non-registration of *ṭalāq* a court would hold that the woman was still married, since her husband had not gone through the complete statutory procedure for obtaining a valid divorce. Courts acted on the belief that the objective of the MFLO was to protect women from the ill-effects of arbitrary divorce, and the subsequent waiting period of 90 days was held to place some limitation and restraint upon the husband's unilateral and arbitrary right to divorce. This safety net had been set out with an eye to the social structure of Pakistan, where a divorced woman is akin to a pariah, with little support or respect both within her family and the wider social circle. However, with the promulgation of the Prohibition of *Zina* Ordinance, the insistence upon the provision of the MFLO that only a *ṭalāq* duly written and notified would be effective became a *dis*advantage to women. Vindictive former husbands who had failed to send a written notice to the Arbitration Council could now allege that a former wife who, after being divorced, had remarried was in fact not married, guilty of adultery, and liable to be accused of *zinā'* an offence punishable with lashes and/or stoning to death.[123] The courts finally declared that failure to notify the authorities of a *ṭalāq* did not invalidate the *ṭalāq*. In a landmark judgement, Naseem Hassan Shah CJ held that where a wife *bona fide* believing that her previous marriage with her former husband stands dissolved on the basis of a *talaqnama* although the husband has not got it registered with the Union Council enters into a second marriage, neither the second marriage nor the fact of her living with the second husband will amount to *zinā'* because of her *bona fide* belief that her first marriage stood dissolved.[124]

Such judgements were 'damage containment' responses by courts to the interaction of the MFLO and the Hudood laws. While these have saved women from the disastrous consequences of being found guilty of *zinā'*, they have in effect nevertheless nullified those provisions of the MFLO that offered some relief to women against arbitrary and unregistered *ṭalāq*. An important point to note for our purposes is that the dynamics in this area of law reside in the differing interpretations of 'Islamic' law which gave rise to the MFLO and the Prohibition of *Zina* Ordinance, and in the judiciary's changing response to the cases before them under pressure from both conservative and modernizing constituencies. Legal pluralism has also played a decisive role by playing provisions of the codified family law (primarily the MFLO) against literalist, inflexible interpretations of Islamic law and rival versions of 'Islamic' laws, including the Hudood Ordinances. The outcome is case law consisting of contradictory rulings, some declaring the MFLO un-Islamic; others upholding the Islamic nature of the statute. Section 7, requiring registration of *ṭalāq* has alternately been found both 'Islamic'[125] *and* 'un-Islamic'.[126]

Alongside the dynamic of plural Islamic law visible in the formal law making and judicial system, a further layer of complexity has become more visible in recent years. In most postcolonial Muslim jurisdictions, governance issues are often mixed up and confused with Islamic-law issues, and this has led to a nostalgia for a supposed 'Islamic' past that was radically displaced by colonial laws. Customary practices and dispute-resolution forums such as *jirgas* and *panchayats* have been a source of frustration and injustice. A combined assault on laws resulting from reform processes (both colonial and postcolonial) and customary practices has been mounted by 'Islamists' in a number of jurisdictions, including Pakistan. Demands for a return to 'Islam' and 'Islamic law' (*sharia*, as they term it) have become the basis of militancy. The militancy in Pakistan's Swat valley is a good example. There, the Taliban initially built a constituency for themselves upon precisely this basis: a demand for 'Islamic law'. A relentless campaign for women's rights and justice within the family, broadcast on an FM radio channel, created sympathy among people who were frustrated by a lack of action by governmental institutions. By way of example, a widow had been denied her inheritance by her in-laws, and the local government had not acted to help her. Upon complaining to the militant Taliban leader Maulana Fazlullah through her mosque's *imam*, she was assured of her inheritance and her in-laws were threatened with 'dire consequences' if she was not reinstated in the family home. Irrespective of the turnaround in the stance of the Taliban and how women became the prime targets of their version of Islam and Islamic law, the fact remains that in the early days of the militancy, the gap left by formal governance structures, including the judicial system, was filled by the 'rough and ready' justice of the Taliban. They spoke the language of the people, delivered on their promise, and responded to the demands for justice by women and other vulnerable sections of society. The state and government, even after these incidents, failed to respond and rise to the occasion by ensuring rights and effective dispensation of justice. Unsavoury as it may appear to Western, liberal society, the Taliban, at least, in their initial days, offered a bottom-up approach to access to justice, including women's rights in the family. Women did not have to pay fees to lawyers, travel to courts, or suffer the inordinate delays that are a hallmark of the Pakistani and other judicial systems. And they were also assured that what was being given to them was a form of divine justice.

Present by their absence: the thorny issues of family law

Competing perspectives in family law reform have informed debates on the subject, reflecting an ongoing struggle between forces of literalist and conservative Islam and proponents of progressive, interpretative expressions of that same religious tradition. That various constituencies pull the law in different directions is also apparent from case law as well as from law reforms instigated by these individuals and groups. What is bemusing in these varying narratives is the eerie silence over certain thorny issues within Islamic family law that have failed to find champions on any side of the ideological divide, and in particular at the grassroots. These include Islamic conceptions of *halala* marriage, the triple *ṭalāq*, post-divorce maintenance, and the adoption of children. Since it can be argued that any meaningful developments in family law have in a sense transpired through judicial decisions, it is disappointing to note an absence of any serious engagement of courts in these important and challenging, yet little discussed, matters. A good example of such thorny issues is the concept of *halala*.

Halala (Urdu, in Arabic *taḥlīl*) is a short, intervening marriage to a third party, which an ex-wife must go through before remarrying her ex-husband in order to make their remarriage *ḥalāl*. It supposedly emanates from a Quranic verse, the aim of which was to demonstrate the seriousness with which divorce should be treated in a Muslim marriage. In a patriarchal society, the need for *halala* has always been a hugely inhibiting factor on otherwise easily available *ṭalāq* divorce, it being a serious reprimand for a man to have his ex-wife marry another man as a precondition for remarrying him. The Quran in verse 2:230 states:

> And if he divorces her finally, she shall thereafter not be lawful unto him unless if she marries another man. If [by chance this marriage also breaks] and the present husband divorces her, there shall be no sin upon either of them [i.e. the first husband and the divorced wife] to remarry—provided that both of them think that they will be able to be within the bounds set by Allah: and these are the bounds of Allah which He makes clear unto people of innate knowledge.

In Muslim societies including Pakistan, *halala* follows on from the (in)famous practice of the triple *ṭalāq*. More often than not, men who have pronounced the triple *ṭalāq* in haste tend to repent but are told that their wife will have to undergo a *halala* marriage if they are to remarry. Thus the least woman-friendly interpretation of the religious text is employed, to first make a woman lose her husband and home and *then* demand that she go through a marriage with another man only to be divorced promptly in order to marry her first husband. Whilst there is a feeling of unease among ordinary Pakistani Muslims at the injustice of these supposedly Islamic laws, they find themselves unable to accept an alternative interpretation challenging this practice.

The MFLO attempted to address the situation by 'Islamizing' the statutory procedure for dissolution of marriage. As indicated earlier, the most common mode of *ṭalāq* is for the husband to pronounce the triple *ṭalāq*, resulting in immediate termination of the marriage and eviction of the wife from the marital home. The basic protection that section 7 of the MFLO provided is the requirement that the husband follow a procedure for *ṭalāq* by notifying the local authorities. This procedure, without stating so explicitly, incorporates a form of divorce called *talaq-i-ahsan* ('the most laudable *ṭalāq*') in section 7(3) that reads thus: 'Save as provided in sub-section (5), *ṭalāq* unless revoked earlier, expressly or otherwise, shall not be effective until the expiration of 90 days from the day on which notice under sub-section (1) is delivered to the Chairman.' That 90-day period is conterminous with a compulsory waiting period (*iddat*) during which the marriage is suspended but not terminated. By holding the husband to this period, after which the divorce becomes irrevocable, a man's unilateral right to divorce is toned down and chances for reconciliation are kept alive until the waiting period has expired. Section 7(4) requires the parties to appear before an Arbitration Council during the 90 days to attempt reconciliation. Section 7(6) minimizes the requirement for an intervening *halala* marriage by the woman in cases where former spouses wish to remarry. It states that: 'Nothing shall debar a wife whose marriage has been terminated by *ṭalāq* effective under this section from remarrying the same husband, without an intervening marriage with a third person, unless such termination is for the third time effective.' In other words, lack of a *halala* marriage is no bar to a remarriage to the same husband if *ṭalāq* has not been pronounced three times. Muslim women through the centuries have borne the brunt of the need for *halala* (which involved having sex with the intervening husband) resulting from a hasty pronouncement of the triple *ṭalāq*. The MFLO, by providing a breathing space, resulted in respite for women from the humiliation of marrying another man simply to remarry the husband who had so summarily divorced her.

So here we have a seemingly woman-friendly article of family law legislation. Yet a review of reported case law from the Pakistani courts reveals just a few scattered cases on *halala* marriages and the triple *ṭalāq* but very little learned discussion or challenges to the negative interpretations and meanings placed on these terms. By and large, courts engage in damage limitation to save the marriage as best they can. In *Attiq Ahmed Khan v Noor-ul-Saba*,[127] the Quetta Baluchistan High Court declared that a single pronouncement of *khul*ᶜ (upon declaration by a judge) does not constitute an irrevocable divorce and that the wife did not require a *halala* marriage in order to remarry her husband. This ruling, it may be noted, went beyond the position of classical Islamic law on *khul*ᶜ (where a pronouncement by a judge makes it final and irrevocable).[128] In *Ghulam Muhammad v the State*,[129] a man who had divorced his wife became repentant and wanted to resume marital relations with her and revive their marriage. However, since he did not revoke the divorce within the stipulated period but had resumed sexual relations with her, they were accused of *zinā'*. The court decided that the divorce pronounced by the man had become effective, and could not be withdrawn by him. Thus the accused had not 'remarried' the female co-accused and no *halala* had taken place, and cohabitation between the two after their divorce therefore amounted to *zinā'*. Their conviction for *zinā'* was maintained, but in light of their not being aware of the legal consequences of living together after non-withdrawal of the divorce, their sentences were substantially reduced.

Some concluding observations

Family law reform in postcolonial Pakistan (and in other Muslim jurisdictions) is firmly placed within the *wilāya-qiwāma* nexus, resulting in a paradox of equality. Women are perceived as perpetual (legal) minors in need of lifelong guardianship such that no law reform is truly able to break free from this conceptualization. The law-reform project in Pakistan is one of a fractured modernity, oscillating between modernity and tradition. In fact, nowhere in the Muslim world has there been observed a radical departure from the religious text in the law-reform project; neither is there sustained reform based on the principle of equality and non-discrimination. Except for Tunisia and Turkey, polygamy has, at best, been restricted or regulated; inheritance rights have remained untouched, and women's rights to guardianship of children are dependent upon the outcome of court decisions and the precise circumstances of each case.

Islamic 'revivalist' initiatives and movements, too, are endangering law reform, as is evident from the increasingly robust challenges mounted to it within the judiciary as well as at a societal level. This chapter has used Pakistan as a case study, but its broader observations are relevant to the wider Muslim world, as the discourse within these communities and societies as well as at their governmental levels is broadly similar. There is a conscious as well as sub-conscious affinity and legitimacy, albeit to a greater or lesser degree, for varying strands of the Islamic legal traditions as drivers of family law reform.

In the case of Pakistan, there is a misconception that 'Islamization' as a law-reform project was initiated by Zia-ul-Haq through his version of Islamic laws. Perhaps at a less overt level, but more consistently, it is the Pakistani judiciary that has slowly but surely placed Islamic law at the centre of their decisions. It may safely be argued that the distinctive feature of Islamic family law in Pakistan is the development of case law. The 'brand' of Islamic law reflected in judgements oscillates between a conservative, literal application of the sources and a progressive, liberal interpretation in the manner of 'judicial *ijtihād*'. These disparate interventions towards 'Islamizing' laws have led to an incoherent law-reform outcome. It is also suggested that despite attempts at the 'Islamization' of Islamic family law, family law and its reform processes maintain a distinct common-law legacy, remaining reliant on Mulla's *Muhammadan Law* as a definitive, classical text. As a member of the judiciary has put it: 'Mulla is the definitive text and it would take a lot to dislodge it in court!'[130] Lack of clear Islamic-law injunctions and multiple interpretations by various juristic schools and scholars, too, compel courts to turn to principles of common law, justice, equity, and good conscience.

These common-law principles stand 'Islamized' and appropriated by Pakistani judges not simply as common-law principles but as *universal* concepts of justice commensurate with Islamic legal principles.

The substantive content of 'Islamic' family law in Pakistan remains contested and pulled in different directions. Almost five decades of recommendations from four law reform commissions and as many decades of court judgements later, the Federal Sharia Court has struck down provisions of one of the few pieces of progressive legislations in Pakistan, i.e. the MFLO. The Council of Islamic Ideology (CII), a constitutional body tasked with determining the 'Islamic' nature of laws in Pakistan has also put its weight behind those that believe some provisions of the MFLO to be 'un-Islamic'. This leaves law reform initiatives such as the MFLO on shaky ground and in a state of flux.

Islamic family law advocates, whether at the level of society, the courts, or legislature, maintain a tangible silence in areas that affect women at their greatest vulnerability, most prominently those relating to post-divorce maintenance, the triple *ṭalāq*, and *halala* marriage. An increasingly patriarchal, inflexible manifestation of Islamic law is in conflict with egalitarian, progressive, and arguably 'Western-inspired' liberal conceptions of Islam, leading to an ongoing tension between different articulations of an inherently plural legal tradition. Until the reform process is embedded within gender-equal and woman-friendly social change that internalizes and accepts this reform, law reform remains a matter of 'two steps forward, one step back'. Fazlur Rahman is of the firm view that legal reform can only be effective in changing the status of women in Muslim contexts when there is adequate basis for social change. It is only then that the Quranic objective of social justice in general, and for women in particular, can be fulfilled; otherwise its success will be limited, transitory, and confined to certain social groups.[131]

Increasingly, there appears to be sympathy for a kind of law reform instigated in a number of Muslim jurisdictions through what are termed 'repugnancy clauses', meaning that where a legal norm is not *prohibited* in Islamic law, it must by default be *permitted*. These changes, however, are confined to matters of state and government, as well as commercial and financial transactions, where wider berth for discretion is countenanced. The principle of 'repugnancy' and this broad discretion are not observed in the area of family law, in view of an obsessively protective attitude towards this as the last bastion of Muslim identity. For example, questions of post-divorce maintenance do not have to be prohibited because these are not *un*repugnant to Islamic law principles, yet opposition to extending the period of alimony has been very fierce in Egypt; neither have they been accepted in family law reforms in Pakistan, or by the courts.[132]

To what extent is family law reform informed and driven by people on the ground? Although the constituencies, interlocutors, and intermediaries have expanded beyond government, parliament, and the courts and now include women's-rights and other pressure groups, law reform remains an elusive, inadequate process. More inclusivity is required of people whose voices are not likely to be heard in decision-making forums where reform is initiative, discussed, and decided.

Is there a consistent vision for the politics of family law and its reform among the governments of Islamic countries? It seems far more likely that there are only piecemeal legislative attempts to calm acute social problems by reactionary law making that is itself, in turn, tugged back and forth between conservative and liberal understandings of Islamic law, and between disputed versions within those traditions, without a clear vision of where society is to go or what it is to be.

Notes

1 A A An-Na'im (ed), *Islamic Family Law in the World Today: A Resource Book* (Zed Books 2002) xi-xii; Ziba Mir-Hosseini, 'Justice, Equality and Muslim Family Laws' in Ziba Mir-Hosseini and others (eds), *Gender and Equality in Muslim Family Law: Justice and Ethics in the Islamic Legal Tradition* (Tauris 2013) 7; Lynn Welchman (ed), *Women's Rights and Islamic Family Law: Perspectives on Reform* (Zed Books 2004); Ziba Mir-Hosseini, *Marriage on Trial: A Study of Islamic Family Law, Iran and Morocco Compared* (Tauris 2001); Barbara Freyer Stowasser, *Women in the Qur'an, Traditions, and Interpretation* (OUP 1994).

2 In the area of family law in particular, NGOs, women's groups, and human-rights groups have instigated family law reform using progressive interpretations of the religious text in Islam in most Muslim countries including Pakistan, Bangladesh, Morocco, and Egypt, to name a few.

3 Judith Tucker, *Women, Family, and Gender in Islamic Law* (CUP 2008) 159 and n 1.

4 For instance, prohibiting through statute the practice of 'triple *ṭalāq*', where a woman is divorced immediately without any process or attempt at mediation or conciliation; restricting polygamy; requiring judicial process for divorce; and legalizing women's right to divorce, to name a few.

5 The most significant of these changes include an emphasis on controlling women's movements and dress code and undermining their equal rights, for instance the right to testify in court as a witness: in the Sudan, for instance, the so-called 'September Laws' of 1983; in Iran post-1979; and in Pakistan, the 'Islamization of Laws' including criminal law and laws on evidence. The commonality between 'women-friendly' law reform and that of so-called 'Islamic' regimes is that they focus on women as markers of 'Islamization'. 'The different face of 'Islamization' is visible in Sudan where it is being promoted by an authoritarian regime with much more brutal effects . . . women's job and promotions opportunities in the government have been severely restricted, their mobility made dependent on male and state approval at various levels, their rights to land ownership curtailed and even their dress regulated . . . girls and women enrolled in educational institutions are formally subject to a dress code and may be expelled in the event of violation of this code . . . further various state-instituted bodies have been established to patrol streets to ensure appropriate behaviour' (Amina Alrasheed, 'Sudanese Women in Exile Islam Politics and the State' Conference Proceedings: Thinking Gender – the NEXT generation, 21–22 June 2006 e-paper No. 1 available at www.gender-studies.leeds.ac.uk citing (18 October 1997, WLUML Dossier).

6 Whilst the focus of the present chapter is on Pakistan, similar inferences will apply to other Muslim jurisdictions – in particular postcolonial countries.

7 S S Ali, 'Testing the Limits of Family Law Reform in Pakistan: A Critical Analysis of the Muslim Family Laws Ordinance 1961' in A Bainham (ed), *The International Survey of Family Law* (Jordan 2002) 317.

8 The phrase 'paradox of equality' is borrowed from Anver Emon, 'The Paradox of Equality and the Politics of Difference: Gender Equality, Islamic Law and the Modern State' in Mir-Hosseini and others (eds), *Gender and Equality* (n 1) 237–258.

9 See for instance Mir-Hosseini and others (eds), *Gender and Equality* (n 1); Yoginder Sikand, 'Reforming Muslim Personal Laws in India: The Fyzee Formula' (2005) 27 WLUML Dossier 21–26; Leon Buskens, 'Recent Debates on Family Law Reform in Morocco: Islamic Law as Politics in an Emerging Public Sphere (2003) 10 Islamic Law and Society 70–131; Dawoud El-Alami and Doreen Hinchcliffe, *Islamic Marriage and Divorce Laws in the Arab World* (Kluwer 1996); Asifa Quraishi and Frank Vogel (eds), *The Islamic Marriage Contract* (Harvard University Press 2008); Welchman, *Women's Rights and Islamic Family Law* (n 1); An-Na'im (n 1); Lynn Welchman, *Beyond the Code: Muslim Family Law and the Shari'a Judiciary in the Palestinian West Bank* (Kluwer 2000); Mir-Hosseini, *Marriage on Trial* (n 1); Ali (n 7) 317–335; A El-Azhary Sonbol, *Women, the Family and Divorce Laws in Islamic History* (Syracuse University Press 1996); Stowasser (n 1); Tucker (n 3); Irene Schneider, *Women in the Islamic World: From Earliest Times to the Arab Spring* (Steven Rendall tr, Markus Wiener 2014); Saba Mahmood, *The Politics of Piety: The Islamic Revival and the Feminist Subject* (Princeton University Press 2011); A Barlas, *'Believing Women' in Islam: Unreading Patriarchal Interpretations of the Qur'an* (University of Texas Press 2002); A Rab, *Exploring Islam in a New Light: A View from the Quranic Perspective* (Brainbow 2010); Amina Wadud, *Inside the Gender Jihad: Women's Reform in Islam* (Oneworld 2006); John L Esposito and Natana J DeLong-Bas, *Women in Muslim Family Law* (2nd edn, Syracuse University Press 2001).

10 See in particular S S Ali, *Gender and Human Rights in Islam and International law. Equal before Allah, Unequal Before Man?* (Kluwer 2000) 49–50 and generally ch 2.

11 N Hevener, *International Law and the Status of Women* (Westview 1983) 4.

12 Ali (n 10).

13 Ibid.

14 *Mahr* (a sum of money or other property given to the wife by the husband at the time of marriage) has multiple connotations: it is described as a 'gift', but if this were so how can it be taken back if the wife initiates a divorce? For a discussion of the nature of *mahr* see A Moors, *Women, Property and Islam* (CUP 1995); S S Ali, 'Is an Adult Muslim Woman *Sui Juris*? Some Reflections on the Concept of "Consent in Marriage" without a *Wali* (with Particular Reference to the *Saima Waheed* Case)' (1996) 3 Yearbook of Islamic and Middle Eastern Law 156–174; D Pearl and W Menski, *Muslim Family Law* (Sweet & Maxwell 1998) 178–181.

15 Esposito and DeLong-Bas (n 9) 106–108; Fazlur Rahman, 'The Status of Women in Islam: A Modernist Interpretation' in Hanna Papanek and Gail Minault (eds), *Separate Worlds: Studies of Purdah in South Asia* (Chanakya 1982) 285–310; Aziza Al-Hibri, 'A Study of Islamic Herstory: How Did We Get Into This Mess?' (1982) 5 Women's Studies International Forum 201–219.

16 Ibid. See also F Mernissi, *Women and Islam* (Mary Jo Lakeland tr, Blackwell 1991); A A An-Na'im, *Toward an Islamic Reformation* (Syracuse University Press 1990); Riffat Hassan, 'An Islamic Perspective' in J Belcher (ed), *Women, Religion and Sexuality* (WCC 1990); M M Taha, *The Second Message of Islam* (An-Na'im tr, Syracuse University Press 1987).

17 Ali (n 10) 48-49.

18 Ibid.

19 Ibid. 49.

20 See Fazlur Rahman, *Islam and Modernity: Transformation of an Intellectual Tradition* (University of Chicago Press 1982); L P Sayeh and A M Morse Jr, 'Islam and the Treatment of Women: An Incomplete Understanding of Gradualism' (1995) 30 TIJL 311 and accompanying footnotes; Ali (n 10) 79–85; N Salem, 'Islam and the Status of Women in Tunisia' in F Hussain (ed), *Muslim Women* (St Martin's 1984); Al-Tahir Al-Haddad, *Our Women in the Law and in Society* (Routledge 2007).

21 Ali (n 10) 72–73.

22 *Asbāb al-nuzūl* or 'context of revelation' of *Quranic* verses is often employed to support the 'text and context' argument. Proponents of this approach argue that the context of the revelation informs application of a particular *Quranic* verse/s.

23 Verse 4:34 of the *Quran* is most frequently cited when justifying wife beating. For a challenging feminist perspective of this verse, see Riffat Hassan's analysis and interpretation in a paper presented at a *Quranic* interpretation meeting held in Karachi, Pakistan (8–13 July 1990) under the auspices of Women Living Under Muslim Laws (paper on file with the author). For a detailed and incisive discussion see Lisa Hajjar, 'Domestic Violence and Shari'a: A Comparative Study of Muslim Societies in the Middle East, Africa and Asia' in Welchman, *Women's Rights and Islamic Family Law* (n 1) 233–268.

24 The works of Muslim scholars including A A An-Na'im, Riffat Hassan, Asma Barlas, Aziza Al-Hibri, Ziba Mir-Hosseini, Saba Mahmoud, Asghar Ali Engineer, and S S Ali, to name just a few, have provided alternative interpretations arguing that a contextual reading of the *Quranic* text displaces gender hierarchies as the only reading. Reading the *Quranic* verses on polygamy through a contextual and feminist lens, these writers question polygamy as a general, unconditional right of the husband. Law reform in some Muslim jurisdictions, too, reflects this by restricting polygamy. See Pakistan's MFLO 1961, Morocco's Mudawwana 2004, and the Tunisian Family Code. Regarding verses permitting the beating of a disobedient wife, this contradicts other verses as well as clearly remaining contingent upon the economic superiority of the husband.

25 Mir-Hosseini, *Gender and Equality* (n 1).

26 The concept of 'restitution of conjugal rights' incorporated into family law in colonial codes continues to this day.

27 Masud defines *wilāya/walāya* as 'the legal authority to manage the affairs of another person who lacks the required capacity', M K Masud, 'Gender Equality and the Doctrine of Wilaya' in Mir-Hosseini and others (eds), *Gender and Equality* (n 1) 128.

28 For a detailed exposition of the various Sunni juristic schools of thought, see Masud (n 27); Mannan (ed), *Mulla's Muhammadan Law* (PLD Publishers first publ 1905); Pearl and Menski, *Muslim Family Law* (Longman 1998); Fyzee, *Outlines of Muhammadan Law* (4th edn, OUP 1974).

29 Masud (n 27) 132–144.

30 Ibid. 140.

31 Ibid. 143.

32 Haider Ala Hamoudi, 'The Death of Islamic Law' (2010) 38 Georgia Journal of International and Comparative Law 293.

33 Ibid.

34 Ibid.

35 Precolonial, colonial, and postcolonial.

36 See Ibn S Jung, *The Administration of Justice in Islam* (Law Publishing 1980) 57–88 for details regarding the administration of justice in India during early Muslim and Mughal rule.

37 For this line of argument see O Siddique, *Pakistan's Experience with Formal law: An Alien Justice* (CUP 2013); D Washbrook, 'Law, State, and Agrarian Society in Colonial India' (1981) 15 Modern Asian Studies 649, cited in M R Anderson, 'Islamic Law and the Colonial Encounter in British India' in C Mallat and J Connors (eds), *Islamic Family Law* (Graham & Trotman 1990) 206.
38 Anderson (n 37) 208 and accompanying footnotes.
39 Ibid. 209.
40 See J D M Derrett, 'Justice, Equity and Good Conscience' in J N D Anderson (ed), *Changing Laws in Developing Countries* (Allen & Unwin 1963), cited in Anderson (n 37) 209.
41 *Waghela v Sheikh Musludin* [1887] 14 IA 89, 96 as cited in Anderson (n 37).
42 For example, Code of Civil Procedure (Act VIII of 1859); Indian Penal Code (Act XLV of 1860); Criminal Procedure Code (Act XXV of 1861); Indian Evidence Act (Act I of 1872).
43 This is a puzzling contradiction in terms. Historically, the common-law legacy is celebrated for its responsiveness to society; hence the difficulty in understanding why this undue emphasis was placed on the 'written law'. It may well be that imperial and colonial imperatives drove this approach.
44 A twelfth-century text of Central Asian origin that relied mainly on Abu Yusuf and Al-Shaybani.
45 A collection of *fatāwā* (legal opinions) in the *fiqh* tradition commissioned by the Mughal Emperor Aurangzeb was translated as N Baillie, *Baillie's Digest of Moohammudan Law* (1865).
46 S A Kugle, 'Framed, Blamed and Renamed: The Recasting of Islamic Jurisprudence in Colonial South Asia' (2001) 35 Modern Asian Studies 304.
47 Siddique (n 37).
48 S S Ali, 'Overlapping Discursive Terrains of Culture, Law and Women's Rights: An Exploratory Study on Legal Pluralism at Play in Pakistan' in J Bennett (ed), *Scratching the Surface: Democracy, Traditions, Gender* (Heinrich Böll Foundation 2007) 77–78.
49 Ali (n 10) 92.
50 For a detailed overview and analysis of local dispute resolution forums, see Ali and Rehman, *Indigenous Peoples and Ethnic Minorities of Pakistan Constitutional and Legal Perspectives* (Curzon 2001).
51 The assault against *wakf* became a rallying point for Muslims, and the Wakf Validating Act 1913 simultaneously affirmed a scripturalist version of Islam as it protected the economic interests of certain propertied classes.
52 Act No 26/1937 of 7 October 1937, Indian Official Gazette (Part 4) of 9 October 1937, 50–51.
53 An-Na'im (ed), *Islamic Family Law in a Changing World: A Global Resource Book* (Zed Books 2002) 204.
54 M R Anderson, 'Islamic Law and the Colonial Encounter in British India' in Mallat and Connors (n 37) 222.
55 Emphasis added. Muslim women's groups have consistently held that it is the customary practices and cultural perspectives of Islam that affect women adversely, whereas Islamic law is empowering and gives them rights; family law reform in postcolonial Pakistan continued this trend.
56 Indian Official Gazette (Part 4) 9 October 1937, 50.
57 Ibid.

58 In the Punjab, the Muslim Personal Law (Shariat) Application Act 1948 was only passed by the Punjab Assembly when women demonstrated outside the Assembly building urging members to vote in favour of the bill. Their reluctance stemmed from the fact that the majority belonged to the landed class and were not prepared to give away immovable property to female heirs.

59 For example, see s 26 of Regulation IV, 1827: 'the law to be observed in the trial of suits shall be Acts of Parliament and Regulations of Government applicable to the case: in the absence of such Acts and Regulations, the usages of the country in which the suit arose; if none such appears, the law of the defendant, and in the absence of specific law and usage, justice, equity and good conscience alone.'

60 Act VIII of 1939 of 17 March 1939, Indian Official Gazette (Part 4) 25 March 1939, 131–133.

61 The DMMA was amended twice by the Muslim Family Laws Ordinance 1961 (MFLO). These amendments provided the added ground for dissolution where the husband took an additional wife in contravention of the procedure laid down in the MFLO. It also allowed women to repudiate marriages contracted by their guardians before they attained the age of 16 (as opposed to 15 as set out originally in the Act).

62 Thus the MPL and DMMA were considered a victory for Indian Muslims in their quest for Islamic law. The laws regulating family issues in Pakistan include the Majority Act 1875, the Guardians & Wards Act 1890, the Child Marriages Restraint Act 1929, and the Muslim Personal Law (Shariat) Application Act 1937.

63 The Commission on Marriage and Family Laws was appointed by the Government of Pakistan under Ministry of Law Resolution No F17(24)/55-Leg, 4 August 1955. Its report was published 20 June 1956 in the Gazette of Pakistan Extraordinary under notification No F9(4)/56-Leg. Other reports on family law and women's rights include that of the Pakistan Women's Rights Committee 1976, the Status of Women (Zari Sarfraz) Commission 1985, and the Commission of Inquiry for Women 1997.

64 Muslim Personal Law (Shariat) Application Act 1962, Muslim Personal Law (Shariat) Application (Removal of Difficulties) Act 1975, Muslim Personal Law (Shariat) Application (Removal of Doubt) Ordinance 1972, Dissolution of Muslim Marriages Act 1939, Muslim Family Laws Ordinance 1961, West Pakistan Rules under the Muslim Family Laws Ordinance 1961, West Pakistan Family Courts Act 1964 (amended 2002), West Pakistan Family Court Rules 1965, Dowry and Bridal Gifts (Restriction) Act 1976, Dowry and Bridal Gifts (Restriction) Rules 1981.

65 Pearl and Menski (n 28) 29.

66 An-Na'im (n 53) 18.

67 Ann Black, Hossein Esmaeili, and Nadirsyah Hosen, *Modern Perspectives on Islamic Law* (Edward Elgar 2013) 108.

68 This is present in the form of various law codes, both substantive and procedural, promulgated during the colonial era (including Code of Civil Procedure (Act VIII of 1859); Indian Penal Code (Act XLV of 1860); Criminal Procedure Code (Act XXV of 1861); Indian Evidence Act (Act I of 1872)) as well as in the structures of courts.

69 B Turner, *Weber and Islam: A Critical Study* (Routledge and Kegan Paul 1974) 119.

70 The prolific writer and scholar A Ala Maududi challenged what he termed 'western-inspired' law reforms in the political, social, and economic spheres. As founder of *Jamaat-I-Islami*, a right-wing political party, and initially opposed to the idea of Pakistan as an independent Islamic state, he and his colleagues immediately engaged with post-independence law making and the political scene. He criticized family law reform on the basis that Islam had created a dichotomy between the public and private

spheres, with women belonging to the private sphere, with the male as head of the household, and with women as protected persons. See Maududi's relevant works: *Haquq uz Zojjain* (1943); *Khawateen aur Deeni Masayl* (2000); *Purdah* (2003); *Purdah and The Status of Woman in Islam* (Al-Ashari tr/ed, 1975).

71 Siddique (n 37) 41.

72 'A well rounded analysis of the weaknesses of this approach requires a contextual approach to the issue exploring legal, sociological, historical, political and economic aspects. History from below, living law, subaltern studies and some recent literature in the field is beginning to make an impact on how we approach this area of research', ibid.

73 Ibid. 41.

74 Kugle (n 46) 283.

75 As Kugle states: 'The effects of British rewriting have created a lens of texts, terms and experiences which continue to distort the view of Shariah today', ibid. 304.

76 Cf British policy on the subject: Kugle (n 46) 270, 272.

77 See Banuri and others (eds), *Dispensation of Justice in Pakistan* (OUP 2003); T Banuri and M Mahmood, 'Learning from Failure: Institutional Reform for Human Resource Development' in Banuri, Khan and Mahmood (eds), *Just Development: Beyond Adjustment with a Human Face* (OUP 1998).

78 For instance, girls' rights to education are undermined by the argument that their exposure to the outside world might lead to untoward 'Western' influences; also, a wife's right to include a clause whereby she may exercise a right of divorce is discouraged as being against the spirit of Islam (recalling a *hadith* of the Prophet Muhammad that divorce is the most abhorrent permissible act).

79 The Commission on Marriage and Family Laws (the Rashid Commission) was appointed by the Government of Pakistan under Ministry of Law Resolution No F17(24)/55-Leg, 4 August 1955. Its report was published 20 June 1956 in the Gazette of Pakistan Extraordinary under notification No F9(4)/56-Leg.

80 Pearl and Menski (n 28) 27.

81 See for instance *Mst Farishta v The Federation of Pakistan PLD* 1980 Pesh 47, in appeal *Federation of Pakistan v Mst Farishta PLD* 1981 SC 120; *Mst Zarina Jan v Mst Akbar Jan PLD* 1975 Pesh 252; *Farid v Mst Manzooran PLD* 1990 SC 511; also Abdul Huq, 'Section 4 of the Muslim Family Laws Ordinance 1961: A Critic' (2010) 1 Northern University Journal of Law 7-13; Riaz ul Hassan Gilani, 'A Note on Islamic Family Law and Islamization in Pakistan' in C Mallat and J Connors (ed), *Islamic Family Law* (Graham and Trotman 1990) 339–346.

82 Under Shiite understandings of Islamic law, the 'triple *ṭalāq*' is not permitted and three pronouncements of *ṭalāq* at one sitting are considered as one.

83 In Sunni Hanafi Islamic law, there are three modes of pronouncing *ṭalāq*: *ṭalāq al-aḥsan, ṭalāq al-ḥasan*, and *ṭalāq al-bidᶜa*. The first two offer some scope for reconciliation as the divorce does not become irrevocable for some time. *Ṭalāq al-bidᶜa* is an irrevocable divorce, and as soon as it is pronounced there is no chance of reconciliation. This mode is not the one sanctioned by the Prophet Mohammed, and hence it is rejected by some Muslims.

84 MFLO 1961, s 7.

85 The concept of the wife being able to 'buy' her freedom by returning her dower is technically known as *khulᶜ* and affords a woman the right to get out of an undesirable union.

86 MFLO 1961, s 6.

87 The wife's infertility, insanity, or incapacity to perform marital obligations have been considered 'acceptable' reasons for remarriage (MFLO 1961, WP Rules, s 14).

88 MFLO 1961, s 6.

89 *Abdul Basit v Union Council, Ward No 3, Peshawar Cantt* 1970 SCMR 753; *Inayat Khan v District Magistrate, Sialkot* 1986 PCrLJ 2023; *Mst Ghulam Fatima v Mst Anwar* 1981 CLC 1651.

90 MFLO 1961, s 4. This also amended the Child Marriages Restraint Act 1929 by raising the legal age of marriage for females from 14 to 16, and from 18 to 21 for males (see MFLO 1961, ss 10 and 12, though s 12 was revoked by the Federal Laws (Revision and Declaration) Ordinance (XXVII of 1981).

91 An-Na'im (n 51) 234.

92 For a detailed exposition see M A Mannan (ed), *D F Mulla's Principles of Mahomedan Law* (PLD Publishers 1995) 84–150.

93 *Yusuf Abbas v Mst Ismat Mustafa* PLD 1968 Kar 480, 508.

94 PLD 1980 Pesh 47.

95 Upon appeal, cited as *Federation of Pakistan v Mst Farishta* PLD 1981 SC 120.

96 Ibid. 127.

97 *Allah Rakha v Federation of Pakistan* PLD 2000 FSC 1, 7.

98 In *Mst Fazeelat Jan v Sikandar* PLD 2003 SC 475, 476, where the court ruled that: 'The trial Court was wrong in holding that the grandson, under the traditional Muslim Law of Inheritance was excluded from the inheritance of his grandfather due to the absence of his own father'.

99 See n 63. In 1975 the Pakistan Women's Rights Committee was set up, chaired by Yahya Bakhtiar, then Attorney General of Pakistan, and reported in 1976. Nothing came out of this exercise, as the report came when the government of the day was caught up in a political crisis that eventually brought it down. A third report, the Report of the Commission on the Status of Women 1985, chaired by Begum Zari Sarfaraz, also made some useful recommendations, but the government declared it a classified document and it was only when a new government came into power in 1988 that it was made public. The latest in the series of reports is that of the Commission of Inquiry for Women submitted in 1997. See also case law on s 5 MFLO 1961 on registration of marriages, *Habib v The State* PLD 1980 Lah 791; *Abdul Kalam v The State* 1987 MLD 1637; *Muhammad Akram v Mst Farman Bi* PLD 1989 Lah 200; on the failure to seek permission of an existing wife for a subsequent marriage see *Abdul Basit v Union Council, Ward No 3, Peshawar Cantt* 1970 SCMR 753; *Inayat Khan v District Magistrate, Sialkot* 1986 PCrLJ 2023; *Mst Ghulam Fatima v Mst Anwar* 1981 CLC 1651 above.

100 Shirkat Gah Women's Resource Centre, *Women's Rights in Muslim Family Law in Pakistan: 45 Years of Recommendations vs. the FSC Judgement* (January 2000) Special Bulletin February 2000, 26 <http://pk.boell.org/sites/default/files/downloads/Women_s_Rights_in_Muslim_Family_Law.pdf> accessed 3 September 2014.

101 Verse 4:3.

102 A R I Doi, *Shariah: The Islamic Law* (Ta Ha 1984) 146 outlines the various circumstances for which he considers polygamy to be the 'best solution'. These include the wife suffering from a serious disease, being barren, of unsound mind, old and infirm, of irreparable 'bad character', moving away from her husband's place of residence, being disobedient and difficult to live with, and as a result of many men dying during war leaving behind a large number of widows. The final circumstance that Doi advances as justifiable is where a husband feels he cannot do without another wife and

is capable of providing equal support to all. Doi in effect gives *carte blanche* to a man to marry if he feels like it, but this is hardly consonant with the contextual rationale behind the *Quranic* verse.

103 Verse 33:32, 50. For example, while the Prophet encouraged widows and divorcees to remarry, his own wives were not to be remarried after his death. They were considered 'the mothers of all believers', and no believer may marry his mother. However, as the Prophet grew older he gave his wives the choice to leave and marry another male, more fulfilling perhaps of husbandly duties. All but one wife refused to leave him. See Al-Hibri (n 15) 216 (citing J Al-Afghani (1945) 79).

104 See Al-Hibri (n 15) 216 for this line of argument; Fazlur Rahman, 'The status of women in Islam: a modernist interpretation' in G Nashat (ed), *Women and Revolution in Iran* (Westview Press 1983) 45–49 (this is a revised version appearing in a collection edited by H Papanek and G Minault). Law reform in Muslim jurisdictions in the twentieth century has relied upon these interpretations.

105 Al-Hibri (n 15) 216 and accompanying footnotes.

106 Doi (n 102) ch 8, especially 147–150.

107 Ibid.

108 Tunisia is an example. Turkey has a secular legal system that prohibits polygamy.

109 Martin Lau, *The Role of Islam in the Legal System of Pakistan* (Nijhoff 2006).

110 Ibid. 1.

111 Ibid.

112 For an incisive analysis of *Farishta*, see Lucy Carroll, 'The Pakistan Federal Shariat Court, Section 4 of the Muslim Family Laws Ordinance, and the Orphaned Grandchild' (2002) 9 *Islamic Law and Society* 70-82; for case law see *Mst Farishta v The Federation of Pakistan* PLD 1980 Pesh 47; *Mst Zarina Jan v Mst Akbar Jan* PLD 1975 Pesh 252; *Farid v Manzooran* PLD 1990 SC 511.

113 Law and Justice Commission of Pakistan, *Federal Shariat Court Annual Report 2003*, 1 <www.federalshariatcourt.gov.pk/Annual%20Report/Final%20Annual%20 Report%202003.pdf> accessed 14 November 2014.

114 PLD 1967 SC 97.

115 The oft-quoted case of *Jamila*, who sought dissolution of marriage on the basis that she did not like her husband's looks and considered him ugly.

116 *Mst Khurshid Bibi v Mohammed Amin* PLD 1967 SC 97.

117 For example in *Safia Begum v Khadim Hussain* 1985 CLC 1869 and *Syed Mohammed Rizwan v Mst Samina Khatoon* 1989 SMCR 25.

118 See e.g. *Aali v Additional District Judge I, Quetta* 1986 CLC 27; *Raisa Begum v Mohammed Hussain* 1986 MLD 1418.

119 1988 MLD 427.

120 Lau (n 109) 5.

121 The most virulent and most often used was the Prohibition of *Zina* (Enforcement of Hudood) Ordinance 1979. Some changes were also made in existing laws including the Evidence Act, in 1984, where evidence of a woman in financial matters was given half the evidentiary weight to that provided by a man. It is beyond the scope of the present chapter to engage in detailed discussion on this law, so suffice it to say that it undermined women's position in society, albeit at a formal level because, insofar as evidence in court was concerned, judges continued as before and accepted women's evidence as equal to men. In other words, the lower evidentiary value of women's testimony, as required by the modified law of evidence, was simply ignored.

122 For instance, the *Zina* Ordinance failed to distinguish between rape and consensual sex, requiring four adult male Muslim witnesses to the actual act of penetration!

123 Leading cases include *Shera v The State* PLD 1982 FSC 229; *Muhammad Siddique v The State* PLD 1983 FSC 173; *Mirza Qamar Raza v Mst Tahira Begum* PLD 1988 Kar 169; *Muhammad Sarwar v The State* PLD 1988 FSC 42.

124 *Mst Bashiran v Muhammad Hussain* PLD 1988 SC 186.

125 *Mst Kaniz Fatima v Wali Muhammad* PLD 1989 Lah 490; *Ayaz Aslam v Chairman Arbitration Council* 1990 ALD 702.

126 *Mirza Qamar Raza v Mst Tahira Begum* PLD 1988 Kar 169; *Allah Dad v Mukhtar* 1992 SCMR 1273; *Allah Rakha v Federation of Pakistan* PLD 2000 FSC 1.

127 2011 CLC 1211.

128 A similar question was raised before the court in *Ghulam Abbas v Station House Officer* (2009) YLR 201 Lahore High Court, leading to a similar outcome.

129 1994 PCrLJ 1856 FSC.

130 Personal communication, the identity of the informant to remain confidential at their request.

131 Rahman (n 15) 308.

132 Hamoudi (n 32) 6–7. For a very detailed discussion of post-divorce maintenance in Pakistan and its case law, see Shahid, 'Post-Divorce Maintenance for Muslim Women in Pakistan and Bangladesh: A Comparative Perspective' (2013) 27 International Journal of Law, Policy and the Family 197–215; Shirkat Gah, *Women's Rights* (n 100).

3 Family law, fundamental human rights, and political transition in Tunisia

Monia Ben Jémia

At the end of the nineteenth century and early on in the twentieth century, legal reforms in Tunisia had permeated all areas, except the law of personal status, i.e. family and succession law. While law was secularized as codes were enacted in civil, commercial, and criminal matters, personal status had remained under the domain of religion. Tunisian Muslims were governed by Islamic law and under the jurisdiction of Sharia courts, while Jews were governed by Mosaic law and under the jurisdiction of rabbinical courts.

At independence in 1956 the law of personal status was reformed and codified, and family law unified. It became applicable to all citizens regardless of their religious denomination, and religious courts were abolished and their competence given to secular national courts. The main patriarchal institutions of polygamy and repudiation were abolished. Reforms continued until the 1970s, reaching the point that custody could now be attributed to the father or the mother according to the sole criterion of the best interests of the child. Although women continue to inherit half the share of men, in 1959 the legislator adopted a rule whereby the whole estate could devolve to the sole daughter, while under Islamic law the daughter as the sole heir had to share the estate with the treasury. Adoption was introduced in 1958. From the late 1970s, the process of reform slowed, partly because of the arrival of the Islamist movement on the political scene. In case of divorce, the father remained the sole guardian of his minor children, but the mother shared some responsibilities with him. If the father died, guardianship was awarded to the mother (under the reform of 1993). An optional community property regime was established in 1998. In 2008, a law allowed parents to share their properties during their lifetime as they wish, with donations between ascendants and descendants being exempted from taxes. In 2010, the nationality law was reformed to allow Tunisian women married to foreigners, and whose children were born abroad, to transfer their Tunisian nationality.

From the fall of the former regime in January 2011, Tunisia entered a democratic transitional stage. The transition from a totalitarian to a rule-of-law regime put the legality and legitimacy of previous laws in question. The Constitution of 1959 having been repealed (March 2011), international treaties on human rights became the basis of the legal system and it is in their light that laws must be interpreted. This rule of law is in effect a regime that protects human rights in accordance with the Universal Declaration of Human Rights (UDHR) and the International Covenant on Civil and Political Rights (ICCPR). More specifically, the United Nations defines the rule of law as:

> . . . a principle of governance in which all persons, institutions and entities, public and private, including the State itself, are accountable to laws that are publicly promulgated, equally enforced and independently adjudicated, and which are consistent with international human rights norms and standards. It requires, as well, measures to ensure adherence to the principles of supremacy of law, equality before the law, fairness in the application of the law, separation of powers, participation in decision-making, legal certainty, avoidance of arbitrariness and procedural and legal transparency.[1]

The Tunisian Code of Personal Status (CSP), enacted in 1956 at independence, should therefore be read and interpreted in the light of these principles. The Court of Appeal of Tunis so held in a judgement of 2 May 2013[2] on the issue of freedom of international movement and the right to a passport: 'The 1959 Constitution remains in force in its provisions guaranteeing fundamental rights and freedoms as these, because of their nature, cannot be abrogated in accordance to the ICCPR in 1966, ratified by Tunisia in Law No 30 of 20 November 1968.' This judgement places fundamental human rights at the apex of the hierarchy of norms and makes them the formal source to which the judge is entitled to refer to interpret the law. Although this judgement does not refer explicitly to personal status, the principle is applicable in all areas, including family law, especially as it is in accordance with international standards governing political transitions and, more precisely, transitional justice.[3]

The new Constitution, adopted on 26 January 2014, takes its place as the fundamental law, with the international treaties on human rights subsidiary to it (Constitution, Article 20). Considering the situation before the revolution, the fundamental principles that were used to interpret the CSP were equality between men and women, freedom of conscience, and the best interests of the child. If the first principle unanimously allowed for the exclusion of foreign norms relating to polygamy and repudiation, which were banned in the CSP, we can cast doubt about the validity of the second principle. However, the latest decisions consolidated the principle of freedom of conscience[4] and re-established it as a pillar of the Tunisian legal system. The third principle, the best interests of the child, has, with the consolidation of the first two principles, flourished.

Even if the interpretation of the CSP in accordance with human rights principles was inconsistent during the transitional period before the adoption of the Constitution, the new Constitution, despite its ambiguities, has opened the way for a unified interpretation of these values.

Fundamental human rights and personal status before the promulgation of the 2014 Constitution

Before the revolution, the Tunisian jurisprudence had evolved in the direction of guaranteeing the principles of non-discrimination on grounds of religion or gender as well as the interests of the child. The application of these principles, however, has declined sharply during the transition period preceding the adoption of the Constitution.

Tunisian jurisprudence on the eve of the transition

There is no religious discrimination in the CSP. At independence, the justice system and the laws were unified, religious courts were abolished, and the CSP applied to all Tunisians whatever their religion. Civil status also did not contain any indication of religious affiliation and nationality and was granted without reference to religion. But the judiciary and the administration have introduced religious discrimination, with reference to the first Article of the Constitution of 1959, which provided: 'Tunisia is a free, sovereign and independent State; its religion is Islam, its language is Arabic and the Republic its regime.'

The legal status of interreligious marriages, adoptions, successions, and custody cases illustrate this very well. The marriage of Tunisian Muslim women to non-Muslim men was prohibited by a ministerial circular in 1975. The circular was addressed to registrars and civil servants, requiring them not only to refuse to perform interreligious marriages, but also to dissolve such marriages. If such marriages were concluded abroad despite the ban, they were not to be recognized in Tunisia. The adoption of a Tunisian Muslim minor by non-Muslims was also prohibited; if performed abroad the adoption would not be recognized in Tunisia. Additionally, a non-Muslim foreigner could not inherit from a Tunisian Muslim. Finally, the judges refused to recognize foreign decisions granting custody of children born to a Tunisian father and a foreign woman to the foreign mother (or a mother domiciled abroad) for religious reasons.[5]

In the late 1990s, courts took another direction and rejected these discriminatory rules, basing themselves mainly on international human rights conventions as well as Articles 5 and 6 of the Constitution of 1959, which guaranteed freedom of conscience (at least in the French version) and the equality of citizens. These cases established freedom of conscience as a fundamental choice of the Tunisian legal system. The courts also used arguments drawn from the unification of the Personal Status Law, namely the failure to prove the religion of individuals and the prohibition of interference in their freedom of conscience.[6] Ali Mezghani has raised the question of 'secularization' and discusses whether in light of this remarkable evolution of jurisprudence, one could speak of a real turnaround, or revolution.[7]

This new direction was not followed in every case, as some judges continued to discriminate. But they were increasingly a minority. Although some continued to draw on the religious reference, they allowed more liberal interpretation of it.

For example, if they continued to maintain that according to Islamic law the disparity of religion was an impediment to inheritance, they allowed the People of the Book (Jews and Christians) to inherit from a Muslim.[8] If international adoptions of Muslims by non-Muslims continued to be prohibited, it was not for religious reasons (at least it was not displayed), but for reasons relating to the best interests of the child and for avoidance of international human trafficking. Gradually, freedom of conscience was recognized and elevated to a fundamental basis of the Tunisian legal system. Equally the best interests of the child became the underlying principle in respect of adoption. Finally foreign decisions awarding custody to the foreign mother of children born from Tunisian fathers and living abroad were recognized regardless of religious factors, solely taking into account the best interests of the child.[9]

The personal status law in the transition

Because of the institutional crisis experienced by Tunisia, the publication of judicial decisions reduced and decisions from this transitional period are scarce. But a judgement of the Court of Appeal of Sousse[10] that cancelled a marriage between a Tunisian woman and an Italian man reveals the sharp increase of religious discrimination and, more generally, the desire to challenge the reforms introduced in the CSP. The decision came at a moment where three draft constitutions were drawn up by the National Constituent Assembly (NCA) which, while maintaining the first Article of the Constitution as enacted in 1959, froze its interpretation by maintaining the principle that Islam is the religion of State after a consensus resulted in the decision to not include 'the Sharia' as a source of law. As for freedom of conscience, it was not established in the drafts, although the protection of the sacred and religion were, and the preamble of the constitution draft based it on Islam.

The situation remained unclear. The 'secular hypothesis' put forward by Ali Mezghani was confirmed in a case involving a marriage celebrated in 2010, before notaries, between a Tunisian woman and an Italian man. The question of religion was not addressed; no requirement for a certificate of Islamization of the spouse was required. Later the husband petitioned for divorce unilaterally; he obtained it on the application of Tunisian law. The wife appealed, seeking an increase of her allowances. The court, however, set aside the trial judgement declaring that the divorce proceedings were inadmissible 'because there was no marriage'. 'Sexual relations between a man and a woman cannot be qualified as a contract', the court held, 'even less a marriage contract, if the husband is not a Muslim because the prohibition for the Muslim woman to marry a non-Muslim is one of the most essential and most fundamental impediments to marriage.' And if the court was willing to admit that 'religion is a personal matter between God and his creature', it added that 'all converge to consider the husband non-Muslim as his name is Giuseppe, and has an Italian nationality and is domiciled in Italy.' Furthermore, the court criticized the notaries who confirmed the marriage 'without ensuring the religion of the husband who is probably Christian.'

It is therefore compellingly clear that the decision relies on religious prescriptions and from this emerges the willingness of the judiciary to challenge the CSP, specifically its legitimacy. The judgement cites Article 5 of the CSP, which states that the future spouses must be free of legal (*sharʿī*) impediments to marriage, but it interprets the term *sharʿī* as referring to impediments provided by the 'Sharia' and not only by statutory law. In addition, the reference to the second sentence of Article 5 is a reference to the version in place before the reform of 2007, which changed the minimum age of marriage to 18 years for both men and women. And the flaw may be in this omission, as we draw from the CSP what we want and the rest is ignored.

The judgement furthermore ignores Article 14 of the CSP, which sets out the impediments to marriage and does not include the disparity of faith. However, the draft constitutions that had emerged at the time of the decision had all established that 'the provisions of this Constitution are understood and interpreted as a harmonious entity', an obvious principle for interpretation, valid for all texts, including the CSP. Article 5 of the CSP cannot be read detached from Article 14 of the CSP and cannot be interpreted in its sole light as Article 14 sets the concrete impediments to marriage and, as with any exception, has to be interpreted strictly. The judgement ignored the law as well as Tunisian doctrine when it said that the disparity of faith as an impediment to marriage is unanimously accepted in the doctrine and jurisprudence. This ignores the many dissenting voices on this issue.[11] The judgement ignored the only attachment criterion allowed in the CSP and the Code of Private International Law, namely the criterion of nationality. When it addresses the woman it never refers to her as a Tunisian, but as a Muslim. The Court of Appeal also ignored gender equality in the free choice of spouses, as men are not under such an obligation to marry only within their faith. And when it says that sexual intercourse between a man and a woman cannot be qualified as an agreement, one is taken aback. If it is not an agreement, a sexual act is rape, because there was no consent. That sex in these circumstances may not be an agreement is liable to result in the criminalization of many.

The many violations of the CSP are evident. The decision attempts to undermine the very foundations of the code. Unfortunately this is repeated in other decisions. In some cases judges have jeopardized the fundamental principle of the conclusion of marriage in Tunisia according to which marriage is concluded as a solemn act whose validity depends on the involvement of civil authorities. In an internal context, marriages that do not abide by this rule, i.e. informal marriages, have multiplied and are justified or trivialized in the name of compliance with the religion, although they are criminalized by state law. Disregarding this, the court of first instance of Tunis[12] recognized a religious marriage concluded in Italy between a Tunisian woman and a Moroccan man, on the basis that it had been registered in the Italian civil status records and the Consulate of Tunisia in Italy. This was done in contradiction to Tunisian laws prohibiting such recognition and public policy considerations that forbid the recognition of a marriage that is concluded in defiance of the fundamental choices of Tunisian law. It must be borne in mind that the reason for the institution of a formal marriage is mainly the protection of women. Formal requirements for the marriage ensure compliance with the prohibition of polygamy and the right of women to obtain a divorce on an equal footing with men. Recognizing informal marriages paves the way for polygamous marriages and the possibility of non-judicial marriage dissolution, unilaterally and at the discretion of the husband.

Finally, international adoption was still impossible in the transitional period when the prospective adopters were non-Muslim foreigners, although the danger of child trafficking could be avoided by the ratification of the Hague Convention on International Adoption (1993), which establishes coordination between the states signatories to protect the child against any risk of trafficking. There are many children awaiting adoption and domestic adoption is stigmatized for religious reasons.

Will the Constitution of 27 January 2014 end the decline of the application of human rights standards in favour of the religious reference?

The Personal Status Code and the Constitution of 2014

The new Constitution provides for freedom of conscience and equality of rights and duties of all citizens, men and women. The enshrinement of these principles in the Constitution was the result of a tremendous mobilization of civil society, after heated and often violent debates, inside and outside the National Assembly. But even if these principles have been enacted, they remain vague and ambiguous (1) and allow controversy on their interpretation (2).

An ambiguous constitution

Equal rights and duties of all citizens are guaranteed in the preamble and in Article 21 of the chapter on rights and freedoms: 'All citizens, male and female, have equal rights and duties, and are equal before the law without any discrimination. The state guarantees freedoms and individual and collective rights to all citizens, and provides all citizens the conditions for a dignified life.'[13]

Articles 22–48 provide individual and collective rights and freedoms, with the exception of those relating to the family. According to Article 46 of the Constitution 'the state commits to protect women's accrued rights and work to strengthen and develop those rights.' The text does not, however, specify that these rights must be provided for in statutory law. Unlike the Constitution of 1959, which introduced during its revision in 1997 the requirement for political parties to comply with the principles of the CSP (Article 8), such a requirement was not stated explicitly in the new Constitution. If it is clear that equality in political, economic, social, and cultural rights is guaranteed without discrimination of gender, it is not the same for private and family rights. The equality in private and family relationships between men and women remains therefore ambiguous: the Constitution refers explicitly to the rights attached to the quality of citizen (right to vote and to be eligible, the right to work, health, etc) for women, as they are citizens. However, it is only in the wording of Article 46 that the expression of *citizen* is substituted with that of *woman.*[14] But if these rights referred to matters of personal status, why not say it clearly?

Further one can cast doubt on whether the Constitution conforms to the UN Convention on the Elimination of All Forms of Discrimination against Women (CEDAW), ratified by Tunisia in 1985. The preamble of the Constitution only recognized the 'higher principles of human rights'. As it seems, some groups do not consider CEDAW to fall into this category. In March 2013, the Minister of Religious Affairs said that 'CEDAW undermines our Arab and Muslim identity'. However, it will be difficult to challenge the validity of CEDAW since Article 20 of the Constitution provides that 'International agreements approved and ratified by the Assembly of the Representatives of the People have a status superior to that of laws and inferior to that of the Constitution.'

In 1980 CEDAW had been approved and signed by the Chamber of Deputies under the former regime. In 2011 the government lifted the Tunisian State reservations made upon the ratification of CEDAW in 1985, including that in respect of Article 16, which guarantees equality in the family. The Constitution refers to the 'family' in Article 7 where it provides that: 'The family is the nucleus of society and the state shall protect it.'

Article 6[15] guarantees freedom of conscience, but it also prohibits the infringement of 'the sacred' and establishes the state as the protector of 'the sacred and religion'. To allow Tunisian women the enjoyment of freedom of conscience in choosing a non-Muslim husband may be considered by some as a violation of 'the sacred'. As the basic unit of society, the family shall guarantee the Arab and Islamic identity of Tunisia to which several provisions of the preamble[16] and of the Constitution (Article 39 on education,[17] in particular) refer. As it is the man who transmits his religion to the family, the marriage of a non-Muslim with a Muslim Tunisian woman could be considered a threat to Tunisian identity. And the same argument can be made with regard to the inheritance rights of non-Muslims from Muslim Tunisians or the adoption of a Tunisian by a non-Muslim.

The impact of ambiguity in the interpretation of the CSP

The ambiguity of the legal texts relating to the equality of men and women in the family will make it challenging to maintain gender equality as a fundamental principle of the Tunisian legal system. The interests of a child in custody or adoption remain under the prerogatives of the father, as their legal guardian (as Kalthoum Méziou has noted[18]), and subordinated to the preservation of the Arab and Muslim identity. 'The disputed childhood', to borrow the title of the thesis of Souhayma Ben Achour,[19] will only be resolved in favour of the interests of the child if religious discrimination is undermined and the principle of equality between men and women properly anchored.

The principle of equality between men and women, however, has been successfully upheld to a certain degree. It has served to reject foreign judgements allowing polygamy and repudiation. The case law was consistent in its refusal to recognize repudiations pronounced abroad for their non-compliance with international human rights standards and the principle of equality between men and women.[20] Reinforced by Article 49 of the Code of Private International Law, which prohibits marriages without prior presentation of a certificate of celibacy by nationals of countries accepting polygamy, the courts did not hesitate to draw on the principle of gender equality law included in the provisions of CEDAW on which Tunisia had made reservations.[21] This is illustrated by a judgement of the Court of Cassation of 21 May 2009.[22] The Court had to adjudicate on a divorce sought by a Tunisian woman from her Egyptian husband residing in Egypt. Although the Tunisian courts were not competent to hear the case, the Court nevertheless accepted the claim and dismissed the argument made by the husband. The court held that 'even if the woman traveled to Egypt and got a divorce, the judgement would not be recognized in Tunisia for its violating Tunisian public order'.[23] The Court considered that even if Egyptian law provided the woman with a divorce based on *khul*ᶜ (i.e. a unilateral divorce against compensation)[24] she would have to renounce all her financial rights, including the *mahr* and the decision would be definite. This divorce, the court held, would be contrary to the fundamental choice of Tunisian law, which is based on the guarantee of the dignity of women and gender equality, respect for freedom to marry and divorce and the principle of double degree of jurisdiction. These, the Court added, are fundamental principles of the Tunisian legal system, as enshrined in Articles 5, 6, and 9 of the Constitution and paragraphs 1a and b of Article 16 of CEDAW. Because the woman cannot obtain an enforceable judgement abroad, Tunisian courts have jurisdiction to decide on the divorce. Thus the Court decided that these considerations justified the competence of the Tunisian courts. As regards custody, which was granted to the mother by the lower court, the Court equally dismissed the appeal. It held that the father, who was domiciled abroad, could not supervise the education of his children regardless of the existence of an Egyptian decision granting it. The Court considered that custody must be granted in accordance with the best interests of the child, which is why the Egyptian decision could not be recognized for its violation of the Tunisian ordre public.

Even though there are dissenting judgements, the jurisprudence that has upheld the principle of equality between men and women and the priority of the best interests of the child in parental care cases has been continuous ever since. In fact, this position can be said to be one of the factors explaining the great uprising of civil society in August 2012 in Tunisia, when a draft for a new constitution, aimed at establishing the notion of 'complementarity' between men and women instead of equality, was published.

Nonetheless, it remains to be seen whether equality will persist as a pillar of the Tunisian legal system or whether the ambiguity of the constitutional provisions on equality in family relationships will pave the way for a reversal on the basis of religious reference. Despite the vagueness of the texts, the principle of monogamy and equality in divorce should continue to support the Court in its interpretation of the CSP. Attempts to introduce a religious reference will infringe Article 49 of the Constitution, which prohibits the limitation of rights and freedom in their essence.[25] Polygamy and repudiation are unequal institutions by definition. But even if equality in the family is not established specifically, the best interests of the child are enshrined in Article 47[26] of the Constitution and the religious reference is placed on the same rank as that of human rights. The preamble of the Constitution does not afford religion a higher rank than the universal principles of human rights, as was the case in the preliminary drafts.

In fact, earlier religious discrimination was based solely on the Article 1 of the Constitution of 1959, which stated that Islam is the religion of the state. The courts and the administration had elevated this principle to a supra-constitutional principle. In its formulation, Article 1 is expressly supra constitutional, but other arrangements are just as important. As such the 'civil state', established in Article 2 of the new Constitution, which refers to a democratic state, as the guarantor of fundamental rights and freedoms in accordance with the provisions of the preamble,[27] cannot not be amended. The same applies to the fundamental rights and freedoms guaranteed by the Constitution (Article 49).

But we are not immune to setbacks. A judgement by the District Court of Mareth of 12 February 2014 attests to this. The court refused to grant an internal adoption on the grounds that the adoption was not in the best interests of the child. It based its decision of Article 47 of the Constitution, which provides that children are guaranteed rights to dignity, health, care, and education from their parents and the state. The state must provide all types of protection to all children without discrimination and in accordance with their best interests. The judgement, having criticized the single mother whose 'behavior was contrary to law, Sharia and the traditions and customs of the region', held that she must assume her responsibilities towards the child; her decision to leave the child with a family (that had asked for the adoption) had been rushed; and that it is in the interests of the child to stay with her, possibly with the help of social services.

It is certainly too early to draw any conclusions from this single decision. One has, however, to bear in mind that the new Constitution calls (more than the previous one) for the reconciliation and harmonization of the various rights and freedoms enshrined within it with the religious reference, and provides that that no hierarchy shall be put in place with respect to these different values. These values have the same constitutional status: they cannot be revised. But the characteristic ambiguity of the previous interpretation of the CSP (secular and religious at the same time)[28] remains. As before, the unification of its interpretation around the values of human rights will not be an easy path.

Notes

1 Report of the Secretary-General on the Rule of Law and Transitional Justice in Conflict and Post-Conflict Societies (S/204/616) <www.un.org/en/ruleoflaw> accessed 17 November 2014.

2 Judgement no 43429, unpublished (all translations from the Arabic are by the author).

3 Louis Joinet, 'Justice transitionnelle: principes et standards internationaux – un état des lieux' (2006) La justice transitionnelle dans le monde francophone: état des lieux, Conference Paper 2/2007, 3 <www.cnudhd.org/rapportjustice.pdf> accessed 17 November 2014.

4 Monia Ben Jémia, 'Le juge tunisien et la légitimation de l'ordre juridique positif par la charia' in Baudouin Dupret (ed), *La charia aujourd'hui: Usages de la référence au droit islamique* (La Découverte 2012) 154ff (and references cited there).

5 Monia Ben Jémia, 'Ordre public, constitution et exequatur' in *Mélanges en l'honneur de Habib Ayadi* (CPU 2000) 271.

6 Monia Ben Jémia, 'Non-discrimination religieuse et Code du statut personnel tunisien' in *Droits et culture: Mélanges en l'honneur du Doyen Yadh Ben Achour* (CPU 2008) 261.

7 Ali Mezghani, 'Religion, Mariage et Succession: L'hypothèse laïque. A propos d'une (R) évolution récente de la jurisprudence tunisienne' in *Droits et culture: Mélanges en l'honneur du Doyen Yadh Ben Achour* (CPU 2008) 345ff.

8 Monia Ben Jémia, 'Le juge tunisien et la légitimation de l'ordre juridique positif par la charia' in Baudouin Dupret (ed), *La charia aujourd'hui: Usages de la référence au droit islamique* (La Découverte 2012) 153; Souhayma Ben Achour, 'L'interprétation du droit tunisien de la famille, entre référence à l'Islam et appel aux droits fondamentaux' in *L'interprétation de la norme juridique, actes du colloque international organisé à Jendouba les 5 et 6 avril 2010, Faculté des sciences juridiques économiques et de gestion de Jendouba*, 17.

9 Monia Benjemia, Souhayma Ben Achour, and Meriem Bellamine, 'L'ordre public en droit international public tunisien de la famille' in Nathalie Bernard-Maugiron and Baudouin Dupret (eds), *Ordre public et droit musulman de la famille en Europe et en Afrique du Nord* (Bruylant 2012) 197.

10 3 May 2013, no 9246, unpublished.

11 Al-Hādī Kirrū, 'Zawāj al-muslima bi-ghayr al-muslim wa muṣādaqat al-dawla al-tūnisiyya ᶜalā ittifāqiyyat nyū yūrk' (1971) 13(2) Al-qaḍā' wa-l-tashrīᶜ (RJL) 11, and Ali Mezghani, 'Réflexions sur les relations du code de statut personnel avec le droit musulman classique' [1975] RTD 53; Monia Ben Jémia, 'Non-discrimination religieuse et Code du statut personnel tunisien' in *Droits et culture: Mélanges en l'honneur du Doyen Yadh Ben Achour* (CPU 2008).

12 3 May 2011, no 76829, unpublished.

13 An unofficial English translation of the Constitution was first prepared by the United Nations Development Programme, and then reviewed by International IDEA, see www.constitutionnet.org/files/2014.01.26_-_final_constitution_english_idea_final.pdf, accessed 1 December 2014 (the following quotes are all taken from this translation, unless stated otherwise).

14 Article 46: 'The state commits to protect women's accrued rights and work to strengthen and develop those rights. The state guarantees the equality of opportunities between women and men to have access to all levels of responsibility in all domains. The state works to attain parity between women and men in elected Assemblies. The state shall take all necessary measures in order to eradicate violence against women.'

15 Article 6: 'The state is the guardian of religion. It guarantees freedom of conscience and belief, the free exercise of religious practices and the neutrality of mosques and places of worship from all partisan instrumentalisation. The state undertakes to disseminate the values of moderation and tolerance and the protection of the sacred, and the prohibition of all violations thereof. It undertakes equally to prohibit and fight against calls for Takfir and the incitement of violence and hatred.'

16 Preamble: '. . . Expressing our people's commitment to the teachings of Islam, to their spirit of openness and tolerance, to human values and the highest principles of universal human rights, inspired by the heritage of our civilization, accumulated over the travails of our history, from our enlightened reformist movements that are based on the foundations of our Islamic-Arab identity and on the gains of human civilization, and adhering to the national gains achieved by our people . . .'

17 Article 39: 'Education shall be mandatory up to the age of sixteen years. The state guarantees the right to free public education at all levels and ensures provisions of the necessary resources to achieve a high quality of education, teaching, and training. It shall also work to consolidate the Arab-Muslim identity and national belonging in the young generations, and to strengthen, promote and generalize the use of the Arabic language and to openness to foreign languages, human civilizations and diffusion of the culture of human rights.'

18 Kalthoum Méziou, '*Tribunal de Première Instance de Grombalia 7 mars 1977*' [1978] RTD 95 (note).

19 Souhayma Ben Achour, *Enfance disputée: Les problèmes juridiques relatifs aux droits de garde et de visite après divorce dans les relations franco-maghrébines* (CPU 2004).

20 *Polygamie et répudiation dans les relations internationales: Actes de la table ronde organisée à Tunis le 16 avril 2004* (AB Consulting 2006).

21 Monia Ben Jémia, '*Tribunal de première instance Tunis no. 34179 du 27 juin 2000*' [2000] RTD 429 (note).

22 No 2009/32561, unpublished.

23 In another judgement delivered on 16 July 2010 (no 2010/40449, unpublished), the Supreme Court refused to recognize a Libyan repudiation on the ground of its opposition to procedural public policy and fundamental principles of procedure, such as the absence of legal proceedings, rights of the defence of women, and the lack of respect for the adversarial principle. The court also rejected the repudiation as contrary to public policy, the principle of equality between men and women according to Article 6 of the Constitution, and international treaties ratified by Tunisia.

24 On this matter, see Nathalie Bernard-Maugiron in this volume, Chapter 8.

25 Article 49: 'The limitations that can be imposed on the exercise of the rights and freedoms guaranteed in this Constitution will be established by law, without compromising their essence. Any such limitations can only be put in place for reasons necessary to a civil and democratic state and with the aim of protecting the rights of others, or based on the requirements of public order, national defence, public health or public morals, and provided there is proportionality between these restrictions and the objective sought. Judicial authorities ensure that rights and freedoms are protected from all violations. There can be no amendment to the Constitution that undermines the human rights and freedoms guaranteed in this Constitution.'

26 Article 47: 'Children are guaranteed the rights to dignity, health, care and education from their parents and the state. The state must provide all types of protection to all children without discrimination and in accordance with their best interest.'

27 Preamble: '. . . With a view to building a participatory, democratic, republican system, in the framework of a civil state founded on the law and on the sovereignty of the people, exercised through the peaceful alternation of power through free elections. A political system founded on the principle of the separation and balance of powers, which guarantees the freedom of association in conformity with the principles of pluralism, an impartial administration, and good governance, which are the foundations of political competition, a system that guarantees respect for human rights and freedoms,

independence of the judiciary, equality of rights and duties between all citizens, male and female, and equality between all regions; . . .'

28 Monia Ben Jémia, Souhayma Ben Achour, and Meriem Bellamine, 'L'ordre public en droit international public tunisien de la famille' in Nathalie Bernard-Maugiron and Baudouin Dupret (eds), *Ordre public et droit musulman de la famille en Europe et en Afrique du Nord* (Bruylant 2012).

Part II

Legislation

4 Struggling for a modern family law

A Khaleeji perspective

Lena-Maria Möller

Introduction

For Islamic family law, the twenty-first century started with groundbreaking reforms. In January 2000, the Egyptian parliament passed Law No 1 of 2000 governing procedure in personal status cases,[1] Article 20 of which henceforth permitted women to seek judicial divorce without any fault on their husband's part and without his consent. The Egyptian legislature's reinterpretation of the traditional Islamic divorce procedure of '*mukhāla*ᶜ'[2] allows the wife to dissolve her marriage against her husband's will so long as she is willing to ransom herself by paying him financial consideration.[3] These Egyptian reforms were quite famously termed 'the dawning of the third millennium on shariᶜa'.[4]

At the same time, roughly 1,300 miles to the south-east, i.e. in the small Arab Gulf monarchies of Bahrain, Qatar, and the United Arab Emirates (UAE), as well as in Saudi Arabia,[5] family law appeared less dynamic. Rules governing Muslim personal status remained uncodified and questions of family and succession law were guided by the individual judge's own interpretation of the multitude of differing opinions that make up Islamic law. Hence, in the Arab Gulf, women in particular were 'in the anomalous position of enjoying one of the highest standards of living in the world and yet being subject to a law which was developed over a thousand years ago'.[6] In 2005, however, the idea of comprehensively codifying Islamic family law was eventually picked up by the UAE, followed by Qatar in 2006 and Bahrain in 2009.[7] Currently, even Saudi Arabia is debating a draft code of Muslim personal status.[8] Codification as a means for the state to shape family relations has taken root in the Arab Gulf and it is this development that this chapter is concerned with.

Following this introduction, I will first explore the legal setting prior to the codification of family law in Bahrain, Qatar, and the UAE. The focus will be laid on the influence of European notions of codification and Egyptian law – the birthplace of the majority of jurists working in the region – on the development of the legal regimes in the Arab Gulf following their independence. In addition, the family court systems and the few legislative steps already taken by the three governments in the area of family law before the comprehensive codifications were introduced will be assessed. The third section of the chapter is devoted to the codification process itself; both the actors and the debates surrounding the first-time codification of family law will be explored. Finally, the fourth section will trace the approaches to codification and legal reform in the new family codes of Bahrain, Qatar, and the UAE by using selected examples from among the many new statutory rules.

The two main questions that this chapter sets out to answer are as follows: first, how did the three Arab Gulf States approach family law codification approximately 90 years after the very first codification of the field in the Muslim world (i.e. the Ottoman Law of Family Rights of 1917) and, second, did the three legislatures create a 'modern family law' in the sense that it accommodates the current socioeconomic realities of the Arab Gulf monarchies?

The pre-codification legal setting

History of a late codification

Family law codification in the Arab-Muslim world

In terms of codification, family law was a latecomer in the Arab-Muslim world. As opposed to civil, criminal, and administrative law, in the area of personal status Muslim countries were reluctant to adopt codes inspired by European models in order to reform religious law.[9] For one, Muslim jurists (*ᶜulamā'*, sing *ᶜālim*) could already draw upon a large number of rules within the primary sources of Islamic law, the Quran and the *sunna* (the practice of the Prophet Muḥammad), and upon the legal treatises of earlier jurists as a base for their judgements. Therefore, for a long time it remained not the state's, but the jurists' monopoly and area of expertise, and the legislature depended on the religious establishment to legitimize any interference in the sacred law as would result from the enactment of codes.[10] In addition, personal status law was concerned with a more private sphere and was barely connected with the rising presence of foreigners in the region. In many Muslim countries under colonial influence, Muslim personal status law further served as a symbol of national identity and distinction from the European-inspired codes that were introduced under colonial rule. It was not until 1917 that, with the Ottoman Law of Family Rights, a comprehensive codification was developed that not only systematically compiled the rules of traditional Islamic personal status law of the dominant school of law but also reformed family law to a certain degree.[11]

In the mid-twentieth century, when the majority of states in the Middle East and North Africa achieved independence, the idea of family law codification gained momentum in the Muslim world. Especially among Arab countries, legislatures paid considerable attention to comparative legal research during the codification processes.[12] Among the various reasons for governments to embark upon codification were to create state control over the law as well as to achieve greater legal certainty, and to facilitate legal awareness. In the area of family law, states also wanted to exercise control over the private affairs of their citizens. Family law codification thus represents a tool with which governments can address social problems. However, the three Arab Gulf States under review in this article did not follow this twentieth-century trend towards family law codification.

Family law codification in the Arab Gulf

Up until the presence of Great Britain as a so-called 'protective power' in the early twentieth century,[13] administrative systems in the small sheikhdoms of the current nation states of Bahrain, Qatar, and the UAE were 'virtually non-existent'.[14] Apart from tribal councils and religious arbitration tribunals, there were neither institutionalized courts nor codified law. When disputes arose, communities often called upon their tribal leaders, who were well versed in the local customary law. In addition, Islamic scholars – often with some type of formal training obtained in other Muslim countries – adjudicated in civil, criminal, and personal status cases based on traditional *fiqh* works and their own interpretation of Islamic law.[15] Great Britain eventually assumed jurisdiction over (mostly non-Muslim) foreigners in the Arab Gulf region as part of their treaty relations with local rulers. At the same time, those cases involving only Muslim residents in the Gulf sheikhdoms, especially in matters of personal status, continued to be settled by local judges in accordance with Islamic law.[16] When independence was gained in 1971, the three small Gulf monarchies lagged behind the majority of Muslim countries in developing a centralized and formalized legal system.

The political, economic, and social situation changed considerably with the discovery and subsequent extraction of the vast natural oil and gas resources that eventually turned the sheikhdoms in the Arab Gulf into rentier states. When Great Britain proclaimed its withdrawal as a protective power in the region in the 1960s, the Gulf rulers were well aware of the need to establish independent, functioning legal systems to meet changing regulatory needs in their new sovereign nation states. In light of the minimally developed legal and political system, as well as the insufficient educational systems in the Gulf, foreign legal practitioners from other Arab countries (mostly Egypt, Jordan, and Sudan) joined the judicial apparatus in the Gulf.[17] These 'import jurists' were to exercise large influence on the development of the legal systems in the Arab Gulf following independence. In line with the previous trend in other Arab countries, the small Gulf monarchies Bahrain, Qatar, and the UAE followed the civil law idea of codification and enacted codes in most legal areas. A civil law system particularly benefited the political system of authoritarian monarchies existing in all three states with their rulers combining substantial legislative and executive powers.[18]

Muslim personal status, in contrast, remained one of the very few areas of the law to be left uncodified and practised based on the traditional rules of the locally dominant school of Islamic law (*madhhab*)[19] in accord with the individual judge's interpretation. This was despite the many legal practitioners working in the Arab Gulf and originating from other Arab countries already in possession of comprehensively codified family law.

One reason for the apparent neglect of family law reform is the distinctive economic status of all three Arab Gulf States: As rentier states, Bahrain, Qatar, and the UAE are in a position to 'cushion' some of the negative social and economic side effects of traditional Islamic law through generous governmental benefits. In the Arab Gulf, instead of, for example, reforming traditional divorce law, divorced women and their children were for a long time simply granted public housing and pensions.[20] In addition, with the exception of Bahrain, civil society structures hardly emerged in the Gulf countries. The non-governmental women's rights organizations that advocated family law reforms in other Muslim countries basically do not exist in Qatar and the UAE.[21] In these two states, in particular, family law reform would not have been possible without the explicit endorsement of the ruling families who continue to uphold authoritarian models of governance.

Thus, as will be discussed in due course, it was not until the 1990s that debates on family law codification and reform arose. Only in Bahrain, with a more active civil society (largely owing to the two years of political liberalization and parliamentarianism from 1973 to 1975 and the nation's heterogeneous population), were demands for family reform voiced as early as in the 1980s. In 1997, the Gulf Cooperation Council (GCC) issued a draft personal status law, the Muscat Document, as a non-binding model text for its member states.[22] Shortly thereafter, Oman passed its first Code of Personal Status,[23] and the smaller Gulf monarchies of Bahrain, Qatar, and the UAE followed suit in the 2000s. At around the same time, Bahrain, Qatar, and the UAE ratified the United Nations Convention on the Elimination of all Forms of Discrimination against Women (CEDAW), albeit with substantive reservations.[24]

Family court systems in the Arab Gulf

Upon their independence, all three Arab Gulf states established dual judicial systems with separate courts adjudicating in matters related to Muslim family and succession law only (often called 'personal status courts', *maḥkamat al-aḥwāl al-shakhṣiyya* or 'family courts', *maḥkamat al-usra*). Personal status cases of (mostly foreign) non-Muslims are brought before the three states' civil courts instead. As family law codification did not affect the family court systems in Bahrain, Qatar, and the UAE, this duality still characterizes the judicial systems of the Arab Gulf.

In Qatar and the UAE, the Muslim family courts are merely separate chambers within the unified national court systems. Judgements in personal status cases can be appealed before the respective chamber of the appeal courts and the courts of cassation in these two Arab Gulf States. In spite of the general trend of 'nationalization' in the judicial sector, a great number of foreign judges from other Arab countries still serve in the personal status courts of both countries.[25]

In contrast to Qatar and the UAE, a sharper distinction between 'civil' and 'religious' courts can be witnessed in Bahrain, where the two court systems form completely separate entities. The regular Bahraini appeal courts and the Bahraini Court of Cassation are not competent to hear Muslim personal status cases. These cases fall outside the scope of the civil courts system, and judgements in Muslim personal status matters can only be appealed before the High Sharia Court of Appeal. In addition, Bahrain's family courts are divided into separate chambers for each sect.[26] Both chambers are staffed with religious jurists, a large majority of whom hold a degree in Islamic legal studies (Sharia and *fiqh*, i.e. Islamic jurisprudence) as opposed to law.[27] They are mostly trained abroad, with potential Sunni judges often studying in either Saudi Arabia or Egypt, and Shiite students receiving professional training in Iran, Iraq, or in private Shiite institutes (sing *hawza*) in Bahrain.

It is precisely this dual legal system that Bahraini women's rights groups have identified as being primarily responsible for the lack of legal certainty in personal status cases prior to the codification of Sunni family law in the kingdom. Until 2009, the religiously trained judges, with only a vague knowledge of the procedural law in force,[28] merely applied uncodified Islamic family and succession law in accord with their own interpretation. In combination with the large numbers of cases brought before them,[29] this resulted in extremely lengthy processes, as well as arbitrary judgements and only fuelled women's rights groups' demands for family law codification and reform.

The duality of Bahrain's judicial system can, for one, be ascribed to the confessional division between Sunni and Shiite citizens of Bahrain. Secondly, it is the outcome of the absence of judicial reforms already undertaken in the other two Arab Gulf states. While a similar duality in the legal system of Qatar was dissolved in 2003,[30] there is no indication that Bahrain's court system will be unified any time soon.

Pre-codification legislation

One might ask whether the late codification means that both rulers and citizens in the Arab Gulf found the rules of traditional Islamic family law to be perfectly equipped to regulate matters of Muslim personal status in their rapidly changing societies. The piecemeal legislation that has been introduced prior to the comprehensive codification of family law does not necessarily suggest so. Instead, we can note that Bahrain, Qatar, and the UAE did in fact resort to legislative measures to combat what they perceived as social wrongs. Hence, while the Arab Gulf States took a rather reluctant stance towards comprehensive codification of family law, it is equally true that uncodified Islamic family law alone did not meet the many questions and regulatory needs arising from the socioeconomic change that the entire region had been facing since the mid- to late-twentieth century as will be shown below.

In the UAE, legislative measures were particularly directed at limiting the soaring costs of marriage and its alleged consequences, such as a rising amount of male exogamy and an increasing population of women never marrying, which Emirati society had struggled with since oil revenues brought a sudden increase of wealth to the country.[31] The first reaction came in the form of a federal law only two years after the UAE became independent. Law No 12 of 1973[32] limited the dower (*mahr*) to a total of AED 10,000. Henceforth, spouses were prohibited from setting a prompt dower (paid upon the conclusion of the marriage) of more than AED 4,000 and a deferred dower (usually due upon the dissolution of the marriage or the death of the husband) of more than AED 6,000.[33] In Article 2, however, the law took a procedural route to curb rising costs of marriage. Claims exceeding the statutory limit could not be asserted in court. In 1997, the law was repealed by Law No 21, which raised the maximum dower to a total of AED 50,000 (the upper limit was set at AED 20,000 for the prompt dower and at AED 30,000 for its deferred portion).[34] In addition, the law limited the permissible wedding expenses, prohibiting wedding celebrations of more than one day and the slaughter of more than nine camels.[35] The new law copied its predecessor's procedural hurdle but also excluded anyone violating its provisions from the financial benefits offered by the Emirati Marriage Fund that had been established in 1992.[36] The Marriage Fund represents the second major legislative attempt at combating the high costs of marriage in the UAE. Its functions are manifold,[37] but at the heart of the fund lies an interest free loan that an Emirati man may apply for when he faces difficulty in financing his marriage to a fellow Emirati citizen. Through such a loan and a variety of educational programs, the Marriage Fund hopes to curb male exogamy and promote marriage among nationals.

Qatar, too, has recently discussed establishing such a marriage fund,[38] but in the late 1980s it took a different route to reduce male exogamy and promote marriage among nationals in order to preserve local culture in light of the overwhelming presence of foreigners in the small Gulf monarchy. In 1989, a law was introduced that prohibited certain categories of state employees and students studying abroad from marrying a foreign citizen.[39] The option for all other male Qataris to marry a non-Qatari woman was made incumbent upon the approval of the Ministry of Interior.[40] The very few exceptions to these rules included women from other GCC countries and daughters of a Qatari mother and a foreign father.[41]

As opposed to Qatar and the UAE, both focused on with whom and at what cost their citizens would conclude a marriage, Bahrain tried to achieve formalization and state control over matters of personal status prior to the comprehensive codification of family law. In 2005, a decree regulating the work of the official marriage notaries (sing. *ma'dhūn sharʿī*) was passed before being repealed two years later by Decree No 45 of 2007.[42] The latter, among other aspects, sets the minimum age to register a marriage at 15 for girls and 18 for boys[43] and allows a woman of legal majority to conclude her own marriage without a marriage guardian (*walī*).[44] The law further requires that a husband's repudiation (*ṭalāq*) of his wife occurs in court,[45] although, at the same time, it also allows for the registration of an extrajudicial *ṭalāq*.[46] All of these provisions are 'hidden' in a procedural law. By introducing new procedural rules, Bahrain endeavoured to reform its substantive law, and thus followed the Egyptian approach to legislative reforms,[47] most likely also inspired by the many Egyptian legal professionals working in the kingdom.

It can be concluded from the foregoing that, until recently, legislative activities in the area of family law were fragmentary. A broader vision of family law was clearly missing in all three Arab Gulf States and gave rise to demands for reform.

Struggling for codification: actors, debates, and identity politics

The codification of Muslim personal status in Bahrain was preceded by a broad societal discussion on family law reform and its content. A comparable process was not witnessed in the other two Gulf States: in the UAE and Qatar, the new family codes were drafted almost exclusively within the confines of governmental circles.*

Qatar and the United Arab Emirates

As non-governmental organizations do not exist in Qatar and the UAE, it was mainly the government and its affiliated women's rights groups that were in a position to impact the outcome of codification. Both Qatar and the UAE have official governmental bodies charged with issues of women's rights and the family: respectively, the Supreme Council for Family Affairs (*al-majlis al-aᶜlā li-shu'ūn al-usra*, SCFA) in Qatar and the General Women's Union (*al-ittiḥād al-nisā'ī al-ᶜāmm*, GWU) in the UAE. The two organizations – both headed by the monarchies' former first ladies and the mothers of the current rulers – actively supported the codification of Muslim personal status law.

In the UAE, the state's federal structure and the constitutionally guaranteed independence of each individual emirate in matters of personal status[48] for a long time stood in the way of a federal code of personal status. Nonetheless, in 1979, a draft federal code of personal status was developed, although never formally adopted or (at least to the author's knowledge) even mentioned in pre-codification judgements.[49] According to the GWU, the codification of family law has not been among the top priorities of either the government or the GWU itself. At the same time, however, the co-existence of different schools of Islamic legal thought that prevail in the seven emirates[50] produced incoherencies with regard to the applicable family law in the UAE. Women's access to judicial divorce and the duration of female child custody, for example, varied depending on the emirate in which the case was brought before the family court (and even depending on the individual judge charged with the case). These differences were among the reasons why, in the early 2000s, both the Emirati government and the GWU started to favour reforms and the unification of substantive law. Those in support of codification hoped for more legal certainty, consistency in family court judgements across the UAE, and a law that citizens could more readily access and comprehend; in short, a law that would meet the regulatory needs of the modern Emirati family.

In Qatar, we find the most homogeneous local population among the three Arab Gulf States under review. While, again in the absence of any procedural restrictions, Qatari judges – like their Emirati counterparts – were in theory free to judge in accordance with their own Muslim school of law or that of the parties, Hanbali law dominated pre-codification family law in reality. Nonetheless, even with one main school of law, the outcome of a case was by no means easily predictable for the parties, and there were very few ways to take action against an arbitrary judgement or a case pending in court for a long time. While there was a defined hierarchy of courts and first-instance family court judgements could be appealed against, it remained difficult to claim an incorrect application of the law in the absence of any clear rules, and even the appeal hearing was likely to produce an equally arbitrary judgement given the fact that the appeal judge would, again, adjudicate based on his own reading of the various traditional Hanbali rules. Hence, in light of these deficiencies and under the influence of both codification efforts in neighboring UAE and the recent passing of the Muscat Document, the Qatari government, too, decided to codify family and succession law.

The draft committees that were set up by both governments were male dominated and composed of family court judges, Muslim *ᶜulamā'*, and other legal personnel, but without the inclusion of the two governmental women's rights bodies. The GWU and SCFA only became involved in the codification process once the first draft laws had been finalized. Members of the two organizations (as well as other legal practitioners) were then asked to comment on the draft codes. This means that while the GWU and SCFA did have a chance to suggest amendments (some of which were actually included), the overall direction that the two codes were to take was decided without their assistance.

Bahrain

Due to its more heterogeneous population and its particular political context following independence in 1971, Bahrain enjoys a comparatively active civil society. Demands for family law reform started as early as the 1980s, i.e. only one decade after the smallest Arab Gulf monarchy became independent. Nonetheless, Bahrain was the last country to pass a comprehensive family code in the Arab Gulf. This is mainly attributed to confessional frictions, the majority Shiite country being ruled by the Sunni Khalifa dynasty. In the end, it was only the Sunni draft that passed the parliament while the Shiite part of the family code was rejected by Shiite clerics and political groups[51] alike. The turbulent process of family law codification in Bahrain thus became a symbol of the kingdom's 'identity politics'.[52]

Until the early 2000s, it was mostly non-governmental women's rights activists who promoted a codification of the rules governing Muslim personal status. In the 1980s and 1990s, advocates of family law reform founded the so-called Personal Status Committee (*lajnat al-aḥwāl al-shakhṣiyya*), but failed to gain the support (or even the recognition) of the government.[53] It was not until the accession of the current King Hamad Al Khalifa to the throne in 1999 that issues of women's rights were put on the government's agenda. Upon his coming into power, Hamad Al Khalifa set himself to modernizing the country in many regards,[54] among them being an enhancement of women's legal status in society. In 2001, he established a governmental women's rights body, the Supreme Council for Women (*al-majlis al-aᶜlā li-l-mar'a*, SCW)[55] and soon after, in 2002, assembled a first committee to draft a family code.

Initially, this committee was mostly composed of (all male) family court judges and only upon the request of the SCW included female lawyers as well. The committee was originally charged with drafting two parts of a prospective family code, i.e. one part for Sunnis and one part for Shiites. However, once it became apparent how few confessional differences there were (mostly concerning inheritance, temporary marriage, and the age limits for female custody), the drafting committee opted for a unified code instead.[56] Notwithstanding the three Shiite family judges who were involved in the drafting process of the unified code, the draft raised considerable criticism from Shiite *ᶜulamāʾ* once it was published in fall 2003. The minister of justice, under whose supervision the drafting committee had worked, resigned and the government seemed to backtrack from the reform project.[57] Bahrain's monarchy no doubt began to realize how emotionally and politically charged potential family law reforms were in the heterogeneous kingdom with its recent troubled history of sectarianism.

While the Al Khalifa-led government seemed to withdraw from their codification efforts, women's rights groups were not willing to sacrifice their vision of family law reform to the sectarian conflict. In 2004, the governmental SCW conducted a public opinion survey on Muslim personal status reform and two non-governmental organizations, the Bahrain Women's Union (*al-ittiḥād al-nisāʾī al-baḥraynī*, BWU) and the Women's Petition Committee (*lajnat al-ᶜarīḍa al-nisāʾiyya*, WPC), joined the campaign for family law codification. At the centre of the women's rights activists' criticism were the many lengthy court proceedings as well as what they perceived to be biased judgements in favour of men delivered by Bahraini family court judges of both sects.[58]

The SCW's public opinion survey on family law reform showed clear support for codification among Bahraini citizens (73.7 per cent), with most respondents (97 per cent) being in favour of a code based on Islamic principles. While approximately one third of the respondents (34.6 per cent) supported a unified code (with different rules in contested areas), another third (29.8 per cent) argued in favour of two separate codes for Sunnis and Shiites.[59] In line with the respondents' overall endorsement of codification, the SCW launched a new campaign in support of a Bahraini family code. The government, too, again took up codification efforts and formed a second drafting committee, this time, however, comprising only family court judges and without any participation from female legal professionals.[60]

By then the issue of family law codification and the question of who had the right to interpret Shiite family law in Bahrain had become a symbol of growing sectarian tensions. Tens of thousands of vigorous opponents of any state interference in what was perceived to be one of the last remaining areas of Shiite autonomy took to the streets.[61] Shiite clerics and politicians further demanded the inclusion of a constitutional guarantee that any potential code of Shiite personal status could enter into force or be amended only with the explicit approval of the *ᶜulamāʾ*. Interestingly enough, in 2009, when the final drafts were put to the vote before Bahrain's lower house (*majlis al-nuwwāb*), the Sunni-dominated government could have passed both parts despite the fierce opposition by Shiite political groups, who did not form the majority of members of parliament. Two drafts were on the table, and it was only shortly before the final vote that the government decided to withdraw the Shiite draft and instead pass only the Sunni part of the new family code to avoid further sectarian conflicts.

With its decision to draft two separate sets of rules and pass the Sunni part only, Bahrain missed the opportunity to enact a unified code and to follow a model that was introduced by Iraq as early as 1959. Having a similar confessional makeup, the Iraqi government under Abd al-Karim Qasim opted for a single Code of Personal Status[62] that applies to its Sunni and Shiite citizens alike. Iraq's unified code has been considered both a 'viable compromise',[63] with the potential to stabilize the country after the 2003 fall of Saddam Hussein and the country's subsequent political reorganization,[64] as well as 'a blueprint for a world debate to come'.[65]

The latter statement refers to the fact that also in Iraq the unification of family law was not devoid of fierce debates, and, similar to Bahrain, discussions had not revolved around the code's actual content but mainly concerned the question of which faction of society has the right to interpret family law. In Iraq, too, Shiite *ᶜulamā'* were reluctant to lose their monopoly and authority over matters of Muslim personal status within their sect.[66] Currently, ten years after the demise of Saddam Hussein's regime, the Iraqi Code of Personal Status has lost its stabilizing and unifying effect. Iraq's law of personal status is likely to again be divided along confessional lines given that a draft Shiite Code of Personal Status, initiated by the Iraqi Minster of Justice Hassan al-Shammari, was approved by the Council of Ministers in late October 2013 and is now (March 2014) being forwarded to Iraq's parliament.[67]

The international impetus for reform

In addition to the domestic impetuses for family law reform in the Arab Gulf, there is the international component, namely the accession of Bahrain, Qatar, and the UAE to CEDAW in the 2000s.[68] Bahrain and the UAE ratified CEDAW before comprehensive family codes were passed. However, only Bahrain submitted its first country report before the introduction of the new family code.[69] In the official hearing before the CEDAW Committee, Bahrain was criticized for its gendered and patriarchal family law and its failure to initiate reforms already undertaken in other Muslim-majority countries.[70] In contrast, the UAE delegation did not face the CEDAW Committee until the Emirati Code of Personal Status had entered into force. Nonetheless, the ratification of CEDAW by both Bahrain and the UAE clearly underscored the importance of reforming family law through codification. Qatar, on the other hand, might have wanted to make sure that there would be a comprehensive family code already in force by the time it acceded CEDAW.

The ratification of CEDAW in 2002 also offered a chance for Bahrain's non-governmental women's rights organization to pressure their government to fulfil its international treaty obligations by codifying a more egalitarian family law. In addition, those organizations not involved in the drafting of the official state report could now submit so-called shadow reports[71] and thus voice their demands at an international level. One shadow report prepared by the non-governmental Bahrain Human Rights Watch Society, for example, contained a letter to the UN Secretary-General by Ghada Jamsheer, chairwoman of the Women's Petition

Committee. In her statement, Jamsheer pointedly asked the Secretary-General and the CEDAW Committee that they support the ongoing demands for the codification of family law. Jamsheer strongly criticized both the Bahraini government's longstanding reluctance to introduce any family law reforms as well as the Shiite *ᶜulamā'*'s opposition to the Bahrain draft family code. In particular, Jamsheer explained how clerics used the law to ignite sectarian tensions within Bahrain.[72]

Legal reforms and legal realities: three approaches to family law codification

In many Arab-Muslim countries enacting codifications from the mid-twentieth century on, a combination of three approaches to family law reform can be recognized: first, the 'traditional approach' by which the particular legislature merely chooses selected rules from the vast body of Islamic jurisprudence on family relations and codifies them without any substantive reform; second, the 'comparative approach', i.e. the reform of certain aspects of family law through inner-Arab and inner-Islamic comparative research; and third, the 'innovative approach', which creates new trends and developments in Islamic family law and which challenges established patterns. Upon their first time codification of family law, the three Arab Gulf States too followed this tendency as will be shown below.

The traditional approach: Khaleeji views on marriage

The three Arab Gulf States' traditional approach to codifying family law is most noticeable in the area of marriage. The rules governing marriage in Bahrain, Qatar, and the UAE are conservative, gendered, and fail to adopt reforms already undertaken in other majority Muslim countries. Two features of the new family codes exemplify the traditional approach to marriage: first, the pivotal role of a woman's marriage guardian, her *walī*, in concluding the marriage and, second, the minimal restrictions on polygamy.

Guardianship in marriage

Maliki jurisprudence is particularly strict when it comes to guardianship in marriage, traditionally even prohibiting an adult woman from concluding her own marriage.[73] Especially the Emirati Code of Personal Status, being mainly inspired by and prioritizing Maliki law, adheres to this doctrinal stance and considers a marriage concluded without a guardian void (*bāṭil*).[74] Moreover, according to the new Emirati code, the two parties (*ᶜāqidān*) between whom the marriage is concluded are the fiancé and the marriage guardian (not the woman herself).[75] While Bahrain and Qatar stipulate that a marriage is concluded between the two spouses-to-be, they too are unambiguous in demanding that the marriage of a female be formally concluded by her guardian on her behalf.[76]

All three family codes do, however, allow for a woman to petition the court and substitute the approval of a judge for her guardian's permission to marry, should he deny this.[77] Whereas in Bahrain, Decree No 45 of 2007 allowed for a woman of legal age and without a close relative available to serve as her guardian to conclude a marriage herself,[78] the Bahraini Family Code now curtails this right for all Sunni Bahraini females. Under no circumstances may a woman conclude her own marriage, even if she has reached the age of legal capacity or has been married previously. At the same time, however, it should be noted that the strict rules on marriage guardianship do not mean that women may be coerced into marriage without their approval. All codes unequivocally require the future wife's consent.[79] Women in Bahrain and the UAE also confirmed that during the religious ceremony, the Imam will usually take the bride aside and inquire about her free intent to marry.

Throughout the Arab Gulf there are cases of women either suing their guardian (usually their father) for his permission to marry or turning to the courts to seek the judge's approval, but the fact that these cases are sometimes even covered in local media indicates that it is still uncommon for women to marry without or against their guardian's will.[80] In addition, the role and position of the marriage guardian was not a major point of debate during the codification process. Accordingly, the resulting question is whether marriage guardianship is still considered necessary in the Arab Gulf. Whereas the practice of women concluding their marriage only through their guardian remains widely acknowledged, it is important to note that marriage guardianship is upheld also for traditional reasons. Therefore, instead of adopting the rigid viewpoint of the Maliki School of law, the Arab Gulf States could have taken a comparative approach that would have allowed for more flexible rules. In this regard, Morocco, also being a predominantly Maliki Muslim country, could have served as an example.

In its far-reaching reforms of 2004, Morocco did away with marriage guardianship as a requirement and instead made '*al-wilāya* the woman's right, which she exercises upon reaching majority according to her choice and interests'.[81] Studies on the implementation of Morocco's Family Code of 2004 also show that many families continue to adhere to guardianship in marriage, mostly for traditional reasons.[82] At the same time, the law guarantees a woman the freedom to conclude her own marriage. A similar model would have been feasible in the Arab Gulf. Women would then have been free to decide whether they want to conclude their marriage through their guardian or not. In addition, courts would not have been bothered with cases in which the regular guardian is not available or does not consent to the marriage. Such rules would have also helped to reduce the workload of family courts which, especially in Bahrain, has often been criticized during the codification process.

Polygamy

Notwithstanding a growing criticism within the Arab Gulf region as to the effects of multiple marriages, restrictions on polygamy remained limited. The Emirati Code of Personal Status, for example, only demands fair treatment of all wives and specifies that co-wives may not be obliged to take up a common residence.[83]

Bahrain and Qatar did introduce mechanisms that – while not restricting a man's right to entering a polygamous union – are designed to at least inform any existing wives, as well as the new wife-to-be, of the polygamous union that is at hand. The Qatari code requires the marriage notary to inform the prospective wife to a polygamous union should she have concerns about the financial capability of the husband to support multiple wives. In addition, any previous wife will be informed that her husband has entered into another marriage.[84] In Bahrain, it is not upon the marriage notary, but upon the husband himself to inform his previous wife of his intention to take a co-wife. However, he only has to do so if the spouses – upon concluding the marriage – entered a stipulation to that effect in their marriage contract.[85] In all the Arab Gulf States, women can also demand a delegated right to divorce (*ṭalāq al-tafwīḍ*) should their husband take another wife, but at the same time, none of the three countries have standard clauses in their official marriage documents that point to this possibility. As such many women may not even be aware of their right to do so.

In order to understand the three Arab Gulf States' cautious stance towards restricting polygamy, one must be aware that polygamous unions still occur at rather high rates compared to most other Muslim countries. This is, for one, due to the high levels of wealth in the region and the relative ease of supporting multiple wives. Whereas financial concerns as well as various legislative steps have helped to limit polygamy in other Muslim countries, this is not the case in Bahrain, Qatar, and the UAE. Polygamous unions are estimated to constitute 5 to 7 per cent of all marriages in the Gulf.[86] Most Gulf rulers live in polygamous unions themselves, thus adding further legitimacy to the practice.

While a severe restriction of polygamy is unlikely to be implemented in the near future, the UAE should at least have introduced legislative measures that allow for both the new wife-to-be as well as any previous wife to be aware of their husband's prospective polygamous union. In addition, all three countries should have added a delegated divorce clause to their official marriage documents or should at least raise awareness about the possibility women have to terminate a polygamous union. In addition, the financial benefits received by newly weds could be restricted to monogamous couples as is the case with the Emirati Marriage Fund. Such reforms would have allowed for an incorporation of polygamy as a social reality in the Arab Gulf while at the same time protecting women who do not wish to live in such a union.

The comparative approach: towards an egalitarian divorce

The comparative approach of all three Arab Gulf legislatures is most notable in the area of divorce. Traditional Islamic divorce law is gendered in the sense that it does not grant husbands and wives equal options to divorce. Divorce law reforms in many Muslim countries have therefore focused on limiting men's right to unilateral *ṭalāq* on the one hand while granting women broadened access to divorce on the other. Upon the codification of family law, Bahrain, Qatar, and the UAE have followed this path by introducing an amended version of *khulᶜ*, largely based on the Egyptian version already mentioned, as well as compensation that a divorcée is now entitled to after having been repudiated by her husband.

Khul^c^

Traditional Islamic family law conceives *mukhāla^c^* as a consensual divorce procedure. The majority of early scholars held that *khul^c^* will be valid only if the husband agrees to pronounce the *ṭalāq*, i.e. he cannot be coerced into this form of divorce.[87] The Egyptian legislature did away with this established principle of mutual agreement as a prerequisite for *khul^c^* and allows for the wife to seek divorce against her husband's will so long as she is willing to ransom herself by paying him financial consideration (*badal*). If spouses fail to settle amicably, and if the wife petitions for *khul^c^* by waiving all her legal (*shar^c^ī*) financial rights and returning the dower (*mahr*) which she was given upon concluding the marriage, the court must grant the divorce.

Similar provisions have been adopted in both Bahrain and Qatar, where the dower (or rather the waiving thereof) constitutes a central element of *khul^c^*. In both codes, *khul^c^* is first and foremost considered a divorce by mutual consent with the woman reimbursing her husband financially.[88] If, however, *khul^c^* cannot be reached amicably, the courts can now intervene at the request of either spouse. Once reconciliation has failed in court, the judge will grant divorce and establish the amount of consideration to be paid by the wife.[89] Both codes also define an upper limit to the consideration that women have to pay. In Bahrain, the wife cannot be obliged to return more than her dower.[90] The Qatari provision is modelled after the Egyptian version so that the court will order the wife to waive all her financial rights and to return the prompt dower.[91] With separation of property still being the rule in all Arab Gulf states and without any general claim to post-divorce maintenance, the wife's 'financial rights' are in essence the deferred dower, which her husband would have to pay in case of a 'regular' repudiation. As a result, despite the different wording, the statutory provisions in Bahrain and Qatar essentially require the court to specify an amount of consideration that is in line with the dower agreed upon by the two parties.

The Emirati Code of Personal Status, in contrast, contains a slightly different version of *khul^c^*. The idea of introducing a divorce mechanism that would allow women to seek divorce without any fault on their husbands' part was highly controversial in the UAE. The Explanatory Memorandum, a first official commentary to the Family Code of 2005, explicitly states that the UAE did not intend to follow other Arab states – Egypt and Jordan in particular – in making *khul^c^* an individual act on the part of the wife.[92] For this reason, the first four paragraphs of Article 110 of the Emirati Code of Personal Status deal with *khul^c^* as a mutual agreement between the spouses. It is only the final paragraph (5) which states that if the husband persistently opposes the divorce, and if it is therefore feared that the spouses will transgress the limits of God, the court will rule for divorce and determine 'appropriate consideration' (*badal munāsib*) owed to the husband.[93]

What is worth noting with regard to the Emirati version of *khul*ᶜ is that the consideration to be determined in a judicial *khul*ᶜ has no statutory upper limit. There is no reference to the dower or any other financial rights of the wife in paragraph (5) of Article 110 of the Emirati Code of Personal Status.[94] This is particularly interesting as the UAE is the only state under review in which the dower has been limited by law.[95] If the new rules regulating judicial *khul*ᶜ were also to refer to the dower when discussing the maximum consideration, the UAE would be the first country to effectively limit the *khul*ᶜ consideration to a particular amount. It will therefore be of great interest to examine how courts in the UAE interpret 'appropriate consideration'.

In its traditional form, *khul*ᶜ was commonly practised before the codification of family law in all three states under review. Being a mutual agreement of the spouses, however, cases concerning *khul*ᶜ would only be brought before the personal status courts if there was disagreement about the amount of consideration agreed upon or the effect of *khul*ᶜ (e.g. whether it was a revocable or irrevocable divorce). It should also be noted that prior to any family law codification it was not uncommon that a *khul*ᶜ agreement would see women not only give up their own financial rights, but also waive their children's entitlement to maintenance from their fathers in order to gain a divorce. Moreover, some judges would even consider the waiving of custody rights by the mother as valid *khul*ᶜ consideration.[96] Both forms of consideration were done away with in all three states when family law was codified. According to the new rules regulating *khul*ᶜ in Bahrain, Qatar, and the UAE, waiving custody rights or child support may not serve as consideration in a *khul*ᶜ agreement, even if it is mutually agreed upon.[97]

An evaluation of judgements in cases of *khul*ᶜ brought before the personal status courts in the UAE prior to the reforms of 2005 indicates that consideration amounts mutually agreed upon exceeded the dower significantly. Reports from Bahrain point to a similar practice. *Khul*ᶜ, even though in theory settled amicably, usually required women to ransom themselves not only by returning their dower, but also by paying the husband whatever amount of money he demanded for pronouncing the repudiation.[98] As such, it does not come as a surprise that some authors describe *khul*ᶜ divorce as 'the hard way out'.[99]

In 2011, five years after the codification of family law, 60 per cent of Qatari men still opposed judicial *khul*ᶜ.[100] Nonetheless, statistics show that Qatari courts do apply the new statutory rules and indeed rule for *khul*ᶜ if women persistently demand divorce. In 2007, one year after the new Qatari Family Code entered into force, 4 per cent of all divorces granted in Qatar's personal status courts were *khul*ᶜ. The number rose to 7.4 per cent in 2008,[101] and according to recent divorce statistics for 2010, *khul*ᶜ accounted for 5.9 per cent of all divorces.[102] Also in the UAE, despite the controversy during the codification process surrounding the introduction of a judicial divorce permissible against the husband's will, *khul*ᶜ appears to be accepted by the Emirati judiciary. Both the Dubai and the Abu Dhabi Court of Cassation have clarified that if a marriage is irretrievably broken, the union should be dissolved by *khul*ᶜ even if the husband does not consent to the divorce or the particular consideration determined by the court.[103]

As mentioned earlier, the codes of Bahrain and Qatar clearly spell out the consideration that is to be determined by the court, i.e. the return of the prompt dower and the waiving of any entitlement to the dower's deferred portion. In contrast, judges in the UAE are more flexible in determining what they consider 'appropriate consideration'. While pre-codification judgements from the UAE indicate that the average *khulᶜ* consideration was significantly above the dower, post-codification judgements differ considerably. Even when presented with a divorce case against the husband's will, Emirati judges have thus far determined rather moderate amounts of *khulᶜ* consideration.

Although the Emirati Code of Personal Status grants substantial discretionary powers to the individual judge in determining the appropriate consideration a wife is to pay her husband, most judgements referred to the dower alone. Women were either asked to return their dower and waive any remaining claims,[104] or they were even allowed to keep the prompt dower that they received when the marriage was concluded and only had to waive their entitlement to its deferred portion.[105] Women's rights groups confirm a similar trend for Bahrain. While prior to the codification of family law men would demand considerations significantly above the dower, the introduction of judicial *khulᶜ* has limited the financial burden women have to carry in order to be granted a divorce against their husbands' will.[106] The reform of *khulᶜ* has thus facilitated the chances for women to petition for divorce even without any fault on their husbands' part.

Mutᶜat al-ṭalāq

The second aspect of divorce law reform introduced in the Arab Gulf is *mutᶜat al-ṭalāq* (short *mutᶜa*), a compensation the husband is obliged to pay to his former wife after unilaterally repudiating her.[107] Similar to *khulᶜ*, *mutᶜa* finds its basis in the primary sources of Islamic law and was already acknowledged in early Islamic jurisprudence. Its current form, however, is largely owed to a re-interpretation and modification of the classical rules. The majority of Muslim countries nowadays attach financial consequences to any *ṭalāq* deemed arbitrary and most family codes do so by providing for compensation in the form of *mutᶜa* (some countries refer to it as *taᶜwīḍ*) for women divorced against their will and without any fault on their part.[108] In Tunisia, the only Arab country that provides a uniform divorce mechanism for both spouses regardless of their sex, *mutᶜa* is owed to each spouse divorced against his/her will and without any fault on his/her part.[109]

In contrast, the Quran, in Sura 2, verse 336, only demands compensation for any divorcée with whom the marriage has *not* been previously consummated.[110] This Quranic version of the *mutᶜa* dominated family law jurisdiction in the Arab Gulf states until recently. In contrast, the codes of Bahrain and Qatar now provide that *every* woman divorced through repudiation at her husband's will and without any fault on her part is entitled to compensation in the form of *mutᶜa*.[111] The maximum amount of compensation in Bahrain is equivalent to the annual maintenance of the woman in question. In Qatar, the upper limit of the *mutᶜa* is the equivalent of three years of maintenance. In both countries, divorcées will also be entitled to regular maintenance during their waiting period (*nafaqat al-ᶜidda*).[112] In the UAE, the rules differ slightly in that the new Emirati code rules out any maintenance claim of a wife repudiated irrevocably. Even if she did not cause the marital discord, she will not be entitled to maintenance during her waiting period.[113] She can, however, be awarded compensation with an upper limit of one year's maintenance consistent with the Bahraini provisions.[114]

In all three states, it is now incumbent upon the courts to determine the appropriate amount of compensation. At the same time, it should be noted that, as opposed to *khulᶜ* consideration, *mutᶜa* does not automatically become part of an in-court divorce proceeding. As the *ṭalāq* can as well be pronounced extra-judicially, women have to file a separate case in order to be awarded post-divorce compensation, and a husband's right to unilaterally repudiate his wife remains unchallenged. It is merely the financial consequences that have been reformed. In addition, there remains too little knowledge about the new rules among citizens of the Arab Gulf states. As opposed to other areas of the new laws, such as *khulᶜ* divorce and limits on polygamy, the statutory rules on *mutᶜa* have not raised much attention or public discussion following the implementation of the new family codes. Therefore, cases of *mutᶜa* are still limited in numbers. At the same time, some preliminary conclusions can already be drawn from an evaluation of judgements in court cases concerning *mutᶜa*.

Appeal case no 42/2009 brought before the Abu Dhabi Court of Cassation in 2009[115] is a good example of how the new rules on *mutᶜa* have indeed served as an effective source of financial security for those women not responsible for the marital breakdown. The particular case concerned a woman repudiated against her will by means of an extra-judicial *ṭalāq*. The judgement confirmed the woman's entitlement to her deferred dower and placed her former husband under the obligation to cover her housing expenses during the waiting period. The court further decided that the woman was entitled to a total *mutᶜa* of AED 18,000, payable in monthly installments of AED 1,500 over a one-year period.

The ruling confirmed a judgement issued earlier by the first instance court, whereas the intermediate Abu Dhabi Court of Appeal had followed the husband's claim that the divorce occurred by mutual consent. The Court of Cassation, in contrast, required the husband to present evidence that he was not solely responsible for the marital breakdown. As there was no indication of any fault on the side of the wife, the Court of Cassation overruled the Court of Appeal's judgement. The Court of Cassation further clarified that the duration of the marriage, the arbitrary repudiation by the husband (without any attempt to seek reconciliation) as well as the psychological harm that the wife suffered were to be taken into consideration in determining the amount of *mutᶜa*. Due to the financial and emotional injury that the repudiation thus caused the woman under these particular circumstances, she was awarded a comparably high compensation that equalled the amount of *khulᶜ* consideration that women have to pay in order to be granted a divorce at their wish.

The innovative approach: custody and the best interests of the child

At first glance, the new statutory rules governing parental care in the three Arab Gulf States reflect traditional Islamic law in the sense that they ascribe different roles and functions to men and women in the upbringing of children. First, the father's right to guardianship (*wilāya*) remains unchallenged. Second, the three codes distinguish between age and gender and tend to place younger children in their mother's custody (*ḥiḍāna*) while requiring male custody for older children. Whereas these rigid age and gender limits do not, at least theoretically, leave much space for a decision based on the individual welfare of the child, the new family codes introduce the concept of 'the best interests of the child' (*maṣlaḥat al-maḥḍūn*) as the central benchmark in determining the eligibility for and allocation of custody. By doing so, Bahrain, Qatar, and the UAE grant family court judges substantial discretionary powers and follow a very recent development in Islamic family law. This stance contrasts with another innovative, albeit stricter, approach to regulating custody: rules precluding non-Muslim mothers from exercising custody over their Muslim children.

The best interests of the child

In all three Arab Gulf States, children's welfare was a reoccurring theme among legal professionals, scholars of law and women's rights groups involved in the codification process. This is for one due to the ratification of the United Nations Convention on the Rights of the Child by Bahrain, Qatar, and the UAE in the 1990s.[116] What is more important, however, is the fact that by introducing the concept of the best interests of the child, the three legislatures were able to tone down rigid gender differences that prevailed in the pre-codification period without infringing on the substance of Islamic jurisprudence on family relations.

Especially in Qatar and the UAE, the statutory rules governing custody follow a particular structure: typically, the article starts with a general rule, mostly in line with the prevailing opinion on custody in the traditional Islamic family law of the dominant school of law. Such a rule would, for example, state that the female custodian will lose her right to custody following a divorce should she marry a 'stranger' (*zawj ajnabī*),[117] i.e. a person who could (in theory) marry the child, or that female custody ends when boys reach the age of 11 (in the UAE) or 13 (in Qatar) and when girls reach the age of 13 (in the UAE) or 15 (in Qatar).[118] The article then goes on to state something along the lines of 'except for those cases in which the court, in considering the best interests of the child, decides to the contrary' (*'illā idhā qaddarat al-maḥkama khilāfa dhalika li-maṣlaḥat al-maḥḍūn'*)[119] and thus empowers the individual judge to disregard the forgoing rule and decide the custody case at hand solely based on the individual interests of the child. In contrast, in Bahrain, the best interests of the child is more of an abstract benchmark not included in each individual article and often not designed to allow for a deviation from the general rule. Even though the new Bahraini code, in its Article 134, contains a general clause that judges shall consider the best interests of the child when deciding on custody, such decisions may not, however, contradict the previous articles which contain many decisive rules on custody, such as age limits and religious affiliation of the custodian.[120]

While all codes refer to the best interests of the child as a concept, Qatar's code stands out in determining how the court is to assess what is in the best interests of the child. Accordingly, the judge is to consider the custodian's affection for the child and the ability to raise him/her as well as to provide a sound environment, education, and medical care.[121] In Bahrain and the UAE, it is upon the judiciary to define the term 'the best interests of the child'.[122]

In Qatar, two judgements issued by the Court of Cassation, one from the pre-codification period, the other from 2007, illustrate the adoption of the concept of the best interests of the child by the judiciary and how it has been used to bring judgements more in line with the individual needs of the child in question. The first case of 6 June 2006 (i.e. shortly before the new family code entered into force) concerned a Shiite Qatari national claiming custody of his son.[123] The father argued that according to Shiite jurisprudence, female custody for boys ends when they have reached the age of seven at the latest (which his son had). The court rejected the father's claim, arguing that it was not the mere age of the child that determined custody but that the court might as well consider the overall welfare of the child. In its ruling, however, the court then goes on to discuss the varying age limits that exist among the multiple Islamic schools of law and reasons that these differing opinions give the judiciary multiple options to choose from depending on the circumstances of the particular case. Hence, the Qatari Court of Cassation did not discard the idea of allocating custody based on age limits altogether, but reserved for itself the discretion to select from among the various rules that Islamic law recognizes.

In 2007, however, a similar case had quite a different outcome. Here again, a father petitioned for custody of his son, this time with reference to the new statutory age limits, arguing that the boy had turned 13 and that his mother's custody should thus be terminated.[124] In its judgement, the Qatari Court of Cassation did not refer to age limits or solely to an extension thereof, but rather discussed the particular circumstances of the case at length. The court concluded that the mother's custody should be extended, particularly so that the boy may remain with his older sister for whom the mother still assumed custody. In addition, the court decided that, as opposed to what the children's father claimed, the frequent travels of the mother did not compromise the children's welfare and that in consideration of all aspects of the case, she was to be considered the most suitable custodian. This reasoning demonstrates how, within only one year, the Qatari Court of Cassation went from defining the best interests of the child solely within the framework of Islamic jurisprudence to a consideration of the individual interests of the child and the particular circumstances of the case at hand.

Interreligious custody cases

All three family codes discriminate against non-Muslim mothers of Muslim children. Bahrain's new code contains the most unambiguous rule in making Islam an inevitable prerequisite for exercising custody.[125] The Emirati Code of Personal Status, too, prohibits non-Muslims from having custody for a Muslim child, but allows for the court to order an, albeit shorter, period of female custody if exercised by the mother herself and if in the best interests of the child. Specifically, the court may grant custody to a Jewish or Christian mother of a Muslim child so long as motherly care is in the best interests of the child, but only until the child reaches the age of five.[126] In Qatar, the non-Muslim mother (but no other female) may serve as custodian as long as she is not an apostate from Islam and only until the child 'understands about the religions' ('*hattā yaᶜqilu al-ṣaġīr al-adyān*') or until the child runs the risk of following a religion other than Islam. In any case, the entitlement of a non-Muslim mother to custody ends once the child is seven years of age.[127] Interestingly enough, at least the Islamic school of law that influenced the new Bahraini and Emirati codes the most, i.e. Maliki jurisprudence, does not consider the religious affiliation of the mother a condition for the allocation of custody.[128] Hence, it can be assumed that the reason for the legislatures' restrictive stance towards interreligious custody does not originate from a strict rule laid down in primary sources but instead from social concerns that are peculiar to the Arab Gulf States.

As mentioned earlier, male exogamy is a key concern of all three Arab Gulf States. Since Islamic law permits Muslim men to marry women of Christian and Jewish faith, male exogamy may very well lead to interreligious marriages. As one of the alleged negative consequences of Gulf nationals marrying foreign women is the loss of 'national culture', interreligious marriages in particular prompt such concerns. Hence, the new rules on custody may have two motives: first, to secure a culturally specific, in essence Muslim, upbringing of children born into mixed marriages and, second, to discourage non-Muslim women from concluding an interreligious union, as they know that they might lose custody upon the breakdown of the marriage.

Conclusion

By comprehensively codifying family law, the Arab Gulf legislatures have claimed for themselves the authority to interpret and reform Islamic law and bring it in line with what they considered to be their societies' regulatory needs. Despite having enjoyed considerable leeway in the pre-codification period, courts in the Arab Gulf have accepted the state's new interpretative authority over family law and have largely followed the new statutory rules. In Qatar and the UAE as well as among Bahrain's Sunni population, Muslim clerics similarly did not voice significant criticism against the codification, even though this, of course, needs to be understood against the background of the largely authoritarian rule that all three monarchies uphold. The public media coverage that all three codes receive in the Arab Gulf further suggests that the three countries' citizens are actively engaged in the current debate on family law and that, in the future, they might thus be able to trigger further reforms.

As for the new statutory rules themselves, we can note that the approaches to family law codification and legal reform differ according to the subject matter in question: with regard to the rules governing marriage, the approach is a largely traditional and gendered. This neither corresponds with women's economic and social participation nor with the ongoing attempts of all three states in empowering women. If Bahrain, Qatar, and the UAE were to adopt a comparative approach in the area of marriage, they could follow the model of other Arab-Muslim states in introducing more flexible rules; rules that allow for the incorporation of Islamic legal concepts, such as marriage guardianship, while at the same time guaranteeing that men and women enter into marriage on an equal footing. Additionally, raising legal awareness among future spouses could help all parties entering into a marriage to make more informed choices. Information duties by the marriage notary for example could ensure that parties are aware whether their union is monogamous or polygamous.

As regards the dissolution of marriage, Bahrain, Qatar, and the UAE have created more egalitarian divorce mechanisms in particular with the introduction of *khul*ᶜ and *mut*ᶜ*a*. These mechanisms now also enable the wife to insist unilaterally on a judicial divorce. Since the codification of family law, the amount of consideration a woman has to pay in a judicial *khul*ᶜ has fallen below the average consideration agreed upon in amicable out-of-court agreements reached before the new family codes entered into force. This suggests that the idea of women having a 'right' to divorce has been accepted by the judiciary and that judges in the Arab Gulf feel no need to punish women financially for exercising this right. Notwithstanding the efforts made, a unification of *khul*ᶜ consideration and *mut*ᶜ*a* would further a more egalitarian divorce system in all three Arab Gulf states. Reforms could include the introduction of a general obligation to compensate the spouse not responsible for the marital breakdown. Such a rule would be in line with Tunisian family law. However, making divorce a wholly judicial process in the Arab Gulf would be an inevitable requirement for such reforms. As a result, while first steps have been taken, it is still a long way towards a completely egalitarian divorce law in Bahrain, Qatar, and the UAE.

The rules governing custody are most likely to correspond to the Arab Gulf societies' regulatory needs. The chosen approach is rather innovative: the inclusion of the concept of the best interests of the child in the codes has given the courts broad discretionary powers to consider and incorporate changing perceptions of family relations. The fact that within only one year after the new family code was introduced, Qatar's Court of Cassation construed the best interests of the child without reference to the framework of traditional Islamic law and with sole consideration of the individual case at hand demonstrates the flexibility that the new rules create.

As a whole the process of codification must be hailed and can be rightly seen as a step towards a 'modern' law for the Gulf family. Many steps, however, lie ahead. It is now up to the government and non-governmental actors to raise awareness among citizens and train legal personnel in the new statutory rules. In this way, all members of society will not only know their rights, but may also voice their concerns and demands in future debates on how to further reform family law and bring it more in line with the needs of Arab Gulf societies.

Notes

1 Law No 1 of 2000 of 29 January 2000 Regulating Certain Litigation Procedures in Personal Status [*qānūn tanẓīm ba*^{c}*ḍ awḍā*^{c} *wa ijrā'āt al-taqāḍī fī masā'il al-aḥwāl al-shakhṣiyya*], Official Gazette no 4 (a) of 29 January 2000, 5–30.

2 More often referred to as '*khul*^{c}' which is the type of divorce established through the procedure of *mukhāla*^{c}.

3 For the Egyptian reforms of *khul*^{c} and the debates surrounding them see e.g. Oussama Arabi, 'The Dawning of the Third Millennium on Shari^{c}a: Egypt's Law No. 1 of 2000, or Women May Divorce at Will' (2001) 16 ALQ 2; Nathalie Bernard-Maugiron and Baudouin Dupret, 'Breaking Up the Family: Divorce in Egyptian Law and Practice' (2008) 6 HAWWA 52; Nadia Sonneveld, 'The Implementation of the "Khul^{c} Law" in Egyptian Courts: Some Preliminary Results' (2004) 21 Recht van de Islam 21.

4 Arabi (2001) 16 ALQ 2; soon after the reforms in Egypt, judicial *khul*^{c} was also introduced in Jordan in 2001, see Art 126 Law No 61 of 1976 on the Law of Personal Status [*qānūn al-aḥwāl al-shakhṣiyya*], Official Gazette no 2668 of 1 December 1976, 2756–2777, as amended by Temporary Law No 82 of 2001; for the controversies surrounding the introduction of judicial *khul*^{c} in Jordan and the subsequent reforms of 2010, see Lynn Welchman, 'Musawah, CEDAW, and Muslim Family Laws in the 21st Century' in Mark S Ellis, Anver M Emon, and Benjamin Glahn (eds), *Islamic Law and International Human Rights Law: Searching for Common Ground?* (OUP 2012) 309, 314f.

5 The straight-line distance between Egypt's capital Cairo and Qatar's capital Doha is 1,281 miles.

6 Doreen Hinchcliffe, 'Women and the Law in the United Arab Emirates' in Ian R Netton (ed), *Arabia and the Gulf: From Traditional Society to Modern States* (Croom Helm 1986) 239.

7 UAE Federal Law of Personal Status No 28 of 2005 [*qānūn al-aḥwāl al-shakhṣiyya*], Official Gazette no 439 of 30 November 2005, 9–118 (hereafter: Emirati Code of Personal Status); Qatar Family Law No 22 of 2006 [*qānūn al-usra*], Official Gazette no 8 of 28 August 2006, 31–99 (hereafter: Qatari Family Code); Bahrain Family Law No 19 of 2009 [*qānūn al-usra (al-qism al-awwal)*], Official Gazette no 2898 of 4 June 2009, 5–30 (hereafter: Bahraini Family Code); the law applies to Bahrain's Sunni Muslim minority only. The second part of the law, which was to codify Shiite family law, was rejected by parliament. For a discussion of the controversies and confessional tensions surrounding the codification of family law in Bahrain see the third section of this chapter.

8 In December 2013, the Saudi Consultative Assembly (*majlis al-shūrā*) debated a draft law of personal status, which, among other things, would set the minimum age of marriage at 18, see Huyā Sahlī, 'Al-aḥwāl al-shakhṣiyya qayd al-taṣwīt bi-l-sa^{c}ūdiyya wasṭ i^{c}tirāḍāt' [Saudi vote on personal status amid protests] *Al-Jazīra* (28 December 2013) <www.aljazeera.net/news/pages/2cf8f699-911c-42ef-bb4b-5c5ec2666476> accessed 13 March 2014.

9 For the history of codification in Muslim countries see e.g. James ND Anderson, 'Codification in the Muslim World: Some Reflections' (1966) 30 RabelsZ 241; Ann Elizabeth Mayer, 'The Sharī^{c}ah: A Methodology or a Body of Substantive Rules?' in Nicholas Herr (ed), *Islamic Law and Jurisprudence* (University of Washington Press 1990) 177; Rudolph Peters, 'From Jurists' Law to Statutory Law or What Happens

When the Shariᶜa is Codified' in BA Roberson (ed), *Shaping the Current Islamic Reformation* (Frank Cass 2003) 82; Joseph Schacht, 'Problems of Modern Islamic Legislation' (1960) 12 Studia Islamica 99.

10 Peters (n 9) 90.

11 For the Ottoman Law of Family Rights see e.g. Judith Tucker, 'Revisiting Reform: Women and the Ottoman Law of Family Rights, 1917' (1996) 4 Arab Studies Journal 4; it should be noted that a code compiled by the Egyptian jurist Muḥammad Qadrī Bāshā in 1875 predates the Ottoman Law. However, Qadrī Bāshā's code merely compiled the majority views in matters of personal status as expressed by scholars of the Hanafi school of law without any reference to differing opinions in other Muslim schools of law. Although never promulgated as law, the code did serve as an important reference for Egyptian jurists.

12 Lynn Welchman, 'Women, Family and the Law: the Muslim Personal Status Law Debate in Arab States' in Robert W Heffner (ed), *The New Cambridge History of Islam*, vol 6: *Muslims and Modernity: Culture and Society since 1800* (CUP 2011) 411, 415. For a long time, Egyptian family law of the 1920s was used as a model for future codification projects in other Arab countries.

13 Great Britain's role as a protective power was established through a series of treaties between the British government and local rulers in the sheikhdoms along the Persian Gulf from the nineteenth century onwards. The first treaties were concluded between local rulers and the East India Company, which was mostly interested in safeguarding its trade routes against piracy. Later treaties explicitly established Great Britain as a protective power with political agents in the region and extra-territorial jurisdiction. See e.g. Husain M Al Baharna, *British Extra-Territorial Jurisdiction in the Gulf 1913–1971: An Analysis of the System of British Courts in the Territories of the British Protected States of the Gulf during the Pre-Independence Era* (Archive Editions 1998); Glen Balfour-Paul, 'Kuwait, Qatar and the United Arab Emirates: Political and Social Evolution' in Ian R Netton (ed), *Arabia and the Gulf: From Traditional Society to Modern States* (Croom Helm 1986) 156–75; James Onley, *Britain and the Gulf Shaikhdoms, 1820–1971: The Politics of Protection* (Georgetown University School of Foreign Affairs 2009).

14 Sultan BA Al-Muhairi, 'The Development of the UAE Legal System and Unification with the Judicial System' (1996) 11 ALQ 121.

15 Nathan Brown, *The Rule of Law in the Arab World: Courts in Egypt and the Gulf* (CUP 1997) 130f; A Nizar Hamzeh, 'Qatar: The Duality of the Legal System' (1994) 30 MES 79, 80ff; Frances Hasso, *Consuming Desires: Family Crisis and the State in the Middle East* (SUP 2011) 53f; Fu'ad Ishaq Khuri, *Tribe and State in Bahrain: The Transformation of Social and Political Authority in an Arab State* (University of Chicago Press 1980) 35, 68; Al-Muhairi (1996) 11 ALQ 120–24.

16 Al-Muhairi (1996) 11 ALQ 124f; Hamzeh (1994) 30 MES 82. The application of British extraterritorial jurisdiction over foreign Muslims in the Arab Gulf region remained controversial due to the different conceptions of the scope of application. For the British, it was mostly a question of nationality, whereas Gulf rulers perceived it as a matter of interreligious law, with the British (Christian) power having jurisdiction over non-Muslim residents in their sheikhdoms, see Brown (n 15) 133f.

17 Brown (n 15) 137, 155ff; for the UAE in particular see Al-Muhairi (1996) 11 ALQ 128.

18 Brown (n 15) 154f, 185.

19 Bahrain's Sunni minority for whom the Family Code of 2009 was passed is predominantly Maliki. The Maliki school of law is also prevalent in the two largest emirates

of the UAE, i.e. Abu Dhabi and Dubai. The five smaller emirates (Ajman, Fujairah, Ras al-Khaimah, Sharjah, and Umm al-Quwain) and Qatar are primarily Hanbali. Therefore, the family law applied prior to the codification differed between the three Arab Gulf States to some degree. It can be assumed that litigants would frequent a judge of their respective school of law and that judges would generally apply the rules of the particular school of law to which the litigants belonged. At the same time, the absence of codified (procedural) law did allow for more flexibility in this regard.

20 Lena-Maria Möller, ‘Family Law in the Arab Gulf: Recent Developments and Reform Patterns’ (2013) 9 JISPIL 22, 24f; for Qatar see Hans-Georg Ebert and Assem Hefny, ‘Katar’ in Bergmann, Ferid and Henrich (eds), *Internationales Ehe- und Kindschaftsrecht* (looseleaf service, in German, R 1 April 2010); for the UAE see Dhabya Al Mehairi, ‘Ministry helps thousands of divorced women in Abu Dhabi “find their way”’ *The National* (Abu Dhabi, 7 November 2013) <www.thenational.ae/uae/ministry-helps-thousands-of-divorced-women-in-abu-dhabi-find-their-way> accessed 11 March 2014, as well as the web pages of Dubai’s and Abu Dhabi’s social services <www.cda.gov.ae/ar/socialcare/SocialBenefits/Pages/default.aspx>, <www.abudhabi.ae/egovPoolPortal_WAR/appmanager/ADeGP/Citizen?_nfpb=true&_pageLabel=p20172&lang=ar> accessed 11 March 2014.

21 JE Peterson, ‘The Political Status of Women in the Arab Gulf States’ (1989) 43 MEJ 34, 38f; Munira Fakhro, ‘Gulf Women and Islamic Law’ in Mai Yamani (ed), *Feminism and Islam: Legal and Literary Perspectives* (NYU Press 1996) 258; Leila Devriese, ‘Renegotiating Feminist Praxis in the Arabian Gulf’ (2008) 20 Cultural Dynamics 73, 75.

22 Muscat Document of the GCC Common Law of Personal Status 1997 [*al-niẓām (al-qānūn) al-muwaḥḥad li-l-aḥwāl al-shakhṣiyya li-duwal majlis al-taʿāwun li-duwal al-khalīj al-ʿarabiyya*], see Middle East Partnership Initiative, <www.maktabatmepi.org/node/1222> accessed 20 March 2014 (hereafter: Muscat Document).

23 Royal Decree No 32/1997 on the Law of Personal Status [*qānūn al-aḥwāl al-shakhṣiyya*], Official Gazette no 601 of 15 June 1997, 6–56.

24 Bahrain in 2002, UAE in 2004, and Qatar in 2009. Upon ratifying CEDAW, all three Arab Gulf States entered substantive reservations to Arts 2, 9, 15, and 16 CEDAW. These reservations either referred to national laws and/or Islamic law to limit the application of the rules contained in these four articles, which deal with policy measure (Art 2 CEDAW), nationality (Art 9 CEDAW), equality before the law and legal capacity (Art 15 CEDAW), and equality in marriage and family relations (Art 16 CEDAW). For a discussion of similar reservations to CEDAW entered by the majority of Muslim states, see e.g. Rebecca J Cook, ‘Reservations to the Convention on the Elimination of All Forms of Discrimination Against Women’ (1989/90) 30 Virginia Journal of International Law 643; Jane Connors, ‘The Women’s Convention in the Muslim World’ in Christine Chinkin and others (eds), *Human Rights as General Norms and a State's Rights to Opt out* (BIICL 1997) 85; Amira Sonbol, ‘A Response to Muslim Countries’ Reservations Against Full Implementation of CEDAW’ (2010) 8 HAWWA 348.

25 For Qatar’s judicial system see e.g. Douglas Clouatre, ‘Qatar’ in Herbert M Kritzer (ed), *Legal Systems of the World: A Political, Social, and Cultural Encyclopedia*, vol 4 (ABC Clio 2002) 1350, and Hamzeh (1994) 30 MES 79 (albeit without reference to the judicial reforms of 2003); see also ‘Qatar’ in Marci Hoffman (ed), *Foreign Law Guide* (Brill Online 2014) <http://referenceworks.brillonline.com/browse/foreign-law-guide> accessed 19 March 2014; for the UAE see

e.g. Al-Muhairi (1996) 11 ALQ 116; Sultan BA Al-Muhairi, 'United Arab Emirates' in Herbert M Kritzer (ed), *Legal Systems of the World: A Political, Social, and Cultural Encyclopedia*, vol 4 (ABC Clio 2002) 1688; Essam Al Tamimi, *Practical Guide to Litigation and Arbitration in the United Arab Emirates* (Kluwer Law Intl 2003) 1–18.

26 For an in-depth analysis of Bahrain's dual legal system see Hassan Radhi, *Judiciary and Arbitration in Bahrain* (Kluwer Law Intl 2003) 75–167.

27 In Qatar and the UAE, most judges currently in office are law school graduates.

28 Such as Decree No 26 of 1986 on Procedure before the Sharia Courts [*marsūm bi-qānūn bi-sha'n al-ijrā'āt amām al-maḥākim al-sharciyya*], Official Gazette no 1726 of 25 December 1986, 5–17.

29 In 2009, Bahrain had a population of 1.2 million. A study from the same year demonstrates that between 15 to 20 new cases were brought before Bahrain's family courts per day, and between 3,500 and 5,000 per year, see Freedom House, *Women's Rights in the Kuwaiti Personal Status Law and Bahraini Shari'a Judicial Rulings (Practical Part)* (2009) 17.

30 Qatar's dual legal system has been unified by Law No 10 of 2003 on the Judicial Authority [*qānūn al-sulṭa al-qaḍā'iyya*], Official Gazette no 9 of 1 October 2003, 11–12.

31 Jane Bristol-Rhys, 'Weddings, Marriage, and Money in the United Arab Emirates' (2007) 2 Anthropology of the Middle East 20; Diane Singerman, 'The Economic Imperatives of Marriage: Emerging Practices and Identities among Youth in the Middle East' (2007) Middle East Youth Initiative Working Paper 6/2007, 27f.

32 UAE Federal Law No 12 of 1973 Limiting the Dower [*qānūn ittiḥādī fī sha'n taḥdīd al-mahr fī caqd al-zawāj*], Official Gazette no 12 of 2 August 1973, 118.

33 Art 1 Law No 12 of 1973.

34 Art 1 UAE Federal Law No 21 of 1997 Limiting the Dower and Wedding Expenses [*qānūn ittiḥādī fī sha'n taḥdīd al-mahr fī caqd al-zawāj wa maṣārīfuhu*], Official Gazette no 312 of 31 December 1997, 43–45.

35 Art 3 Law No 21 of 1997.

36 UAE Federal Law No 47 of 1992 Establishing the Marriage Fund [*qānūn ittiḥādī fī sha'n inshā' ṣundūq al-zawāj*] Official Gazette no 246 of 21 December 1992.

37 For the many topics that the Emirati Marriage Fund addresses see Paul Dresch, 'Debates on Marriage and Nationality in the United Arab Emirates' in Paul Dresch and James Piscatori (ed), *Monarchies and Nations: Globalisation and Identity in the Arab States of the Gulf* (IB Tauris 2005) 136, 147–49.

38 Muhannad al-Shūrbajī, 'Ṣundūq al-zawāj mashrūc fāshil' [The marriage fund is a failed project] *Al-Rāya* (5 May 2009) <www.mohamoon-qa.com/Default.aspx?action=DisplayNews&ID=4541> accessed 13 March 2014.

39 Art 1 Law No 21 of 1989 Concerning the Regulation of Marriage to Foreigners [*qānūn bi-sha'n tanẓīm al-zawāj min al-ajānib*], Official Gazette no 16 of 31 December 1989, 7–10; the UAE considered the introduction of such a law as well, see Dresch (n 37) 146f, 151, 155f.

40 Art 2 Law No 21 of 1989.

41 The Qatari Nationality Law of 2005 deems only those children born to a Qatari father to be Qatari by birth. Children born to a Qatari mother and a non-Qatari father will automatically acquire their father's foreign citizenship. They will, however, be given priority when applying for naturalization. The same rules were contained in the previous Nationality Law No 2 of 1961, which was later repealed by the current Nationality

Law No 38 of 2005 [*qānūn al-jinsiyya al-qaṭariyya*], Official Gazette no 12 of 29 December 2005, 33–38. The nationality laws of Bahrain and the UAE contain similar provisions.

42 Decree No 45 of 2007 Concerning the Marriage Notary and the Notarization of Documents Pertaining to Matters of Personal Status [*qarār bi-sha'n lā'iḥat al-ma'dhūnīn al-sharᶜiyyīn wa aḥkām tawthīq al-muḥarrirāt al-mutaᶜalliqa bi-l-aḥwāl al-shakhṣiyya*], Official Gazette no 2812 of 11 October 2007, 15–25.

43 Art 10 Decree No 45 of 2007.

44 Art 8 Decree No 45 of 2007.

45 Art 14 Decree No 45 of 2007.

46 Art 16 Decree No 45 of 2007.

47 Egypt is among the few majority Muslim countries that did not pass a comprehensive family code but instead a series of piecemeal legislative acts, many of which can be classified as procedural law, such as Law No 1 of 2000 (n 1), see Alim/Yassari, in this volume.

* Unless otherwise noted, the information in this chapter was gathered by the author during field research in the Arab Gulf in 2012 and 2013. During this time, the author met with and interviewed various actors involved in the codification process in Bahrain, Qatar, and the UAE. Among those individuals were legal practitioners, such as lawyers and family court judges, women's rights activists, and members of the Bahraini parliament.

48 The Emirati Constitution lists all affairs in which the Union has exclusive legislative and executive jurisdiction; matters of personal status are not included and hence fall within the jurisdiction of each individual emirate, see Arts 120, 121 Constitution of the United Arab Emirates [*al-dustūr li-l-imārāt al-ᶜarabiyya al-muttaḥida*], Official Gazette no 1 of 19 December 1971, 1–39, as amended by Law No 1 of 1996.

49 Draft Code of Personal Status of 1979 [*mashrūᶜ qānūn ittiḥādī li-sanat 1979 bi-iṣdār qānūn al-aḥwāl al-shakhṣiyya*] (on file with author); the author wishes to thank Hans-Georg Ebert for providing her with a copy of the draft code.

50 See n 19.

51 Official political parties are not permitted in the kingdom.

52 Jane Kinninmont, 'Framing the Family Law: A Case Study of Bahrain's Identity Politics' (2011) 1 JAS 53.

53 Kinninmont (2011) 1 JAS 55; Sandy Russel Jones, *God's Law or State's Law: Authority and Islamic Family Law Reform in Bahrain* (publicly accessible dissertation, University of Pennsylvania 2010) 28f.

54 Most notably expressed through Bahrain's 'National Action Charter' [*mīthāq al-ᶜamal al-waṭanī*] of 2001, see e.g. Katja Niethammer, 'Opposition Groups in Bahrain' in Ellen Lust-Okar and Saloua Zerhouni (eds), *Political Participation in the Middle East* (Lynne Rienner 2008) 143, 144ff.

55 See <www.scw.gov.bh> accessed 14 March 2013; in an interview with the author, a female Shiite MP said that the establishment of the SCW was a watershed moment for women's rights activists in Bahrain as they realized that the new King Hamad Al Khalifa was indeed willing to support their demands and to promote women's legal status, Manama, January 2013.

56 Russel Jones (n 53) 192f.

57 Russel Jones (n 53) 29f; Lynn Welchman, *Women and Muslim Family Laws in Arab States: A Comparative Overview of Textual Development and Advocacy* (Amsterdam University Press 2007) 22.

58 See e.g. Freedom House (n 29) 17; Al-Ittiḥād al-Nisā'ī al-Baḥraynī, *Al-aḥwāl al-shakhṣiyya wa-l-usriyya wa-l-qānūniyya li-l-mar'a al-baḥrayniyya* [The Legal Status of Bahraini Women in Personal Status Matters] (2008) 12, 69, 71; Women's Petition Committee, 'Bahrain: Women Victims of Political Agenda and Propaganda' <www.wluml.org/node/5773> accessed 13 March 2014; Women Living under Muslim Laws, 'Bahrain: Young Divorcee is Threatened for Speaking out against Sharia Courts, Politicized Judges and the Lack of a Personal Status Law' <www.wluml.org/action/bahrain-young-divorcee-threatened-speaking-out-against-sharia-courts-politicized-judges-and-l> accessed 13 March 2014; until today, women's rights activists criticize the lack of legal certainty in the Shiite family courts where judges – in the absence of a codified family law – continue to apply their interpretation of traditional (Shiite) Islamic law in personal status matters.

59 Freedom House (n 29) 22; Welchman, 'Gulf Women and the Codification of Muslim Family Law' in Amira El-Azhary Sonbol (ed), *Gulf Women* (Bloomsbury Qatar Foundation 2012), 376f; another third (30.1 per cent) favoured a completely uniform code without any distinction whatsoever on the basis of sect.

60 Russel Jones (n 53) 43.

61 Freedom House (n 29) 21f; Kinninmont (2011) 1 JAS 64.

62 Law No 188 of 1959 on Personal Status [*qānūn al-aḥwāl al-shakhṣiyya*], Official Gazette no 280 of 30 December 1959, 889–906.

63 'Tragfähigen Kompromiss', see Hans-Georg Ebert, 'Zum Personalstatut im Irak: Besonderheiten und Perspektiven' in Irene Schneider and Thoralf Hanstein (eds), *Beiträge zum Islamischen Recht V* (Peter Lang 2006) 85, 98.

64 Ebert (n 63) 114.

65 Chibli Mallat, 'Shi'ism and Sunnism in Iraq: Revisiting the Codes' in Chibli Mallat and Jane Connors (eds), *Islamic Family Law* (Kluwer Law International 1990) 71, 91.

66 Mallat (n 65) 77f, 80f.

67 Draft Code of Shiite (Ja'fari) Personal Status of 2013 [*mashrūᶜ qānūn al-aḥwāl al-shakhṣiyya al-jaᶜfariyya*] (on file with author); also see Mushraq Abbās, 'Qānūn al-aḥwāl al-jaᶜfariyya . . . marra ukhrā!' [Ja'fari Personal Status Code . . . once again!] *Al-Monitor* (3 March 2014) <www.al-monitor.com/pulse/ar/contents/articles/originals/2014/03/iraq-justice-minister-push-shiite-personal-status-law.html> accessed 17 March 2014. Update (as of May 2015): Ultimately, however, the draft Shiite Code of Personal Status did not enter into force in Iraq for two reasons. First, it was heavily criticized not only for its content, but also for its many technical flaws and inconsistencies. Second, soon after the draft code was forwarded to the Iraqi parliament, the country plunged into political chaos following the capture of multiple Iraqi cities by the extremist group known as the Islamic State of Iraq and the Levant. For a detailed and insightful analysis of the draft Shiite Code of Personal Status see Haider Ala Hamoudi, 'The Political Codification of Islamic Law: A Closer Look at the Draft Shi'i Personal Status Code of Iraq' (2016) Arizona Journal of International and Comparative Law (forthcoming), available at SSRN: <http://ssrn.com/abstract=2603811> accessed 7 May 2015.

68 Also see Möller (2013) 9 JISPIL 33f.

69 CEDAW, Combined initial and second periodic report Bahrain (CEDAW/C/BHR/2) (12 December 2007).

70 See e.g. CEDAW Committee, Consideration of reports submitted by State parties: Bahrain (CEDAW/C/SR.861).

71 Two shadow reports were submitted to the CEDAW by Bahraini NGOs, see Bahrain Human Rights Watch Society (BHRWS), Shadow Report submitted to the United

Nations Committee on the Elimination of Discrimination against Women (CEDAW) in response to the Kingdom of Bahrain Periodic Report (Combined initial and second periodic report of States parties) (August 2008) <www2.ohchr.org/english/bodies/cedaw/docs/ngos/HRWS_Bahrain.pdf> accessed 17 March 2014; Bahrain Women's Union, Shadow Report on the Implementation of CEDAW (September 2008) <www2.ohchr.org/english/bodies/cedaw/docs/ngos/Bahrainwomenunion42.pdf> accessed 17 March 2014.

72 BHRWS (n 71) 16–28.

73 Laleh B Bakhtiar, *Encyclopedia of Islamic Law* (ABC Intl 1996) 423; Muhammad Tabiu, 'Unlawful Marriages and their Effect in Islamic Law of the Maliki School' (1992) 31 Islamic Studies 319, 324, 326.

74 Under Art 39 Emirati Code of Personal Status, however, the filiation (*nasab*) of children born from such a union is established.

75 Art 38 (1) Emirati Code of Personal Status.

76 Art 26 (a) Bahraini Family Code; Art 28 Qatari Family Code.

77 Art 12 (c), 14 Bahraini Family Code; Art 30 Qatari Family Code; Art 34f Emirati Code of Personal Status.

78 See section two above.

79 Art 24 Bahraini Family Code; Art 28 Qatari Family Code; Art 39 Emirati Code of Personal Status.

80 See e.g. the case of a 27-year-old Emirati woman suing her father for his permission to marry, Salman al-Amir, 'Woman sues her father so she can marry' *The National* (Abu Dhabi, 10 July 2011) <www.thenational.ae/news/uae-news/courts/woman-sues-father-so-she-can-marry> accessed 20 March 2014.

81 Art 24 Law No 70.03 on the Family Code [*qānūn bi-mathābat mudawwanat al-usra*], Official Gazette no 5184 of 5 December 2004, 421–452.

82 Katja Zvan-Elliott, 'Reforming the Moroccan Personal Status Code: A Revolution for Whom?' (2009) 14 Mediterranean Politics 213.

83 Arts 55 (6), 77 Emirati Code of Personal Status; the same is true for Bahrain and Qatar, see Arts 37 (d), 60 (a) Bahraini Family Code; Arts 57 (6), 67 Qatari Family Code.

84 Art 14 Qatari Family Code.

85 Art 17 Bahraini Family Code.

86 Munira Fakhro, 'Gulf Women and Islamic Law' in Mai Yamani (ed), *Feminism and Islam: Legal and Literary Perspectives* (NYU Press 1996) 259; for more recent figures see Ebert and Hefny (n 20) 17.

87 Arabi (n 1) 8ff.

88 Art 97 (a) Bahraini Family Code; Art 118 Qatari Family Code.

89 Art 97 (b) Bahraini Family Code; Art 122 Qatari Family Code.

90 Art 97 (c) Bahraini Family Code.

91 Art 122 Qatari Family Code.

92 Explanatory Memorandum to the Emirati Code of Personal Status, Official Gazette no 439 of 30 November 2005, 199–478, notes to Art 110.

93 Art 110 (5) Emirati Code of Personal Status.

94 Only Art 110 (2) Emirati Code of Personal Status states that *khul*^{c} consideration can be everything that could also serve as a valid dower, thus rather pointing towards the type of consideration (e.g. cash benefit or in-kind benefit).

95 See above n 32.

96 Other pre-codification judgements clearly opposed any waiving of custody rights as valid *khul*^{c} consideration, see the Bahraini judgements of 2006 (Sunni personal status

chamber) cited in Freedom House, *Women's Rights in the Kuwaiti Personal Status Law and the Bahraini Shari'a Judicial Rulings (Theory Part)* (2009) 181.

97 Art 98 (a) Bahraini Family Code; Art 120 Qatari Family Code; Art 110 (2) Emirati Code of Personal Status.

98 Manager of the BWU in a personal interview with the author (Manama, Bahrain, 15 January 2013).

99 Suad Hamada, 'The Hard Way Out: Divorce by Khula' *The WIP* (18 March 2010) <http://thewip.net/2010/03/18/the-hard-way-out-divorce-by-khula/> accessed 19 March 2014.

100 '66 khala^{c}na azwājahunna khilāl ^{c}ām' [66 (Women) Dissolved Their Marriage through *Khul*^{c} This Year] *Al Arab Newspaper* (Doha, 23 October 2011) <www.alarab.com.qa/details.php?docId=175831&issueNo=1164&secId=31> accessed 19 March 2014.

101 Al Arab (n 100).

102 State of Qatar, *Marriages and Divorces (Review & Analysis)* (Statistics Authority 2010) 54, 57; out of 1,172 divorces, 69 were through *khul*^{c}, with the majority of divorces still being unilateral repudiations by the husband.

103 Abu Dhabi Court of Cassation (personal status chamber), appeal no 69/2008 of 31 March 2008 (on file with author); Dubai Court of Cassation (personal status chamber), appeal no 67/2008 of 20 January 2009 (on file with author).

104 See e.g. Dubai Court of Cassation (personal status chamber), appeal no 77/2007 of 25 December 2007 (on file with author); Dubai Court of Cassation (personal status chamber), appeal no 90/2008 of 24 March 2009 (on file with author).

105 Abu Dhabi Court of Cassation (personal status chamber), appeal no 61/2007 of 28 November 2007 (on file with author).

106 Manager of the BWU in a personal interview with the author (Manama, Bahrain, 15 January 2013).

107 The word '*mut*^{c}*a*' means both pleasure and compensation. In Shiite jurisprudence it is used to denote temporary marriage, which is not recognized in Sunni jurisprudence.

108 See Jamal JA Nasir, *The Islamic Law of Personal Status* (3rd edn, Brill 2009) 135f.

109 Art 31 Tunisian Code of Personal Status [*majallat al-aḥwāl al-shakhṣiyya*], Official Gazette no 66 of 17 August 1956, 1544–54, as amended by Law No 7 of 1981.

110 Mājid Abū Rakhiyya and ^{c}Abdallāh M Jabūrī, *Fiqh al-zawāj wa-l-ṭalāq* [The law of marriage and divorce] (Maktabat Jāmi^{c}a 2006) 181ff, citing sura 2, verse 236; see also Dawoud El Alami, 'Mut^{c}at al-Talaq under Egyptian and Jordanian Law' (1995) 2 YIMEL 54f.

111 Art 52 (d) Bahraini Family Code; Art 115 Qatari Family Code.

112 Art 52 (b) Bahraini Family Code; Art 70 Qatari Family Code.

113 The husband does, however, have to provide housing for his irrevocably divorced wife during her waiting period, see Art 69 Emirati Code of Personal Status; if the irrevocably divorced wife is pregnant when observing her waiting period, she will be entitled to maintenance until she delivers.

114 Art 140 Emirati Code of Personal Status.

115 Abu Dhabi Court of Cassation (personal status chamber), appeal no 42/2009 of 9 June 2009 (on file with author).

116 Bahrain in 1992, Qatar in 1995, and the UAE in 1997.

117 Art 168 (1) Qatari Family Code; Art 144 (1) Emirati Family Code; this rule also applies in Bahrain, see Art 131 (a) Bahraini Family Code.

118 Art 173 Qatari Family Code; Art 156 (1) Emirati Code of Personal Status.

119 See e.g. Art 144 Emirati Code of Personal Status.

120 At the same time, female custody ends at a relatively late age in Bahrain, i.e. 15 years for boys and 17 years for girls, at which point children may decide themselves whether they wish to remain with their mother, see Art 128f Bahraini Family Code.
121 Art 170 Qatari Family Code.
122 For an evaluation of Emirati high courts' interpretation of the best interests of the child see Lena-Maria Möller, 'Custody Regulations in the United Arab Emirates: Legal Reforms and Social Realities' (2013) 11 HAWWA 41.
123 Court of Cassation (personal status chamber), appeal no 30/2006 of 6 June 2006 (on file with author).
124 Court of Cassation (personal status chamber), appeal no 8/2007 of 27 March 2007 (on file with author).
125 Art 130 (a) Bahraini Family Code.
126 Art 145 Emirati Code of Personal Status
127 Art 175 Qatari Family Code.
128 Bakhtiar (n 73) 471; Nasir (n 108) 164, 165.

5 Between procedure and substance

A review of law making in Egypt

Nora Alim and Nadjma Yassari

Introduction

Muslim countries have come to develop various devices to reform family law. Roughly speaking, these devices fall into one of three categories.[1] The codification of substantive family law is one of these classifications.[2] Hereby, legislatures have been using different methods of traditional Islamic law: one is *takhayyur*, which consists of choosing from among the various schools of law the one interpretation of the holy texts which seems most appropriate, the other method is *talfīq*, i.e. the combination of rules from various schools of Islamic law.[3] The second category of reform involves the enhancement of women's rights by means of private autonomy, reflected in the emergence of stipulations in marriage contracts – provisions that include a delegation of the right to divorce by the husband to the wife[4] or the restriction or prohibition of polygamous marriages.[5] In Iran, and to a lesser degree in Pakistan, party autonomy has, for example, been strengthened by the introduction of standardized marriage contracts.[6] The third classification refers to procedural devices. For example, many Muslim countries have introduced judicial divorce proceedings, preventing men from repudiating their wives in a purely private manner. This étatisation of divorce proceedings has been reinforced by regulations on the registration of all matters of personal status.[7] This last device, i.e. reform through procedural law, is well known and often used by the Egyptian legislature.[8] This chapter aims to shed some light on the process of law making by procedural device in Egypt by turning to the examples of paternity and marriage, as well as the law on testamentary dispositions.

A short review of codification of family law in Egypt

The Egyptian legislature was one of the first legislatures in Muslim jurisdictions to take up the codification of family law. The first codifications of substantive family law were adopted in 1920[9] and 1929[10] and mainly amended in 1985[11] and 2000[12]. In 1875, family law rules had been compiled for a first time in a comprehensive manner by the Egyptian lawyer and Minister of Justice Muhammad Qadri Pasha (1821–86)[13] during the reign of the Osman viceroy of Egypt Ismail Pasha.[14] Qadri Pasha's work *Kitāb al-Aḥkām al-Sharʿiyya fī al-Aḥwāl al-Shakhṣiyya ᶜalā Madhhab Abī Ḥanīfa al-Nuᶜmān*, known as the Qadri-Pasha-Compilation,[15] was, however, never enacted as a law and thus never came into force in Egypt,[16] even though it was essentially a collection of family law regulations of the Hanafi school of law. Interestingly, when codifying law in 1920 and 1929, the Egyptian legislature did not opt for a comprehensive code, but rather chose to codify short laws that would address specific legal issues. This can partly be explained by the fact that when conceiving a family law codification, the Egyptian law makers had to strike a balance between the interests of conflicting groups.[17] The internal stakeholders, on the one side, were state 'centralizing'[18] elites that, in particular during the course of the nineteenth and twentieth centuries, endeavoured to 'recast local legal systems along Western lines'.[19] On the other side, beyond being generally opposed to the import of foreign law, Islamic elites lobbied in particular against its adoption in areas of family and succession law, as these fields were perceived as being the last stronghold of Islamic law under their competence.[20] Consequently, a state-initiated comprehensive family law codification, even if based on Islamic law, would have meant a loss of their position of power. These conflicts inhibited, to a large extent, the emergence of a uniform law modernization process in Egypt. In fact, while codification of civil and administrative law as well as procedural law was comprehensive and mainly based on European models,[21] the codification of family law remained piecemeal and fragmentary.

As regards family law, the legislature's *modus operandi* was twofold. Its main endeavour was certainly directed to codifying and thereby forming and reforming substantive family law. In fact, the laws of 1920 and 1929 contain primarily regulations of substantive nature, based mainly on Hanafi law, with some borrowing from other *madhhabs*, namely the Maliki school of law.[22] Law No 25 of 1920 in its original version had 13 articles, dealing with issues of alimony (*nafaqa*) and the waiting period (*ᶜidda*),[23] and also the right of the wife to divorce in case of non-payment of alimony,[24] in case of desertion (Arts 7–8), and in case of sickness or disease of the husband.[25] Law No 25 of 1929, encompassing 25 articles, also primarily dealt with issues of substantive law, such as the conditions under which the repudiation of the wife was permissible,[26] and the conditions for a divorce because of harm,[27] for desertion, and because of the husband's imprisonment.[28] Further, it contained regulations on alimony during the waiting period,[29] on the time period of maternal custody,[30] and on the declaration of death.[31]

Simultaneously, the legislature also enacted regulations of a procedural nature that influenced substantive family law considerably. As early as 1880, a first Decree-Law on the Organization of the Sharia Courts[32] was enacted, fundamentally regulating the procedure before the Sharia courts that at that time were competent to adjudicate on family law.[33] Amongst the 190 articles of this law one could find regulations on the registration of marriages in courts and the duties of the *ma'dhūn*, i.e. the civil servant in charge of registration.[34] In 1897, the law was amended.[35] The new law (and all subsequent Decree-Laws on the Organization of the Sharia Courts up until abolishment of the courts in 1955[36]) contained specific rules precluding courts from entertaining litigation whenever certain formalities concerning the legal act in question were not met.[37] The 1897 Decree-Law on the

Organization of the Sharia Courts, for example, stated that actions with regard to marital claims filed after the husband's death must be based on documentary evidence; otherwise the courts were barred from admitting the case to court.[38] Over the course of time, the types of lawsuits that would be admissible in court only upon documentary evidence were continuously increased. In 1931, the subsequent Decree-Law on the Organization of the Sharia Courts[39] stated that marital claims were not admissible in court if one party denied their existence and their existence could not be based on an official state document. In the same vein, Article 15 of Law No 25 of 1929 precluded the admissibility of paternity claims which could not be proven by documentary evidence, and in 1946, the legislature used this device in the field of testamentary dispositions, rejecting the admissibility of testate inheritance claims based on an oral will.

The family law reforms of 1985 and 2000 also introduced procedural regulations. Law No 100 of 1985 inserted a new Article 5(b) into Law No 25 of 1929 regarding the requirement of a written certificate for divorce notarized by a civil servant who was also given information duties vis-a-vis the to-be-repudiated wife.[40] Equally, a new Article 23(b) subjected the husband and the notary to punishment by imprisonment for any contravention of Article 5(b). Law No 1 of 2000 took this aspect even further and introduced a multitude of procedural rules. *Prima facie*, these rules aimed to organize court procedure, as is illustrated by Articles 9–15 on the jurisdiction of family courts. Additionally, the legislature reiterated the rules on the inadmissibility of lawsuits based on an unregistered marriage, as well as marriages by minors.

Why procedural law?

Procedural law is an area of law that has been codified in Egypt, mainly on the basis of law imports from the West. From the late nineteenth century on, Egypt enacted a number of codes based mainly on the French model, including a commercial and a penal procedure code,[41] as well as two comprehensive codes on the organization of the courts, the *Code civil mixte* in 1875 and the *Code civil indigène* in 1883.[42] The reception of foreign codes of procedure was mainly prompted by the urgent need to quickly install a functioning and more unified court system. At the same time, the import of procedural law was not met with great resistance as it was perceived as a value-neutral area and thus not as contentious a battlefield between the ideologies of secular and religious groups.[43]

Further, the concept of *siyāsa sharᶜiyya*, i.e. the right of the Muslim ruler to introduce regulations in the public interest and particularly in the absence of Islamic provisions, fostered the idea of using procedural tools to tackle substantive law issues. The principle of *siyāsa sharᶜiyya* had been called upon in Egypt since the time of Ottoman rule in order to regulate in particular (but not exclusively) legal procedure.[44] Also, in line with his authority, the ruler had the right to define the competence of the courts and thus restrict certain judges from hearing certain cases.[45] There was thus a long tradition of involvement of the legislature in procedural matters.[46]

Against this background the Egyptian legislature chose to have recourse to procedural devices to reform family law. In the first place it intended to strike a balance between the different, often conflicting interests it had to consider: it chose to leave Islamic law untouched in its essence, but at the same time limited state protection.[47] By restricting access to justice the legislature intended to deter people from their traditional practices and 'reshape' their 'social behaviour',[48] to prevent them from concluding marriages outside the state's control and to educate them to abide by the new formal standards.[49] Equally, the introduction of registration duties for matters of personal status was meant to enhance the information and control by the state of its citizens and to support the building of a strong central state.[50] Moreover, the move helped to enforce protective legal measures such as the observance of the minimum ages for marriages (and the avoidance of minor marriages) and also the compliance with (potential) restrictions on polygamous marriages and divorce. Overall, the Egyptian legislature aimed at ensuring greater legal certainty and avoiding the falsification of civil status.[51]

The scheme of the chosen devices was always the same: certain types of claims were disqualified from being heard in court whenever they were not based on documentary evidence. The provisions thus had two fundamental pillars: first, they were based in the law of evidence, which was itself subject to remarkable reforms as the preference previously given to testimonial evidence under Islamic law was replaced in favour of documentary evidence. Secondly, the legislature restricted the admissibility of court suits to claims established by these new evidentiary means. By considering the examples of unregistered marriage, children born outside the legal presumption of paternity and the form of testamentary dispositions, it shall be investigated next whether the legislature has been successful in reaching his set aims.

Examples

Who is my spouse? The legal status of informal marriages

According to all Islamic schools of law, a Muslim marriage can be concluded without the state's participation or documentation.[52] A marriage is valid if its essential requirements are fulfilled. Those are the articulations of offer and acceptance by prospective spouses who have legal capacity. Under Sunni laws the declarations of intent must further be pronounced in the presence of two witnesses, whose role is mainly to give testimony over the conclusion of the marriage in case of doubt.[53] There are no further formalities to be observed. In particular the drawing of a written document is not required.

Notwithstanding these requirements, in the course of the twentieth century, modern legislatures in almost all Muslim countries introduced the requirement of registering the conclusion of a marriage with state authorities. As stated above, the main objective was to ensure a higher degree of legal certainty and establish a better control of personal status matters. However, most of the jurisdictions refrained from explicitly designating the consequences of non-compliance with the registration rules. Tunisia is an exception as under the Tunisian Code of Personal Status a marriage performed without the assistance of the state is null and void (*bāṭil*).[54] Most of Muslim jurisdictions, by contrast, have chosen a different solution. This consists of linking the registration requirement to the rules of evidence and understanding registration as a matter of proof. Accordingly, in Iran,[55] Pakistan,[56] and Morocco,[57] for example, an informal marriage (i.e. a marriage performed according to religious law but without being registered with state authorities[58]) is principally valid and a claim based on such a marriage will be admissible in court, with the reservation that the conclusion of the marriage must be proven first.[59] Accordingly an Iranian, Pakistani, or Moroccan woman who concluded a marriage in private according to Islamic law can address the courts to request her dower or alimony or to ask for the establishment of the filiation of her children. The courts must look into the case and may accept any evidence as to the existence of the marriage.

The third solution that can be observed is the position of the Egyptian legislature, which – just as the Tunisian case – is unique. While staying silent on the validity of informally concluded marriages, Egyptian law rejects the right to base any marital claim on such a marriage in court by restricting the admissibility of such actions to claims based on a marriage certified by an official document, i.e. registration. Consequently, according to Article 17 para 2 of Law No 1 of 2000, marital claims based on informal marriages are inadmissible in court.[60] Thus, a religiously married woman will be considered married by her community, but she will not be able to petition for any marital right if her marriage is not registered with state authorities.

Who is my child? Establishing filiation

The establishment of filiation is yet another example of the use of procedural law to indirectly affect substantive law. Article 15 of Law No 25 of 1929 regulates the establishment of filiation in cases of denial. Accordingly, a lawsuit regarding the establishment of paternity cannot be heard by the courts if it is established that the mother of the child did not have intercourse with her husband after the marriage was concluded or if the child was born one year after the husband's disappearance or the divorce of the parents or the death of the husband. It has to be borne in mind that under traditional Islamic law paternity is established on the basis of a blood relation between the child and the married parents.[61] Legitimate paternity is thus established for a 'child of the marital bed' (*walad li-l-firāsh*).[62] Parenthood outside this frame is principally unacceptable, ignored at best and penalized at worst. Classical jurists were, however, aware of the fact that adherence to these strict rules would leave a multitude of children without established filiation and provoke severe legal and social problems. The Islamic schools of law have therefore conceived of legal fictions to mitigate the effects of the principle of *firāsh*. Amongst them is the theory of the sleeping embryo (*al-rāqid*),[63] according to which the female gestation period can range anywhere from six months to seven years.[64] As a consequence a child born later than the biological gestation period of nine lunar months after the death of the husband of the mother or after their divorce could still be considered a legitimate child of this man.[65]

The Egyptian legislature did not adhere to these extended Islamic rules, as they obviously contradict medical realities. But it took up the rationale of the rule, i.e. the protection of children in dubious filiation circumstances, and extended the gestation period to one year. However, the rule refrains from defining the status of children borne outside the legal time period of Article 15 of Law No 25 of 1929. The only legal effect of Article 15 is to preclude paternity claims by such children. In the same vein, Article 7 of Law No 1 of 2000 provides that contested paternity suits filed after the potential father's death are to be heard by the courts only if filiation is proven by some documentary or other unambiguous proof. Sufficient evidence is adduced by three means: official documents, handwritten documents signed by the deceased, or other decisive evidence (*aw adilla qaṭᶜiyya jāzima*).[66] This third alternative was introduced upon the suggestions of the Islamic Studies Academy of Al-Azhar in Cairo in light of illiteracy rates in Egypt and in order to broaden the admissibility of paternity claims in line with the more generous rules of traditional Islamic law.[67] The possibility to prove paternity by three different means broadens the sphere of action of the child as compared to the sole alternative that a wife is given to prove her marriage. Therefore, a child born to an informally married couple may address the court for the establishment of filiation to his father by using any 'decisive evidence' whereas the mother is barred from using such alternatives to establish the existence of her marriage.

Who is my heir? The form of testamentary dispositions

The final example is that of the oral will. Under traditional Islamic law the principle of informality is generally adhered to as regards the form of testamentary dispositions.[68] Accordingly, no specific form is required for the formal validity of a last will: it may be oral, in writing, or conveyed by signs.[69] The intention to bequeath suffices, provided it is ascertained clearly and without ambiguity. In fact, in traditional Islamic law the validity of a will could be assured by witness testimony, as oral testimony was considered more valuable than written documentation. The preference of oral over written wills is generally explained by the Arab people's lived tradition of oral transmission, as exemplified in the scholarship of the prophetic traditions[70] as well as in the absence of a culture of writing in the early formation period of Islamic law.[71]

Egypt codified the law on testamentary dispositions in a comprehensive manner in 1946.[72] Law No 71 of 1946 contains 82 articles and regulates testamentary dispositions in a very detailed manner, including their form. Article 2 sentence 1 of Law No 71 of 1946 states that a testator may express his will orally or in writing and, if he cannot speak or write, by unequivocal symbols.[73] This apparent irrelevance of the form of the will is however challenged by Article 2 sentences 2 and 3, according to which in case of dispute over the validity of the will the courts may admit the case only if the action is based on documentary evidence.[74] 'Documentary evidence' means any authenticated documents,

documents handwritten and signed by the testator, or documents carrying the authenticated signature of the testator. As with informal marriage, the requirement of documentary evidence does not strictly speaking touch upon the validity of the will. Rather, it is a condition for the admissibility of the claim in court. Just as an informal marriage is theoretically valid, an oral will is valid, but no judicial relief is available in the courts for claims based on such an oral will if it is not also proven by documentary evidence. As a matter of fact, the same pattern observed in the previous examples unfolds. Instead of clearly determining the legal status of oral wills, the legislature has chosen a procedural device to curtail access to justice.

Evaluation of the Egyptian approach

Legal nature of the provisions

Because of the indirect approach via procedural law, the question arises whether the enacted provisions are of procedural or substantive nature. In other words, a major issue is the question whether these rules have also had an impact on substantive law in the sense that they have indirectly reformed substantive family law in Egypt and *de facto* settled the question of the validity of the legal institutes at issue. The provisions themselves do not state anything about the validity of the legal institutions in question. However, they severely undermine state protection for claims arising of these institutions and thus restrict access to justice. This is clearly illustrated by the judgement of the Egyptian Court of Cassation in the case of oral wills: the requirement of written documentation, the Court held, is merely of a procedural nature, leaving intact the possibility to bequeath by any means.[75] But where does this leave a person claiming her share of the estate based on such a will? The fact remains that the rule of Article 2 sentences 2 and 3 of Law No 71 of 1946 largely deprives oral wills of any sphere of operation. This – it is assumed – is also true for informal marriages and – to a certain extent – paternity claims, even if these questions have not yet been settled as clearly by Egyptian courts, leaving their legal status vulnerable.[76]

A clarification on the nature of the rules in Article 15 of Law No 25 of 1929 (on the establishment of paternity) and Article 17 of Law No 1 of 2000 (on informal marriage) would, further, be important in two fields: first in internal cases involving inter-religious conflict-of-law rules and second in private international law cases. Egypt's family law is inter-religiously split. Accordingly, the substantive religious law associated with the religion of an Egyptian individual must apply in matters of personal status.[77] This does, however, not extend to procedural law as it is applicable to all Egyptians independent of their religious affiliation. If, therefore, Article 17 of Law No 1 of 2000 or Article 15 of Law No 25 of 1929 were qualified as procedural rules, then they would be applicable to all (thus also non-Muslim) Egyptians. Conversely, in private international cases the result of this characterization would lead to the non-applicability of Article 17 of Law No 1 of 2000 and Article 15 of Law No 25 of 1929 whenever Egyptian law governs an international family law case in a non-Egyptian court, as procedural law is a matter of the *lex fori*.[78]

Unfortunately these questions are hardly addressed in Egyptian literature. As far as the nature of Article 17 of Law No 1 of 2000 is concerned, however, one can draw some conclusions from the existing analysis of the literature on the earlier provision in Article 99 para 4 of Decree-Law No 78 of 1931 on the Organization of the Sharia Courts.[79] The prevailing opinion in Egyptian scholarship is that Article 99 para 4 of Decree-Law No 78 of 1931 (and by extension Article 17 of Law No 1 of 2000) is to be characterized as a substantive rule, basically because it contains a rule on evidence but not on the procedure of the court.[80] It follows from this approach that Article 17 would not be applicable in domestic conflict-of law cases, i.e. it would not be applicable to non Muslim Egyptians. Therefore a Muslim Egyptian wife who is married only religiously would be barred from addressing the courts, whereas a non-Muslim Egyptian woman could address the court to claim, for example, marital maintenance based on her religious law without regard to whether her marriage was registered or not.

Commentators of private international law, on the other hand, argue that Article 99 para 4 of Law No 78 of 1931 relates to the law of evidence and that as a consequence, for the sake of private international law, it must be considered in questions regarding the form of a marriage.[81] Generally, in private international law the formal validity of a legal act is established if the formal requirements of the law which is applicable to the legal relationship forming the subject matter of the legal act or, alternatively, the law of the country in which the act is performed, are satisfied.[82] It follows from this that Article 17 of Law No 1 of 2000 must be observed as a formal requirement when a foreign court has to rule on the validity of a marriage performed in Egypt.[83] Therefore, a marriage concluded in Egypt without being registered will not, for example, be recognized in a German court as a basis on which marital claims can be petitioned for.[84] Although this might not be of immediate interest to the Egyptian legislature *per se*, it is of interest to Egyptians living abroad, and it illustrates the problems on the international level stemming from the ambiguity of the national Egyptian provisions.

Reality check: did the legislature achieve its goals?

With the introduction of these provisions the Egyptian legislature did not intend to facilitate or enhance the quality of court procedures. Clearly its aim was to enforce substantive family law reforms regarding marriage, paternity, and last wills. Indeed, legislating on the level of procedure instead of addressing substantive family law is a potentially interesting choice. On the national level it can help minimize conflicts between different social streams and their diverging emphasis on the implementation of Islamic law. The legislature avoids a clear positioning and reserves for itself an – albeit frail and ambiguous – margin to manoeuvre on a case-to-case basis.[85] In the Egyptian context this kind of manoeuvring was also chosen with the endeavour to structure family law more efficiently and to bring matters of personal status under state control for purposes of greater legal certainty. An unequivocal confirmation of the validity of unregistered marriages or oral wills would therefore have been counter-productive. Outlawing informal marriages or oral wills, on the other hand, would have meant a clear break with religious precedents. The compromise that was struck was to choose a value-neutral area such as procedural law in order to gradually and unobtrusively bring about change and tackle existing social problems indirectly. The question remains whether the Egyptian legislature has in fact been successful?

This question shall be examined in more depth with reference to the example of informal marriages. In the mid-1950s *Yvon Linant de Bellefonds* affirmed the successful implementation of the family law policy regarding the registration of marriages. 'Today in Egypt', he stated, 'all marriages are being registered' out of fear of being left without judicial remedy in case of litigation.[86] However, in 2015 the situation is quite a different one. According to unofficial statistics the number of informal marriages has constantly increased over the last decades. In fact, the figures suggest that the number of registered marriages in any single year coincides with the number of informal marriages concluded privately.[87] Interestingly, the debates on informal marriages that preoccupy Egypt today do not revolve around the permissibility of formal registration. In fact religious and secular groups concur that the registration of matters of personal status is important and must be supported, and very few contest the significance of legal certainty that is ensured with more state control in matters of personal status.[88] In this sense the legislature has been successful in implementing a paradigm shift in matters of marriage. Moreover, the greatest opponent of informal marriages today is the religious establishment, for whose appeasement the procedural device was – ironically – chosen in the first place. Religious figures contest quite loudly the increase of informal marriages and voice their concern with regard to the declining morality of society.[89] This decline is particularly exemplified by the growing numbers of informal marriages concluded between university students who often, away from their families, marry secretly, primarily to 'overcome sexual repression, but in Islamic form'.[90] The informality of traditional Islamic law allows them to marry religiously and thus to have licit sexual relationships while at the same time staying outside the scope of the legal and financial consequences of an official marriage. In fact, the legal loophole created by the frictions between religious and procedural law has generated opportunities that the religious establishment considers to be immoral.

However, the reasons for marrying informally have often little to do with morality. There are obviously cases where the spouses are not aware of the registration requirement or the legal problems they might encounter by not registering. But very often the non-registration is intentional in order to avoid the consequences of a registered marriage. For example polygamous marriages are frequently concluded privately to avoid the legal (state-imposed) conditions for their conclusion and to keep the union secret. Also, economic interests are at stake. The high costs of weddings and housing that generally accompany official marriages can be avoided by an informal marriage that is also kept secret. Equally, the potential loss of other financial claims linked to the marital status can be avoided by an informal marriage, e.g. where a widow wishes to remarry but not lose the pension of her late husband.[91] Mention needs to be made, furthermore, of the nasty phenomenon of 'marriage tourism' engaged chiefly by men from the Gulf States,[92] who for their limited stay in Egypt marry young, often underage Egyptian girls from a low social status whose parents are willing to agree to such unions in return for financial compensation.[93] Unfortunately, most of these men do not (religiously) divorce their wives upon their return to their home countries, leaving their brides in a legal limbo as they consider themselves married and thus unable to remarry.[94] Beside their social implications these phenomenon also show that one major reason for contracting informal marriages and for the rise of the figures are economic problems faced by Egyptians and less a general defiance of registration obligations imposed by state law.

Against this background and in view of the fading resistance of the religious establishment, it is time to re-evaluate the measures taken by the Egyptian legislature and think of alternative options. As far as oral wills are concerned, one could think of admitting them to court and having them proven by other means of evidence, such as obligatory witness testimony by a certain number of persons. This model would, on the one hand, match traditional Islamic law of evidence favouring oral over documentary evidence and, on the other hand, would offer more legal certainty, provided it is accompanied by a state measure to enhance legal awareness and knowledge of the law. Further, the categorical refusal to hear cases related to informal marriages and (overdue) paternity claims in court has ultimately not led to a decrease in these social phenomena as intended by the state, but has created a series of other severe problems. Assuming – as is suggested here – that one of the main reasons for staying outside the legal framework is economic in nature, the legislature could start by re-visiting the financial backbone and economic configuration of family law. Also, some very basic legal problems encountered by both informally married women and children born outside the legal framework can be linked to the fact that administrative affairs, such as the issuance of a national identification card or passport, are frequently dependent on the permission or involvement of the father. If the father refuses to cooperate or denies his paternity, mothers may encounter great obstacles in obtaining those documents.[95] This has wider implications than merely the lack of an identity card as access to a series of public social transfers and the use of state facilities – such as public medical care and free subscription in schools – is often dependent on the Egyptian nationality of the child. Until 2004, nationality laws in Egypt discriminated against Egyptian mothers, as they could not transmit their nationality to the child. Hence a child born to an informally married Egyptian mother and a foreign father would have no access to these services. In 2004, the right of a mother to pass on her nationality to her child was introduced by Law No 154 of 2004.[96] In doing so, the Egyptian legislature has taken a step in the right direction.[97] In order to realize further and significant changes, the legislature's sensitivity to the repercussions of law reform patterns – whether procedural or substantial – must be sharpened, and it is desirable that he adopt a more audacious and problem-solving position.

In fact, the legislature has shown courage, for instance in Law No 1 of 2000 with its provisions on *khul*ᶜ.[98] Article 20 of Law No 1 of 2000 introduced the right of a wife to initiate divorce proceedings on the basis of a *khul*ᶜ without and even against the express will of the husband. This provision is rather unique in the Muslim world[99] as the Egyptian *khul*ᶜ divorce aligns the right of the wife to dissolve her marriage without reason with the right of the husband to repudiate his wife.[100] It was therefore not surprising that the introduction of the *khul*ᶜ provision caused a great uproar in the legal and religious community, indeed in Egyptian society at large,[101] and it remains to be seen whether the new political elites in Egypt will continue to abide by this law.[102] Nevertheless, it must also be emphasized that the introduction of the *khul*ᶜ provision withstood the compatibility test of Article 2 of the Egyptian constitution, according to which the principles of Islamic Sharia are the main source of law. The Supreme Constitutional Court of Egypt upheld the validity of the provision and confirmed its compatibility with the constitution.[103]

Against this background, there is hope that further, more effective family law reform will follow. For the moment, the legislature would be well advised to initiate reforms in the discriminatory administrative provisions and to equalize in this regard the rights of mothers with those of fathers. This would instantly relieve children and single (providing) mothers from an unfair legal burden, even if the social stigma might continue to stain the status of the child. But as shown by the acceptance of the registration rule by the religious establishment and by the bold introduction of the *khul*ᶜ provisions, attitudes can evolve in response to continued efforts, even in the Middle East.

Notes

1 For a detailed evaluation of the different methods of law reform in the Muslim world, see Mathias Rohe, *Islamic Law in Past and Present* (Gwendolin Goldbloom tr, Brill 2014) 233ff; Norman Anderson, *Law Reform in the Muslim World* (The Athlone Press 1976) 42ff; Norman Anderson, 'Codification in the Muslim World: Some Reflections' (1966) 30 Rabel Journal of Comparative and International Private Law 241; Hans-Georg Ebert, 'Wider die Schließung des "Tores des *iğtihād*": Zur Reform der *šarīᶜa* am Beispiel des Familien- und Erbrechts' (2002) 43 Orient 365–81.

2 Chibli Mallat, *Introduction to Middle Eastern Law* (OUP 2009) 239ff; Aharon Layish, 'The Transformation of the *Sharī'a* from Jurists' Law to Statutory Law in the Contemporary Muslim World' (2004) 44 Die Welt des Islams 85ff; on the recent family law codification in the Arab Gulf States, see Lena-Maria Möller, *Die Golfstaaten auf dem Weg zu einem modernen Recht für die Familie?* (Mohr Siebeck 2015).

3 On *takhayyur and talfīq* see Birgit Krawietz, 'Cut and Paste in Legal Rules: Designing Islamic Norms with *Talfīq*' (2002) 42 Die Welt des Islams 3ff.

4 On stipulations in marriage contracts, see generally Ali Reda Bariklou, 'The Wife's Right of Divorce on the Basis of the Delegation Condition under Islamic and Iranian Law' (2011) 25 International Journal of Law, Policy and the Family 184ff; Muhammad Munir, 'Stipulations in a Muslim Marriage Contract with Special Reference to *Talaq Al-Tafwid* Provisions in Pakistan' (2005–06) 12 Yearbook of Islamic and Middle Eastern Law 235ff; Lynn Welchman, 'Special Stipulations in the Contract of Marriage: Law and Practice in the Occupied West Bank' (1994) 11 Recht van de Islam 55ff;

Ron Shaham, 'State, Feminists and Islamist State – the Debate over Stipulations in Marriage Contracts in Egypt' (1999) 62 Bulletin of the School of Oriental and African Studies 462ff; on stipulation of the matrimonial property regime, see M Siraj Sait, Chapter 11.

5 Polygamy is explicitly forbidden only under Tunisian and Turkish law, and a polygamous marriage will be considered void. In all other Muslim countries polygamous marriages are restricted but not banned. On the Islamic foundations of polygamy see Ahmed E Souaiaia, 'From Transitory Status to Perpetual Sententiae: Rethinking Polygamy in Islamic Traditions' (2004) 2 Hawwa 290–300.

6 Nadjma Yassari, *Die Brautgabe im Familienvermögensrecht* (Mohr Siebeck 2014) 111f.

7 With regard to Egypt see Ron Shaham, 'Custom, Islamic Law, and Statutory Legislation: Marriage Registration and Minimum Age at Marriage in the Egyptian Sharīᶜa Courts' (1995) 2 Islamic Law and Society 264ff.

8 Substantive law refers in this article to the *corpus juris* that defines and describes the rights and obligations of individuals. Procedural or adjective law is the body of legal rules that governs the organization of the judicial system as well as the process by which the rights of parties are determined.

9 Decree-Law No 25 of 1920 of 12 July 1920 Regarding Maintenance and Some Questions of Personal Status, Official Gazette no 61 of 15 July 1920, 52–55.

10 Decree-Law No 25 of 1929 of 10 March 1929 Regarding Certain Personal Status Provisions, Official Gazette no 27 of 25 March 1929.

11 Law No 100 of 1985 of 3 July 1985 Regarding the Amendment of Certain Personal Status Provisions, Official Gazette no 27 *tābiᶜ* of 4 July 1985. There have also been some occasional amendments to these laws since 2000.

12 Law No 1 of 2000 of 29 January 2000 Regulating Certain Litigation Procedures in Personal Status, Official Gazette No 4 *mukarrar* of 29 January 2000, 5–30.

13 On Qadri Pasha see Hans-Georg Ebert, *Die Qadrî-Pâshâ-Kodifikation – Islamisches Personalstatut der hanafitischen Rechtsschule* (Peter Lang 2010) 11ff. Qadri Pasha also compiled the Hanafi penal law, the law of contract and the regulations regarding *waqf.* None of his compilations ever entered into force, Layish (2004) 44 Die Welt des Islams 89f.

14 Cl Huart, 'ISMĀᶜĪL-PASHA', *Enzyklopädie des Islam*, vol 2 (Brill 1927) 585f. Ismail Pasha from the dynasty of Muhammed Ali, also known under the patronym Ismail the Magnificent, was the viceroy of Egypt from 1863–79.

15 Muḥammad Qadrī Bāshā, *Kitāb al-Aḥkām al-Sharᶜiyya fī al-Aḥwāl al-Shakhṣiyya ᶜalā Madhhab al-Imām Abī Ḥanīfa al-Nuᶜmān* (4th edn, Maṭbaᶜa Hindiyya 1900); for an English translation, see Mohammed Kadri Pasha, Code of Mohammedan Personal Law According to the Hanafite School (Wasey Sterry and N Abcarius tr, Spottiswoode & Co Ltd 1914) (hereinafter: QPC).

16 Nathalie Bernard-Maugiron and Baudouin Dupret, 'From Jihan to Susanne – Twenty Years of Personal Status Law in Egypt' (2002) 19 Recht van de Islam 2.

17 On the formation of the modern Egyptian legal system, see Clark B Lombardi, *State Law as Islamic Law in Modern Egypt* (Brill 2006); Nathan J Brown, *The Rule of Law in the Arab World* (CUP 1997); Nathan J Brown, 'Retrospective Law and Imperialism: Egypt in Comparative Perspective' (1995) 29 Law & Society Review 103.

18 Brown, 'Retrospective Law and Imperialism' (n 17) 106.

19 Brown, 'Retrospective Law and Imperialism' (n 17) 106ff, who points out that legal reform had already been initiated in Egypt before European penetration.

20 Lombardi (n 17) 70.
21 On the reception of foreign law in Egypt in general, see Baudouin Dupret and Nathalie Bernard-Maugiron, 'Introduction: a General Presentation of Law and Judicial Bodies' in Nathalie Bernard-Maugiron and Baudouin Dupret (eds), *Egypt and Its Laws* (Kluwer 2002) xxiv ff; Kilian Bälz, 'Das Moderne arabische Recht' in Hans-Georg Ebert and Thoralf Hanstein (eds), *Beiträge zum Islamischen Recht II* (Peter Lang 2003), 175ff.
22 On *takhayyur* in Egyptian divorce law, see Nathalie Bernard-Maugiron, Chapter 8; see also Ron Shaham, 'Judicial Divorce at the Wife's Initiative: The Sharīᶜa Courts of Egypt, 1920–1955' (1995) 2 Islamic Law and Society 260.
23 Arts 1–3 Law No 25 of 1920.
24 Arts 4–6 Law No 25 of 1920.
25 Arts 9–11 Law No 25 of 1920.
26 Arts 1–5 Law No 25 of 1929.
27 Arts 6–11 Law No 25 of 1929.
28 Arts 12–14 Law No 25 of 1929.
29 Arts 16–18 Law No 25 of 1929.
30 Arts 20 Law No 25 of 1929.
31 Arts 21 Law No 25 of 1929.
32 Decree-Law on the Organization of the Sharia Courts of 17 June 1880, Official Gazette no 923 of 24 August 1880.
33 Bernard-Maugiron and Dupret, (2002) 19 Recht van de Islam 2; Norman Anderson, 'Law Reform in Egypt: 1850–1950' in PM Holt (ed), *Political and Social Change in Modern Egypt* (OUP 1968) 209, 218.
34 See for a detailed account of the role of the *ma'dhūn* in Egyptian law, Nora Alim, 'Egypt's Marriage Laws – Ensuring Flexibility or Enhancing Confusion?' (Dissertation, forthcoming 2016).
35 Regulation on the Organization of the Sharia Courts and the Related Procedures of 27 May 1897, Official Gazette no 61 of 6 June 1897.
36 In 1955, these courts were abolished and competence over matters of personal status was transferred to national courts, Law No 462 of 1955 of 21 September 1955 on the Abolition of the Sharia Courts and the *Milliyya* Courts, Official Gazette no 73 of 24 September 1955; see also Yüksel Sezgin, *Human Rights under State-enforced Religious Family Laws in Israel, Egypt and India* (CUP 2013) 130, who points to the fact that the abolition of the Sharia courts was a procedural step without accompanying reforms on substantive law.
37 Norman Anderson, 'The Significance of Islamic Law in the World Today' (1960) 9 American Journal of Comparative Law 191.
38 Decree-Law of 27 May 1897 as cited in Y Linant de Bellefonds, 'Immutabilité du droit musulman et réformes législatives en Egypte' (1955) 7 Revue Internationale de Droit Comparé 5, 29.
39 Decree-Law No 78 of 1931 of 12 May 1931 on the Organization of the Sharia Courts and their Proceedings, Official Gazette (special issue) no 53 of 20 May 1931.
40 For an English translation of Law No 100 of 1985, see Dawoud El Alami, 'Law No 100 of 1985 "Amending Certain Provisions of Egypt's Personal Status Laws"' (1994) 1 Islamic Law and Society 117.
41 Anderson, 'Law Reform in Egypt' (n 33) 217.
42 See Joseph Aziz, *Concordance des Codes égyptiens mixte et indigène avec le Code Napoléon* (Penasson 1886). The codes contained substantive as well as procedural

rules; for an annotated French version of the *Code civil mixte*, see Gabriel Bestawros, *Code civil égyptien mixte annoté* (Librairie générale de droit et de jurisprudence 1929); Kilian Bälz, '*Shari'a* and *Qanun* in Egyptian Law: A Systems Theory Approach to Legal Pluralism' (1995) 2 Yearbook of Islamic and Middle Eastern Law 44; BA Roberson, 'The Emergence of the Modern Judiciary in the Middle East: Negotiating the Mixed Courts of Egypt' in Chibli Mallat (ed), *Islam and Public Law* (Graham and Trotman 1993) 107–39.

43 See Linant de Bellefonds (1955) 7 Revue Internationale de Droit Comparé 26; Ebert, 'Wider die Schließung des "Tores des *iğtihād*"' (n 1) 371f.

44 See Norman Anderson, 'The State and the Individual in Islamic Law' (1957) 6 International and Comparative Law Quarterly 51; Émile Tyan, 'Méthodologie et sources du droit en Islam (*Istiḥsān, Istiṣlāḥ, Siyāsa šarᶜiyya*)' (1959) 10 Studia Islamica 101ff.

45 Omaia Elwan, 'Die Form von zwischen Ägyptern und Deutschen in Ägypten geschlossenen Ehen aus dem Blickwinkel des deutschen Kollisionsrechts' in Heinz-Peter Mansel, Thomas Pfeiffer, and Christian Kohler (eds), *Festschrift für Erik Jayme*, vol 1 (Sellier 2004) 158; Muḥammad bin ᶜAbdallāh bin Muḥammad al-Marzūqī, *Sulṭat Walī al-Amr fī Taqyīd Sulṭat al-Qāḍī* [The Authority of the *Walī al-Amr* in Restriction of the Authority of the Judge] (Maktabat al-ᶜabīkān 2004) 170f.

46 Anderson (1960) 9 American Journal of Comparative Law 191ff.

47 Anderson, 'Law Reform in Egypt' (n 33) 223.

48 Shaham (1995) 2 Islamic Law and Society 275.

49 Lynn Welchman, *Women and Muslim Family Laws in Arab States* (Amsterdam University Press 2007) 54.

50 See Marnia Lazreg, *The Eloquence of Silence* (Routledge 1994) 88, on the introduction of registration duties in Algeria by the French colonial powers in the late nineteenth century for purposes of political 'expedience and control'; see also Mounira M Charrad, *States and Women's Rights* (University of California Press 2001) 137, who points to the fact that the introduction of registration duties was primarily directed to facilitating the work of the French courts.

51 Welchman, *Women and Muslim Family Laws* (n 49) 53.

52 Majdi Chakroun, 'La condition de la femme en Tunisie: de l'humanitaire au partenariat' (2009) 43 Revue juridique Thémis 109, 137; Arts 5–7 QPC; Aḥmad Maḥmūd Khalīl, *ᶜAqd al-Zawāj al-ᶜUrfī, Arkānuhu wa Shurūṭuhu wa Aḥkāmuhu* [Informal Marriages] (Munsha'at al-Maᶜārif 2002) 20; M Hidayatullah and Arshad Hidayatullah (eds), *Mulla's Principles of Mahomedan Law* (19th edn, LexisNexis Butterworths Wadhwa Nagpur 2008) s 252; AB Srivastava and SI Jafri (eds), *B.R. Verma's Commentaries on Mohammedan Law (In India, Pakistan & Bangladesh)* (9th edn, Law Publishers (India) Pvt Ltd 2006) 67f.

53 ᶜAbla ᶜAbd al-ᶜAzīz ᶜĀmir, *Al-Zawāj fī al-Sharīᶜa al-Islāmiyya wa-l-Qānūn al-Miṣrī* [Marriage in the Islamic Sharia and Egyptian Law] (Dār al-Nahḍa al-ᶜArabiyya 2010) 30ff. The Shiite school of law does not require any witnesses for the conclusion of marriage, Sayyid Muṣṭafā Muḥaqqiq Dāmād, *Barrisī-i Fiqhī-i Ḥuqūq-i Khānivādih – Nikāḥ va Inḥilāl-i ān* [Islamic Studies on Family Law – Marriage and Its Dissolution] (12th edn, Markaz-i Nashr-i ᶜUlūm-i Islāmī 2005) 170.

54 See Article 36 Tunisian Code of Personal Status of 13 August 1956, Official Gazette no 66 of 17 August 1956.

55 See on Iranian law, Court of Cassation, Judgement No 666 of 8 June 2004, Case No 8–1382, (2004–05) 10 Muẕākirāt va Ārā'-i Hay'at-i ᶜUmūmī-i Dīvān-i ᶜĀlī-i

Kishvar 121ff; see also Mahdī Shahīdī, *Ḥuqūq-i Madanī* [Civil Law], vol 1 (3rd edn, Intishārāt-i Majd 2003) 117.

56 On Pakistani law see *Syed Farman Ali v Abid Ali* PLD 1995 Lah 364; M Farani, *Manual of Family Laws* (Lahore Law Times Publications 1989) 7, who points to the fact that the registration of marriage is absolutely necessary under s 5 of the Muslim Family Laws Ordinance 1961, but the consequence of non-registration is solely that there is a 'doubt on solemnization of such marriage'.

57 On Moroccan law, see Art 16 of Law No 70.03 of 2004 of 3 February 2004 on the Family Code (Mudawwana), Official Gazette no 5184 of 5 February 2004; Andreas Börner, 'Die Eheschließung im marokkanischen Recht – Form und Beweis' [1993] Das Standesamt 377, 383.

58 For a discussion of the notion of informal marriages, see Nadia Sonneveld, 'Rethinking the Difference between Formal and Informal Marriages in Eygpt' in Maaike Voorhoeve (ed), *Family Law in Islam – Divorce, Marriage and Women in the Muslim World* (Tauris 2011) 81f.

59 For a comparative analysis of registration rules and the consequences of non-compliance in Muslim countries, see Yassari (n 6) 114ff.

60 A sole exception applies to divorce claims and claims on marriage annulment if the marriage can be proven through any written document.

61 Choukri Kalfat, 'Les aspirations conflictuelles du droit de l'adoption' [1994] Revue Algérienne des sciences juridiques, économiques et politiques 7, 13.

62 Daniel Pollack and others, 'Classical Religious Perspectives of Adoption Law' (2004) 79 Notre Dame Law Review 693, 734.

63 This theory has no basis in the Quran or the *sunna*. It was mainly devised by the Maliki school of law, whose founder *Mālik ibn Anas* appears to have been himself a 'sleeping foetus', Susan Gilson Miller, 'Sleeping Fetus', *Encyclopedia of Women & Islamic Cultures: Family, Body, Sexuality and Health* (2006) vol 3, 421ff.

64 The Sunni school of law envisages female gestation periods from two to four years and the Maliki school up to even seven years, Choukri Kalfat [1994] Revue Algérienne des sciences juridiques, économiques et politiques 21. The Shiite consider ten lunar months as the limit, Norman Anderson, 'Islamic Family Law', *International Encyclopedia of Comparative Law* (2007) vol 4, 73; Noel James Coulson, *A History of Islamic Law* (Edinburgh University Press 1964) 174.

65 Based on this theory, an unmarried mother escaped the penal sanction for adultery in Nigeria, see Elias J Groll, 'Radcliffe Fellow Defends Nigerian Woman Using Sharia Law' *The Harvard Crimson* (24 November 2008) <www.thecrimson.com/article/2008/11/24/radcliffe-fellow-defends-nigerian-women-using> accessed 1 December 2014.

66 Note the development of the terminology in paternity-related cases: while Law No 25 of 1929 used the term of 'not hearing' (*lā tusma*^{c}) the case, Law No 1 of 2000 uses the term of 'not admitting' (*lā tuqbal*) a case. The new terminology serves in the first place the unification of Egyptian legal terminology.

67 Essam Fawzy, 'Muslim Personal Status Law in Egypt: the Current Situation and Possibility of Reform through Internal Initiatives' in Lynn Welchman (ed), *Women's Rights and Islamic Family Law* (Zed Books Ltd 2004) 15, 61. The Azhar scholars had expressly proposed to admit blood tests as permissible evidence. Consequently, Art 7 Law No 1 of 2000 was altered, but without giving any concrete examples of 'other decisive evidence'.

68 See on the forms of last wills in selected Muslim jurisdictions, Nadjma Yassari, 'Testamentary Formalities in Islamic Law and their Reception in the Modern Laws of

Islamic Countries' in Kenneth GC Reid, Marius J de Waal, and Reinhard Zimmermann (eds), *Comparative Succession Law*, vol 1 (OUP 2011) 282–304.

69 Muṣṭafā Muḥaqqiq Dāmād, *Vaṣiyat, Taḥlīl-i Fiqhī va Ḥuqūqī* (3rd edn, Markaz-i Nashr-i ᶜUlūm-i Islāmī 1999) 198; Muḥaqqiq ḥillī, *Sharāyiᶜ al-Islām*, vol 2 (Mu'assasa-i Intishārāt va Chāp-i Dānishgāh-i Tihrān reprint 1985) 383; André Colomer, *Droit musulman*, vol 2: *La succession – le testament* (Éditions La Porte 1968) 194; Faiz Badruddin Tyabji, *Muslim Law: The Personal Law of Muslims in India and Pakistan* (Muhsin Tayyibji ed, 4th edn, NM Tripathi Private Limited 1968) 790; Jules Roussier, 'Le Livre du Testament dans le nouveau code tunisien du statut personnel' (1961) 15 Studia Islamica 89, 93f; Khalil (Ibn Ishaq), *Code musulman* (N Seignette tr, Augustin Challamel 1911) 636.

70 Roussier (1961) 15 Studia Islamica 93.

71 Anwarullah, *The Islamic Law of Evidence* (2nd edn, Kitab Bhavan 2006); Brinkley Messick, 'Commercial Litigation in a Sharīᶜa Court' in Muhammad K Masud, Rudolph Peters, and David S Powers (eds), *Dispensing Justice in Islam: Qadis and their Judgments* (Brill 2006) 203ff; Wael Hallaq, *Sharīᶜa: Theory, Practice, Transformation* (Harvard University Press 2009) 350.

72 Law No 71 of 1946 on Testamentary Dispositions of 24 June 1946, Official Gazette no 65 of 1 July 1946. In 1943, the law on intestate succession had already been comprehensively codified in Law No 77 of 1943 on Testate Succession of 6 August 1943, Official Gazette no 92 of 12 August 1943.

73 Sami A Aldeeb Abu-Sahlieh, *Les successions en droit musulman: Cas de l'Égypte* (TheBookEdition 2009) 33. A written will may be in the handwriting of the testator or a third party. In both cases the will has to be signed by the testator, ibid.

74 This rule had already existed in Egyptian law since 1931 as part of the Decree-Law on the Organization of the Sharia Courts (see n 39).

75 See the decision of the Egyptian Court of Cassation of 4 November 1969, Appeal Case No 193, 35th judicial year, (1969) 3(179) Majmūᶜāt al-Aḥkām al-Ṣādira min al-Hay'a al-ᶜĀmma li-l-Mawādd al-Madaniyya wa-l-Tijāriyya wa min al-Dā'ira al-Madaniyya wa min Dā'irat al-Aḥwāl al-Shakhsiyya 1159f, confirmed in the decision of 21 March 1979, Appeal Case No 7, 47th judicial year, (1979) 2(166) Majmūᶜāt al-Aḥkām al-Ṣādira min al-Hay'a al-ᶜĀmma li-l-Mawādd al-Madaniyya wa-l-Tijāriyya wa min al-Dā'ira al-Madaniyya wa min Dā'irat al-Aḥwāl al-Shakhsiyya 903f.

76 For an account of the jurisdiction of Egyptian courts from the 1920s until 1955 see Shaham, 'Custom, Islamic Law, and Statutory Legislation' (n 7) 258–81.

77 Art 6 of Law No 462 of 1955 of 21 September 1955 on the Abolition of the Religious Courts, Official Gazette no 73 *mukarrar (b)* of 24 September 1955; see Hans Wehr, 'Urkunden' (1958) 5 Die Welt des Islams 254ff; Maurits S Berger, 'Secularizing Interreligious Law in Egypt' (2005) 12 Islamic Law and Society 394–418; Imen Gallala-Arndt, '"Inconvenient Loves": The Mismanagement of Interfaith Marriages in Lebanon and Egypt' in Marie-Claire Foblets and Nadjma Yassari (eds), *Approches juridiques de la diversité culturelle – Legal Approaches to Cultural Diversity* (Brill 2013) 581f.

78 Omaia Elwan, 'Qualifikation der Unzulässigkeit von Klagen aus 'urfi-Ehen im ägyptischen Recht' in Herbert Kronke and Karsten Thorn (eds), *Grenzen überwinden – Prinzipien bewahren: Festschrift für Bernd Hoffmann zum 70. Geburtstag* (Gieseking 2011) 101; Elwan, 'Die Form von zwischen Ägyptern und Deutschen in Ägypten geschlossenen Ehen' (n 45) 163.

79 The following account is mainly drawn from an analysis of Egyptian academic literature by Elwan, 'Qualifikation der Unzulässigkeit von Klagen aus 'urfi-Ehen' (n 79) 101ff.

80 Elwan, 'Qualifikation der Unzulässigkeit von Klagen aus 'urfi-Ehen' (n 79) 103; but see Hans-Georg Ebert and Assem Hefny, 'Ägypten' in Alexander Bergmann, Murad Ferid, and Dieter Heinrich (eds), *Internationales Ehe- und Kindschaftsrecht* (looseleaf service, in German, R 15 July 2008), who categorize Law No 1 of 2000 as a law which applies to all Egyptians.

81 Elwan, 'Qualifikation der Unzulässigkeit von Klagen aus 'urfi-Ehen' (n 79) 106.

82 See for example Art 11 of the German EGBGB (Introductory Act to the Civil Code) of 21 September 1994, Federal Law Gazette I, 2494, last amended by Article 12 of the Act of 23 May 2011, Federal Law Gazette I, 898.

83 Rohe (n 1) 269.

84 Rohe (n 1) 269.

85 Rohe (n 1) 269, who points to an unpublished judgement of the Cairo Court of Appeal on 24 May 2006 where the paternity of a man was established notwithstanding his having denied being the father and informally wedded husband of the mother.

86 Linant de Bellefonds (1955) 7 Revue Internationale de Droit Comparé 31: '. . . il est certain qu'actuellement tous les mariages font en Egypte l'objet d'une transcription authentique. . . . l'acte authentique est également recherché par ceux qui savent qu'un mariage purement consensuel est valable, mais qui ne veulent pas courir le risque de n'avoir un jour que des droits sans actions.'

87 The figures diverge considerably: according to Ebert and Hefny (n 81) 25, around 700,000 informal marriages are concluded per year; Andreas Jacobs and Fabian Metzler, 'Wilde Ehe auf Ägyptisch' (country report of the *Konrad Adenauer Foundation*, January 2008) <www.kas.de/aegypten/de/publications/12726> accessed 5 May 2011, indicate 400,000 marriages per year. Moreover, Jacobs and Metzler estimate there to be several million informal marriages in Egypt altogether.

88 The impact of informal marriages was widely discussed in the public in the context of the amendments of Law No 1 of 2000, see Welchman, *Women and Muslim Family Laws* (n 49) 56ff; see also Fawzy (n 68) 60, on the discussion regarding the requirement of registering marriages by the Egyptian Islamic Studies Academy.

89 Jacobs and Metzler (n 88).

90 Sami Zubaida, *Law and Power in the Islamic World* (IB Tauris 2005) 180.

91 Jacobs and Metzler (n 88); Fawzy (n 68) 42.

92 Maha AZ Yamani, *Polygamy and Law in Contemporary Saudi Arabia* (Duke University Press 2008) 49.

93 Bernard Botiveau, 'Le statut personnel des musulmans égyptiens au XXe siècle: régulations autoritaires et réponses sociales' (1993) 27 Annales islamologiques 86: 'mariages "saisonniers" ou même "touristiques"'.

94 Fawzy (n 68) 42. The legislature tackled this problem in a very 'Egyptian' manner, as the courts can dissolve informal marriages under Law No 1 of 2000 even if no marital claim can be based on such a marriage. As a result, the courts may dissolve a marriage that otherwise has no legal effect.

95 For example, childbirth is traditionally reported by the father (Art 15 para 1(1) Law No 12 of 1996 of 25 March 1996 on Child Law, Official Gazette no 13 of 28 March 1996 as amended by Law No 126 of 2008 of 15 June 2008, Official Gazette no 24 *mukarrar* of 15 June 2008). If the mother is to report the birth alone, she has to first

prove her marriage (Art 15 para 1(2) Law No 12 of 1996) in order to be allowed to include the father's name in the birth certificate. If she cannot provide any proof, the child will be barred from obtaining free-of-charge vaccinations (Art 25 Law No 12 of 1996) and denied the right to free education in public schools (Art 54 Law No 12 of 1996). It may also happen that the child is left without a means of obtaining a surname.

96 Art 2 Law No 154 of 2004 of 14 July 2004 Regulating the Amendments of Some Regulations of Law No 26 of 1975 with Regard to Egyptian Nationality, Official Gazette no 28 *mukarrar (a)* of 14 July 2004, 11ff.

97 Equally, the new Egyptian Constitution of 2014 articulates in Article 6 that 'Citizenship is a right to anyone born to an Egyptian father or an Egyptian mother. Being legally recognized and obtaining official papers proving his personal data is a right guaranteed and organized by law.' An unofficial translation of the constitution is available online at <https://www.constituteproject.org/constitution/Egypt_2014.pdf>.

98 On the Egyptian *khul*^{c} provision, see Nathalie Bernard-Maugiron, Chapter 8.

99 This rule has also been incorporated in the Code of Personal Status of the United Arab Emirates, see Lena-Maria Möller, 'Family Law in the Arab Gulf: Recent Developments and Reform Patterns' (2013) 9 Journal of Islamic State Practices in International Law 22, 27.

100 Before the introduction of judicial *khul*^{c}, an Egyptian woman could contract an extra-judicial *khul*^{c} with her husband and have the divorce registered with the *ma'dhūn* (Art 39 of the Decree of 4 January 1955 on the *ma'dhūn*, Official Gazette no 3 *mulḥaq* of 10 January 1955). In essence, the *khul*^{c} was a consensual divorce until 2000, see Nathalie Bernard-Maugiron and Baudouin Dupret, 'Breaking Up the Family: Divorce in Egyptian Law and Practice' (2008) 6 Hawwa 52, 58.

101 See in more detail Nadia Sonneveld, *Khul' Divorce in Egypt – Public Debates, Judicial Practices, and Everyday Life* (American University in Cairo Press 2011) 35ff.

102 Recent years have seen dramatic changes in Egypt's political system and the coming into force of two Constitutions. The overthrow of the Mubarak regime in 2011 was first followed by the Islamist presidency of Mohammed Mursi and, after his removal by the military, the election of Abdel Fattah el-Sisi in 2014. While, as of now, the focus lies on more pressing political and economic issues than on questions of family law reform, *khul*^{c} has in fact been on the political agenda after the revolution of 2011, especially on part of more conservative and religious political forces who called for a revision of Law No 1 of 2000. See e.g. Heba Saleh, 'Egyptian women fear regression on rights' (*Financial Times online*, 1 October 2012) <www.ft.com/cms/s/0/b203c126-06f5-11e2-92ef-00144feabdc0.html#axzz3lunU20I7> accessed 16 September 2015; Ahmed Fekry Ibrahim, *Pragmatism in Islamic Law* (Syracuse University Press 2015), 212, 226.

103 See judgement of the Supreme Constitutional Court of 15 December 2002, 23rd judicial year, Case No 201 (on file with author); Nathalie Bernard-Maugiron, 'The Judicial Construction of the Facts and the Law – The Egyptian Supreme Constitutional Court and the Constitutionality of the Law on the *khul*^{c}' in Baudouin Dupret, Barbara Drieskens, and Annelies Moors (eds), *Narratives of Truth in Islamic Law* (Tauris 2008) 241ff.

6 The financial relationship between spouses under Iranian law

A never-ending story of guilt and atonement?

Nadjma Yassari

Introduction

Iranian family and succession law was codified in a comprehensive manner in the Iranian Civil Code in 1935 (CC). The regulations mainly rest on the Shiite Jafari school of law and reflect the traditional perception of the family as a unit to which both spouses have to contribute according to their supposed strengths and weaknesses. Consequently, under Iranian law the husband is the head of the family[1] and must provide for his wife and children, including marital maintenance (*nafaqih*)[2] and a dower (*mahr*),[3] i.e. an asset of economic value for his wife. The wife, on the other hand, has to obey her husband and provide a comfortable home. Financial solidarity is limited to the duration of marital life. With the dissolution of marriage financial duties come to an end, as traditional Islamic law knows neither post-marital claims nor generally the concept of community of property. Against this background, until very recently under Iranian law a divorced wife had only one source of financial support, her *mahr*. The situation has evolved since the early 1990s, when the Iranian legislature endeavoured to strengthen the financial situation of divorced women (and widows) by reforming existing instruments and introducing new legal concepts. This chapter critically examines the steps taken by the legislature to reshape the financial relationship between the spouses. It will consider the traditional instruments of financial security, such as *nafaqih* and the *mahr*, and investigate if and how new means of support, such as *ujrat ul-mis̱l*, have had an impact on the economic structure of the family. In addition, the concept of the matrimonial property regime will be discussed as to its potential to level the financial relationship of spouses. Finally, a glance will be thrown at the amendments to the intestate succession rights of surviving wives.

Marital claim

Nafaqih

Marriage creates an obligation on the part of the husband to provide maintenance for his wife (*nafaqih*) and to give her a dower (*mahr*). Maintenance in Iranian law comprises all the material needs of the wife, such as housing, clothing, food, household goods, medical care, as well as domestic staff (*khādim*) in so far as the wife is used to it or where it is required because of illness or need.[4] In 2002 some minor amendments were introduced,[5] but they were essentially of a clarifying nature and did not derogate from the basic understanding of maintenance under traditional Islamic Shiite Law. The right to be maintained is an absolute legal right, from which the spouses cannot deviate. It is basically gendered, as the obligation is only borne by the husband. The failure to provide for the wife enables her to petition for divorce.[6] On the other hand, the wife's right to be provided for is directly linked to her duty to obey (*tamkīn*) her husband. If she disobeys, he can retain maintenance; if he fails to maintain her, she can be disobedient.[7] Therefore, in the event of dispute the paramount question is which spouse started to disregard his or her duties, justifying the withholding of duties by the other. As a result, *nafaqih* and the consequences of the failure to provide for it are intrinsically linked to the personal effects of marriages and are bound together by the principle of fault.

Mahr

The *mahr* is the second financial obligation that is created at the time of marriage. The codification of *mahr* regulation in the Civil Code in 1935[8] reflects, basically, the Shiite rules. The rules remained substantially untouched until 1998 when the Inflation Adaption Law[9] was enacted. In addition, in 2013 new regulations on the *mahr* were introduced in the Family Protection Act 2013.[10]

The *mahr* is a legal institution of a hybrid nature: it has both a legal and a contractual basis. It is of contractual nature as the agreement on the *mahr* is considered a separate contract agreed upon in the course of the conclusion of the marriage. Therefore, the validity of the marriage is not impaired by the invalidity of the *mahr* agreement. On the other hand, if the marriage is invalid, the *mahr* will be invalid too, as its raison d'être lies in the existence of a valid marriage (with exceptions for specific circumstances, such as the erroneous cohabitation (*al-waṭ' bi-shubha*),[11] which creates the right to a *mahr*). In addition, the contractual character is exemplified by the fact that the spouses are free to agree on its subject matter, quantity, and due time.[12] The *mahr* is defined in respect of its subject as a property (*māliyat*) of monetary value.[13] Another important point is the requirement that the *mahr* be determined or at least determinable.[14] Typically, Iranian *mahr* consist of a sum of money or an amount of gold coins.

Furthermore, the right to a *mahr* comes about *ex legem*. This is shown by the figure of the proper dower (*mahr ul-mis̱l*). It is rather unusual for the spouses to fail to stipulate the *mahr* when marrying. This is because marriage certificates are standardized in Iran. The marriage must be registered with state authorities and is written down in a booklet that contains various rubrics, including one for the *mahr*. Where the nomination of a dower is omitted or where the nominated *mahr* is – for whatever reason – invalid, and also where the *mahr* is expressly rejected by the prospective spouses, the duty to provide a dower does not come to an end.[15] Rather, the husband is obliged to provide for a so-called proper dower, i.e. a usual dower,[16] the exact amount of which is determined by experts appointed by the court.[17]

The value is then determined with due consideration of various factors, including the social status of the wife and her family, the comparable dowers paid in her family, and custom.[18] Generally the scope of application of the proper dower is very limited, so that average values of the proper dower are difficult to assess.[19] In practice, the courts decide on a case-to-case basis.

The *mahr* is a potentially powerful instrument for securing financial support in several respects. First, because of the lack of post-marital maintenance rights and regulations on matrimonial property under traditional Islamic family law, the *mahr* stands out as the wife's most important financial claim against her husband. Second, the claim to the *mahr* is established with the conclusion of the marriage and its extent is known at the beginning of marital life. The wife has thus a certain degree of certainty as to the financial cushion she can rely on in case of need. Further, the fact that the right to a *mahr* is created when the marriage is concluded means that it is – as a concept – not a post-marital claim, even though over time in many Muslim jurisdictions the practice of deferring the *mahr* has become common. In Iran, however, the *mahr* is generally not deferred. Statutes and the standard clause in the marriage certificate specify that the *mahr* is due on the wife's demand,[20] even though in practice wives rarely ask for the *mahr* during marital life, particularly when the marriage is a happy one. Thirdly, and most importantly, the right to the *mahr* is based on a system of strict liability where issues relating to marital misbehaviour, the wife's needs, and the financial capability of the husband, are irrelevant. The *mahr* is an absolute right of the wife and not linked to the question of fault, and is therefore due even in cases where the wife has breached or failed to perform her marital duties. The linking of the right to maintenance to female obedience is not applicable in the case of the *mahr*.

The importance of the *mahr* as a financial instrument in marriage law is also acknowledged by the legislature. As Iranian *mahr* are often designated as an amount of money, the extreme devaluation of the Iranian currency Rial from the 1980s on led to a substantial loss of purchasing power in the *mahr*. To secure the value of the *mahr* the legislature enacted, in 1997, the Inflation Adaption Law.[21] This law enables the courts to adapt the amount of the *mahr* stipulated in Rial to the inflation rate at the time the *mahr* is claimed.[22] There was, however, uncertainty as to whether the law would apply to *mahr* agreements dating from before its enactment. According to art 4 CC new laws have no retroactive power and are applicable from the moment they come into force, if the law itself does not provide otherwise.[23] As the Inflation Adaption Law was silent on this issue, there were diverting views on the matter.[24] In 2000, the Iranian Supreme Court clarified the situation. It held that, notwithstanding the silence of the law, its *ratio legis* is directed towards the protection of *mahr* agreement that effectively had suffered from the devaluation of the Rial.[25] A retroactive law was thus intended and did not conflict with the general principle of art 4 CC.[26]

The majority of commentators welcomed the law,[27] as it addressed a severe problem. In fact, because of the lack of financial claims after divorce, the *mahr* had developed into an important source of support for divorced women, a source that would have dried up if the legislature had not intervened to stabilize its value. On the other hand, the increase in the value of the *mahr* also had its downside: according to unofficial statistics the average size of the *mahr* had risen continuously in the last few decades. Whereas in 1985 an average was 150 gold coins *bahār āzādī*,[28] by 2004 the amount had climbed to 260–350 and, in 2009, to 300–450.[29] This growth reflects the increase in the female level of education: in 2009, the *mahr* of women of a low educational background amounted to an average of 52 gold coins, the *mahr* of women with a school education to 208 gold coins and educated women's *mahr* to between 400 and 500 gold coins.[30] These increases did not, however, match the general economic growth in Iran. For years the Iranian economy had stagnated,[31] as had wages and salaries. On the other hand, the average cost of living had continuously increased, with housing prices rocketing. The economic sanctions against Iran have exacerbated the situation further. In December 2010 the price for fuel quadrupled, as the government was not able to renew state subsidies.[32] These circumstances affected the significance of the *mahr* for both the wife and the husband. For the woman the *mahr* increasingly constituted privately financed support in the absence of a functioning state welfare system.[33] For the husband the *mahr* became a heavy burden in two respects. First, he alone bore the burden of financial support for his wife and, second, he faced imprisonment for failing to abide by this duty as, under art 2 of the Act on the Enforcement of Debts,[34] a debtor can – on the demand of the creditor – be imprisoned for non-performance. In fact, the number of husbands detained in Iran for non-payment of the *mahr* has continuously increased.[35]

Against this background, a number of legislative proposals have been discussed both in public and in the Iranian Parliament in the last decade. The main theme of these debates was the question of whether and, if so, how the size of the *mahr* should or could be regulated and a cap limit set. For example, in 2005 a proposal was made to designate regional maximum amounts according to the living cost of each Iranian province.[36] Further, an income tax on the *mahr* was considered, payable at the time of marriage, in order to deter spouses from agreeing on a very high *mahr*.[37] Both proposals were rejected.[38] As further amendments were equally criticized, in April 2011 Parliament announced that limitations to the *mahr* would not be the subject of any draft law and that it was the state's duty to provide educational measures to change the prevailing attitudes towards the *mahr*.[39]

In March 2012, after some years of negotiations, corrections, and amendments, a final draft for a new Act on the Protection of the Family (FPA 2013) was presented to Parliament, and came into force in April 2013.[40] The FPA 2013 is the third act of this name.[41] The main reason for its introduction was the uncertainty that surrounded the validity of the former Family Protection Act of 1975. In fact, except for art 15 FPA 1975 (which was abolished in 1979),[42] no article of the FPA was removed and no other law explicitly abolished or replaced the FPA 1975. The FPA 2013, it was said, was necessary to consolidate and clarify the legal situation, as it was meant to replace the FPA 1975 and ensure legal certainty.[43] The insecurity, however, remains: the list of legislation that became obsolete with the new FPA does not include the FPA 1975.[44]

The new act was mainly concerned with procedural rules on marriage, divorce, and child law. Furthermore, it contained one article on the *mahr*. This article was neither concerned with imposing taxation, nor did it explicitly establish a maximum size for the *mahr*. Rather the legislature chose an indirect way to get to grips with the pressing problem of the extremely high *mahr*. Without infringing on the spouses' right to determine the *mahr* as they wish, art 22 FPA 2013 states that art 2 of the Act on the Enforcement of Debts is only applicable to a *mahr* that does not exceed 110 *bahār āzādī* gold coins (or its corresponding monetary value) whereas the exceeding amount can only be claimed if the husband is financially capable of effecting the payment. The article also clarifies that the Inflation Adaptation Law continues to apply.

In fact, the legislature did not introduce a cap limit for the *mahr*. Rather, art 22 operates on the enforcement rules. The legislature left untouched the autonomy of the spouses to determine the *mahr*, but levelled the degree of judicial protection afforded to the wife by dividing the *mahr* in two parts: one that is independent of the financial capability of the husband, and one that is – *contra legem islamicum* – dependent on it. Whereas *mahr* agreements of up to 110 gold coins can be enforced directly and without court proceedings, the amount exceeding 110 gold coins must be pleaded in court and will only be granted if the husband is capable of effecting the remaining payment. In the event that he is financially unable to provide for the rest, the court can order him to make payments by instalments.

This regulation reveals the legislature's concern to primarily address the increase in imprisoned husbands who had failed to pay the *mahr*. In addition, it reflects a careful balancing of the interests of the parties: on the one hand, it strengthens the right of the wife to directly enforce (at least) 110 gold coins of her *mahr*, emphasizing hereby her interest in a predictable and secure financial future. It has to be borne in mind that in April 2013, 110 *bahār āzādī* gold coins had a monetary value of approximately 31,000 Euros.[45] On the other hand, the legislature also displayed political realism by connecting the remainder of the *mahr* to the realities of the general economic situation and therefore to the capability of the husband to pay the *mahr*. In doing so, the legislature considered the arguments of both the advocates and opponents of a cap limit for the *mahr* and created, *de facto*, a legal average for the *mahr*.

Matrimonial property regimes

Matrimonial property is an unknown concept in traditional Islamic law.[46] Marital property is mainly seen through the lens of a woman's independence in managing her assets without the interference of her relatives or husband.[47] As a consequence, modern family law codes in Muslim jurisdictions generally do not refer in any detail to a matrimonial property regime.[48] Rather, it is assumed that the regime of separation of property reigns supreme. Art 1118 CC, for example, states that a woman can dispose of her property in whatever way she wishes. Marriage is therefore not a ground for the assimilation of the spouse's assets. Each spouse remains the owner of the assets he or she owned at the time of marriage and of all property acquired during marriage. This principle is generally acknowledged without any further investigation into matrimonial property as a concept.[49] Only where specific items cannot directly be allocated to the one or other spouse a gender-specific rule applies: assets generally owned by women will be given to the wife and vice versa.[50]

On the other hand, Iranian law allows the spouses to regulate their marital relationship contractually, as long as their agreements are compatible with the nature of marriage.[51] As such, art 1119 CC sets out the spouses' possible options: they may, for example, agree on further grounds for a divorce by the wife and thereby bypass certain statutory law limitations.[52] In addition, art 1114 CC states that the designation of the marital home (a responsibility lying generally with the husband) may be contractually delegated to the wife. Against this background arises the question of whether the liberty to opt out of statutory provisions also extends to the financial rights and responsibility of the spouses. On first sight there does not seem to be any reason to prohibit such agreements, as long as the agreement does not undermine the very nature of marriage. As such, for example, stipulations negating the right of the wife to be maintained financially during marriage would not be enforceable,[53] as the right to maintenance is seen as mandatory counterbalance to the wife's obedience duty. There is, however, room for manoeuvre. In fact, marriage as understood in Iranian Shiite Law (and for that matter also in Sunni schools) is a civil contract with a wide range of contractual liberties. Marriage certificates in Iran acknowledge this freedom as they contain pre-printed standard clauses (*sharāyiṭ-i żimn-i ᶜaqd yā ᶜaqd-i khārij-i lāzim*), pertaining in particular to the abrogation of certain personal effects of marriage but also to the expansion of divorce grounds for the wife.[54] The introduction of these clauses into the marriage certificate goes back to an initiative of Imam Khomeini to strengthen the rights of women.[55] Interestingly, the alternative contractual grounds for divorce in the standardized marriage certificate are based on the FPA 1975, in particular art 8, which explicitly sets out the reasons giving rise to divorce. With their signature the spouses can opt into any of these clauses, if they wish to do so.

Amongst these, a clause was introduced in the 1980s, according to which the spouses could agree on a financial claim of the wife against her husband, amounting to up to half of the assets he acquired during marriage, whenever he divorces her, and without her giving him any reasons for it.[56] The conditions of the clause must be fulfilled simultaneously. The husband must petition for the divorce, whereas the wife must be innocent as regards the breakdown of the marriage. The relevant period is the duration of the marriage (*ayām-i zanāshūyī*) and only assets acquired by the husband during the marriage may be divided.[57] Property owned at the time of marriage, the growth of those assets, and assets acquired through inheritance during marriage, are excluded from division.[58] According to the wording of the clause, the courts have a wide margin of appreciation when determining the precise amount of the claim.[59] This vague formulation was chosen to allow for a consideration of the specific circumstances of each case, including factors such as the duration of marriage, the material and immaterial contribution of the wife to marital life, and the size of the *mahr*,[60] in order to adjust the claim to the financial needs of the wife. Moreover, the vagueness of the clause must be read against the background of the anticipated difficulty of persuading husbands to sign the clause.[61] A rather indefinite and adjustable formulation was preferred in order to ensure its practicability. A precise determination of the amount was thus intentionally avoided.[62]

Although the clause was conceived of as a protective measure to support women financially, it suffers from a systematic deficiency as only an innocent and unwillingly divorced wife can bring such action. The claim thus does not stem from the idea of marriage as an economic partnership to which both spouses contribute to its financial viability and to which, therefore, both are entitled to a share, but is conceived of as a sort of compensation for the wife only for an arbitrary divorce instigated by her husband. In this sense, it cannot be accounted for as a change to the matrimonial property regime, but it is rather meant to deter arbitrary divorce by the husband and provide a ground for compensating the wife for perceived abusive behaviour. In fact, the concept of 'guilt and atonement' transcends also the other financial post-marital claims that the Iranian legislature has conceived of in the last few decades, as will be seen next.

Post-marital claims

Post-marital maintenance claims

In the last 50 years, new post-marital financial claims have been introduced in almost all Muslim jurisdictions.[63] These claims, called *mutᶜat al-ṭalāq*, are generally granted to the divorced wife only where the husband initiated the divorce or caused the breakdown of the marriage. To obtain any such financial support, the wife must thus prove that she was not at fault, which may prove to be a difficult endeavour. Moreover, post-marital financial claims are often limited to a certain amount and to certain periods of time.

In 1975 the Iranian legislature also introduced such a claim in its FPA 1975. According to art 11 FPA 1975, the court could oblige the spouse who had caused the breakdown of the marriage to pay a monthly sum to the innocent ex-spouse. The amount of this payment was to be determined by considering the specific circumstances of each case, the age of the spouses, the duration of the marriage, the needs of the applicant, and the financial status of the respondent.[64] In addition, changes in the personal circumstances of the parties would lead to changes in the calculation of the monthly sum.[65]

Art 11 FPA 1975 addressed the applicant in a gender-neutral manner (*har yik az ṭarafayn*, any of the parties). The academic literature, however, was not unanimous as to whether both the husband and the wife could claim post-marital annuity. According to *Kātūziyān*, art 11 FPA 1975 could only be used by the wife, as it implied that the cause of the breakdown of the marriage was marital misconduct. As men could divorce women without giving any reason, art 11 could only apply whenever the woman petitioned for divorce, with the behaviour of the husband being the ground for both the divorce and post-marital annuity.[66] Further, the claim was conceived of as compensation for damages suffered (*jubrān-i żarar*) because of the loss of marital maintenance.[67] Marital maintenance, however, is exclusively the duty of the husband and the dissolution of the marriage does not mean a financial loss for him.[68] Conversely, *Ṣafā'ī* and *Imāmī* emphasize that art 11 FPA 1975 was also grounded in the concept of marriage as a community of solidarity, which in return was the basis of post-marital maintenance claims. This idea would be evident in the further parts to art 11, which provided for post-marital claims on a strict liability basis for specific groups of needy spouses, such as physically and psychologically impaired spouses, without consideration of the reason for the breakdown of the marriage. In addition, the amount of the annuity was calculated not only with due consideration to the damage suffered by the innocent spouse but also the financial needs and capabilities of the spouses. Therefore, they concluded, art 11 FPA 1975 had to be considered as a kind of maintenance (*yik naw*ᶜ*-i nafaqih*), which until 1975 had been unknown in Iranian law.[69]

This dispute shows the difficulty of constructing a post-marital claim in a family law system that in its foundational spirit ignores post-marital claims. In fact, the financial annuity under art 11 FPA 1975 was based on a hybrid legal ground, partly informed by concepts of tort law with an compensatory character (damage for financial loss) and partly by concepts of post-marital solidarity based on the idea of continuous post-marital support duties of spouses according to the need of the applicant and the capability of the respondent. Meanwhile, the definite nature of art 11 FPA 1975 remains unresolved, as do the insecurities with regards to the persistence of the Act as a whole, as the new FPA 2013 did not explicitly repeal its predecessor.

Nonetheless, it seems that in practice art 11 FPA has been largely ignored by the courts.[70] It is therefore difficult to assess the impact of these rules on the financial relations of spouses. Some writers suggest that between 1975 and 1979 the amount of the *mahr* stipulated in Iranian marriage certificates decreased considerably. Accordingly, the spouses would afford a rather symbolic value to the *mahr*, designating it as a number of flowers or candy sugar.[71] Whether the decrease in the value of the *mahr* was related to the possibility of obtaining a post-marital annuity cannot be stated with certainty. This short trend may also be an outcome of the general secularization of the Pahlavi area of the late 1970s.

Beside art 11 FPA 1975 Iranian law did not recognize any other ground for post-marital claims. It was only in 1992 that the Iranian legislature conceived of a new ground for a claim to provide financial support to divorced women. This new claim was innovative in that it used basic tenets of civil law and, in particular, the law on wage compensation, as shall be shown next.

Ujrat ul-Miṣl*: the compensation for household works*

In 1992, the Iranian legislature introduced, in the Act on the Reform of Divorce (Divorce Act),[72] a new legal institution, *ujrat ul-miṣl*,[73] enabling the wife to ask for compensation for household work done voluntarily during the course of the marriage. The conditions of *ujrat ul-mis̲l* were rather tight: the wife could ask to be compensated for household work that she had done on the demand of her husband, without being legally (and religiously) obliged to do so, and without the intent to do so gratuitously. Further, *ujrat ul-mis̲l* could only be claimed in cases where the husband had asked for divorce and where the wife had not caused the breakdown of the marriage. Finally, the regulation only applied where the spouses had not agreed otherwise.[74]

The legislature had used different concepts of Shiite law to justify this new regulation. Shiite law generally distinguishes between the general (*tamkīn-i ᶜāmm*) and specific duties of the wife (*tamkīn-i khāṣṣ*).[75] Whereas the last relates to the wife's duty to cohabit with her husband,[76] the first comprehends the general duties of the wife to obey her husband in his decisions with regard to her residence,[77] or her employment, for example.[78] Shiite law, and by extension Iranian family law, however, does not foresee any other specified marital duty for the wife. Therefore, household works, such as cleaning, shopping, and cooking are not included in a wife's marital responsibilities.[79] Moreover, the wife has no duty to nurse the newborn[80] nor must she educate them after they have reached a certain age.[81] Therefore, it was argued, if the wife had performed these duties on the demand of her husband and without the intention of doing them gratuitously, she had to be compensated if he divorced her through no fault of her own. The amount of compensation was to be determined by experts, who had to consider the duration of the marriage and the kind of work undertaken to assess the wage commonly paid for such works. In addition, the income of the husband and the lifestyle of the spouses had to be taken into consideration.[82]

The strict conditions under which *ujrat ul-mis̲l* could be claimed made it extremely difficult for woman to access this right. One major problem was that *ujrat ul-mis̲l* was only due when the husband had petitioned for divorce and the wife had been innocent as regards the breakdown of the marriage.[83] Although the general theme of the claim seemed to suggest that the foundation of *ujrat ul-mis̲l* was a compensation for the *innocent* wife, *ujrat ul-mis̲l* was not due when it was the innocent wife who applied for divorce for good reason.[84] This very formalistic interpretation of the conditions of *ujrat ul-mis̲l* considerably narrowed its scope of application.

Another problem lay in the fact that *ujrat ul-mis̲l* could only be claimed where the spouses had not agreed otherwise. The wording of the article remained quite vague and Iranian academic literature discussed, controversially, whether the claim to *ujrat ul-mis̲l* was displaced by the standard clause in Iranian marriage certificates according to which a woman can be entitled to half of the marital assets of her husband in the event of an innocent divorce.[85]

Finally, the major deficiency of the new rule was its inconsistency in respect of the general regulations on wage claims under the Iranian Civil Code.[86] According to art 336 CC, a person who at the order of another person performs an act for which usually a wage is due is entitled to adequate remuneration. Applying this rule, the wife could have asked for compensation without having to prove the strict conditions of *ujrat ul-mis̱l* under the Divorce Act. Whereas this ground had not been referred to in divorce proceedings before 1992, interestingly, the enactment of the Divorce Act led to the revival of art 336 CC in Iranian family courts. Seemingly aware of the difficulties of establishing the grounds for *ujrat ul-mis̱l* under the Divorce Act, the courts made use of art 336 CC to grant the wife post-marital compensation for work done in the household.[87]

In 2001 the Iranian Parliament again took up the issue of *ujrat ul-mis̱l*. A draft law was proposed to accept a claim to *ujrat ul-mis̱l* also in the event of the death of the husband.[88] This was, however, rejected. Instead, in 2007, after the intervention of the Expediency Council,[89] art 336 CC was amended to include a new paragraph. According to art 336 para 1 CC, wives who on the demand of their husband had done household tasks (which they were not legally obliged to do) had a right to be adequately remunerated.[90] In contrast to the regulations in the Divorce Act, the new paragraph does not link the right to compensation to the dissolution of the marriage, hereby widening its scope of application. As the right to wage compensation is generated by the performance of the tasks, by its legal nature this right is not exclusively a post-marital claim, but may be asked for during marriage as well. In addition, the original intent of the legislature to grant *ujrat ul-mis̱l* in the event of the death of the husband could also be achieved as, according to art 231 of the Act on Non-Contentious Matters, the liabilities of a person become due at his death.[91] Therefore, the widow now had a legal base to claim compensation for household work against the estate of her late husband as well.[92] An important difference between *ujrat ul-mis̱l* under the Divorce Act and wage compensation under art 336 para 1 CC, however, remained: whereas under the Divorce Act the courts had to consider *ujrat ul-mis̱l ex officio*, the right under art 336 CC would only be heard if pleaded by the wife.

Notwithstanding these reforms, the legal situation remained unclear, as all three grounds (art 336 CC, art 336 para 1 CC and the Divorce Act) existed alongside each other until 2013, when the new Family Protection Act was enacted. The FPA 2013 repealed the Divorce Act.[93] At the same time, art 29 FPA 2013 states that the claim to *ujrat ul-mis̱l* must to be adjudicated under art 336 CC. As a result, the strict conditions under the Divorce Act of *ujrat ul-mis̱l* were abolished. It is assumed that the reference to art 336 CC is directed to art 336 para 1 CC, it being the *lex specialis* to the general rule in art 336 CC. It is further assumed from the wording of art 29 FPA 2013 that the courts have to take up the issue of *ujrat ul-mis̱l ex officio*, as the registration of the divorce will not be processed if all financial claims of the wife are not clearly dealt with in the divorce judgement.

Notwithstanding these clarifications, there remain reservations as to the potential of *ujrat ul-mis̱l* as a means for securing financial support for divorced women. For one its application is socially disputed.[94] Public polls point to the fact that a majority of women deem it humiliating to ask for it, as they feel downgraded to the status of a cheap labourer. In a survey conducted in 2004, most interviewees maintained that they would not petition for it.[95] In addition, uncertainty as to its precise amount places *ujrat ul-mis̱l* on shaky grounds. Finally, the burden of proof lies with the wife, putting additional weight on her shoulders. Notwithstanding these shortcomings, the Iranian legislature used the technical scheme of *ujrat ul-mis̱l* to establish yet another financial claim, thus far inexistent in Iranian law, i.e. the reimbursement of expenses incurred by the wife, as will be shown next.

Reimbursement of expenses incurred by the wife

According to art 30 FPA 2013, the wife has the right to claim for expenses that she incurred during the course of the married couple's common life (*hazīnih barāy-i makhārij-i muta*ᶜ*ārif-i zindigī-i mushtarak*), either that she undertook on the demand of her husband or with his permission without having the intent to do so gratuitously. The wife bears the burden of proof that she acted in accordance with her husband's demands, whereas the husband can reject the claim only if he proves that the wife had the intention to perform these tasks gratuitously.

This article is inserted into the chapter on divorce,[96] and has to be regarded as a post-marital claim. This can also be deduced from the Parliamentary debates on the draft article that initially stated that this right should apply only to adversary divorce proceedings, but not to consensual divorces.[97] As enacted, the article does not refer to the kind of divorce and establishes the right to be reimbursed for the expenses incurred without recourse to the principle of fault. This right comes as a specific flanking measure to the instrument of *ujrat ul-mis̱l*. Both claims are meant to compensate the wife for services that she rendered without being under a legal obligation to do so, be it for services rendered *in naturales* as under *ujrat ul-mis̱l*, or for other expenses as under art 30 FPA. It is, however, not clear from the wording of the article ('if the wife proves in court . . .'), whether the claim under art 30 FPA must be explicitly pleaded by the wife or whether it falls under the competence of the court to raise it *ex officio*. The impact of this article cannot yet be gauged as the law has been in force for only two years.

Succession rights

Finally, some light shall be shed on the succession rights of the surviving spouses. Under traditional Islamic law, and by extension in Iranian law, the surviving spouse is considered a Quranic heir, i.e. an heir designated in the Quran on the basis of a fractional share in the estate.[98] As such, the surviving spouse is never excluded and he or she inherits together with the blood relatives of the deceased. Whereas the right of both spouses to inherit is acknowledged irrespective of their gender,[99] their respective shares vary according to their gender and the presence of descendants. Thus, in the presence of descendants, the portion of the husband is one-quarter, and, in their absence, one-half. The share of the surviving wife is exactly half of these portions.[100]

As far as the inheritable property is concerned, Shiite law makes a distinction between the movable and immovable portions of the estate. This rule has no basis in the Quran and is derived from various Shiite hadiths.[101] The general thrust of these narratives is that the bond between husband and wife is based on affinity and not blood.[102] From this premise discussions followed as to whether it was reasonable to allow the widowed wife to inherit land owned by her deceased husband, as on her re-marriage to an outsider that land could be extracted from the late husband's family property. The predominant opinion amongst Shiite jurists was thus to deprive women of any share in the immovable property of their deceased husband's estate.[103]

This rule, which was applicable in Iran until recently, resulted in particular hardship for rural women in respect of the transfer of agricultural land. Only when the estate included land with buildings or trees could the widow claim the equivalent of her respective Quranic share of the value of the buildings or trees, but she could claim neither the land itself nor its value.[104] In 2009 the Iranian legislature initiated debates on that rule, based on other minority opinions held by Shiite jurists. In fact, some had argued against that rule, as it had no basis in the Quran,[105] while others had opted to limit the prohibition against the succession of land to residential sites and to acknowledge the widow's rights to other types of property, especially agricultural land. Further, there was the view that the prohibition could only apply to childless widows, as there are no descendants to whom the property could pass.[106] Finally, there was also the opinion that the wife should be excluded from inheriting the land itself, but that she ought to be awarded a corresponding right to its value, according to her share. The discussions in Iran culminated in an intervention by the Supreme Religious Leader, Ayatollah Ali Chamenei, who issued a fatwa adopting the latter view in January 2009.[107] The Iranian Parliament accordingly amended the relevant articles of the Iranian Civil Code, which now award the surviving wife a right to the value of immovable property, according to her share.[108] As a result, Iranian women still do not inherit immovable property *in rem*, but will receive a fractional share of the value of the land.

Thus, the right of the surviving wife to the estate of her late husband remains limited in three respects: first, it is gendered, as the share of a surviving wife is half of that of the surviving husband and, second, she has no right *in rem* as regards land. Also, Iranian succession laws favour the surviving husband over the surviving wife, as her share is limited (in the presence of descendants) to a maximum of one-eighth, a share that may be split amongst all surviving wives where the deceased practised polygamy.[109] Finally, as matrimonial property regimes are not foreseen by law, a share in the marital assets is not possible under the scheme of Iranian succession law.

Evaluation

This survey has shown the evolution of financial claims between spouses under Iranian law. Generally, the regulations of the Civil Code rest on the Shiite school of law and reflect largely the traditional conception of husband and wife and their respective rights and duties. In fact, the conventional system of traditional Islamic law has its logic and operates in interaction with all fields of family law: the man is the head of the family, bearing the financial burden of maintaining it and having a greater share in the estate, be it as the son of the deceased in relation to his sisters, be it as the surviving husband vis-à-vis his late wife. The rights and duties of the wife correspond to that scheme. What binds together reciprocal spousal rights and duties is the question of fault: whichever party's rights have been infringed by the other can withhold his or her own responsibilities. The question of fault is thus a central theme in traditional Islamic law.

This mode of operation may have suited a traditional society with a clear distribution of roles. It is, however, disconnected from the reality of modern Iranian society in the twenty-first century. Woman are more and more literate, have entered the workforce, and provide for themselves and their families.[110] The age of marriage has risen considerably[111] and the choice not to marry has become a real option for many women. The careful balance of the gendered family is under threat and a new young generation is formulating new demands. In particular, when maintenance is shouldered *de facto* by both spouses the grounds for favouring men over women in succession law lose strength. The Iranian legislature chose to address these inconsistencies in an inherently Islamic discourse: rather than opening the floor to a comprehensive re-evaluation of the system of family and succession law in consideration of the changing societal attitudes and realities, it operated on the basis of the traditional roles of man and wife. By strengthening the right of the wife to be compensated for maintenance and other services, it reinforced the idea of men as providers and women as being largely outside any familial financial responsibility and, as such, of marriage essentially as a 'providing institution'. This attitude is also reflected in the formulation of the standard clause in marriage certificates. The wife's entitlement to monetary compensation is conceived of as a sort of compensation for the wife for being arbitrarily divorced and fails to transcend the emerging idea of marriage as an economic partnership to which spouses contribute for it to be financial viable.

The intent of the legislature is certainly praiseworthy as it has attempted to better the immediate financial situation of the wife. The reforms, however, remain framed mostly within the concept of guilt and compensation and are inherently gendered. This direction bears great social risks, as it does not reflect on the new trend that – born out of economic necessity – boosts the idea of marriage as a partnership that the spouses shape together. Whereas young families have come to realize that the given framework no longer provides for adequate answers and that they have to forge a new common frame of reference, the law reinforces the gendered divide between the spouses and inhibits the connection of the law with social changes. What is missing is a vision for a restructuring of family and succession law as a system, a reshaping of ascribed gender roles that would be the logical consequence of the acknowledgement of changing societal attitudes and realities.

Notes

1 Art 1105 CC.
2 Art 1106 CC.
3 Arts 1078–1101 CC.

4 Art 1107 CC as amended on 10 November 2002.

5 Law on the Amendment of Some of the Articles of the Civil Code (arts 1107 and 1110 CC) of 10 November 2002, Official Gazette no 16834 of 11 December 2002.

6 Arts 1111–1112, 1129 CC.

7 Art 1108 CC.

8 Art 1078–1101 CC.

9 Act on the Addition of a Paragraph to Article 1082 Civil Code of 20 July 1997, Official Gazette no 15287 of 25 August 1997 (hereinafter: Inflation Adaption Law).

10 Family Protection Act of 19 February 2013, Official Gazette no 19835 of 11 April 2013.

11 'Erroneous co-habitation' denotes a cohabitation that took place between persons who wrongly believed that they were married. On this concept see Muḥammad Javād Maghniyyih, *Aḥvāl-i Shakhṣiyyih – Al-Fiqh ʿalā al-Madhāhib al-Khamsa* (M Jabbārī and ḤM Sarā'ī tr, Intishārāt-i Qaqnūs 2000) 96–98; *Encyclopaedia of Islamic Law and Jurisprudence*: *Islamic Law and Family* (2010) vol 4, 212–13.

12 Arts 1080, 1083 CC.

13 According to art 1078 CC, anything with a market value that can be owned can be designated as *mahr*, see Sayyid Ḥusayn Ṣafā'ī and Asadullāh Imāmī, *Ḥuqūq-i Khānivādih*, vol 1 (11th edn, Mu'assasih-i Intishārāt va Chāp-i Dānishgāh-i Tihrān 2009) 166–67; Nāṣir Kātūziyān, *Ḥuqūq-i Madanī, Khānivādih*, vol 1 (5th edn, Bahman Burnā 1999) 140.

14 Art 1079 CC; on the determinability of the subject-matter of a contract see Nāṣir Kātūziyān, *Ḥuqūq-i Madanī, Qavāʿid-i ʿUmūmī-i Qarārdādha*, vol 2 (6th edn, Bahman Burnā 2004) 177ff; Sayyid Muṣṭafā Muḥaqqiq Dāmād, *Barrisī-i Fiqhī-i Ḥuqūq-i Khānivādih – Nikāḥ va Inḥilāl-i Ān, Mavādd-i 1034–1157 Qānūn-i Madanī* (12th edn, Markaz-i Nashr-i ʿUlūm-i Islāmī 2005) 219; Sayyid ʿA Ḥā'irī-Shāhbāgh, *Sharḥ-i Qānūn-i Madanī*, vol 2 (Ganj-i Dānish 1997) 959f; Ṣafā'ī and Imāmī, *Ḥuqūq-i Khānivādih* (n 13) 169. The courts have interpreted this rule rather generously. In 2009, for example, the Court of Appeal of Tehran considered the agreement of a *mahr* amounting to an 'apartment in the city of Hamburg' as being adequately determinable by referring to the general rules of contractual interpretation: it held that in the case where the subject of the agreement was not specified in detail, an average value had to be considered. Accordingly, the husband was obliged to provide his wife with an average-sized apartment in an average area in Hamburg, Iranian Court of Cassation of 10 August 2009, file no 24/360 (unpublished, on file with author).

15 Art 1087 CC.

16 Art 1087 CC.

17 Mehrāngīz Kār, 'Mahriyih' (1997) 34 Zanān 50.

18 Art 1091 CC; Sayyid Ḥusayn Ṣafā'ī and Asadullāh Imāmī, *Mukhtaṣar-i Ḥuqūq-i Khānivādih* (28th edn, Nashr-i Mīzān 2011) 169.

19 According to online media a quantity of between 100 and 200 gold coins were designated as proper dower see *Fuẓih Mīrbāqirī*, 'Dar Bārih-i Mahr ul-Misl va Niḥlih' *Jām-i Jam* (26 November 2009) <www.jamejamonline.ir/papertext.aspx?newsnum=100923597105> accessed 1 March 2011.

20 Art 1082 CC.

21 See n 9.

22 The Iranian Central Bank publishes regularly the current inflation rates on <www.cbi.ir/page/4930.aspx> accessed 1 May 2012.

23 Art 4 CC.

24 Ibrāhīm Pūlādī, *Mahriyih va Taᶜdīl-i Ān (Muḥāsibih-i Mahriyih bi Nirkh-i Rūz)* (2nd edn, Nashr-i Dādgustar 2009) 176, points to diverting judgements. The Legal Office of the Ministry of Justice (*Idārih-i Kull-i Umūr-i Ḥuqūqī va Tadvīn-i Qavānīn-i Quvvih-i Qaẓāy*) first denied a retroactive effect of the Act, see statement by the Legal Office of the Ministry of Justice No 1762 of 17 December 1998, quoted in Yadallāh Bāzgīr, *Qānūn-i Madanī dar Ā'īnih-i Ārā-i Dīvān-i ᶜĀlī-i Kishvar – Ḥuqūq-i Khānivādih*, vol 1 (2nd edn, Intishārāt-i Firdawsī 2001) 173; siehe auch Ibrāhīm Gulistānī, 'Tūżīḥī bar Māddih -i Vāḥidih-i Ilḥāq Yik Tabṣirih bi Māddih-i 1082 Qānūn-i Madanī' (2000) 17 Ḥuqūq-i Zanān 59; Ḥasan Ḥamīdiyān, 'Farāz va Nishībhā-i Mahriyih bi Nirkh-i Rūz' in Ḥasan Ḥamīdiyān (ed), *Majmūᶜih-i Maqālāt-i Ḥuqūq-i Khānivādih* (Intishārāt-i Dādgustar 2011) 210, 215.

25 Judgement no 647 of 18 January 2000, file no 26–1378, Official Gazette no 16036 of 12 March 2000, 4.

26 See Gulistānī (2000) 17 Ḥuqūq-i Zanān 59.

27 Nāzanīn Shāhruknī, 'Darbārih-i Taṣvīb-i Ṭarḥ-i Muḥāsibih-i Mahriyih bi Nirkh-i Rūz' (1997) 33 Zanān 60, 61ff; Humā Mihrī, 'Mahr – Dīrūz Imrūz' (1999) 8 Ḥuqūq-i Zanān 12ff; Ḥamīdiyān (n 24) 210ff.

28 The *bahār āzādī* gold coin (BA) is the official gold coin of the Islamic Republic of Iran. It weighs 8.136 g with a purity of 900 per cent <www.bullionweb.de/artikel/gold/pahlavi-azadi.html> accessed 16 July 2015. The price of gold is steadily increasing. In 1985, the rate stood at 350 US-Dollars/ounce (1 ounce equals 31.1 g), one *bahār āzādī* was worth 90 US-Dollars; in 2004, the rate was 400 US-Dollars/ounce (1 *bahār āzādī* being worth 114 US-Dollars) and, in 2009, the price rose to 1,000 US-Dollars/ounce (1 *bahār āzādī* being worth 260 US-Dollars) <www.was-war-wann.de/historische_werte/goldpreise.html> accessed 1 April 2014.

29 Evaluation of interviews conducted with 1,500 men and women (*International Women & Family News Agency (iwna.ir)*, 3 February 2009) <www.iwna.ir/pages/showneews.aspx?newsid=15795> accessed 8 June 2009.

30 Ibid.; Sayyid Vakīlī, 'Increase in Husbands Imprisoned for Failure to Pay the *Mahr*' (*The Bankers*, 7 September 2010) <www.thebankers.ir> accessed 1 March 2011 (in Persian).

31 Rolf Weitowitz, *Wirtschaftstrends kompakt – Iran* (Germany Trade & Invest 2009) 1 <www.heilbronn.ihk.de/ximages/1408495_wirtschaft.pdf> accessed 16 July 2015.

32 One litre of fuel amounted then to 30 cents instead of 7.5 cents.

33 See Sayyid Mahdī Jalālī, 'Naqd va Barrisī-i Mahriyih dar Lāyiḥih-i Ḥimāyat az Khānivādih' (2010) 48 Muṭāliᶜāt-i Rāhburdī-i Zanān 1, 4.

34 Act on the Enforcement of Debts of 1 November 1998, Official Gazette no 15666 of 7 December 1998.

35 See Farjullāh Hidāyat Niyā, 'Arziyābī-i Qāvānīn-i Khānivādih' (2004) 25 Muṭāliᶜāt-i Rāhburdī-i Zanān 1, 9: in half of the evaluated files the husband had been imprisoned on the basis of art 2 of the Act on the Enforcement of Debts.

36 Art 5 para 1 Draft-Law of 28 December 2004, Session no 43 of 28 December 2004 [2004–2005] Muẕākirāt-i Majlis-i Shūrāy-i Islāmī, Annexe to Official Gazette no 17456 of 25 January 2005, 9ff; see also online interview with members of Parliament (*Ensaf*, 4 February 2005) <http://ensaf.blogfa.com/post-61.aspx> accessed 18 January 2011.

37 Art 25 Draft-Law No 36780/68357 of 23 July 2007 <http://rc.majlis.ir/fa/legal_draft/states/720519> accessed 1 May 2012; on this draft law see Arzoo Osanloo, 'What a Focus on "Family" Means in the Islamic Republic of Iran' in Maaike Voorhoeve (ed),

Family Law in Islam – Divorce, Marriage and Women in the Muslim World (Tauris 2012) 51, 52f, 68ff.

38 See online news on iwna.ir: 'The Limitation of the Mahr Has No Effect on the Divorce Rate' (*iwna.ir*, 24 May 2008) <www.iwna.ir/pages/shownews.aspx?newsid=12375>; 'Low Mahrs Do Not Decrease Divorce Rate' (*iwna.ir*, 13 July 2008) <www.iwna.ir/pages/shownews.aspx?newsid=12998>; 'High Mahrs Are a Sign for Mistrust between Spouses' (*iwna.ir*, 7 February 2009) <www.iwna.ir/pages/shownews.aspx?newsid=15866>; see also two interviews with *Ayatollah Ṣāniʿī*: 'Taxation of the Mahr Is Not Permissible as a Tool to Avoid High Mahrs' (*iwna.ir*, 4 August 2008) <www.iwna.ir/pages/shownews.aspx?newsid=13246> and 'The Taxation of the Mahr Is to the Detriment of Women' (*iwna.ir*, 2 September 2008) <www.iwna.ir/pages/shownews.aspx?newsid=13555> all accessed 22 May 2009 (in Persian).

39 *Mehrnews.com*, 13 April 2012 <www.mehrnews.com/fa/newsdetail.aspx?NewsID=1286844> accessed 1 June 2012.

40 See n 10.

41 The FPA 1967 and 1975; Family Protection Act 1967 of 15 June 1967, Official Gazette no 6516 of 4 July 1967, repealed by the Family Protection Act 1975 of 4 February 1975, Official Gazette no 8785 of 3 March 1975. On the FPA 1967 see Gholam-Reza Vatandoust, 'The Status of Iranian Women During the Pahlavi Regime' in A Fathi (ed), *Women and the Family in Iran* (Brill 1985) 107, 114–21; on the FPA 1975, see Nadjma Yassari, 'Iranian Family Law in Theory and Practice' (2002–2003) 9 Yearbook of Islamic and Middle Eastern Law 43, 49–50.

42 Art 15 FPA 1975 allowed the court to nominate the mother as the *valī* of her children, Law on the Abolishment of Articles That Are in Contradiction with the Civil Code in Respect of Guardianship of 7 October 1979, Official Gazette no 10094 of 18 October 1979.

43 Draft-Law No 36780/68357 of 23 July 2007 <http://rc.majlis.ir/fa/legal_draft/states/720519> accessed 1 May 2012.

44 Art 58 FPA 2013.

45 On 1 January 2014 gold rates stood at 1,200 US-Dollars/ounce, one full *bahār āzādī* gold coin was thus worth 314 US-Dollars or 228 Euros <www.was-war-wann.de/historische_werte/goldpreise.html> accessed 1 May 2012.

46 Marie-Claude Najm, '*Cour de cassation, première chambre civile, 22 novembre 2005, n° 03–14.961*' (2006) 4 Journal du Droit International 1366 (note); Kalthoum Meziou, 'Le régime de la communauté des biens entre époux' in Mohamed Charfi (ed), *Mélanges en l'honneur de Mohamed Charfi* (Centre de Publication Universitaire Tunis 2001) 439; G-H Bousquet, *Précis de Droit Musulman principalement mâlékite et algérien* (2nd edn, La Maison des Livres 1950) 123: '[L]a théorie des régimes matrimoniaux n'existe pas en droit musulman.' On matrimonial regimes in Muslim jurisdictions see Sait in this volume.

47 Cf Ayatollah Morteza Motahari, *Stellung der Frau im Islam* (Iranian Embassy 1982) 70f; Morteza Hosseini-Téhérani, *Le statut de la femme mariée en droit shyite* (Loviton 1935) 152.

48 See Sami A Aldeeb Abu-Sahlieh, 'Les régimes matrimoniaux en droit arabe et musulman' in Andrea Bonomi and M Steiner (ed), *Les régimes matrimoniaux en droit comparé et en droit international privé* (Librairie Droz 2006) 279, 282; Lotfi Chedly, 'Les relations pécuniaires entre époux – Cinquante ans après l'entrée en vigueur du Code du statut personnel tunisien' (2007) 59 Revue internationale de droit comparé 551, 576; A-M Amirian, *Le Mouvement législatif en Iran „Perse" et le Mariage en*

droit & en fait: sa réforme (2nd edn, Librairie générale de droit & de jurisprudence 1938) 35.

49 See Amirian (n 48) 34: 'L'institution des régimes matrimoniaux est étrangère à la Législation iranienne'; similarly Tannaz Jourabchi Esmailzadeh, *Mariage permanent et Mariage temporaire – Etude comparative du mariage en droit iranien et en droit suisse* (Schulthess 2010) 192.

50 Nāṣir Kātūziyān, *Ḥuqūq-i Madanī, Amvāl va Mālikiyat* (21st edn, Nashr-i Mizān 2008) 209. If the distribution cannot be made in accordance with this principle, co-ownership is assumed.

51 Sayyid Mahdī Mīrdādāshī, *Shurūṭ-i Żimn-i ᶜAqd-i Izdivāj* (Intishārāt-i Jangal 2011–2012) 97–100.

52 See on the contractual divorce grounds in the Iranian marriage certificate Humā Mihrī, 'Sharṭ-i Żimn-i ᶜAqd-i Izdivāj – Mufīd amā Nākāfī' (2000) 14 Ḥuqūq-i Zanān 6–7, 41.

53 Amirian (n 48) 36.

54 For an English translation of these clauses see Jürgen Basedow and Nadjma Yassari (eds), *Iranian Family and Succession Laws and their Application in German Courts* (Mohr Siebeck 2004) 173–75.

55 See Ali Reda Bariklou, 'The Wife's Right of Divorce on the Basis of the Delegation Condition under Islamic and Iranian Law' (2011) 25 International Journal of Law, Policy and the Family 184, 187.

56 See ᶜAbbās Jaᶜfarī Dawlat Ābādī, 'Barrisī-i Ḥuqūq-i Mālī-i Zawjih dar Mavārid-i Ṣudūr-i Ḥukm-i Ṭalāq bi Darhāst-i Zawj' <http://hbadvi.farsedu.ir/portal/show.aspx?page=10748> accessed 11 May 2011.

57 Statement by the Legal Office of the Ministry of Justice no 7/1271 of 23 May 2005 <http://www.moi.ir> accessed 13 July 2012.

58 Javād Ḥabībī Tabār, *Gām bi Jam bā Ḥuqūq-i Khānivādih* (3rd edn, Nashr-i Gām bi Gām 2007) 269; see also the statement of the Ministry of Interior, Office of Women's Affairs, 'Shurūṭ-i Band-i Alif-i Sanad-i Izdivāj Āmil-i Chih Mabāḥisī Ast?' <http://www.moi.ir/Portal/Home/ShowPage.aspx?Object=Faq&CategoryID=aabeeff6-1bb1-45ca-93e3-8a8da02822ef&LayoutID=db38baa2-c527-4f2f-8927-5dffe0413f20&ID=0a6a8e00-f40d-4a99-9698-c0eebf6074f7> accessed 13 July 2012.

59 M Rizāy, 'Irtibāt-i Ujrat ul-Misl va Sharṭ-i Tanṣīf-i Dārāyī' *Rūznāmih-i Mardum-i Sālārī* (Tehran, 17 August 2008).

60 Ḥabībī Tabār (n 58) 269.

61 On the difficulties of persuading the husband to sign the clause see Mehrangiz Kar and Homa Hoodfar, 'Personal Status Law as Defined by the Islamic Republic of Iran: An Appraisal' (1996) 1 Women Living Under Muslim Laws (Special Dossier) 7, 15f.

62 Z Fihristī and M Chāvshīhā, 'Shurūṭ-i Mundarij dar Sanad-i Izdivāj' (2008) 17 Faṣlnāmih-i Bānūvān-i Shīᶜih 109, 110.

63 E.g. Egypt (art 18bis Decree-Law No 25 of 1929 Regarding Certain Personal Status Provisions of 10 March 1929, Official Gazette no 27 of 25 March 1929); Algeria (art 52 Law No 11 of 1984 on the Family Code of 9 June 1984, Official Gazette no 24 of 12 June 1984 as amended by Law No 2 of 27 February 2005, Official Gazette no 15 of 27 February 2005); Morocco (art 84 Law No 70.03 of 2004 on the Family Code (Mudawwana) of 3 February 2004, Official Gazette no 5184 of 5 February 2004); Tunisia (art 31 Personal Status Law of 13 August 1956, Official Gazette no 66 of 17 August 1956); Libya (art 51 Law No 10 of 1984 on Personal Status of 19 April 1984, Official Gazette no 16 of 3 June 1984); Oman (art 91 Law No 32 of 1997 on Personal Status of 4 June 1997, Official Gazette no 601 of 15 June 1997); Jordan

(art 155 Law No 36 of 2010 on Personal Status of 26 September 2010, Official Gazette no 5061 of 17 October 2010); Kuwait (art 165 Law No 51 of 1984 on Personal Status of 7 July 1984, Official Gazette no 1570 of 23 July 1984); UAE (art 140 Federal Law No 28 of 2005 on Personal Status of 19 November 2005, Official Gazette no 439 of 30 November 2005); Bahrain (art 52(d) Law No 19 of 2009 on the Family Code (pt 1) of 27 May 2009, Official Gazette no 2898 of 4 June 2009); Iraq (art 39 para 3 Law No 188 of 1959 on Personal Status of 19 December 1959, Official Gazette no 280 of 30 December 1959); Syria (art 117 Law No 59 of 1953 on Personal Status of 17 September 1953, Official Gazette no 63 of 8 October 1953) and Qatar (art 115 Law No 22 of 2006 on the Family Code of 29 June 2006, Official Gazette no 8 of 28 August 2006).

64 Such a claim was only foreseen in adversary proceedings. If the marriage was dissolved by consensual divorce under one of the schemes of *khulʿ* or *mubārāt* (art 1146, 1147 CC), art 11 FPA 1975 did not apply, see Ṣafā'ī and Imāmī, *Ḥuqūq-i Khānivādih* (n 13) 300.

65 See Ṣafā'ī and Emāmī, *Ḥuqūq-i Khānivādih* (n 13) 301.

66 Kātūziyān, *Ḥuqūq-i Madanī, Khānivādih* (n 13) 476.

67 Ibid. 478, 488.

68 Ibid. 486.

69 Ṣafā'ī and Imāmī, *Ḥuqūq-i Khānivādih* (n 13) 302.

70 See Farīdih Shukrī, 'Muqarrarī-i Māhānih va Jāyigāh-i Ān dar Niẓām-i Ḥuqūqī-i Īrān' (2010) 51 Faṣlnāmih-i Fiqh va Ḥuqūq-i Khānivādih 1, 3.

71 See also Ziba Mir-Hosseini, *Marriage on Trial – A Study of Islamic Family Law* (2nd edn, Tauris 2000) 74f.

72 Act on the Reform of Divorce of 19 November 1992, Official Gazette No 13914 of 10 December 1992 (hereinafter: Divorce Act). This Act was repealed in 2013, the claim to *ujrat ul-mis̱l* was reiterated in art 29 FPA 2013.

73 Art 1 para 6(a) Divorce Act.

74 Next to *ujrat ul-mis̱l* the Divorce Act also introduced an institution called *niḥlih* (art 1 para 6(b) Divorce Act), which could be claimed for whenever the conditions for a claim to *ujrat ul-mis̱l* were not met. The amount of *niḥlih* was to be determined by the courts with due consideration of the duration of marriage, the works undertaken, and the financial possibilities of the husband, see Ḥabībī Tabār (n 58) 249. Although the Divorce Act has been repealed by the FPA 2013, the legal ground for *niḥlih* was exempted: the Divorce Act is repealed with the exception of art 1 note 6(b) of the Divorce Act (art 58 FPA 2013).

75 Ghulāmriżā Ṣadīq Ūriʿī, *Tamkīn-i Bānū – Riyāsat-i Shūhar* (Shurāy-i Farhangī – Ijtimāʿī-i Zanān 2001) 57; Ḥabībī Tabār (n 58) 248.

76 Ṣafā'ī and Imāmī, *Ḥuqūq-i Khānivādih* (n 13) 146; ṣadīq Ūriʿī (n 75) 47.

77 Art 1114 CC.

78 Art 1117 CC.

79 Ṣadīq Ūriʿī (n 75) 47; Ghulāmriżā Muvaḥidiyān, *Ḥuqūq va Ravābiṭ-i Mālī-i Zawjayn* (3rd edn, Mu'assasih-i Farhangī Intishārātī-i Nigāh-i Bīnih 2009) 76–77; MA Ansari-Pour, 'Remuneration for Work Done by a Wife under Islamic and Iranian Law' (2001–2002) 8 Yearbook of Islamic and Middle Eastern Law 108, 110f.

80 Art 1176 CC; see also SN Ebrahimi, 'Child Custody (*Hizanat*) under Iranian Law: An Analytical Discussion' (2005–2006) 39 Family Law Quarterly 459, 468 fn 51.

81 Ansari-Pour (2001–2002) 8 Yearbook of Islamic and Middle Eastern Law 111; Nadjma Yassari, 'Who is a child? Consideration of tradition and modernity in Iranian

Child Law' in Susan Rutten (ed), *Recht van de Islam 22. Teksten van het op 18 juni 2004 te Leiden gehouden tweeentwintigste RIMO-symposium*, vol 22 (Rimo 2005) 17, 22ff.

82 Ḥabībī Tabār (n 58) 249; Nadjma Yassari, 'Überblick über das iranische Scheidungsrecht' [2002] Zeitschrift für das gesamte Familienrecht 1088, 1094.

83 This condition has been strongly criticized by academic literature, see Manīzhih Dānāy ᶜAlamī, 'Naqdī bar Qānūn-i Iṣlāḥ-i Muqarrarāt-i Marbūṭ bi Ṭalāq Kānūn-i Vukalā' (1993–1994) 6–8 Kānūn-i Vukalā 437, 443f; Hidāyat Niyā (2004) 25 Muṭāliᶜāt-i Rāhburdī-i Zanān 14ff.

84 Muvaḥidiyān (n 79) 75.

85 See e.g. Muvaḥidiyān (n 79) 74, who states that the standard clause in the marriage certificate eliminates the right to *ujrat ul-mis̱l*; for a dissenting view see Ansari-Pour (2001–2002) 8 Yearbook of Islamic and Middle Eastern Law 113, who differentiates between the rational of these agreements and claims that only an agreement that explicitly relates to compensation for household work can displace the legal claim to *ujrat ul-mis̱l*, whereas the clause related to the right of the wife to the marital assets has a different basis.

86 Ṣafā'ī and Imāmī (n 13) 150.

87 Court of First Instance Qom, Dept 5, judgement of 4 September 1999, file no 956; Court of First Instance Qom, Dept 5, judgement of 5 November 2000, file no 1712–1711; Court of Appeal of Qom, judgement of 2 January 2002, file no 111286, all quoted in Hidāyat Niyā (2004) 25 Muṭāliᶜāt-i Rāhburdī-i Zanān 15.

88 Draft-Law in View of the Amendment of Article 948 CC of 27 August 2001, registration no 320, <www.dadkhahi.net/modules.php?name=News&file=print&sid=439> accessed 26 March 2009.

89 Statement of the Expediency Council of 13 January 2007, Official Gazette no 18049 of 13 February 2007.

90 Act on the Addition of a Paragraph to Article 336 CC of 13 January 2007, Official Gazette no 18049 of 13 February 2007.

91 See also statement by the Legal Office of the Ministry of Justice no 7/3335 of 12 August 2007, in Riyāsat-i Jumhūrī (ed), *Majmūᶜih-i Qānūn-i Madanī* (8th edn, Muᶜāvinat-i Tadvīn-i Tanqīḥ va Intishārāt-i Qavānīn va Muqarrarāt 2011) 130; statement by the Legal Office of the Ministry of Justice no 7/3622 of 2 September 2008, in Riyāsat-i Jumhūrī (ed), *Majmūᶜih-i Qānūn-i Madanī* (8th edn, Muᶜāvinat-i Tadvīn-i Tanqīḥ va Intishārāt-i Qavānīn va Muqarrarāt 2011) 131.

92 See Decision of the Court of Appeal of Tehran of 21 June 2003, file no 517/31/3/82, in Muḥammad Riżā Zandī (ed), *Ujrat ul-mis̱l – Khisārat, Raviyih-i Qażāyī dādgāhhāy-i Badavī va Tajdīdnaẓar-i Ustān Tihrān dar Umūr-i Madanī* (Intishārāt-i Jangal 2012) 13–14.

93 With the exception of art 1 para 6(b) Divorce Act.

94 See Maryam Aḥmadiyih, 'Ujrat ul-Mis̱l az Nigāhī Dīgar' (1998) 6 Ḥuqūq-i Zanān 12f.

95 Hidāyat Niyā (2004) 25 Muṭāliᶜāt-i Rāhburdī-i Zanān 14; Aḥmadiyih (1998) 6 Ḥuqūq-i Zanān 12.

96 Ch 4, art 24–39 FPA 2013.

97 Parliamentary debates, Session no 231 of 5 September 2010 [2010–2011] Muẕākirāt-i Majlis-i Shūrāy-i Islāmī, Annexe to Official Gazette no 19092, 2, 9.

98 Art 896 CC.

99 Art 861 CC.

100 Art 846 CC.

101 In particular, the hadiths compiled by the Shiite scholar Sheikh al-Hurr al-^{c}Āmilī (died 1693 AD).

102 For a comprehensive overview, see Nadjma Yassari, 'Die iranische Reform des Ehegattenerbrechts – Ein Beispiel für die Wandelbarkeit des islamischen Rechts' (2009) 73 Rabel Journal of Comparative and International Private Law 985–1004.

103 See Afsānih Zamānī-Jibārī, 'Irs̱-i Zan az Dārāyī-i Shūhar' (1999) 11 Ḥuqūq-i Zanān 18.

104 Former art 947 CC: 'The wife inherits the value of the buildings and trees, and not their corpus; it shall be presumed that the buildings and trees are entitled to remain on the land free of charge.'

105 For a discussion of these issues, see Ḥusayn Mihrpūr, *Barrisī-i Mīrās̱-i Zawjih dar Ḥuqūq-i Islām va Īrān* (Intishārāt-i Iṭṭilā^{c}āt 1997).

106 For a detailed discussion, see Zamānī-Jibārī (1999) 11 Ḥuqūq-i Zanān 18.

107 See the Parliamentary debates related to the promulgation of the amendments of arts 946, 947, and 948 CC, Session no 60 of 25 January 2009 [2008–2009] Muẕākirāt-i Majlis-i Shūrāy-i Islāmī, Annexe to Official Gazette no 18623, 3–4.

108 Official Gazette no 18651 of 11 March 2009.

109 Art 942 CC.

110 See Mahdi Majbouri, 'Female Labor Force Participation in Iran: A Structural Analysis' (2015) 11 Review of Middle East Economics and Finance 1–23, who shows that in the last three decades, women's education levels in Iran have consistently increased while fertility rates have fallen rapidly; see also Ida A Mirzaie, 'Females' Labor Force Participation and Job Opportunities in the Middle East' < www.aeaweb.org/aea/2015conference/program/retrieve.php?pdfid=847> accessed 1 July 2015.

111 According to statistics, in 2005 the average age for the first marriage in Iran was between 22–29 years for women and 27–34 years for men, Iranian Parliament, Protocol of Session no 43 of 28 December 2004 [2004–2005] Muẕākirāt-i Majlis-i Shūrāy-i Islāmī, Annexe to Official Gazette no 17456 of 25 January 2005, 9, 10.

Part III

Judiciary

7 Les pouvoirs du juge tunisien en droit de la famille (The powers of the Tunisian judge in family law)

Salma Abida

English summary

In Tunisia, personal status law was historically divided along confessional lines. Muslim and Jewish Tunisians were subject to their respective religious laws, and matters of personal status were adjudicated by religious tribunals. Yet with the realization of national independence in 1956, there came a will to codify, unify, and modernize this field of law. Consequently, the religious tribunals were abolished and the judiciary unified. All Tunisians were subjected to one universal personal status law, as codified in the Code of Personal Status (CPS). The CPS represented a revolution in Arab and Islamic countries. It espoused an approach founded on the promotion of gender equality and the protection of the child. For instance, polygamy was abolished and subject to penal sanction. Divorce, through a judge, became the only legal manner in which to terminate a marital relationship. Moreover, a minimum age of marriage was set. And, no less importantly, this modernist approach did not come to a halt with the promulgation of the CPS; instead, it continued in subsequent amendments, such as the 1993 amendment that abolished the duty of the wife to obey her husband and introduced equal partnership between spouses as a founding principle of the Tunisian family.

Although the legislative texts are liberal and modernist, their actual impact depends on their application by the courts. In fact, the legislature has given judges an important role in the field of personal status. It has intentionally kept significant provisions of the law ambiguous, leaving ample room for judicial discretion.

This article looks into the practice of Tunisian judges as to their attitudes towards implementing the CPS. The basic question is whether Tunisian judges have followed the spirit of gender equality and freedom in their interpretation of the law, or whether they have chosen a more conservative approach. The examination of the case law produced during the 60 years since the promulgation of the CPS shows that the position of the courts has fluctuated between a liberal and modernist approach on the one hand and a conservative and traditional approach on the other.

Conservative and traditionalist judges have adopted Islamic law as their main frame of reference when interpreting vague provisions of law and when deciding how to use their discretionary power. Thus, courts have referred to Islamic law to interpret and clarify the provisions in the CPS. For example, according to Islamic law a difference in religion is an impediment to both marriage and succession. Such a difference, however, is not expressly mentioned in the relevant Tunisian legal provisions as a barrier to either matrimony or inheritance (CPS articles 5, 14, and 88). In 1966 the Court of Cassation decided the famous case of Hourya, and for the next 20 years Tunisian courts consistently followed this ruling. In that decision, the Court of Cassation held that as Islamic law was the exclusive source of the CPS, unclear provisions of the Code must be interpreted in accordance with Islamic tenets. As a consequence, the courts have considered a difference in religion to be an impediment to both marriage and succession. In evaluating the concerned persons' commitment to Islam, lower tribunals have subsequently fluctuated between strictness and leniency. With respect to paternity, Tunisian case law established (in accordance with Islamic law) that legitimate paternity requires the existence of a marriage, even if the marriage turns out to be invalid. If the child is born out of wedlock, an acknowledgement of paternity alone is not enough to establish filiation.

Interestingly, in the field of child law, the legislature has endowed judges with significant discretionary power. As such, the legislature has departed from traditional Islamic law by giving judges discretion in the granting of custody and the concretization of the child's best interests. Many judges have chosen a religious-based approach in determining the best interests of the child. Thus, in many decisions, judges have stated that the best interests of a child born to a Muslim father (and thus a Muslim child) dictate that he or she grow up in a Muslim and Arab milieu. In the same vein, Tunisian judges have refused to recognize foreign decisions granting custody of a Muslim child to a non-Muslim mother. They have argued that the protection of the Arab and Muslim identity is an element of Tunisian public policy.

This conservative approach can also be found in the context of adoption. Contrary to the laws of almost all Islamic countries, the Tunisian legislature allowed and regulated adoption in 1959. The legislature did not provide that, as a condition of adoption, the adopting parents be Muslim. Nevertheless, Tunisian case law has generally emphasized that parents adopting a Tunisian Muslim child must be Muslim because this is in the child's best interests.

Finally, Tunisian judges also have discretionary power to evaluate the allegation of harm on which a claim for divorce relies. For instance, courts have considered that the conversion of an initially Muslim husband to Christianity represents apostasy and thus a harm to the wife. They have also held, in line with traditional Islamic law, that cohabitation is a duty whose infringement justifies divorce on the grounds of harm.

Since the end of the 1980s, Tunisian case law has shown a tendency to detach itself from religious arguments and instead have recourse to fundamental rights. Accordingly, a difference in religion has no longer been considered an impediment to marriage or succession. In addition, courts have, more recently, also interpreted the concept of the best interests of the child consistent with fundamental rights.

In the last two or so decades courts have emphasized that Tunisian law does not contain any provision according to which religion constitutes an impediment to marriage or succession. Rather, these judges have relied on fundamental rights, such as freedom of religion and the principle of equality as enshrined in the Tunisian Constitution and in the international conventions ratified by Tunisia. More specifically, modernist judges have invoked the New York Convention on Consent to Marriage, Minimum Age for Marriage and Registration of Marriages (December 1962). In some cases, even the Court of Cassation has followed this approach. Moreover, in this open-minded vein, Tunisian judges have concretized the best interests of the child without any reference to Islamic law in a number of decisions concerning paternity. These cases have seen courts ground their decisions exclusively on statutory law, interpreted in the light of the UN Convention on the Rights of the Child (November 1989). In accord with this approach, judges have, contrary to earlier rulings, concluded that the filiation of a child can be established, even in the absence of a marriage between the parents, based solely on the acknowledgement of the father. They have also argued that it could be in the best interests of the child to remain with his or her mother, even where the latter is a non-Muslim. In an adoption-related decision, the court accepted the adoption of a Tunisian child by an American couple without requiring a certificate of conversion to Islam.

The trend towards liberalism is, however, not constant. The dominant case law remains traditionalist and conservative with vague provisions of the CPS often being interpreted by reference to Islamic law. Not surprisingly, Tunisian society is itself divided on the nature of the Tunisian family. There is no general consensus as to whether the family should be founded on principles of freedom and equality or whether it should enforce traditional family roles as formulated by religious patterns. For the sake of legal certainty, it is recommended that the legislature intervene and provide for clear solutions, guided by the spirit of modernism that initially inspired the enactment of the CPS. For this effort it remains essential that judges be given the opportunity to (i) become more acquainted with international fundamental rights standards and (ii) specialize in the adjudication of personal status matter more stringently.

Introduction

La matière de statut personnel était longtemps en Tunisie « le domaine privilégié des droits non codifiés d'origine religieuse ».[1] En effet, jusqu'à la veille de l'indépendance, et compte tenu des différentes confessions des citoyens tunisiens à l'époque, le droit applicable en matière de statut personnel était caractérisé par la diversité de ses sources faisant qu' « à chacun sa religion, à chacun son droit ».[2] Ce pluralisme législatif avait ses répercussions sur le système juridictionnel, étant donné qu'une pluralité de juridictions était compétente en matière de statut personnel. La grande majorité des tunisiens était musulmane et ses litiges relevaient des tribunaux charaïques qui appliquaient le droit musulman.[3] Les différends qui opposaient les Tunisiens israélites relevaient de la compétence des tribunaux rabbiniques et étaient soumis à la loi mosaïque. Les tribunaux français implantés en Tunisie étaient habilités à trancher les litiges lorsqu'au moins l'une des parties au litige n'est pas de nationalité tunisienne et appliquaient quant à elles le droit français.

A l'indépendance, les premiers piliers de la modernisation de la société et de l'émancipation de la femme ont été mis en place grâce à la promulgation du Code du statut personnel (CSP) le 13 août 1956,[4] considéré par la doctrine comme étant « un monument législatif »,[5] « un modèle de progrès social »,[6] voire « la constitution civile des tunisiens ».[7] Les choix mis en œuvre lors de l'élaboration de ce Code étaient bien clairs et bien précis, à savoir l'unification, la codification et la modernisation du droit de la famille. La codification s'est réalisée par l'adoption d'un Code unique du statut personnel le 13 août 1956. Ce Code assurait l'unification du droit familial puisqu'il régissait le statut personnel et familial de tous les Tunisiens quelles que soient leur croyance et leur confession. Ce Code « a mis fin au pluralisme, a pris acte de l'appartenance nationale en faisant prévaloir la nationalité sur la confession ».[8] Cette unification du droit fondamental du statut personnel s'est accompagnée d'une unification de la justice. Les juridictions religieuses ont été supprimées.[9]

Un seul ordre judiciaire est depuis compétent pour connaître des litiges du statut personnel pour tous les citoyens. La chambre civile du statut personnel auprès du tribunal de première instance a une compétence de principe en la matière et le juge cantonal est exclusivement compétent pour connaître des actions relatives aux pensions alimentaires et à l'adoption.[10] La justice tunisienne a ainsi achevé sa mutation. Tous les Tunisiens sont désormais justiciables des mêmes juridictions et le droit applicable est le même pour tous.

L'unification du statut personnel s'est suivie d'une modernisation de la matière. En effet, le législateur tunisien ne s'est pas contenté seulement de la codification, mais il a agi également sur le contenu du droit, et ce dans le but de « faire évoluer la société et de transformer en profondeur les structures familiales ».[11] Le Code du statut personnel a été toujours qualifié comme étant révolutionnaire et avant-gardiste dans la sphère des législations gouvernant le droit de la famille dans les pays arabo-musulmans. Adoptant un contenu moderne en la matière, ce Code a consacré une approche fondée essentiellement sur la promotion de l'égalité homme-femme et la protection de l'enfant. Ainsi, et depuis 1956, la législation tunisienne a interdit la polygamie et en a fait une infraction pénale (art 18 du CSP). Elle a fixé un âge minimum pour le mariage tout en imposant la vérification du consentement des futurs époux lors de la célébration du mariage. Elle a abolit la répudiation. Elle a attribué à la mère, en cas du décès du père, le droit de tutelle sur les enfants mineurs et a imposé le mariage authentique (art 4 du CSP) et le divorce judiciaire comme l'unique procédure de dissolution du lien conjugal valablement formé entre les époux vivants (art 30 du CSP).

Depuis, « le législateur n'a cessé d'aller de l'avant ».[12] Le Code du statut personnel a connu entre 1958 et 2010, douze amendements dont le plus important est celui du 12 juillet 1993[13] qui a introduit le principe du partenariat et de la coresponsabilité parentale au sein de la famille tout en supprimant le devoir d'obéissance de la femme envers son époux.[14] Plusieurs textes matériellement extérieurs au Code l'ont aussi complété. Il en est ainsi de la loi n° 57–3 du 1 août 1957 relative à l'état civil et à la forme du mariage;[15] de la loi n° 58–27 du 4 mai 1958 relative à l'adoption ou encore la loi du 28 octobre 1998 relative à l'attribution d'un nom patronymique aux enfants abandonnés ou de filiation inconnue[16] et la loi n° 91 du 9 novembre 1998 relative à la communauté des biens entre époux.[17]

Toutefois, aussi révolutionnaire qu'elle puisse paraître, la refonte du droit du statut personnel ne saurait à elle seule atteindre les objectifs visés et réaliser les résultats escomptés, à savoir la construction d'un Etat moderne qui rompt avec un modèle traditionnel de société, si l'œuvre législative n'est pas complétée par l'œuvre prétorienne. En effet, « appelé à interpréter les normes textuelles du Code du statut personnel, à combler ses lacunes ou encore à adapter ses standards juridiques au gré des espèces »,[18] le juge devait avoir un rôle essentiel pour préciser et amplifier la volonté du législateur. Ainsi, la détermination des contours définitifs de la règle législative dépendra dans une large mesure de son appréhension par le juge.

En matière de statut personnel beaucoup plus que dans autres matières, le législateur comptait sur le rôle du juge dans l'approfondissement des réformes déjà entreprises. En fait, et « pour bien ménager les transitions et à fin d'éviter de heurter le front traditionnaliste de l'opinion publique »,[19] le législateur de 1956 est resté muet sur certaines questions capitales comme celle de savoir si la disparité de culte constituait un empêchement à mariage et successibilité, ou celle de savoir si l'adoption d'un enfant tunisien par un étranger était possible etc. Le mutisme du texte a été considéré par la doctrine comme étant un choix délibéré du législateur qui, pour ne pas fermer la porte à d'autres réformes,

> a adopté des textes ambigus ou gardé des silences révélateurs pour permettre à la jurisprudence de compléter plus tard la réforme législative par des interprétations adéquates. Il a presque cultivé l'art du silence ou de l'ambiguïté dans l'espoir que la loi ayant fait l'essentiel, les juges seront à la hauteur pour achever son œuvre.[20]

Le juge tunisien a-t-il été à la hauteur de l'attente du législateur? Dans sa mise en œuvre des textes du statut personnel, le juge tunisien a-t-il choisi la voix de l'innovation et de la réforme déjà entreprise par le législateur? Ou a-t-il, au contraire, cherché à la contrecarrer en adoptant des solutions traditionnelles qui rompent avec l'esprit innovateur du texte et neutralisent la volonté de changement voulu par ses rédacteurs?

L'examen de la pratique judiciaire tunisienne, après plus de 50 ans d'application du Code du statut personnel, révèle un flottement au niveau des positions des juridictions entre un flux de modernisme qui se tourne vers les droits fondamentaux pour interpréter les dispositions dudit Code et un reflux de conservatisme qui cherche l'éclairage, en cas d'ambiguïté ou de silence du texte, par référence au droit musulman.

Le reflux du conservatisme: la référence systématique au droit musulman

En dépit de son contenu révolutionnaire, le Code du statut personnel « demeure laconique et lacunaire sur certains points, ambigu sur d'autres et présente certaines incohérences ».[21] Ainsi, et lorsque « la puissance normative du droit écrit s'affaiblit, le juge est appelé à intervenir pour en déterminer le sens, en combler les lacunes ou encore l'adapter aux besoins de la situation concrète qui lui est soumise ».[22]

Certaines juridictions tunisiennes puisent l'éclairage des dispositions floues ou des notions à contenu variable par référence aux prescriptions du droit musulman. L'examen de la pratique judiciaire révèle une nette propension des juridictions du fond et de la Cour régulatrice à recourir à un référentiel traditionnel qui comprend « non seulement l'ensemble des règles et principes du droit musulman, mais également les valeurs de l'Islam que les juges n'hésitent pas à mettre au premier plan pour expliquer et justifier leurs solutions ».[23] Ce recours est doublement paradoxal. D'une part, et contrairement à d'autres législations arabes comparées,[24] le Code du statut personnel se caractérise par une totale absence de référence expresse au droit musulman en tant que source formelle du droit en matière de statut personnel. D'autre part, les règles générales d'interprétation prévues par le Code des obligations et des contrats[25] en réfèrent exclusivement, après la loi, à l'analogie et aux principes généraux de droit et ne se réfèrent point au droit musulman ou à ses principes en tant que source de droit. Le recours au référentiel traditionnel a largement influencé l'exercice des pouvoirs du juge en droit de la famille aussi bien son pouvoir discrétionnaire que son pouvoir d'interprétation.

Le pouvoir d'interprétation et le référentiel traditionnel

L'appel au référentiel traditionnel a été la démarche entreprise par le juge tunisien en vue d'interpréter le sens ambigu d'une disposition textuelle ou encore en vue d'en combler les lacunes. Les exemples en la matière sont abondants. La disparité de culte ainsi que l'établissement de la filiation sont parmi les exemples les plus expressifs et les plus révélateurs du recours inconditionnel et systématique du juge aux prescriptions du droit musulman.

La disparité de culte

Il est incontestable que selon le droit musulman, la disparité de culte est considérée, dans certains cas, comme cause d'empêchement à mariage, et dans tous les cas comme cause d'indignité successorale.[26] La disparité de culte doit-elle être considérée de même, comme un empêchement à mariage et comme une cause d'indignité successorale, en droit positif tunisien? L'ambiguïté des textes qui régissent la matière, à savoir les articles 5 et 88 du CSP qui traitent, respectivement, des cas d'empêchement à mariage et des cas d'interdiction a successibilité, a suscité une large controverse au niveau de la jurisprudence.

Dans sa version française, l'article 5 du CSP prévoit que « les deux futurs époux ne doivent pas se trouver dans l'un des cas d'empêchements prévus par la loi ». Le texte arabe qui seul fait foi[27] emploie les termes « empêchement charaïques (*mawāni^c shar^ciyya*) ». Le sort de la question est tributaire alors du sens du terme charaïque employé par le législateur. S'il vise la loi, l'interdiction n'existe pas. S'il renvoie aux empêchements prévus par la *sharī^ca* (le droit musulman), « alors la prohibition reprend ses droits ».[28] Quant à l'article 88 du même Code, tel que libellé en français, il édicte expressément que « l'homicide volontaire constitue un empêchement à la successibilité ». En revanche, la rédaction arabe de cet article est très polysémique. L'homicide volontaire semble y être inscrit comme « une des causes d'empêchements à successibilité ». Le texte arabe débute par le terme « *min* » qui signifie « parmi ». L'homicide volontaire a donc été interprété comme n'étant qu'une hypothèse d'empêchement successoral et qu'il fallait d'autant plus compléter le texte par référence au droit musulman surtout que la matière successorale est supposée être reprise dans sa quasi-intégralité du droit musulman. Formulation lapidaire de l'article 88 du CSP, « elle permet le retour du refoulé, le droit musulman, et sa règle sur la disparité confessionnelle comme cause d'empêchement à successibilité ».[29]

Ainsi, depuis 1966, la Cour de cassation dans un arrêt de principe, arrêt *Houria,*[30] a considéré qu'en employant le mot « parmi », la liste des causes d'indignité successorale contenue dans l'article 88 du CSP n'est pas limitative mais simplement indicative. La formule employée par ce texte suggère de compléter la liste des indignités successorales par référence au *droit musulman, lequel droit constitue, au regard de la Cour Suprême, la source exclusive du code du statut personnel.* La Cour en conclut que, dès lors qu'elle est comptée parmi les causes d'interdiction à la successibilité en droit musulman, l'apostasie, doit inéluctablement, être comprise dans la liste de l'article 88 susvisé. Toutefois, le mariage de la dame ne saurait, à lui seul, présumer de son apostasie et qu'il convient d'apporter la preuve que l'épouse s'est convertie à la religion de son époux non musulman. Par ailleurs, et étant donné que la question de la disparité de culte comme étant un empêchement à mariage se pose de façon indirecte à propos d'affaires successorales, la Cour de cassation a considéré dans l'affaire *Houria* que le mariage de la musulmane avec un non-musulman est l'un *des pêchés les plus graves au regard de la loi musulmane* qui entache le dit mariage *d'une nullité absolue*. Il est à remarquer à cet égard, que si la succession s'est ouverte après la promulgation du Code du statut personnel, le mariage en question a eu lieu bien avant. La Cour n'a pas déclaré nul un tel mariage par application de l'article 5 du CSP mais seulement par référence au droit musulman.

Cette position de la Cour de cassation va faire une jurisprudence constante pendant plus que vingt ans. Dans l'arrêt *Louise CHARLOTTE,*[31] la Cour déclare avec fermeté, « manifestement non sérieux le moyen invoqué par les auteurs du pourvoi et tiré de ce que la disparité de culte ne doit pas être considérée, en droit Tunisien, comme une cause d'interdiction à la successibilité par cela seul qu'elle n'a pas été explicitement prévue par l'article 88 du CSP et formellement incluse dans la liste des causes d'indignités successorales qu'il contient ».

Les juges du fond et ceux de la Cour suprême estiment que les articles 5 et 88 du CSP renvoient aux empêchements de la *sharīʿa*, ont maintenu, dans plusieurs décisions, la disparité de culte comme étant un empêchement à mariage et à successibilité. Il en est ainsi, tout d'abord de l'arrêt de la Cour de cassation en date du 8 juin 2006[32] qui a affirmé que la liberté de religion consacrée par l'article 5 de la constitution tunisienne ne saurait être considérée comme écartant la disparité de culte en tant que cause d'indignité successorale et que cette position ne porte pas atteinte au principe de l'égalité devant la justice. Il s'agit ensuite de l'arrêt de la Cour de cassation en date du 16 janvier 2007[33] qui a confirmé d'une manière non équivoque que

> la disparité de culte est l'une des causes d'indignité successorale et qu'il n'y a point de succession entre communauté différente et ce conformément aux dispositions de l'article 88 du CSP et à la position constante de la doctrine et de la jurisprudence.

Enfin, l'arrêt de la Cour de cassation rendu le 30 juin 2009[34] est revenu à une interprétation extensive de l'article 88 du CSP et y trouve de nouveau une référence religieuse.

Il y a lieu de citer comme étant un exemple significatif de la jurisprudence conservatrice, un arrêt tout récent de la cour d'appel de Sousse rendu le 3 mai 2013,[35] qui a annulé un mariage entre une Tunisienne et un Italien pour disparité au culte musulman de la femme. Il s'agissait en l'espèce d'un mariage célébré en 2010 à Sousse, par deux notaires, entre une Tunisienne et un Italien, sans que la question du culte n'ait été envisagée, c'est-à-dire sans exigence de certificat d'islamisation de l'époux.[36] Le mari demande peu après le divorce par volonté unilatérale, il l'obtient par application de la loi tunisienne et, conformément à celle-ci des indemnités sont accordées à la femme. La femme interjette appel pour demander l'augmentation de ses indemnités. La cour d'appel infirme le jugement de première instance en déclarant

> l'action en divorce irrecevable parce qu'il n'y a pas de mariage ; et que les relations sexuelles entre un homme et une femme ne peuvent être qualifiées de contrat, et encore moins de contrat de mariage, si l'époux n'est pas musulman car parmi les empêchements les plus essentiels et les plus fondamentaux, figurent l'interdiction pour la musulmane d'épouser un non musulman.

La cour ajoute que

> si la religion est une question personnelle entre Dieu et sa créature, tous les indices convergent pour considérer l'époux comme non musulman (son prénom, son pays d'origine, sa nationalité, son domicile en Italie) et ce d'autant plus que les notaires qui ont célébré ce mariage ne se sont pas assurés de la religion de l'époux et n'ont pas exigé sa conversion à l'Islam, celui-ci étant sans doute chrétien.

Cet arrêt a été qualifié par la doctrine[37] comme étant un retour « avec beaucoup de force aux interdits religieux. L'impression qui se dégage de cette décision, est la remise en cause même du Code du statut personnel, plus précisément de sa légitimité ». L'arrêt cite bien l'article 5 du CSP, mais il l'interprète comme renvoyant aux empêchements prévus par la *sharīʿa* tout en ignorant l'article 14 du même Code qui fixe les empêchements à mariage et n'inclut guère parmi eux la disparité au culte musulman.

> Pourtant, les avants projets de la constitution qui avaient vu le jour au moment où la décision a été rendue avaient tous institué la règle selon laquelle « les dispositions de la présente constitution sont comprises et interprétées comme un tout harmonieux », principe évident en matière d'interprétation valable pour tous les textes, y compris pour le Code du statut personnel. L'article 5 ne peut être lu détaché de l'article 14, il ne peut être interprété qu'à sa seule lumière puisque c'est l'article 14 qui fixe les empêchements au mariage que ceux-ci comme toute exception sont d'interprétation stricte.[38]

Il est à noter à ce niveau que le courant conservateur considère que l'empêchement à mariage disparait si le futur époux se convertit à l'Islam.

À l'intérieur de ce bloc, la jurisprudence oscille aussi entre souplesse et sévérité dans l'appréciation de la conversion à l'Islam. Un premier clivage considère que la conversion à l'Islam, même tardive et toute proche de la date du décès reste valide. Elle peut être prouvée par tous moyens.[39] Une deuxième tendance jurisprudentielle plus sévère a maintenu qu'il n y a point de succession entre musulmans et non-musulmans et qu'il est nécessaire, pour surmonter l'obstacle religieux, d'apporter la preuve probante de la conversion à l'Islam tel que le certificat d'islamisation délivré par le Mufti de la République.[40]

L'établissement de la filiation

L'article 68 du CSP prévoit que la filiation ou le *nasab* (dans la version arabe) est établie par « la cohabitation,[41] l'aveu du père, ou le témoignage de deux ou plusieurs personnes honorables ». Ainsi formulé, cet article pourrait permettre à l'enfant naturel d'établir sa filiation par l'un des deux derniers modes de preuve à savoir l'aveu ou le témoignage. En effet,

> et à partir du moment où le législateur a prévu trois moyens de preuve dont le mariage, les deux autres moyens doivent être considérés comme des moyens indépendants du mariage sinon on tombe dans des tautologies. La simple analyse grammaticale du texte permet d'affirmer que le mariage n'est qu'un mode de preuve et que ce mode n'est pas nécessaire.[42]

La doctrine tunisienne[43] a considéré que, par ladite formulation de l'article 68 susindiqué, le législateur ouvrait en 1956, la voie de l'établissement de la filiation paternelle légitime aux enfants nés hors mariage afin qu'ils puissent intégrer par la suite la catégorie des enfants légitimes.

Néanmoins, et « au lieu de profiter de cette matière, du silence du législateur sur la condition du mariage des parents et de venir ainsi au secours des enfants innocents qui ont besoin de protection »,[44] la majorité des juridictions tunisiennes ont méconnu cette alternative en considérant qu'il n'y a de *nasab* que s'il y a mariage fût-il nul. Cette solution est largement inspirée des thèses du droit musulman fondées principalement sur un hadith du prophète selon lequel « l'enfant appartient au lit, l'amant doit être lapidé ». Ce hadith a été interprété par les jurisconsultes musulmans comme signifiant que seul le mariage peut établir la filiation. Les rapports hors mariage ne le permettent pas.[45] Cette interprétation a été retenue par la majorité écrasante des juges tunisiens. En effet, l'examen de la jurisprudence dominante relative à l'aveu de paternité légitime laisse entrevoir l'idée générale que l'aveu du père ne saurait établir un lien de *nasab* qu'autant qu'il aura reposé sur l'existence d'un mariage. Ainsi, dès que la nature illicite des rapports entre les parents de l'enfant apparaît, la filiation légitime ne peut être établie.

Depuis déjà 1963, la Cour de cassation[46] a affirmé que l'aveu de paternité ne saurait en aucune manière établir *nasab* dès lors qu'il a laissé apparaitre les origines illicites de la naissance de l'enfant. Cet aveu est selon la Cour suprême « nul et non avenu parce que contraire à l'ordre public et aux bonnes mœurs ». En adoptant cette solution, « la jurisprudence a privé de leur filiation, les enfants dont la paternité était reconnue à l'occasion par exemple des poursuites pénales contre le père pour détournement de mineure par application de l'article 227 bis du code pénal »[47].

Cette position a été également maintenue dans un arrêt en date du 12 mars 1981.[48] La Cour de cassation a rappelé d'une manière expresse que « *la quasi-totalité des règles contenues dans le Code du Statut Personnel dont l'article 68 relatif aux modes d'établissement de la filiation ont été puisées dans le droit musulman* ». Elle a affirmé qu'entre autres conditions à remplir pour que l'aveu du père soit fructueux et opérant, il en est une qui fait interdiction à l'avouant de dévoiler l'origine illicite de la filiation. A l'appui de sa thèse, la Cour suprême n'hésitera pas à faire référence directement, dans l'un de ses attendus, à un auteur contemporain du droit musulman, en l'occurrence le Cheikh Mohamed Abou Zahra. De même, la Cour suprême affirme dans un arrêt rendu le 13 juin 1989[49] que « l'aveu de l'article 68 du CSP est un aveu fondé sur l'existence d'un mariage même nul et non celui fondé sur l'existence des relations de concubinage ».

Cette même interprétation conservatrice a été adoptée concernant le témoignage. Ce dernier n'a point été considéré comme étant un moyen distinct du *firāsh* c'est-à-dire des relations licites entre les parents de l'enfant. La jurisprudence[50] a décidé fermement que les témoins doivent prouver l'existence d'une relation licite entre les parents consistant sinon en un mariage valable, du moins en un mariage nul parce que non célébré en la forme authentique.

Fortement influencés par les préceptes du droits musulman, les juges tunisiens ont refusé de conférer à l'aveu du père ou au témoignage le rang de mode de preuve indépendant et autonome de la paternité légitime alors même que d'après l'exégèse de l'article 68 du CSP, mariage et aveu du père ou témoignage constituent, en matière d'établissement du *nasab*, des procédés autonomes et indépendants l'un de l'autre.[51] Méconnaissant cette alternative, la jurisprudence tunisienne a contribué « à diminuer de l'efficacité de l'aveu de paternité légitime, à freiner la cadence et à en ralentir le rythme par l'affaiblissement de sa force probante ».[52]

Il est à noter à ce niveau que cette interprétation constante, excluant l'aveu et le témoignage comme moyens de preuve indépendants du *firāsh*, de la filiation légitime, ne s'est pas limitée seulement au domaine prétorien. Elle a même guidé les orientations législatives en la matière. En effet, par la loi n° 1998–75 en date du 28 octobre 1998 relative à l'attribution d'un nom patronymique aux enfants abandonnés ou de filiation inconnue, le législateur a prévu, dans son article 3, que l'aveu, le témoignage et l'analyse génétique sont des moyens de preuve de la filiation naturelle. Celle-ci n'ouvre à l'enfant que le droit à l'établissement de la filiation naturelle à l'égard de ses parents, à la pension alimentaire et aux droits découlant de la garde et la tutelle. La preuve de la filiation naturelle ne pourrait accorder à l'enfant le droit à l'héritage de son père naturel. Le droit à la succession reste tributaire de l'établissement de la filiation légitime laquelle nécessite la preuve du mariage.[53]

Le pouvoir discrétionnaire et le référentiel traditionnel

Beaucoup plus que dans d'autres matières, le législateur tunisien a accordé au juge en matière de statut personnel un large pouvoir discrétionnaire principalement dans l'appréciation de l'intérêt de l'enfant et en matière de divorce. L'examen de la pratique judiciaire démontre l'omniprésence du référentiel traditionnel dans l'exercice de ce pouvoir.

L'intérêt de l'enfant

La notion de l'intérêt de l'enfant est au cœur du droit du statut personnel tunisien. Cette notion ne figurait pas dans le Code du statut personnel au moment de sa promulgation en 1956. L'article 67 relatif à la garde de l'enfant ne consacrait pas ce critère d'une manière explicite. C'est la jurisprudence qui, depuis un arrêt de la cour d'appel de Tunis du 29 mai 1958[54] puis un arrêt de la Cour de cassation du 24 août 1966,[55] a estimé que le critère essentiel à prendre en considération dans l'attribution de la garde c'est l'intérêt de l'enfant. Cette notion a été ensuite consacrée par la loi du 3 juin 1966 qui a modifié l'article 67 du CSP en retenant l'intérêt de l'enfant comme seul critère pour l'attribution de la garde. L'intérêt de l'enfant est une notion si « incontournable qu'il est difficile d'en donner le contenu exacte ».[56] Le doyen Carbonnier estimait qu'elle est « une notion magique » qui « à la limite finirait par rendre superflues toutes les institutions du droit familial . . . rien de plus fuyant, rien de plus propre à favoriser l'arbitraire judiciaire ».[57]

Notion à contenu variable, les juges tunisiens ont fait recourir pour l'appréciation de l'intérêt de l'enfant aux règles de droit musulman aussi bien en matière d'attribution de la garde qu'en matière d'adoption.

EN MATIÈRE D'ATTRIBUTION DE LA GARDE

L'article 67 du CSP dispose que le juge confie la garde à l'un des deux époux ou à une tierce personne « en prenant en considération l'intérêt de l'enfant ». Ce faisant, le législateur a opté pour une solution qui s'éloigne du droit musulman,[58] consistant à accorder au juge un pouvoir discrétionnaire dans l'attribution de la garde qui s'exerce au regard du critère exclusif de l'intérêt de l'enfant.[59]

Alors que le Code du statut personnel opte dans son article 67 pour une solution pragmatique qui conditionne l'exercice du droit de la garde au seul critère de l'intérêt de l'enfant, le juge tunisien va, à maintes reprises, conférer à ladite notion une coloration religieuse en faisant appel au référentiel islamique. Depuis l'année 1979,[60] la Cour de cassation a considéré que

> l'enfant est d'obédience musulmane puisqu'il est né d'un père tunisien musulman. Il est donc incontestable que le déplacement de l'enfant dans un environnement qui diffère du sien dans sa religion et sa civilisation, présente le danger de le déraciner de ses attributs originels.

Cette même idée a été reprise dans plusieurs décisions rendues par les juridictions du fond. Dans un jugement du tribunal de première instance de Sfax rendu le 30 mai 1997,[61] le juge a considéré que « l'intérêt du mineur impose d'attribuer sa garde à son père par crainte que la mère de nationalité roumaine, n'imprègne la personnalité de l'enfant par des idées non islamiques ».

En outre, nombreuses sont les décisions qui avaient refusé d'accorder l'exequatur à des jugements étrangers attribuant la garde à un parent ayant la nationalité et résident dans un pays non-musulman pour contrariété à l'ordre public au sens du droit international privé. L'ordre public, a reçu, dans toutes ces décisions

> une forte connotation religieuse puisque le refus de l'exequatur est justifié par le fait que l'éducation d'un enfant né d'un père tunisien et musulman devrait se faire dans le respect des traditions de la culture arabe et de la religion musulmane.[62]

À cet égard, il convient de citer un arrêt de la cour d'appel de Tunis en date du 16 octobre 1996[63] qui a rappelé que

> la jurisprudence est constante à considérer que le déracinement de l'enfant du milieu dans lequel il a grandi et dont il parle et écrit la langue et qui s'est imprégné de ses habitudes et traditions, de même que son détachement de son milieu social arabe et musulman sont de nature à faire de lui un exilé permanent coupé à la fois de la religion et donc apostat, ainsi que de sa patrie, ce qui viole absolument l'ordre public du pays et s'oppose aux prescriptions de sa constitution.

Toujours au niveau des juridictions du fond, le tribunal de première instance de Tunis[64] a considéré que « l'attribution de la garde de l'enfant à sa mère italienne heurte l'ordre public tunisien qui a parmi ses composantes l'arabité et l'Islam lesquels forment les fondements de la souveraineté tunisienne d'après la constitution ».

Au niveau de la Cour suprême, dans un arrêt en date du 3 juin 1982,[65] il a été décidé que

> l'attribution de la garde à la mère française vivant en France amène au déracinement de l'enfant du milieu dans lequel il a grandi et dont il parle et écrit la langue, de même qu'elle conduit à rompre avec les coutumes et les traditions de ce milieu, de même encore, cette solution emporte le fâcheux inconvénient de détacher l'enfant de son *milieu arabe et musulman* ce qui est susceptible de faire de lui un exilé permanent qui se trouve en rupture avec sa religion et sa patrie.

De même, dans un autre arrêt en date du 4 janvier 1999,[66] la Cour de cassation a considéré que

> viole l'ordre public international tunisien, le jugement belge qui attribue la garde à la mère étrangère alors que l'enfant est de nationalité tunisienne, de confession musulmane du fait qu'il descend d'un père tunisien musulman et qu'il a vécu une période en Tunisie où il s'est adapté aux spécificités de son environnement familial et national et qu'il a assimilé spirituellement et en s'attachant à sa patrie.

Une décision plus récente de la Cour de cassation est venue « conforter cette approche culturaliste de la notion d'intérêt de l'enfant »[67] en soulignant que

> les juges du fond ont motivé leur décision d'attribuer la garde de l'enfant à son père par le fait que cet enfant préfère rester avec son père qui s'est converti à l'Islam et qui a convolé en seconde noce avec une femme de nationalité tunisienne . . . ; les juges du fond estimant qu'une pareille situation est de nature à procurer à l'enfant une vie stable tant sur le plan matériel, que sur le plan moral, que motivant leur décision de la sorte, les juges du fond ont sauvegardé l'intérêt de l'enfant.[68]

EN MATIÈRE D'ADOPTION

À l'exception de tous les pays arabo-musulmans,[69] le législateur tunisien a autorisé dès les premières années de l'indépendance, l'adoption avec la loi du 4 mars 1958 relative à la tutelle publique, la tutelle officieuse et à l'adoption. En vertu de cette loi, le législateur a opté pour une adoption plénière de telle sorte que l'enfant adopté devient, pour l'adoptant assimilé à un enfant légitime avec tout ce que cela comporte comme droits et obligations réciproques[70] notamment les vocations successorales réciproques entre l'adopté et la famille adoptive. Sur le plan extra-patrimonial, l'adoption confère à l'adopté le nom de l'adoptant. La tutelle ainsi que le droit de garde appartiennent aux parents adoptifs. De plus, le législateur a précisé dans cette loi les conditions de l'adoption, parmi lesquelles ne figure guère la condition de croyance ou de la religion de l'adoptant. D'ailleurs, même lorsqu'il ouvre au Tunisien la possibilité d'adopter un étranger, il ne fait aucune référence à sa croyance ou à la croyance de l'enfant adopté.

Néanmoins, la rupture entre le droit tunisien et le droit musulman a subi la résistance de la pratique. « Chassé par un législateur audacieux et laïc, le facteur religieux est réintroduit par un juge timide et conservateur ».[71] En effet, pour décider de l'adoption, le législateur a attribué au juge un large pouvoir d'appréciation compte tenu de l'intérêt de l'enfant. Cette notion a reçu également en la matière une connotation religieuse « aboutissant ainsi à une sorte d'islamisation de l'adoption »,[72] résultat pour le moins curieux, puisqu'il s'agit d'une institution prohibée par l'Islam.[73]

D'abord, « l'islamisation de l'adoption » par le juge apparaît à travers la condition d'islamité qu'il a exigé pour l'adoption d'un Tunisien musulman par un étranger. Une telle adoption n'est possible, selon les juges tunisiens, qu'à la condition que l'étranger soit musulman. Ainsi, le tribunal cantonal de Tunis dans une décision du 26 décembre 1974[74] relative à la validité d'une adoption d'un enfant tunisien par des époux français, a fait de l'islamisation du couple une condition pour l'acceptation de l'adoption. Dans une deuxième décision rendue par le tribunal de première instance de Tunis le 26 juin 2000,[75] le juge a considéré que « le droit tunisien ne permet pas à l'étranger d'adopter un tunisien et que l'adoption ne peut être prononcée dans la mesure où rien, dans le dossier, ne permet de constater que le demandeur s'est converti à l'Islam ». Il s'agissait en l'espèce d'un jugement autrichien qui avait prononcé l'adoption d'un tunisien par un autrichien. L'adoptant s'adresse aux juridictions tunisiennes à fin de demander l'exequatur de la décision autrichienne. Le tribunal estime que « les dispositions relatives à l'adoption concernent l'ordre public et que la décision autrichienne est contraire à l'ordre public et ne peut recevoir la forme exécutoire ». Si l'on tente de donner une lecture plus large à la solution retenue par les tribunaux, on peut conclure que l'adoption d'un musulman n'est possible que si l'adoptant est musulman.

Ensuite, « l'islamisation de l'adoption » se vérifie au niveau de sa révocation. La loi du 4 mars 1958 précitée ne s'est pas prononcée clairement sur la révocation de l'adoption. Elle n'a prévu ni prohibition expresse, ni permission conditionnée contrairement à son homologue français.[76] La jurisprudence tunisienne était partagée sur la révocabilité de l'adoption et ce jusqu'à un arrêt de la Cour de cassation du 23 mars 1993[77] qui a déclaré que l'adoption était révocable sur le fondement de l'intérêt de l'enfant.

Bien avant cet arrêt, certaines juridictions[78] se sont référées pour accepter la révocation de l'adoption sur le droit musulman qui constitue le fondement même du droit tunisien du statut personnel et qui est prohibitif de cette institution. Cette islamisation de l'adoption relève selon la doctrine[79] de la « schizophrénie juridique » : Voici une norme à la fois laïque et religieuse, une règle qui rejette l'Islam et s'y réfère à la fois.

En matière de divorce

Le législateur tunisien a attribué au juge de la famille un large pouvoir d'appréciation en matière de divorce aussi bien dans la phase de conciliation au cours de laquelle il peut ordonner, au besoin d'office, les mesures provisoires concernant la résidence des époux, la pension alimentaire, la garde des enfants et le droit de visite, que dans la phase contentieuse dans laquelle il doit se prononcer sur le divorce et sur tous les chefs qui en découlent tels que la garde des enfants et le droit de visite, la pension alimentaire, la rente et la résidence des époux.

Plusieurs exemples illustrent à ce niveau la forte pénétration du référentiel traditionnel dans l'exercice du pouvoir discrétionnaire du juge. En effet, l'article 31 du CSP prévoit que « le tribunal prononce le divorce à la demande de l'un des époux en raison du préjudice qu'il a subi ». Dans ce dernier cas, il est statué sur la réparation du préjudice matériel et moral subi par l'un ou l'autre des époux et résultent du divorce prononcé dans les deux cas prévus aux 2ème et 3ème alinéas du même article.

L'appréciation du préjudice subi par l'un des époux relève du pouvoir discrétionnaire du juge qui s'exerce parfois par référence au droit musulman. Un jugement rendu par le tribunal de première instance de Tunis le 3 décembre 2007[80] est à cet égard très expressif. Il s'agissait en l'espèce d'une présentation par une femme d'une demande en divorce pour préjudice au motif que son mari qu'elle a épousé en 1994, a abjuré la foi musulmane pour se convertir au christianisme depuis 2007. Le tribunal accueille sa demande en divorce pour préjudice étant donné que

> l'abandon par l'époux de la religion musulmane qui unissait les deux conjoints au moment de la conclusion du mariage, constitue pour l'épouse un préjudice justifiant l'acceptation de sa demande en divorce étant donné que le changement de confession du mari altère une condition substantielle qui a déterminé l'épouse à consentir au mariage.

Le tribunal ajoute à l'appui de sa position que

> l'époux étant devenu apostat du fait de sa conversion au christianisme, on se trouve alors en présence d'un empêchement religieux et juridique prévu par l'article 5 du CSP, lequel empêchement met obstacle à la pérennité du lien matrimonial entre les deux conjoints.

Ce faisant, la doctrine[81] considère que

> le tribunal de première instance de Tunis opte clairement pour une approche de l'article 5 du CSP à la lumière du droit musulman classique, les termes « *mawāniᶜ sharᶜiyya* », ou « empêchements charaïques » étant entendus ici, comme renvoyant non seulement aux empêchements juridiques prévus par la loi de 1956, mais également aux empêchements religieux entérinés par le droit musulman, au rang desquels figure l'apostasie.

C'est également, dans le sillage de cette mouvance conservatrice que s'inscrit la jurisprudence qui considère la violation du devoir de cohabitation comme étant un préjudice justifiant la demande de divorce. En effet, et malgré la réforme de l'article 23 du CSP par la loi du 12 juillet 1993, qui a supprimé le devoir d'obéissance de la femme et a cantonné la notion de mari chef de famille au paiement de la pension alimentaire, la jurisprudence considère toujours que la femme qui quitte le domicile conjugal et refuse de le réintégrer sans justification est en état de *nushūz* ce qui justifie le divorce pour préjudice.[82] Selon la Cour suprême,[83] la cohabitation est l'objectif principal et essentiel du mariage, c'est même l'une des principales obligations qui pèsent sur la femme. Dès lors, le refus de cohabiter constitue une violation des obligations de l'article 23 du Code du statut personnel. Cette notion de *nushūz* est par excellence une notion empruntée du droit musulman à laquelle le juge tunisien en fait toujours recours, non seulement pour prononcer le divorce pour préjudice subi, mais également pour décider que l'épouse ne doit pas des aliments.

En effet, l'article 38 du CSP ne prévoit que la consommation du mariage comme condition d'obtention de la pension alimentaire. Toutefois, le juge tunisien, et en se référant au droit musulman, a ajouté la nécessité de non-manquement aux obligations conjugales notamment celle de cohabitation des deux époux. Dans un arrêt n° 6155 rendu le 19 janvier 2006,[84] la Cour de cassation a décidé que la pension alimentaire est la contrepartie des obligations pesant sur la femme. Elle suppose la cohabitation de la femme avec le mari au domicile choisi par celui-ci. Par ailleurs, l'épouse qui a volontairement quitté le domicile conjugal sans motif légitime est en état de *nushūz* « défaut injustifié de cohabitation » et n'a pas droit à la pension alimentaire.[85]

Cette position a toutefois évolué vers la distinction entre le droit de la femme à la pension alimentaire et le *nushūz*. La Cour de cassation dans un arrêt rendu le 21 décembre 2000 a décidé que l'appréciation du *nushūz* est en dehors de la compétence du juge des aliments. La demande de la femme de la pension alimentaire est indépendante de toute contestation relative aux obligations conjugales notamment l'obligation de cohabitation des époux. Il convient de souligner à ce niveau que même en se limitant à la seule condition légale prévue par l'article 38 du CSP pour l'obtention de la pension alimentaire, à savoir la consommation du mariage, le juge tunisien s'est fortement inspiré du droit musulman pour dégager les contours de cette notion indéfinie par le législateur.

À cet effet, la Cour de cassation[86] a affirmé que, conformément au rite malékite, la consommation est d'abord un fait qui doit être prouvé comme tel indépendamment de l'acte de mariage. C'est ensuite, un fait a contenu variable, elle suppose la retraite des époux en tête à tête après abaissement des rideaux et fermeture des issues. Cette notion est fortement puisée de la notion de *khulwa* du droit musulman.[87] Cette interprétation a connu, néanmoins, un élargissement afin de garantir les droits de la femme à la pension alimentaire. En effet, et par référence toujours au rite malékite, la Cour de cassation parvient dans un arrêt rendu en date du 15 juillet 1977[88] à asseoir la notion de « *dukhūl ḥukmī* » ou « la consommation fictive ou assimilée », notion directement puisée du droit musulman qui fait application, en la matière, de la théorie de l'Ihtibas (*naẓariyyat al-iḥtibās*) ou le fait pour la femme de s'offrir à son mari et de se mettre à sa disposition entière et exclusive. Ainsi, et selon la Cour suprême la consommation du mariage peut être même fictive ou assimilée lorsque « l'épouse a officiellement demandé par huissier notaire la consommation du mariage à son mari et celui-ci l'a refusée ».

Le flux du modernisme: le détachement du référentiel religieux vers les droits fondamentaux

Depuis la fin des années 80, un temps nouveau s'inaugure dans la jurisprudence tunisienne. L'éclairage des textes ambigus ou lacunaires du Code du statut personnel ne se fait plus par référence à une conception religieuse du droit de la famille mais plutôt par référence aux droits fondamentaux consignés au sein de la constitution et certaines conventions internationales. Ce mouvement libéral a particulièrement marqué le sujet de la disparité de culte. Celle-ci n'est plus un empêchement à mariage ni une cause d'indignité successorale. Le recours aux droits fondamentaux est désormais l'élément essentiel à prendre en considération pour l'appréciation de l'intérêt de l'enfant.

La lecture libérale des articles 5 et 88 du CSP

Plusieurs décisions émanant des juges du fond attribuent aux textes régissant le droit tunisien de la famille, notamment ceux relatif au mariage de la musulmane avec le non musulman et l'empêchement successoral tiré de la disparité de culte, une lecture libérale en les détachant totalement du droit musulman. Au regard de cette tendance moderniste, l'expression usitée par l'article 5 du CSP doit être entendue par référence à la loi positive tunisienne, à savoir le Code du statut personnel lui-même. Ce faisant, et puisqu'on ne trouve à la disparité de culte aucune trace parmi les cas d'empêchement à mariage limitativement énumérés aux articles de 14 à 20 du dit Code, il y a lieu de considérer que la disparité de culte ne peut être retenue comme cas d'empêchement à mariage. Il en est de même pour l'article 88 du même Code dès lors qu'il ne compte pas expressément la disparité de culte parmi les causes d'indignité successorale qu'il édicte.

Cette tendance libérale est amorcée par le jugement du tribunal de première instance de Mahdia qui a considéré dans une décision rendue le 31 octobre 1988[89] que la disparité de culte n'est pas une cause d'indignité successorale et s'est interrogé sur le silence du texte à propos d'une cause « que si elle avait été aussi grave que l'homicide volontaire, n'aurait pas laissé indifférent le législateur ».

Quelques années plus tard, le tribunal de première instance de Monastir dans un jugement rendu le 1 novembre 1994[90] a donné une interprétation restrictive de l'article 88 du CSP et limitative des causes d'empêchements au seul homicide volontaire. « Les croyances religieuses relèvent du sentiment et des convictions intimes, qu'elles ne sont ni matérielles, ni palpables ni – encore moins – quantifiables ».

L'interprétation moderniste de l'article 5 du CSP se confirme par une décision rendue le 29 juin 1993[91] dans laquelle le tribunal de première instance de

Tunis a décidé pour la première fois, que la disparité de culte ne constitue pas un empêchement matrimonial et valide le mariage entre une tunisienne musulmane et un belge non musulman. Les juges se sont fondés à l'appui de cette solution sur *le droit fondamental de toute personne de choisir librement son conjoint* et ce conformément à la convention de New York du 10 décembre 1962 sur le consentement au mariage, l'âge minimum du mariage et l'enregistrement du mariage, ratifiée par la Tunisie.

La vague libérale atteint le domaine des successions moins d'une année après. Une décision du tribunal de première instance de Tunis du 18 mai 2000[92] s'est écartée du droit musulman pour interpréter l'article 88 du CSP. Pour le tribunal,

> l'exclusion de la veuve du de cujus sur la base de ses convictions religieuses contredit les dispositions de l'article 88 du Code du statut personnel qui a fixé les empêchements successoraux et les a limité au seul homicide volontaire. Il ne convient pas d'élargir le domaine de ce texte, et ce conformément à ce que stipule l'article 540 du Code des obligations et des contrats.

La cour d'appel de Tunis, dans trois décisions successives rendues le 14 juin 2002,[93] le 6 janvier 2004[94] et le 4 mai 2004,[95] s'est fondée également sur les règles d'interprétation contenues dans le Code des obligations et des contrats pour interpréter les articles 5 et 88 du CSP tout en apportant à la question de nouveaux contours en introduisant dans l'argumentation générale les principes constitutionnels d'égalité de citoyens devant la loi et de liberté confessionnelle. En effet, les juges considèrent que

> *la non-discrimination sur des bases religieuses est un des principes fondateurs de l'ordre juridique tunisien* et représente un des impératifs de la liberté de conscience. Cet impératif ressort de l'article 5 de la constitution, des articles 2, 16 et 18 de la Déclaration Universelle des Droits de l'Homme, ainsi que des paragraphes 1 et 2 des articles 2 des deux pactes internationaux relatifs, l'un aux droits économiques, sociaux et culturels, l'autre aux droits civils et politiques auxquels la Tunisie a adhéré sans réserve.

Les juges concluent à l'inconstitutionnalité de toute interprétation extensive de l'article 88 du CSP « puisqu'elle équivaut à créer deux catégories de Tunisiens; ceux qui auraient droit d'hériter parce que de même confession que l'auteur et ceux qui en seraient empêchés pour la seule raison qu'ils auraient exercé une des libertés fondamentales ».

Ces décisions ont affirmé avec fermeté le caractère strictement limitatif de l'article 88 du Code du statut personnel qui exclut tout autre empêchement. La cour d'appel ajoute dans l'arrêt du 14 juin 2002 précité que

> l'interprétation de la loi ne peut, sans faux prétexte, induire une inégalité dont on ne trouve trace dans les textes, ni de manière implicite, ni de manière explicite. Les deux principes de la liberté de conscience et de l'égalité devant

> la loi retrouvent leur caractère fondateur du droit tunisien. La garantie de la liberté confessionnelle de l'article 5 de la constitution interdit de lier les droits patrimoniaux au facteur religieux.

Plus encore, les juges se sont déclarés, dans cet arrêt, contre « l'instrumentalisation de la religion dans un conflit patrimonial et contre le fait que la foi devienne un objet de démonstration ».

Le même raisonnement a été repris dans la décision du 6 janvier 2004 précitée qui a affirmé que

> l'intégration de l'élément religieux parmi les empêchements contenus dans les articles 5 et 88 du CSP conduit à contredire l'article 6 de la constitution qui garantit l'égalité entre les citoyens et aurait pour conséquence de créer des catégories de droit différents, d'accorder aux hommes la liberté d'épouser des non-musulmans, sans accorder cette même liberté aux femmes, d'attribuer à certains une aptitude à succéder en raison de l'identité de religion avec le de cujus, et d'en priver d'autres.

Cette tendance se confirme aussi bien dans le domaine du mariage que dans celui des successions. Outre les trois décisions précitées, la cour d'appel de Tunis valide les successions entre musulmans et non-musulmans dans une décision rendue le 15 juillet 2008.

Le mouvement innovateur au niveau des juges du fond a basculé le conservatisme du juge de droit qui, saisit d'un pourvoi en cassation contre la décision de la cour d'appel du 6 janvier 2004 sus-indiquée, a décidé que ladite cour a correctement interprété les articles 5 et 88 du CSP et que cette interprétation est en parfaite adéquation avec les principes contenus au sein de la constitution tunisienne.[96]

Le libéralisme de la Cour de cassation a été confirmé dans une décision de principe rendu le 5 février 2009[97] dans laquelle il a été décidé que l'article 88 du CSP doit être lu et interprété à la lumière des principes fondateurs sur lesquels se fonde l'ordre juridique tunisien tels qu'ils résultent de la constitution et des conventions internationales ratifiées par la Tunisie. Dans cet arrêt, on peut lire les attendus suivants :

- *Attendu* que la liberté religieuse garantie par l'article 5 de la Constitution et l'article 18 du Pacte relatif aux droits civils et politiques impose la distinction entre la jouissance des droits civils et les convictions religieuses.
- *Attendu* que l'affirmation selon laquelle le législateur tunisien garantit d'une part la liberté religieuse et interdit d'autre part la succession entre personnes de confession différente conduit à une contradiction.
- *Attendu* que l'égalité garantie par l'article 6 de la constitution et l'article 26 du Pacte international relatif aux droits civils et politiques impose l'absence de discrimination en raison de considérations religieuses.
- *Attendu* que la garantie de la liberté matrimoniale de la femme à l'égale de celle de l'homme prévue par le paragraphe 1-b de l'article 16 de la Convention

> sur l'élimination de toutes les formes de discrimination à l'égard des femmes ratifiée par la Tunisie interdit toute influence des convictions de la femme sur sa liberté matrimoniale et par voie de conséquence sur sa vocation successorale, les conventions internationales étant supérieures à la loi conformément à l'article 32 de la Constitution.

La nouvelle appréciation de l'intérêt de l'enfant

Le droit fondamental de tout enfant à l'établissement de sa filiation sans égard à l'origine de sa naissance, ainsi que son intérêt de vivre, vu son jeune âge, avec sa mère même si elle est de confession non musulmane, ou encore son intérêt de vivre dans une famille adoptive afin de résoudre au mieux le douloureux problème de l'enfance abandonnée sont désormais les seuls éléments à prendre en considération par certains juges tunisiens dans l'appréciation de l'intérêt de l'enfant.

L'interprétation extensive de l'article 68 du CSP

La pénétration des droits fondamentaux dans l'œuvre jurisprudentielle trouve sa place en matière d'établissement de la filiation. En effet, le tribunal de première instance de Gafsa, dans un jugement rendu le 21 février 1994,[98] a considéré l'aveu du prétendu père comme étant un moyen de preuve indépendant permettant l'établissement de la filiation légitime (*nasab*), et ce quelle que soit la nature licite ou non des relations de ses parents.

De même, le tribunal de première instance de Manouba dans deux décisions qualifiées « d'originales »[99] rendues le 28 octobre 2003[100] et le 2 décembre 2003[101] conclut à l'établissement de la filiation d'un enfant né hors mariage en se référant à l'article 68 du CSP. Le tribunal se fonde à l'appui de sa position d'une part, sur la formulation et la généralité des termes de l'article 68 du Code du statut personnel qui permettent de couvrir aussi bien les cas d'établissement de la filiation légitime que ceux d'établissement de la filiation naturelle. Le texte relatif à la preuve de la filiation

> présente une structure ouverte puisque outre la cohabitation, l'aveu du père et le témoignage de deux ou plusieurs témoins honorables, ce texte supporte l'ajout d'autres moyens de preuve fiables de la filiation tels que les tests d'analyse génétique qui peuvent attester, de manière certaine, d'un rattachement biologique d'un enfant à son père.[102]

D'autre part, cette lecture est consolidée par un appel aux droits fondamentaux de tout enfant à l'établissement de sa filiation nonobstant l'origine de sa naissance tels que consacrés par l'article 6 de la constitution ainsi que l'article 2 paragraphe 2 de la convention de New York du 20 novembre 1989 relative aux droits de l'enfant ratifiée par la Tunisie en vertu de la loi du 29 novembre 1991.[103]

Cette nouvelle interprétation de l'article 68 du CSP qui rompt avec le sens traditionnellement donné par les juges tunisiens à ce texte est en plus en parfaite adéquation avec une idée force qui traverse l'ensemble de la législation tunisienne relative aux droits de l'enfant, à savoir la protection de l'enfant.

Le même tribunal de première instance de Manouba a considéré dans un jugement n° 1525 du 4 mars 2006[104] que l'article 68 du Code du statut personnel tunisien prévoit que « la filiation est établie par la cohabitation ou par l'aveu ou par le témoignage, le mariage n'est donc pas exigé et l'aveu suffit pour établir la filiation quelle que soit sa nature ». Il s'agissait en l'espèce d'une demande d'établissement de la filiation d'un enfant né en Libye et qui y réside. En plus, l'enfant dont on demande l'établissement de sa filiation est né de parents qui ne sont pas mariés. Par application de l'article 52 du code de droit international privé, il convient de choisir entre la loi tunisienne en tant que loi nationale et loi de domicile du défendeur et la loi libyenne en tant que loi de résidence de l'enfant. Le tribunal décide que la loi tunisienne est plus favorable à l'établissement de la filiation de l'enfant puisqu'elle n'exige pas le mariage et se suffit à l'aveu pour établir la filiation quelle que soit sa nature alors que la loi libyenne aboutirait, si elle était retenue, à la non-reconnaissance de la filiation puisqu'elle prévoit que la filiation ne peut être établie que s'il y a mariage valable ou nul, l'aveu ne peut établir la filiation si l'enfant est né d'une relation illicite. Le tribunal en conclut « qu'il convient donc de choisir la loi tunisienne et d'appliquer l'article 68 du CSP pour établir la filiation de l'enfant en vertu de l'aveu du père ». Il est à noter à ce niveau que cette position n'a pas été consolidée par la Cour de cassation ni unanimement adoptée par les juges du fond et ce, contrairement à la position de la jurisprudence tunisienne relative à la garde de l'enfant.

L'évolution de la jurisprudence en matière de garde de l'enfant

En matière de garde, la pratique judiciaire a également largement évolué. Elle ne tient plus compte du seul milieu culturel et religieux dans lequel se développera l'enfant pour apprécier son intérêt. Ainsi, une loi étrangère attribuant la garde au parent étranger et résidant dans un pays non musulman n'est plus envisagée comme étant contraire à l'ordre public. La cour d'appel de Tunis, dans un arrêt n° 48765 du 11 juillet 1998[105] a décidé que « l'attribution de la garde des enfants par le jugement belge à leur mère étrangère résidant en Belgique n'a rien de contraire à l'ordre public international tunisien ».

Ce faisant l'intérêt de l'enfant s'est détaché des seules considérations religieuses. La Cour de cassation, dans un arrêt en date du 2 mars 2001[106] a considéré que

> la décision étrangère remplit l'ensemble des conditions exigées pour l'exequatur. Le droit tunisien prend en considération l'intérêt de l'enfant pour l'attribution de la garde . . . les juges du fond ont accordé la garde de l'enfant à sa mère étrangère en tenant compte de son intérêt. Rien, dans la décision étrangère, ne contredit l'ordre public international tunisien ou la politique législative tunisienne. Seul l'intérêt de l'enfant doit être pris en compte, sans autre considération.

« Se plaçant à contre-courant d'une jurisprudence antérieure bien établie qui avait clairement manifesté son opposition à ce que les enfants des couples tuniso-étrangers soient élevés en dehors de la société tunisienne »,[107] la Cour de cassation et pour la première fois dans cet important arrêt, n'apporte pas l'argumentation classique et a adopté une appréciation in abstracto de l'intérêt de l'enfant fondée sur les principes généraux et les droits fondamentaux.

Par ailleurs, les dispositions des lois inspirées de la religion musulmane, ont même été écartées en raison de leurs dispositions moins favorables à l'intérêt de l'enfant en comparaison avec les dispositions du droit tunisien. En effet, lors du choix de la loi applicable à la garde d'enfants saoudiens résidents en Arabie Saoudite, où la loi tunisienne et la loi saoudienne étaient toutes les deux en concurrence, les juges du tribunal de première instance de Tunis, dans un jugement en date du 11 juillet 2001,[108] ont préféré à la loi saoudienne « tirée de la *Chariaa* islamique », la loi tunisienne « qui se base en premier lieu sur l'intérêt de l'enfant lors de l'attribution de la garde ». La religion musulmane « jadis critère d'attribution de garde et donc de l'évaluation de l'intérêt de l'enfant en droit international privé tunisien, n'a plus la même place en la matière ».[109]

L'évolution en matière d'adoption

L'appréciation de l'intérêt de l'enfant s'est également détachée des considérations religieuses en matière d'adoption. Un jugement en date du 28 octobre 1995 a prononcé l'adoption d'un enfant tunisien par un couple américain sans exiger un certificat d'islamisation des parents. L'adoption est possible selon le juge du moment qu'elle est dans l'intérêt de l'enfant et que la loi de 1958 ne se réfère pas à la religion des parties.[110]

Conclusion

En dépit du flux de modernisme qui a émergé dans la jurisprudence tunisienne et qui ne constitue, ni l'unanimité au niveau des juges du fond, ni une position constante de la Cour de cassation, l'examen de la pratique prétorienne démontre que le courant traditionnaliste et conservateur est resté non seulement omniprésent mais également bien dominant.

L'état des lieux actuel caractérisé par une « turbulence dans l'application judiciaire du code du statut personnel »[111] est une situation qui porte atteinte au principe de la sécurité juridique auquel a droit tout justiciable. En effet, confronté à l'une des questions les plus controversées (disparité de culte, établissement de la filiation d'un enfant né hors mariage, etc), la solution juridictionnelle est nettement imprévisible. Celle-ci dépendra dans une large mesure des prédispositions du juge saisi à accueillir un modèle traditionnel ou bien moderne. Ces prédispositions dépendent de la formation du juge moderne ou classique, de son tempérament conservateur ou innovateur. Cette situation est également une source d'incohérence interne du Code du statut personnel et de l'ensemble des normes du système juridique tunisien.

L'oscillation des juges entre tradition et modernité reflète en fin de compte une oscillation plus générale, celle de la société tunisienne entière entre le modèle traditionnel de la famille patriarcale et musulmane et le modèle libéral de la famille moderne assis sur les principes d'égalité et de liberté.

À ce niveau des solutions peuvent être proposées en vue de pallier à cette situation : D'abord, au-delà des facteurs extra-juridiques (religieux, culturels, sociologiques . . .) qui peuvent influencer la position du magistrat, la formation continue des juges de la famille basée sur les bonnes pratiques et les standards internationaux en la matière est indispensable. Ensuite, la spécialisation des juges statuant en matière de droit de la famille et leur promotion tout au long de leur carrière professionnelle dans la même matière est également de nature à assurer une certaine continuité et stabilité dans les décisions judiciaires. On peut même penser à ce niveau à la création d'un tribunal de la famille au lieu d'un simple espace dédié à la famille au sein des tribunaux. Enfin, l'intervention du législateur est désormais inévitable en vue de clarifier les zones d'ombres qui règnent encore sur les dispositions les plus problématiques du Code du statut personnel surtout avec l'adoption d'une nouvelle constitution pour la République tunisienne le 26 janvier 2014 qui a consacré d'une manière non équivoque la liberté de conscience tout comme l'égalité en droits et en devoirs entre les citoyens et les citoyennes.[112] Cette même constitution engage l'Etat dans son article 46 à protéger « les droits acquis de la femme, à les soutenir et œuvrer à leur amélioration ».

Le gouvernement tunisien a également notifié au secrétaire général des Nations Unis le 17 avril 2014 la levée des réserves relatives aux articles 15(4) et 9(2) et 16(c, d, h, g, k) et 29(1) relatives à la convention sur l'élimination de toutes les formes de discrimination à l'égard des femmes (CEDAW). Toutefois, il est à noter que la déclaration concernant l'article 1 de la constitution de 1959, qui a été repris dans sa même formulation dans la constitution de 2014, n'a pas fait l'objet de la levée des réserves. Or, toutes les discriminations religieuses qui avaient été auparavant établies ont reposé sur le seul article 1 de la constitution de 1959, que la jurisprudence et l'administration avaient élevé au rang de la règle supra-constitutionnelle.

Le terrain semble-t-il être encore propice pour une hésitation des juges entre une conception confessionnelle du droit tunisien de la famille et une conception libérale qui se fonde sur les principes universels des droits de l'Homme en tant que choix fondamental de l'ordre juridique tunisien.

Notes

1 K Meziou, 'Droit de la famille', *Jurisclasseur droit comparé* (2012) Fasc 60, 1.

2 M-M Bouguerra, 'Le juge tunisien et le droit du statut personnel' (2000) 14 Actualités juridiques tunisiennes 14.

3 Scindées en tribunaux malékites et tribunaux hanafites, ces juridictions appliquaient, respectivement, les dispositions du rite malékite et celles du rite hanafite, sur ce sujet voir M Dabbab et T Abid, *La justice en Tunisie : Histoire de l'organisation judiciaire (essai) de 1856 à l'indépendance* (Centre d'Etudes Juridiques et Judiciaires 1998).

4 Décret du 13 août 1956 portant promulgation du code du statut personnel, Journal Officiel n° 104 du 28 décembre 1956, 1742.
5 A Colomer, 'Le code du statut personnel tunisien' [1957] Revue algérienne tunisienne et marocaine de législation et de jurisprudence 117.
6 Y Ben Achour, 'Une révolution par le droit? Bourguiba et le code du statut personnel' in *Politique, religion et droit* (Cérès-CERP 1992) 203.
7 A Mezghani, 'Religion, mariage et succession : L'hypothèse laïque. A propos d'une (R) évolution récente de la jurisprudence tunisienne' in *Droits et culture : Mélanges en l'honneur du Doyen Yadh Ben Achour* (Centre de Publication Universitaire 2008) 345.
8 ibid. 348.
9 Les juridictions françaises ont été supprimées de Tunisie en vertu du décret du 1 juillet 1957.
10 Article 13 de la loi n° 58–27 du 4 mars 1958 relative à la tutelle publique, à la tutelle officieuse et à l'adoption, Journal Officiel n° 19 du 7 mars 1958, 236.
11 Meziou, 'Droit de la famille' (n 1) Fasc 60, 4.
12 Bouguerra (2000) 14 Actualités juridiques tunisiennes 17.
13 Loi n° 93–74 du 12 juillet 1993 portant modification de certains articles du code du statut personnel, Journal Officiel n° 53 du 20 juillet 1993, 1004.
14 Il s'agit notamment de l'obligation faite aux deux époux « de se traiter mutuellement avec bienveillance et de s'entraider dans la gestion du foyer et des affaires des enfants » qui a remplacé la disposition suivante « la femme doit respecter les prérogatives du mari »; le droit de la mère de gérer les affaires de ses enfants en collaboration avec le père, notamment en ce qui concerne l'enseignement, les voyages et les comptes financiers (article 23 nouveau – al 3); le consentement de la mère au mariage de son enfant mineur; l'octroi à la fille mineure mariée le droit de conduire sa vie privée; la création d'un fonds garantissant le versement des pensions alimentaires, au profit de la femme divorcée et de ses enfants. Ce fonds procède au paiement de la pension alimentaire ou de la rente de divorce objet des jugements exécutoires rendus au profit des femmes divorcées et des enfants.
15 Loi n° 57–3 du 1er août 1957 réglementant l'état civil, Journal Officiel n° 2 et 3 des 30 juillet et 2 août 1957, 11.
16 Loi n° 98–75 du 28 octobre 1998 relative à l'attribution d'un nom patronymique aux enfants abandonnés ou de filiation inconnue, modifiée et complétée par la loi n° 2003–51 du 7 juillet 2003, Journal Officiel n° 87 du 30 octobre 1998, 2119.
17 Loi n° 98–91 du 9 novembre 1998, relative au régime de la communauté des biens entre époux, Journal Officiel n° 91 du 13 novembre 1998, 2225.
18 S Bostanji, 'Turbulences dans l'application judiciaire du code tunisien personnel: Le conflit de référentiels dans l'œuvre prétorienne' (2009) 1 Revue internationale de droit comparé 7.
19 M Charfi, *Introduction à l'étude de droit* (Cérès édition 1983) 196.
20 ibid.
21 Meziou, 'Droit de la famille' (n 1) Fasc 60, 6.
22 Bostanji (2009) 1 Revue internationale de droit comparé 14.
23 ibid. 12.
24 Sur ce point, l'exemple tunisien est unique dans le monde arabo-musulman. A titre d'exemple, le Code algérien de la famille du 9 juin 1984 se réfère au droit musulman. Selon l'article 222 du Code algérien de la famille, « en l'absence d'une disposition dans la présente loi, il est fait référence aux dispositions de la chariâa ». De même le

Code soudanais du statut personnel du 24 juillet 1991 précise dans son article 5 al 1 qu'en cas de silence du présent Code, il sera fait application de la doctrine dominante du rite Hanafite.

25 Art 535 du COC.

26 Sur la disparité de culte envisagée comme empêchement à mariage et cause d'indignité successorale en droit musulman classique voir Muḥammad Muḥī al-Dīn ᶜAbd al-Ḥamīd, *Aḥkām al-Mawārīth fī al-Sharīᶜa al-Islāmiyya ᶜalā Madhāhib al-A'imma al-arbaᶜa* (Dār al-Kitāb al-ᶜArabī 1984) 49; Badrān Abū al-ᶜAynayn Badrān, *Al-Fiqh al-Muqāran li-l-Aḥwāl al-Shakhṣiyya bayna al-Madhāhib al-Arbaᶜa al-Sunniyya wa-l-Madhhab al-Jaᶜfarī wa-l-Qānūn*, vol 1: *Al-Zawāj wa-l-Ṭalāq* (Dār al-Nahḍa al-ᶜArabiyya 1967) 115.

27 La loi n° 93–64 du 5 juillet 1993 relative à la publication des textes au Journal Officiel de la République Tunisienne et à leur exécution, Journal Officiel n° 50 du 6 juillet 1993, 931.

28 Mezghani (n 7) 351.

29 S Ben Achour, 'Figures de l'altérité : À propos de l'héritage du conjoint "non musulman"' in *Mouvements du droit contemporain : Mélanges offerts au Professeur Sassi Ben Halima* (Centre de Publication Universitaire 2005) 823.

30 Cass Civ n° 3384 du 31 janvier 1967 (1967) 6 Revue de la jurisprudence et de la législation 43; E de Lagrange [1968] Revue tunisienne de droit 115 (note).

31 Cass Civ n° 10160 du 13 février 1985 (1985) 9 Revue de la jurisprudence et de la législation 102.

32 Cass Civ n° 9658 du 8 juin 2006 (2009) 3 Revue de la jurisprudence et de la législation 135.

33 Cass Civ n° 4487 du 16 janvier 2007 [2007] Les annales des sciences juridiques 297.

34 Cass Civ n° 26905 du 30 juin 2009 (inédit).

35 Cour d'appel de Sousse, arrêt n° 9246 rendu le 3 mai 2013 (inédit).

36 Une circulaire du ministre de la justice du 5 novembre 1973 adressée aux officiers de l'état civil interdit la célébration du mariage d'une Tunisienne musulmane avec un non-musulman; elle est confirmée par la circulaire du ministre de l'intérieur n° 59 du 23 novembre 2004 qui exige des candidats au mariage une attestation d'islamité délivrée par une autorité religieuse officielle, le mufti de la République si le mari est un non-musulman.

37 M Ben Jémia, 'Y a-t-il du nouveau en matière d'ordre public international?' (Présentation au colloque organisé à la faculté des sciences juridiques, politiques et sociales, février 2014, deuxièmes journées Mohamed Charfi de droit international privé, à paraître).

38 ibid. 4.

39 Cass Civ n° 68443 du 6 juillet 1999, Cass Civ n° 2000–3396 du 2 janvier 2001, cités dans le mémoire de K Sghaier, 'L'héritage de la non-musulmane devant les tribunaux tunisiens' (Mémoire de DEA en sciences juridiques fondamentales, Faculté des sciences juridiques, politiques et sociales Tunis 2001–2002) 60, 136.

40 Cass Civ du 28 avril 2000, cité par Sghaier (n 39) 106–107.

41 Dans la version arabe l'expression pour la cohabitation est « *firāsh* », un terme employé par le droit musulman qui signifie la relation licite. L'expression est plus large que le mariage puisqu'elle englobe le mariage valable ou nul.

42 S Ben Halima, 'La filiation naturelle en droit tunisien' (2003) 16 Actualités juridiques tunisiennes (numéro special : L'enfant en droit privé) 28.

43 Bostanji (2009) 1 Revue internationale de droit comparé 19.

44 Charfi, *Introduction* (n 19).
45 Al-Hādī Kirrū, 'Al-walad li-l-firāsh' (1972) 2 Revue de la jurisprudence et de la législation 11.
46 Cass Civ du 31 décembre 1963, arrêt publié en annexe dans le mémoire de M-M Bouguèrra, 'L'établissement de la filiation de l'enfant des fiancés' (Mémoire de DEA en droit, Faculté de droit Tunis 1979).
47 S Ben Halima, 'La filiation paternelle légitime en droit tunisien' (Thèse de doctorat d'État, Tunis 1976) 146.
48 Cass Civ n° 3712 du 12 mars 1981 (1981) 1 Bulletin de la Cour de cassation (partie civile) 99.
49 Cass Civ n° 21419 du 13 juin 1989 (1989) 1 Bulletin de la Cour de cassation (partie civile) 292.
50 Cass Civ n° 51–346 du 26 novembre 1996 (1996) 2 Bulletin de la Cour de cassation (partie civile) 228; Cass Civ n° 49–089 du 7 mai 1996 (1996) 2 Bulletin de la Cour de cassation (partie civile) 231.
51 Ben Halima, 'La filiation paternelle' (n 47) 146.
52 Bouguerra (2000) 14 Actualités juridiques tunisiennes 71.
53 L'article 152 du CSP prévoit que « l'enfant adultérin n'héritera que de sa mère et des parents de celle-ci. La mère et ses parents auront, seuls, vocation héréditaire dans la succession du dit enfant ».
54 Cour d'appel de Tunis, arrêt n° 16980 du 29 mai 1958 (1959) 6 Revue de la jurisprudence et de la législation 54.
55 Cass Civ n° 4875 du 24 août 1966 (1966) 8 Revue de la jurisprudence et de la législation 27.
56 J Bejaoui Attar, 'L'intérêt de l'enfant fondement de l'adoption en droit tunisien' (2003) 16 Actualités juridiques tunisiennes (numéro spécial : L'enfant en droit privé) 85.
57 J Carbonnier, cité in *L'enfant et les conventions internationales* (Actes de colloque, Lyon, 1995), cité par Bejaoui Attar (2003) 16 Actualités juridiques tunisiennes (numéro spécial: L'enfant en droit privé) 88.
58 Conçue comme le prolongement du devoir d'allaitement, le droit musulman fixe un ordre de dévolutaires de la garde favorisant la mère et la ligne maternelle et ne permet au père de reprendre l'enfant que parvenu à un certain âge, Meziou, 'Droit de la famille' (n 1) Fasc 60, 50.
59 Dans les conflits internes, l'intérêt de l'enfant est apprécié au regard de l'audition des parties par le juge et éventuellement à la lumière d'une expertise sociologique.
60 Cass Civ, arrêt n° 2000 du 15 mai 1979 (1979) 1 Bulletin de la Cour de cassation (partie civile) 227.
61 Jugement n° 38339 du 30 mai 1997, in M Ghazouani, *Sommaire de la jurisprudence de droit international privé* (Unité de recherche relations privées internationales, juillet 2006).
62 S Ben Achour, 'L'adoption en droit tunisien : Réflexions sur la "condition d'islamité"' in *Mouvements du droit contemporain* (n 29) 847.
63 Cour d'appel de Tunis, arrêt n° 33745 du 16 octobre 1996, in Ghazouani, *Sommaire de la jurisprudence* (n 61).
64 Tribunal de première instance de Tunis, jugement n° 23843 du 20 avril 1999, in Ghazouani, *Sommaire de la jurisprudence* (n 61).
65 Cass Civ, arrêt n° 7422 du 3 juin 1982 (1983) 9 Revue de la jurisprudence et de la législation 63.
66 Cass Civ, arrêt n° 69523 du 4 janvier 1999 (2002) 1 RJL 167; M Ghazouani [2001] Revue tunisienne de droit (partie en langue arabe) 201 (note).

67 Bostanji (2009) 1 Revue internationale de droit comparé 17.

68 Cass Civ, arrêt n° 18182 du 24 octobre 2002 (inédit).

69 À titre d'exemple, l'article 46 du Code algérien de la famille dispose que « l'adoption est interdite par la chariâa et la loi ». La nouvelle *moudawana* marocaine dispose également dans son article 149 que « l'adoption est considérée comme nulle et n'entraine aucun des effets de la filiation légitime ».

70 Articles 14 et 15 de la loi du 4 mars 1958 précitée.

71 S Ben Achour, 'L'adoption en droit tunisien' (n 62) 846.

72 S Ben Achour, 'L'interprétation du droit tunisien de la famille, entre référence à l'Islam et appel aux droits fondamentaux' in *L'interprétation de la norme juridique, actes du colloque international organisé à Jendouba les 5 et 6 avril 2010, Faculté des sciences juridiques économiques et de gestion de Jendouba*, 8.

73 L'interdiction résulte de deux versets coraniques clairs de la sourate 33 des confédérés (*al-aḥzāb*). Dans le verset 4 nous lisons : « *De vos enfants adoptifs (Allah) n'a point fait vos propres fils. Appelez les (vos fils adoptifs) du nom de leurs pères, cela est juste auprès d'Allah.* » *Coran* (E Montet tr) 530.

74 Tribunal de Justice Cantonale de Tunis du 26 décembre 1974, n° 2272 (1975) 2 Revue tunisienne de droit 117; K Meziou [1975] 2 Revue tunisienne de droit 119 (note).

75 TPI Tunis du 26 juin 2000, n° 34256, in Ghazouani, *Sommaire de la jurisprudence* (n 61) n° 26.

76 Articles 370 et 359 du Code civil français.

77 Cass Civ du 23 mars 1993 [1993] Bulletin de la Cour de cassation (partie civile) 29.

78 Cour d'appel de Monastir, arrêt civil n° 145 du 9 janvier 1986 [1989] Revue tunisienne de droit 117; S Ben Halima [1989] Revue tunisienne de droit 125 (note).

79 S Ben Achour, 'L'adoption en droit tunisien' (n 62) 848.

80 TPI Tunis n° 65760 du 3 décembre 2007 [2008] Revue tunisienne de droit 365.

81 S Bostanji, 'Un cas insoupçonné de divorce pour préjudice en droit tunisien : L'apostasie du conjoint (observations sous le jugement du Tribunal de première instance de Tunis n° 65760 en date du 3 décembre 2007)' [2008] Revue tunisienne de droit 511.

82 Cass Civ n° 6155 du 19 janvier 2006 [2006] Bulletin de la Cour de cassation (partie civile) 289.

83 Cass Civ n° 14649 du 13 décembre 2007 (2007) 1 Bulletin de la Cour de cassation (partie civile) 263.

84 Cass Civ n° 6155 du 19 janvier 2006 [2006] Bulletin de la Cour de cassation (partie civile) 289.

85 Cass Civ n° 17685 du 22 septembre 1987 [1987] Bulletin de la Cour de cassation (partie civile) 229.

86 Cass Civ n° 2300 du 31 mars 1964 [1964] Revue de la jurisprudence et de la législation 591.

87 « Dans le droit musulman, la khulwa est une notion à contenu matériel, voire charnel c'est pourquoi les jurisconsultes exigent des époux leur aptitude physique à l'accomplissement de l'acte sexuel et l'absence entre eux d'empêchements de quelque nature qu'ils soient susceptibles de leur constituer une entrave à l'entretien de relations sexuelles », Bouguerra (2000) 14 Actualités juridiques tunisiennes.

88 Cass Civ n° 1229 du 15 juillet 1977 (1977) 2 Bulletin de la Cour de cassation (partie civile) 81.

89 TPI Mahdia n° 5701 du 31 octobre 1988 (1990) 3 Revue de la jurisprudence et de la législation 119, 130.

90 TPI Monastir n° 8179 du 1 novembre 1994 (2002) 10 Revue de la jurisprudence et de la législation 105.

91 TPI Tunis n° 26–855 du 29 juin 1999 [2000] Revue tunisienne de droit 403; S Ben Achour [2000] Revue tunisienne de droit 407 (note).

92 TPI Tunis n° 7602 du 18 mai 2000 [2000] Revue tunisienne de droit (partie en langue arabe) 247; A Mezghani [2000] Revue tunisienne de droit (partie en langue arabe) 251 (note).

93 Cour d'appel de Tunis n° 82861 du 14 juin 2002 (2002) 10 Revue de la jurisprudence et de la législation 75.

94 Cour d'appel de Tunis n° 120 du 6 janvier 2004 [2005] Journal du Droit International 1193; S Ben Achour [2005] Journal du Droit International 1195 (note).

95 Cour d'appel de Tunis n° 3351 du 4 mai 2004 (2009) 3 Revue de la jurisprudence et de la législation 197.

96 Cass Civ, arrêt n° 3843 du 20 décembre 2004 [2005] Journal du Droit International 1193; S Ben Achour [2005] Journal du Droit International 1195 (note).

97 Cass Civ, arrêt n° 31115 du 5 février 2009 (2009) 3 Revue de la jurisprudence et de la législation 91; M Ghazouani [2009] 3 Revue de la jurisprudence et de la législation 101 (note).

98 TPI Gafsa n° 43979 du 21 février 1994 [1994] Revue tunisienne de droit (partie en langue arabe) 199; S Ben Halima [1994] Revue tunisienne de droit (partie en langue arabe) 202 (note).

99 Bostanji (2009) 1 Revue internationale de droit comparé 23.

100 TPI Manouba n° 16198 du 28 octobre 2003 (inédit).

101 TPI Manouba n° 16189 du 2 décembre 2003 (inédit).

102 Bostanji (2009) 1 Revue internationale de droit comparé 23.

103 Suivant ce paragraphe : « . . . les Etats parties prennent toutes les mesures appropriées pour que l'enfant soit effectivement protégé contre toutes formes de discrimination ou de sanction motivées par la situation juridique de ses parents . . . ».

104 TPI Manouba n° 1525 du 4 mars 2006, in L Chedly et M Ghazouani, *Code de droit international privé annoté* (Édition du Centre d'études juridiques et judiciaires 2008) 641.

105 Cour d'appel de Tunis, arrêt n° 48765 du 11 juillet 1998 (inédit).

106 Cour de cassation n° 7286 du 2 mars 2001 (2002) 1 Revue de la jurisprudence et de la législation 183.

107 S Bostanji, 'L'émergence d'un statut privilégié de l'enfant en droit international privé tunisien' (2003) 16 Actualités juridiques tunisiennes (numéro spécial : L'enfant en droit privé) 157.

108 TPI Tunis n° 32779 du 11 juillet 2000, in L Chedly et M Ghazouani, *Code de droit international privé annoté* (Édition du Centre d'études juridiques et judiciaires 2008) 627.

109 SM Bouyahia, 'La proximité en droit international privé de la famille français et tunisien: Actualité et perspectives (Étude des conflits de lois)' (Thèse de doctorat en droit, Université Paris II Panthéon-Assas et Faculté des Sciences Juridiques, Politiques et Sociales de Tunis 2012) 225.

110 M Charfi, 'Culture et droit dans le monde musulman : L'exemple tunisien' in *Mélanges offerts au Doyen Abdelfattah Amor* (Centre de Publication Universitaire 2005) 349.

111 Bostanji (2009) 1 Revue internationale de droit comparé 8.

112 L'article 21 du chapitre relatif aux droits et libertés dispose que « les citoyens et les citoyennes sont égaux en droits et en devoirs. Ils sont égaux devant la loi sans discrimination aucune. L'Etat garantit aux citoyens les libertés et les droits individuels et collectifs. Il leur assure les conditions d'une vie décente ».

8 Divorce in Egypt

Between law in the books and law in action

Nathalie Bernard-Maugiron

Introduction

Since the beginning of the twentieth century, Egypt has codified and reformed its personal status law. Divorce for various forms of harm[1] was allowed by legislation adopted in 1920[2] and 1929,[3] though the Hanafi school of law, which Egypt follows, does not accept judicial divorce on such grounds. In 1979[4] and 1985,[5] the legislator allowed women to file for divorce in case of prejudice caused by their husband's polygamous remarriages. Finally, a law adopted in 2000[6] introduced a judicial procedure for ending a marriage without a showing of harm (*khulᶜ*). A reading of the explanatory memorandums of these laws reveals that these reforms followed a process of internal overhaul and were legitimated by reference to Sharia principles.[7]

The outcome of the reforms, however, depends on their implementation. Even if these statutory reforms were designed to improve women's legal status, their operation could only be achieved with the support of the judiciary. Judicial divorce under Egyptian law requires that a court assess the nature and degree of harm suffered by the wife. Judges therefore play a vital role as they enjoy a great deal of discretion in their decisions.

Law is not made up of self-applicable rules free of ambiguity. Interpreting the law and settling on its meaning is a highly subjective and creative task, and wives' requests therefore remain subject to the judge's discretionary power of assessment. Finally, the practical effects of a legal provision may not conform to the objective sought by the legislature at the time of the provision's adoption. Various social and economic obstacles may impede the effective implementation of the reforms.[8] The analysis of these three dimensions of divorce in Egypt will help capture both the language of law in the book and law in action.

Dissolving marriage: law in the books

The right to judicial divorce in Egypt was elaborated in three stages: first, the laws of 1920 and 1929 allowed divorce for various forms of harm; second, the laws of 1979 and 1985 dealt with the particular case of divorce for harm caused by a husband's polygamous re-marriage; finally, Law No 1 of 2000 introduced a judicial procedure for the dissolution of a marriage without harm.

Laws of 1920 and 1929: divorce for harm

In the 1920s, the Egyptian legislature authorized women to petition for judicial divorce where it could be proved that they suffered one of the harms stipulated in the law. The reform was justified by reference to principles adopted by various Sunni religious legal schools, showing the will of the legislator to re-establish a certain balance between the two spouses.

The Hanafi school of law, traditionally applied in Egypt, hardly acknowledges any reasons for legal dissolution of the spousal bond by the wife, except for the husband's impotency or castration. Hanafi law does not consider harm suffered by a wife as a reason for divorce, as it believes that it can be dealt with by other means like reprimanding the husband or releasing the wife from her duty of obedience. The Maliki doctrine, on the contrary, is prepared to grant women a divorce on certain grounds. This situation is well-illustrated in the Explanatory Memorandum of Decree-Law No 25 of 1929: 'No opinion in the Abū Ḥanīfa doctrine provides women with the means to exit marriage or foresees any way to bring back the husband on the right path. Each one can harm the other out of vengeance.'[9]

This discord between spouses 'is a source of harm which hurts not only the spouses, but also their offspring, parents, and in-laws'.[10] In order to avoid the crimes and sins provoked by this disharmony between spouses, the explanatory memorandum deemed that 'welfare commands the adoption of Imām Mālik's doctrine in case of discord between spouses'.[11]

In this memorandum, the legislature justifies having recourse to the Maliki doctrine in order to allow women to ask for divorce in case of a husband's extended absence,[12] this being premised on a fear for the abandoned wife's honour and chastity. The explanatory memorandum underlines that 'the Ḥanafī doctrine brings no remedy in such cases, whereas bringing a remedy constitutes a pressing social obligation'. While the Hanafi school has not foreseen such a case, 'the Mālikī School allows the judge to issue the divorce when the husband is absent for more than one year and when the wife complains of his absence, even if he has property from which she can get her maintenance'. In addition, the introduction of a possibility for divorce on account of a failure to provide maintenance[13] by the non-absent[14] or imprisoned[15] husband is equally of Maliki inspiration. In its explanatory memorandum, the legislature justified this last case of enabling divorce with the wish to protect women from risks of adultery: 'It is against nature that a woman live alone and preserve intact her honour and honesty' and 'what matters is the harm suffered by the wife because of her husband's distance from her, whether it is wilful or not on his behalf'.[16]

Additionally, the wife can ask to terminate a marriage if the husband is suffering from a serious and incurable disease if such a defect makes marital life harmful to the woman. She cannot, however, invoke this grievance when it was present before the marriage and she had been aware of it. Her right is also forfeited in cases where the disease appeared subsequent to marriage but she accepted its existence, expressly or tacitly.[17]

Further, art 6 para 1 of Decree-Law No 25 of 1929 foresaw another more general reason for divorce, which is divorce for harm:

> If the wife alleges that she suffered harm from her husband which makes the continuation of life impossible between persons of their condition, she can ask the judge to divorce her. The judge will issue an irrevocable judgment of divorce in her favour when such harm is proven and he could not reconcile the spouses . . .

It will be the wife's responsibility to prove to the court that the injury inflicted upon her by her husband renders life between persons of their social standing impossible. The judge will, on *ad hoc* basis, have to decide upon the existence or non-existence of such harm. Such assessment can vary on a case-by-case basis, contingent upon circumstances and according to the subjective evaluation and discretion of the judge. The assessment criteria for the degree of harm will, in addition, depend on the social status of both spouses. Some acts considered harmful at some social levels will not necessarily be considered as such by the judge for people belonging to other social strata. This reason for divorce is also inspired by the Maliki school, as is underlined by the explanatory memorandum of Decree-Law No 25 of 1929.

To prove the harm and in particular the bad treatment inflicted by her husband, the wife will have to present two persons who have personally witnessed the acts attributed to the husband. Such testimony will be subject to the unconstrained assessment of the judge, who is not obliged to grant the divorce. The proof of harm is consequently difficult to establish, especially when it constitutes a moral harm. This is also true for physical violence, as it often takes place in the bedroom, far from any external witnesses.

Decree-Law No 25 of 1929 did not allow the judge to grant the wife a divorce if investigations by arbitrators proved that she was to be blamed for the discord with her husband. However, under the amendments of 1985, judges were authorized to grant a wife's request for judicial divorce even where the wife is at fault, but in such cases she must forfeit her financial rights and pay compensation to her husband.[18]

In practice, it seems that the grounds most frequently cited by women seeking divorce are the lack of maintenance and the husband's absence.[19]

Laws of 1979 and 1985: the polygamous husband

The laws of 1920 and 1929 remained unchanged for more than half a century. Only in 1979 did President Sadat issue Decree-Law No 44 of 1979 amending those two texts. Among the new provisions introduced was the requirement that the husband's remarriage without the first wife's (or first wives') consent was to be considered harmful *as such*. The first wife would be granted an automatic divorce by the judge (i.e. a divorce not requiring further substantiation), provided she so requested within a year from the day she learned of his marriage.[20] The mere fact that her husband remarried was thus presumed harmful and she could secure a divorce before the courts without the need to prove any concrete harm having been inflicted on her. This law was criticized and challenged as constituting an indirect restriction on polygamy, which – since it is legally and religiously legitimate – should not be considered as a harm suffered by the first wife. Many personal status judges refused to apply this provision and referred the issue to the Supreme Constitutional Court with the argument that the provision violated art 2 of the Constitution according to which the principles of the Sharia are the main source of legislation.[21]

In 1985 Decree-Law No 44 of 1979 was declared unconstitutional, but on procedural grounds: the Supreme Constitutional Court held that using the decree-law procedure, which permits the president of the republic to legislate on urgent matters in the parliament's absence, was not a valid means for amending laws dating back to 1920 and 1929.[22] Two months after the decision of unconstitutionality, a new law was adopted. It still authorized the wife to divorce her husband for polygamy but required her to prove that her husband's remarriage had caused her material or moral harm so as to make continued married life impossible.[23] According to the new law the wife had a one-year grace period from the date she learned of her husband's remarriage to ask for divorce, unless she had consented to it explicitly or tacitly.[24] Since any new marriage must be registered and the previous wife notified of it, it is normally the case that a wife will be informed of any further marriages entered into by her husband.[25]

The legal effects of the amendments introduced by Law No 100 of 1985 are not very far reaching. In fact the situation is close to that which prevailed under Decree-Law No 25 of 1929: A wife can ask to have her marriage dissolved because of the polygamous remarriage of her husband. This right is, however, conditioned upon proof that this very remarriage has caused her harm. As before, the court has to evaluate the evidence on the basis of testimony by witnesses. In this same vein, the explanatory memorandum maintains that the new provisions do not aim to restrict the husband's right to polygamy but rather seek to remedy the harm caused by a polygamous marriage.[26]

The Egyptian legislature has, therefore, allowed wives to obtain a divorce for various grievances, but the request remains subjugated to the judge's discretionary power of assessment. Moreover, a wife needs to provide at least two witnesses to prove that she has suffered harm, whatever its nature. Last but not least, the procedure is often lengthy and costly, and a wife has no guarantee that the years spent before court will result in her marriage being dissolved.

*Law of 2000: divorce without harm (***khul^c***)*

To fight against the court backlogs and lengthy divorce procedures, in 2000 the legislature offered women the possibility of terminating marriage automatically by a procedure called *khul^c* in return for forsaking their financial rights.

Khul^c is a unilateral means of ending a marriage that allows women to dissolve their union in exchange for material compensation. It existed in Egyptian law prior to 2000 but the court did not participate in such a procedure as it took place entirely before a civil state officer (*ma'dhūn*). At that time it was contingent on the husband's express agreement and was a kind of amicable separation agreement or joint divorce request.[27]

In 2000, the legislature gave wives the possibility to ask for an automatic dissolution of their marriage without the judge being empowered to turn their request down, even in cases where the husband opposed the dissolution of the marriage.[28] According to the new law, a wife's declaration stating that she detested life with her husband, that continuation of married life between them had become impossible, and that she feared she would not abide by the 'limits of God' due to this detestation[29] in the event she was compelled to remain with him was deemed sufficient. The law does not require a wife to justify her request nor prove its soundness. As a compensation for her husband, however, she will have to forfeit her right to both alimony (*nafaqa*)[30] and financial compensation (*mutᶜa*),[31] and she will have to both return the dower that was paid at marriage[32] and relinquish its deferred portion (*mu'akhkhar al-ṣadāq*).[33]

The advantages of *khulᶜ* are many: this means of dissolving marriage is more quickly obtained than a normal judicial divorce. The revolutionary character of Law No 1 of 2000, however, lies in the fact that neither the husband's nor the court's consent is necessary. In addition, the modalities of forsaking financial reimbursement are fixed by the legislature and thus not open to negotiation between the spouses. Further, because the wife can divorce without her husband's consent and does not have to prove any harm, she will not be exposed to the embarrassment of disclosing the intimate details of her private life before the court. Unlike in all other cases of judicial divorce, she will not have to produce two witnesses. Moreover, the procedure is quite accelerated, as the obligatory attempt at reconciling the two spouses has to be carried out by the arbitrators within a maximum of three months.[34] If reconciliation is not achieved by the end of the three-month period and the wife still maintains her request, the judge is bound to dissolve the marriage even if it is against the husband's will. The divorce is final and the judge's decision is not subject to any appeal.[35]

On the other side, the economic consequences for the wife are burdensome. Thus, financially speaking, *khulᶜ* is more advantageous to the husband than a normal request for divorce since he does not have to pay alimony or any financial compensation. In addition, he will be reimbursed the part of the dower he paid at the time of the marriage even where it is his conduct (e.g. bad treatment or a new marriage) that led his wife to decide to break the marriage off.

Internal overhaul

It goes without saying that the provisions of Egyptian personal status law are discernibly based on Islamic rules and provisions. From this starting point the Egyptian legislator has strived to adapt them to the modern needs of society and to improve the legal status of women within the family. In doing so, law makers frequently have referred to the principles of the Sharia to legitimate the new provisions and to present their reforms as the fruit of an internal overhaul. To co-opt the support of eminent religious authorities without directly attacking the often rigid rules of the Hanafi school of law, reformers have pointed to rulings of other schools of law, in particular the Maliki school, using the methods of *takhayyur*[36] and *talfiq*.[37] The reforms have thus been placed within a common frame of reference and attacks from the conservative religious circles can be better dealt with.

The results of the reforms of personal status laws have, however, been limited in Egypt. The difficult political context, the endurance of patriarchy, and the influence of conservative and religious circles are some of the factors that have negatively affected the outcome of the reform. Amending traditional rules can induce resistance from society and conservative religious groups and is therefore politically costly in Egypt's patriarchal society. Reform attempts have been rapidly politicized and have immediately led to protest and opposition. Reform of personal status law has become the battlefield of conflicting interpretations of the sacred law, each group referring to the same body of religious rules but adopting different readings of them. In addition to the existing stakeholders, new players such as feminists and women's rights NGOs are raising their voices, challenging Islamic doctrine from within, and are urging that a distinction be drawn between patriarchal tradition and authentic Islam. Rather than emphasizing human rights and international conventions, which opens them to accusations of importing Western cultural and imperialist values, they increasingly base their views on new interpretations of the Sharia in order to legitimize their call for additional legal reforms.[38]

Notwithstanding these struggles, successive law reforms have reinforced women's legal security and rights. Still, they remain fragmentary and touch only on areas most urgently requiring a solution. The issue of their effective implementation remains extremely sensitive.

Divorce before the courts: law in action

In order to exercise their given legal rights, women have to address the court and it correspondingly falls upon judges to assess the nature and degree of harm inflicted on them. Hereby, different courts may be involved in the request for divorce. First, the family courts of first instance will decide on the substance of the case.[39] These courts were established in 2004[40] to bring relief to an over-burdened judicial system by consolidating all aspects of a divorce dispute into a single case and thus speeding up the legal process.[41] They are run by a panel of three judges and their decisions, except in *khul*ᶜ cases where the ruling of the judge is final,[42] can be contested before appeal courts. However, since 2004, rulings in family law can no longer be challenged before the Court of Cassation.[43] The rulings of the Court of Cassation mentioned in this chapter were issued before 2004 and the entry into force of that procedural law.

It should also be mentioned that Law No 100 of 1985, which gives women the right to petition for divorce in case of their husband's polygamous remarriage, and Law No 1 of 2000 on *khul*ᶜ were both challenged before the Supreme Constitutional Court for unconstitutionality. The Court was asked to decide whether the provisions violated art 2 of the 1971 Constitution according to which 'Egypt is an Arab state, its official language is Arabic and Sharia is the main source of legislation'. I shall return to this issue in the coming discussion.

Divorce because of harm and injury

In their implementation of the provision allowing divorce for harm and injury, the Court of Cassation, as well as the lower courts, have defined the concept rather broadly whilst at the same time establishing a distinction on the basis of the social status of the spouses. Further, the implementation of the provision has been limited by the proof requirements established by the Hanafi school.

Interpreting the concept of harm broadly

According to art 6 of Decree-Law No 25 of 1929, if a wife alleges that she has suffered harm (*ḍarār*) from her husband in such a way as to make continuation of marital life between persons of their social standing impossible, she may request a divorce from the judge. She will be granted an irrevocable divorce, provided the maltreatment is established and the judge fails to reconcile the couple. The burden of substantiating before the judge that harm inflicted on her by her husband has rendered the continuation of marital life between persons of their social standing impossible lies with the wife. She will have to convince the judge of the validity of her claim by proving that her husband mistreated her.

The courts of merit are bound by the rulings of the Court of Cassation, but the way the Court interpreted the concept of harm has left judges with a wide margin of discretion. In interpreting the notion of harm, the Court of Cassation consulted the Maliki school's legal literature, as the explanatory memorandum of Decree-Law No 25 of 1929 explicitly refers to the provisions of that school. This approach, however, is in contradiction with Law No 1 of 2000, which provides that in case of legal lacuna courts must refer to the prevalent opinion of the Hanafi school of law. Yet this would have been a meaningless exercise as Hanafi law does not allow divorce based on harm and injury.

The definition of the Court of Cassation is multi-layered: harm is seen as a prejudice inflicted by the husband upon his wife – consisting of deeds or words – which does not suit persons of their social standing. Further, the conduct complained of by the wife must as a matter of custom (*fī al-ᶜurf*) constitute unusual and damaging treatment which can no longer be endured and which renders the continuation of conjugal life impossible for persons of their social standing.[44] In their decisions, courts of merits usually refer to this definition of harm, though they often refer to several other rulings as well.[45]

According to the Court of Cassation harm can be inflicted actively through violence in words or facts, or passively, for example by refraining from sexual intercourse.[46] Harm may be an action, like beating or insulting, but it may also be neglect, like the abandonment (*hajr*) of a wife.[47] The Court of Cassation has, however, not made a clear statement as to the intention of the husband, i.e. whether harm must be intentional or not.[48] The frequency of the harm is not relevant, a single occurrence suffices.[49] The wrongful act will still be considered to fulfil the requirement of harm even if at the time of the examination of the case the mistreatment has stopped; it suffices that it occurred in the past.[50] Thus the Court of Cassation held that the willingness of the wife to come back to the conjugal residence after having suffered harm did not deprive her of the right to claim divorce for harm.[51]

Conversely, the Court of Cassation has recognized the right of the husband to discipline his wife by physical violence, basing itself on a Quranic verse. This right is, however, a means of last resort and can only be legitimately used after the husband has tried to exhort her and has refrained from sexual intercourse as a means of discipline. It should be absolutely necessary and is considered as a detestable permissible act (*ḥalāl makrūḥ*). The assessment of the legitimacy of physical violence lies with the judge of first instance.[52]

The Court of Cassation identified various kinds of injuries that can fulfil the concept of harm in art 6. Amongst these are the desertion of the wife by the husband[53] and the abstention of the husband from sexual intercourse,[54] as in these cases the wife' situation is unclear: she is neither having a proper conjugal life nor is she separated. The absence of her husband renders the wife vulnerable to seduction and she risks committing adultery. The court also granted divorce to a wife who was insulted by her husband and thrown out of the marital home in her night dress while the husband broke her furniture.[55] Sterility of the husband, though, is not enough to justify a divorce because procreation is not the sole purpose of marriage and an absence of children does not prevent a couple from feeling mutual tenderness and compassion.[56]

The analysis of the decisions of the Court of Cassation shows that a divorce proceeding petitioned by the wife promises to be more successful when the harm is a composite of several kinds. In practice, wives thus often refer to a multitude of misbehaviour from their husbands, including polygamy and its effects. For instance, a wife was granted a divorce for harm on the cumulative grounds that her husband failed to pay her maintenance,[57] confiscated her salary, and married another wife without her agreement.[58] In another case divorce was granted because the husband had expelled his wife from the marital home, married another woman, and stopped fulfilling his financial duties towards his first wife.[59] The Court of First Instance of Mansoura granted a divorce to a wife whose husband abandoned her, married another wife, and tried to tarnish her reputation by reporting her to the police.[60]

If a woman can establish the occurrence of both physical violence and mental abuse,[61] her petition will most likely be deemed justified. Also the combination of maltreatment with the refusal to provide financial support has been accepted by the courts as justifying a divorce petition.[62] Equally, the failure to provide a matrimonial domicile, the non-payment of the dower, abusive behaviour, and taking control of the wife's private property and inducing her to engage in prostitution or suffer humiliation have been considered as wrongful acts legitimizing divorce for harm.

The legislature has foreseen special grounds for divorce in case of the imprisonment of the husband[63] and in case of his having a serious and incurable disease, if such an illness has made marital life harmful to the woman.[64] The validity of such claims is, however, conditioned on the ignorance of the wife: if the disease was present before marriage and the wife was aware of it, or if it appeared after marriage with her accepting it, expressly or tacitly, no divorce can be granted.[65]

The social dimension of the concept of harm

A further condition for the application of art 6 of Decree-Law No 25 of 1929 is that the harm caused by the husband must be such as to make marital life between persons of their social standing impossible. The Court of Cassation has repeatedly stated that this criterion is personal (*shakhsī*), meaning that the case has to be judged on its concrete merits and could change according to the background (*bi'at*) of the spouses, their level of education, and their social environment.[66]

Again here, the assessment of this criterion is left to the discretion of the judges of first instance.[67] They must decide what kind of treatment is bearable for which kind of persons. This assessment is grounded on the presumption that the aptitude of women to endure violence and abuse is intimately linked to their social strata. Whereas 'moderate' physical abuse is tolerable for poor or illiterate rural women (on the assumption that violence is widespread and natural in this social stratum), the same level of abuse would be deemed excessive and unacceptable for women of upper-social classes, since well-educated and richer women are accustomed to better treatment. The basic evaluation criterion thus entails a subjective assessment of the judge as to the accepted social norms, culture, socioeconomic background, profession, and the community in which the spouses live.

Cases that give detailed account of these assessments by the lower court judges are very few. From the reported case one can, however, get a glimpse of the evaluation process: the Court of Cassation confirmed a decision of the lower judge who had granted a divorce to a wife on the grounds that her husband had locked the front door of their marital home and refused to let her in by insulting her and shouting at her to get away in front of two other men. Because the spouses came from a respectable family and both had an advanced education level, the court held that such behaviour was damaging to the honour of the wife and a wrong not acceptable for a person of her social strata.[68]

Considering the social strata of the couple can, however, also work in the other direction: thus the divorce request of a wife who felt ashamed because of the imprisonment of her husband was declined as the court argued that within the social level of the couple this did not constitute harm for the wife. The court in particular questioned the impact of the condemnation on the wife as harmful, as she had waited six months before applying for divorce.[69] Similarly, a request for divorce was turned down on the fact that the claimed physical abuse of the wife could not be considered harm in terms of art 6 as this kind of behaviour did not make marital life impossible for persons of their social standing.[70]

These judgements are of critical significance as the taking into consideration of the social rank of a person when assessing the level of harm reinforces stereotypes and induces discrimination on the basis of social class. It also fosters contradictory rulings and makes the outcome of legal proceedings unpredictable for women.

Difficult standards of proof

The wife shoulders the burden of providing evidence of harm. The judges have a wide margin of discretion in their assessment of the proof – this including witnesses' testimony and a judge's appreciation thereof – without having to justify their choices.[71] Adding to this, the standards of proof are very difficult to meet, as harm is mostly proven by witnesses' testimony. According to the Court of Cassation, the principles of the Hanafi school and not those of the Maliki are applicable in determining the conditions for crediting testimony.[72] The prevailing opinion in Hanafi law requires the testimony of two males, or two females and one male,[73] all Muslims[74] because a non-Muslim may not testify in favour of a Muslim.[75] Furthermore, the witnesses must have personally witnessed the harm, hearsay testimony (*tasāmuʿ*)[76] is not allowed; testimony that one has heard of a marital dispute without witnessing the battering or verbal abuse, therefore, is not acceptable. If such witnesses cannot be provided, the wife's request will be rejected.[77]

It is evident that establishing harm by these means is extremely difficult. Physical and mental abuse generally takes place in the privacy of the marital home. Both the couple, as well as the witnesses, may feel ill at ease in disclosing the intimate details of private life and, in particular, of sexual abuse. The Court of Cassation has therefore reacted to this situation and has held that harm can also be established by other evidentiary means, such as letters,[78] documents proving that a husband had stolen his wife's properties,[79] medical certificates, a police report,[80] or the fact that the husband has been convicted of assault and battery.[81]

Courts and divorce for polygamy

Evolution of the statutory provisions on polygamy

In 1979, a revolutionary law was decreed. Law No 44 of 1979 prescribed that a wife could seek a divorce because of harm if her husband remarried without her consent. This right was conferred on the first wife, without her having to substantiate the harm inflicted upon her. The new legal presumption was that polygamous marriages are per se harmful. The law was justified in the explanatory memorandum with reference to Maliki and Hanbali precedents, a Quranic verse (4:35) and the *hadith* '*lā ḍarar wa lā ḍirār*' (no harm, no foul).[82]

The reactions were immediate: the provision was challenged as restricting polygamy, albeit indirectly, and in labelling it harmful despite the fact that polygamy was legally and religiously legitimate. Judges rejected the law and refused its application, considering it unconstitutional and contrary to the Islamic Sharia. The Supreme Constitutional Court was overwhelmed with pleas of unconstitutionality. Decree-Law No 44 of 1979 was declared unconstitutional in 1985, but for procedural reasons rather than on substantive grounds. Specifically, the Court held that the decree-law procedure, which permitted the President of the Republic to legislate in the Parliament's absence for urgent matters, could not be used to amend laws dating back to 1920 and 1929.[83]

Law No 100 of 1985, which was adopted two months after the abrogation of Decree-Law No 44 of 1979, altered the rules. It reiterated the wife's right to divorce because of the polygamous remarriage of her husband, even without an explicit clause in their marriage contract stipulating that he may not marry another wife.[84] The new art 11bis, however, did require the wife to prove that her husband's remarriage caused her material or mental harm, which made marital life amongst persons of their social standing difficult.[85] Again, the explanatory memorandum tried to justify the rule by pointing out that the intention of the law was not to confine the husband's right to polygamy. Rather, it acknowledged that a harm caused by the husband's polygamous remarriage needed a remedy.

As a result the new provision removed the legal presumption that polygamy is harmful per se, and the situation prevailing under Decree-Law No 25 of 1929 was quasi reinstalled.[86] Thus a woman can be granted divorce on the basis of the harm inflicted on her by her polygamous husband, albeit pursuant to some substantial conditions. First, the burden of proof lies on her to substantiate the harm suffered. The judge has a discretionary power to assess the evidence on the basis of testimony by witnesses. Second, the harm must result from the remarriage of the husband; and, third, the harm must make continued conjugal relations 'difficult' (*yata*ᶜ*adhdhar ma*ᶜ*ahu dawām al-*ᶜ*ishra*) amongst persons of their social standing, whereas the general condition for divorce for harm is that marital life becomes 'impossible' (*lā yustaṭā*ᶜ*a ma*ᶜ*ahu dawām al-*ᶜ*ishra*). Another difference is that the wife will lose her right to petition for divorce after one year. And finally, the new law clearly states that the harm may be physical or mental. Its assessment, however, will depend on the social strata of the spouses.

Notwithstanding these changes the mitigated version of the 1985 provision was challenged before the Supreme Constitutional Court for violating art 2 of the Constitution.

The Supreme Constitutional Court upholds the provisions on divorce for polygamy and khulᶜ

In 1994, a bigamous man, whose first wife had asked for divorce on the ground of polygamy, challenged the relevant provision before the Constitutional Court, asking the Court to declare it unconstitutional on the basis that the conditions which it provides jeopardized a man's right as accorded by the Sharia to be married to up to four women simultaneously. The Supreme Constitutional Court, however, refused to confirm that the wife's right to request divorce in case of polygamy violated the Sharia.[87]

Having consideration for a basic principle first established in 1993,[88] the Constitutional Court made a distinction between absolute and relative principles of Islamic Sharia.[89] Only principles 'whose origin and significance are absolute' (*al-aḥkām al-shar*ᶜ*īyya al-qaṭ*ᶜ*īyya fī thubūtihā wa dalālatihā*), i.e. principles which represent uncontestable Islamic norms as to their source or their meaning, cannot be subject to interpretative reasoning (*ijtihād*) and cannot evolve with time. They represent the fundamental principles and the fixed foundation (*thawābit*) of Islamic law.

By way of contrast, the constitutional judges identified a second group of so-called relative rules (*aḥkām ẓanniyya*), either because of their origin or because of their significance or with regard to both. Those rules can evolve over time and space, are dynamic, give rise to different interpretations, and are adjustable to the changing needs of society. It is the duty of the 'person in authority' (*walī al-amr*), i.e. the legislator, to interpret and establish norms in relation to these rules. Bearing in mind the interest of the Sharia, this interpretative endeavour must be based on reasoning and is not limited by any previous view.[90]

Against this background the Supreme Constitutional Court reasoned that notwithstanding a man's right to polygamy as guaranteed by a Quranic verse,[91] it was not made mandatory. Furthermore the exercise of polygamy was subordinated to the fair and equal treatment of all wives. The Court stated that Law No 100 of 1985 had not forbidden polygamy – which would indeed have violated an absolute principle in the Sharia – but had referred to objective grounds, taking into consideration the material and moral suffering of the first wife, for whom such a remarriage could render marital life impossible. It also highlighted that the wife had to prove that she had been harmed by the second marriage. Finally, the ultimate decision would rest upon a judge who has discretionary powers in assessing the harm and who has to try to reconcile the spouses. In view of all these facts, the court concluded that the provision did not violate art 2 of the 1971 Constitution.

The same reasoning was used in 2004 by the Supreme Constitutional Court in its decision concerning Law No 1 of 2000 in regard to *khulᶜ*. In its ruling, the Court declared that *khulᶜ* did not contradict the rules of the Islamic Sharia. It stressed that the woman's right to *khulᶜ* and her right to exit the marriage upon payment of compensation was enshrined in the Quran as a provision of absolute origin. Its implementation, though, had not been fixed in a definite manner. As a matter of fact the various Islamic schools of law and Islamic scholars were in disagreement on the details of *khulᶜ*. Whereas some held that the husband's agreement was indispensable, others deemed it unnecessary. The statutory provision followed the opinion in the Maliki school: the wife could resort to *khulᶜ* in case of necessity, i.e. in case it was impossible for her to continue the marriage. This approach, the Court explained, can be followed as in no way does it contradict the rules of the Sharia. A woman cannot be forced to live with a man. The claim of unconstitutionality was rejected.[92]

Material or moral harm caused by polygamy

Before art 11bis was introduced, a wife could already ask for divorce in case of polygamy within the frame of art 6 of Decree-Law No 25 of 1929. To be successful she had to establish a causality between the remarriage and harm inflicted by her husband: she could argue that the husband did not treat all wives equally,[93] which is a requirement in polygamous remarriages, or that because of the remarriage the husband had refrained from sexual intercourse or had stopped providing maintenance.[94] If the wife failed to establish this causality, she could still base her divorce request on art 6 of Decree-Law No 25 of 1929 with reference to the general concept of harm[95] or on the grounds of the absence of her husband.

According to the interpretation adopted by the Court of Cassation, the concept of harm caused by polygamy must be assessed on the concrete circumstances of the case: the harm caused by the second marriage must be real, not illusory; concrete, not abstract; and established as a matter of fact before the court, not presumed.[96] The first wife must prove that the harm was caused by the polygamous remarriage of her husband. It does, however, not suffice that the purpose of the second marriage was illegitimate.[97] The repulsion a wife might feel for her polygamous husband will also not be sufficient to make a case for divorce.[98] Thus in accordance with these principles, the Court of Cassation overruled the decision of a first instance court that had granted divorce to a wife who felt jealous, miserable, and full of sorrow because of the polygamous remarriage of her husband. The Court deemed that these feelings were not sufficient to prove an occurrence of harm independent from the marriage itself. Jealousy, the Court held, was a 'natural feeling between the two wives of a same man'.[99] The mental effects that the remarriage had on the wife were not held to fulfil the conditions of art 11bis.

Conversely, forcing the first wife to live with the new wife has been held to create a moral and material harm justifying divorce for the first wife.[100] Similarly, a wife was granted divorce as her husband had abandoned her and stopped providing for her after his remarriage.[101] Other aspects of harm are illustrated by a decision of 1999 of the Cairo Appeal Court granting divorce. In that case the husband had remarried and – in order to house his new wife – had ejected the first wife from the marital home, refrained from providing for her, beaten and insulted her, and finally repudiated her only to revoke the pronouncement of the divorce shortly after.[102] Equally, a wife was granted divorce because her husband had refrained from cohabitation and sexual intercourse after having married another wife.[103] Further, the abandonment of the first wife for more than ten months and the non-provision of maintenance to her and their common children after his remarriage,[104] as well as the expulsion of the first wife from the marital home after a polygamous remarriage, have been considered valid grounds to establish harm legitimizing the divorce request of the first wife.[105]

Judges and the implementation of personal status law

The Egyptian legislature has allowed women to obtain a divorce based on various grievances. It has also granted the judiciary a wide margin of appreciation to assess the alleged harm. Judges interpret the legal norms and exercise creative efforts. Thus they play an important role in the process of social regulation and in the evolution of family affairs. Interestingly this role is given to the courts even in personal status law, a field traditionally pertaining to Islamic law. In practice Egyptian judges rarely refer to Islamic norms, as most of them are not trained in Islamic law and thus are not familiar with traditional Islamic jurisprudence. Notwithstanding this fact, according to Law No 1 of 2000 the courts have to follow the most prevalent opinion within the Hanafi school in case of legal lacunae.[106]

Thus, in the silence of the law, the judge must seek, identify, and implement non-codified Islamic norms. It can, however, be observed that even in the absence of a legal rule in the personal status laws or in the decisions of the Court of Cassation, judges have in only limited situations referred to the Hanafi school.[107]

The analysis of the jurisprudence shows that lower court judges have interpreted the concept of harm rather broadly, and wives have managed to secure a divorce on a wide range of grounds. In fact courts have been rather open to women's requests and willing to examine the cases with benevolence. They have drawn a distinction according to the social conditions of the couple in question, but they have not taken into consideration religious factors as such. Further, one has to bear in mind, that until the beginning of 2007, no women were sitting on any Egyptian ordinary courts. The Supreme Constitutional Court was the only court that included a woman in 2003.[108] Additionally, women face a wide range of social and economic difficulties in realizing their legal rights in divorce matters.

Divorce in Egyptian society

The objective sought by the legislature through the enactment of legislation is not always reflected in the practical effects of the law. This is the case with legal reforms related to divorce, which often clash with social and economic considerations.

Social obstacles

In Egyptian society the family is the basic unit of society. The prevailing view is that it must be preserved and protected even at the expense of the individual members. Thus a woman seeking to end her marriage will generally be seen as responsible for destroying the family even if she has good reasons to exit an abusive marriage. This societal conservatism and prejudice against women was plainly apparent during parliamentary debates[109] at the time of the adoption of the law on *khul*ᶜ. Thus, one could hear deputies allege that such a procedure would lead to family dislocation and have detrimental consequences on the children; that women could abuse this right and act mindlessly; that wives would give in to temptation and destroy their homes and throw their children in the streets. Another deputy added that this provision was a menace to the stability of the families and that it would inflame home life. Other criticisms were correspondingly raised in conservative religious circles, which considered any provision not requiring the husband's consent and not involving the judge as being contrary to the Sharia.[110] The fact that the Egyptian People's Assembly included only a handful of women among its members[111] was no doubt a factor that increased the prevalence of such stances.

Social and familial pressures, therefore, strongly dissuade women from dissolving their union, especially if they have children, even if there are valid reasons to do so. Out of fear for marring their as well as their family's reputation, a substantial number of women are reluctant to take advantage of the legal reforms. Further, social shame transcends within the families: some mothers will renounce having recourse to the procedure of *khul*ᶜ because they fear that their daughters will not find any suitors for marriage, according to the adage *like mother like daughter*.[112]

If a man's honour and virility are considered tainted when his wife asks for divorce,[113] it is even worse if she asks for *khul*ᶜ. To avoid the humiliation of being 'repudiated' by his wife, the husband could have recourse to his right of unilateral repudiation. Conversely, however, some husbands may push their wives to initiate *khul*ᶜ because it is financially more advantageous for them. They may also agree to repudiate their wife for financial compensation. This is the 'traditional' conception of *khul*ᶜ that was common before 2000 when it was considered a 'divorce by agreement' performed in front of the *ma'dhūn*. In exchange for the repudiation, the husband often required his wife to forfeit her right to alimony, her compensation claim (*mut*ᶜ*a*), her deferred dower (*mu'akhkhar al-ṣadāq*), and more often than not her furniture as well as the matrimonial domicile.[114]

The lack of education and high illiteracy rates among women undoubtedly play a role in both the knowledge women have in respect of the law and their means to have legal rights in fact respected. One interviewed woman reported that it was only during the reconciliation session of the *khul*ᶜ procedure that she learned that she could still keep the custody of her children, seek alimony for them from their father, and keep her furniture. This was an unpleasant surprise for the husband, who refused to cooperate further, became nervous, and was ultimately asked to leave the premises.[115]

Economic obstacles

Material difficulties are added to social obstacles. Normally a repudiated wife is entitled to compensation, to alimony in the waiting period (for three months), and to the deferred part of her dower. Most of the time, however, the husband will not pay, and she will have to bring a case to court. She will wait for months to get a decision and then face the harshest of difficulties in attempting to enforce it.[116] Thus, over the years the procedure of *khul*ᶜ has proven to be a success, despite considerable controversy at the time of its adoption, when it was criticized as being accessible only to wealthy women of high social standards, since only rich women would be able to reimburse the prompt dower and forsake their other financial rights.

This view fails to see the economic realities of Egyptian society today: in many cases women are the ones who not only provide for their families but also for their unemployed husbands. Instead of wasting time, energy, and money in trying to obtain a judgement ordering their husbands to pay alimony, and wasting even more time in trying to enforce it, women prefer to forsake their financial rights from the very beginning. *Khul*ᶜ is in many cases the lesser of two evils as it releases the wife both from an unhappy marriage and from the burden of providing for an unemployed husband.

Therefore *khul*ᶜ has become a favoured procedure for women wishing to quickly end their marriage. Some even maintain that if financial circumstances did not dissuade women from asking for divorce, the number of *khul*ᶜ divorces would double.[117] Also, the fact that increasingly more wives participate in supporting the family explains why middle-class women and even women of lower social strata have recourse to it as well.

Furthermore one has to bear in mind, that lawsuits involve a financial burden. The attorney's fees and the court dues have to be paid. [118] Law No 1 of 2000 has tried to reduce the fees by granting maintenance claims free of charge, but this exemption does not include divorce claims.[119] This financial obstacle weighs on lower-class women. Some NGOs, being aware of such obstacles, have created a legal service that offers legal help free of charge to women of lower economic status.[120]

Whatever the kind of marriage dissolution, women will face economic difficulties in most cases, since a great number of ex-husbands do not pay alimony and litigation brought against them lingers for years. Such financial difficulty is of course to be expected when the marriage is dissolved by *khul*ᶜ (since there the wife forfeits all her financial rights) or when the wife was repudiated on her request for a divorce in exchange for financial compensation: in such situations she ends up with no financial means. But it is also the case in many instances of judicial divorce, where the husband pays his former wife neither her *mut*ᶜ*a*, alimony nor the deferred dower.

In addition, it is quite often the case that fathers abstain from providing maintenance for their children. According to Decree-Law No 100 of 1985, if the children have no personal resources, fathers have to cover the needs of any minor children who are entrusted into their mother's custody.[121] In practice, few fathers fulfil their financial obligation. Instead mothers have to provide for their children from their own resources, when many can hardly cover their own needs.

Most women have no independent source of income and depend on the financial support of their families and relatives. The most crucial problem for most of them is finding a place to live, especially in big cities like Cairo. Decree-Law No 100 of 1985 allocates the matrimonial domicile to the wife upon divorce if she has custody of the children,[122] but custody ends at the age of 15. Besides, not all women have children or children in custody age. Thus many women find themselves without financial resources when their husband decides to repudiate them in order to marry a younger wife.[123] Moreover, in practice, women are not always successful in having the court decision entitling them to the spousal home enforced;[124] this is in particular when the decision is delivered years after the divorce.

But even when women are employed, their salaries hardly enable them to cover the rent. For support, these women turn to their families, who often lack the place and the means to accommodate extra mouths to feed. It is therefore often the members of her own family who try to convince the wife that her place is beside her husband, striving to minimize the bad treatment to which the wife has been subjected, with mothers presenting the situation as normal for all wives. Some women go and live with their married children, a situation that may equally have a negative impact on the family life of their daughter or son. Others delay the divorce procedure or even withdraw it because they would not have a place to live.[125]

Conclusion

A faithful assessment of access to judicial divorce for harm and injury must take all the mentioned dimensions into consideration. Egyptian personal status law reforms were introduced as the fruit of an internal overhaul and made legitimate by reference to Sharia principles. However limited, these reforms have nevertheless improved women's legal security and improved their rights, even though they were fragmentary and only touched on issues that needed urgent solutions. Thus the legal status of women wishing to end an unhappy marriage has undoubtedly improved through the codification process of personal status law in Egypt in the twentieth century. The practical effects of these legal reforms can, however, be questioned. The codification and unification of norms and the improvement of women's legal status in family relations are but a first step. The second step, however, should be to ensure that they know of their legal rights and to provide an environment that would enable them to use such rights and claim greater protection.

The study of law in general and personal status law in particular needs more focus on practices. It must capture the language of law in action and not only that of law in the books. Law as a social phenomenon cannot be reduced to the mere provisions of a legal code.[126] The effectiveness of such reforms is linked to social acceptance. One should not presume that the mere presence of laws is sufficient to ensure their implementation and respect. The question remains how and how far law can be a vehicle for social change when its implementation is confronted by religious, economic and social norms.

Notes

1 This chapter deals only with personal status law for Muslims. For personal status law for non-Muslims see Nathalie Bernard-Maugiron, 'Divorce and Remarriage of Orthodox Copts in Egypt: The 2008 State Council Ruling and the Amendment of the 1938 Personal Status Regulations' (2011) 18 Islamic Law and Society 356. Cases from the Court of Cassation, the Supreme Constitutional Court, appeal courts, courts of first instance (until 2004), and family courts (after 2004) were reviewed in preparing this submission. Most of the cases were adopted after the 1970s.

2 Decree-Law No 25 of 1920 Regarding Maintenance and Some Questions of Personal Status of 12 July 1920, Official Gazette no 61 of 15 July 1920.

3 Decree-Law No 25 of 1929 Regarding Certain Personal Status Provisions of 10 March 1929, Official Gazette no 27 of 25 March 1929.

4 Law No 44 of 1979 Regarding the Amendment of Certain Personal Status Provisions of 20 June 1979, Official Gazette no 25 *tābiᶜ* (a) of 21 June 1979.

5 Law No 100 of 1985 Regarding the Amendment of Certain Personal Status Provisions of 3 July 1985, Official Gazette no 27 *tābiᶜ* of 4 July 1985.

6 Law No 1 of 2000 Regulating Certain Litigation Procedures in Personal Status of 29 January 2000, Official Gazette no 4 *mukarrar* of 29 January 2000.

7 I have made reference to this process in an earlier paper, see Nathalie Bernard-Maugiron, 'Courts and the Reform of Personal Status Law in Egypt' in Elisa Giunchi (ed), *Adjudicating Family Law in Muslim Courts* (Routledge 2014).

8 For a study of the normative implementation of family law in Egypt see Essam Fawzy, 'Muslim Personal Status Law in Egypt: the Current Situation and Possibilities of Reform through Internal Initiatives' in Lynn Welchman (ed), *Women's Rights and Islamic Family Law: Perspectives on Reform* (Zed Books 2004).

9 Explanatory Memorandum to Decree-Law No 25 of 1929 was published with the law itself, Official Gazette no 27 of 25 March 1929 and can be found in Y al-Shazlī, *Personal Status Laws for Muslims with the Explanatory Memorandums* (al-Maktaba al-Qānūniyya 1987) pt 1 (in Arabic) and in French in (1928–1929) 19 Gazette des Tribunaux Mixtes d'Égypte 115–118.

10 Explanatory Memorandum to Decree-Law No 25 of 1929 (n 9).

11 Ibid.

12 The wife can ask for the divorce in case the husband's absence exceeds a year without any legitimate reason, even if he has left assets from which she can make maintenance expenditures, arts 12 and 13 Decree-Law No 25 of 1929.

13 The husband has a maintenance obligation towards his wife for the entire duration of marriage, including when the wife has personal resources.

14 Art 4 Decree-Law No 25 of 1920.

15 The wife can also seek a divorce if her husband is condemned to jail for more than three years, even if he has property from which she could provide for her maintenance, see art 14 Decree-Law No 25 of 1929.

16 See Explanatory Memorandum to Decree-Law No 25 of 1929 (n 9).

17 Art 9 Decree-Law No 25 of 1920.

18 Art 11 Decree-Law No 25 of 1929 as amended by Law No 100 of 1985.

19 For the reasons invoked before the Sharia courts see Ron Shaham, 'Judicial Divorce at the Wife's Initiative: the Shari'a Courts in Egypt, 1920–1955' (1994) 1 Islamic Law and Society 16. For an analysis of other decisions of the Egyptian Court of Cassation dealing with divorce for injury see Immanuel Naveh, 'The Tort of Injury and Dissolution of Marriage at the Wife's Initiative in Egyptian Mahkama al-Naqd rulings' (2001) 9 Islamic Law and Society 1, 16.

20 Art 6bis para 1.2 Decree-Law No 25 of 1929 as amended by Law No 100 of 1985.

21 Art 2 of the Constitution of 1971 has been reproduced in the new Egyptian Constitution of 18 January 2014, Official Gazette no 3 *mukarrar (a)* of 18 January 2014.

22 Supreme Constitutional Court (SCC) No 28/2, 4 May 1985.

23 Art 11bis 1 Decree-Law No 25 of 1929 as amended by Law No 100 of 1985.

24 Art 11bis 1 Decree-Law No 25 of 1929 as amended by Law No 100 of 1985.

25 If the new wife was ignorant of her husband already being married, she can ask for the divorce.

26 SCC No 35/9, 14 August 1994. In this case, the Supreme Constitutional Court determined this provision to be in conformity with the Islamic Sharia.

27 The Court of Cassation defined in a judgement of 28 October 1937 *khul*ᶜ as an agreement to obtain final separation in exchange for a financial compensation to the husband.

28 Art 20 of Law No 1 of 2000.

29 The law has quoted from *Quran* sura 4 (*sūrat al-baqara*) verse 229.

30 This alimony is paid for a maximum of one year after the divorce is issued, arts 17 and 18 Decree-Law No 25 of 1929. It is due to the wife whether the dissolution of the marriage took place by means of repudiation or by a judicial decision. It must cover her food expenses, clothing, housing, and medical expenses.

31 Since 1985 wives have been entitled to receive financial compensation (*mut*^{c}*a*), the amount of which should not be less than two years of maintenance; it is evaluated according to the husband's financial means, divorce circumstances, and length of marriage. This compensation is only due if the marriage was ended without the wife's consent and without her being responsible for it.

32 The husband-groom must pay to his bride a dower – a sum of money that is totally hers. In Egypt, the custom is to divide the dower in two parts; the first part is paid at marriage while the second part is paid when the marriage is dissolved (either by the husband's death or divorce).

33 Other women's rights are not reappraised. Thus, her right to custody of children is not reconsidered nor is the obligation of alimony that falls on the husband for supporting his children (art 20 para 3 Law No 1 of 2000), nor the right to keep the house until custody of the children comes to an end.

34 Arts 18–20 Law No 1 of 2000. Two attempts have to be carried out if the spouses have children.

35 Art 20 Law No 1 of 2000.

36 A choice of rules between the wide range of opinions advocated by eminent historical jurists within the four Sunni schools of law.

37 A combination of rules from opinions advocated by eminent historical jurists within the four Sunni schools of law to produce new solutions. The legislator also conceived of a device of procedural nature, a restriction of the jurisdiction of the courts, see on this matter Nora Alim and Nadjma Yassasi, Chapter 5.

38 Diana Singerman, 'Rewriting Divorce in Egypt: Reclaiming Islam, Legal Activism and Coalition Politics' in Robert Hefner (ed), *Remaking Muslim Politics: Pluralism, Contestation, Democratization* (Princeton University Press 2005); see also Fawzy (n 8).

39 *Sharia* courts, which had previously ruled in Muslim personal status matters, were abolished by Laws No 461 and 462 of 1955 and their powers transferred to the ordinary courts, in which special circuits dealt with personal status cases.

40 Law No 10 of 2004 Establishing Family Courts of 17 March 2004, Official Gazette no 12 *tābi*^{c} *(a)* of 18 March 2004. These courts were annexed to the more than 200 existing summary courts and eight appeal courts.

41 For a detailed study of the five first years of family courts see Mulki Al-Sharmani, *Recent Reforms in Personal Status Laws and Women's Empowerment. Family Courts in Egypt* (AUC Social Research Center 2008) <www.musawah.org/sites/default/files/Familycourts.pdf> accessed 12 July 2014.

42 Art 20 Law No 1 of 2000.

43 Art 14 Law No 10 of 2004. The explanatory memorandum of the law justified this measure by the special nature of personal status cases and the necessity to rule in as short a timeframe as possible in order to determine the legal status of important questions regarding individuals and the family. Only the public prosecution is, under certain conditions, allowed to bring a personal status case before the Court of Cassation.

44 Court of Cassation No 23/57, 28 June 1988; Court of Cassation No 369/68, 9 March 2002.

45 See Family Court of Shubra No 256/2008, 29 July 2008, which refers to Court of Cassation No 99/59, 5 December 1991 and Family Court of Badrashin No 465/2006, 31 May 2007, which refers to Court of Cassation No 337/67, 13 October 2001.

46 Court of Cassation No 15/47, 2 April 1980.

47 Court of Cassation No 432/64, 29 September 1998 or Court of Cassation No 323/66, 10 March 2001.

48 Court of Cassation No 640/66, 11 June 2001 or Court of Cassation No 163/59, 19 May 1992, where the Court stated that injury shall be wilful; Court of Cassation No 19/48, 21 February 1979, where the Court decided, on the basis of the Maliki school, that the wife was injured even if the husband did not intend to hurt her by abandoning her.

49 Court of Cassation No 23/57, 28 June 1981 or Giza First Instance Court No 3322/2000, 29 January 2001, which refers to the case law of the Court of Cassation in that regard.

50 Court of Cassation No 19/48, 21 February 1979.

51 Court of Cassation No 82/63, 28 January 1997.

52 Court of Cassation No 85/66, 10 February 2001.

53 An absence of the husband is considered as a special ground for divorce under arts 12 and 13 of Decree-Law No 25 of 1929 out of fear for the abandoned wife's honour and chastity. The wife can claim divorce on that ground if the husband's absence is prolonged more than a year without any justified excuse (*ᶜudhr maqbūl*), even if he has left property from which she can secure her maintenance. The explanatory memorandum defines absence of the husband as his taking up residence in a town different from that of the matrimonial residence; an absence is justified if it results from travel for the purpose of study or trade or the breakdown of transportation means. Conversely, absence within the meaning of art 6 of Decree-Law No 25 of 1929 does not require that the residence of the husband be in a different city.

54 Court of Cassation No 50/52, 28 June 1983 or Court of Cassation No 92/58, 18 December 1990.

55 Port Said First Instance Court No 127/1990, 22 December 1992; confirmed by Court of Cassation No 398/63, 27 January 1998.

56 Court of Cassation No 357/63, 29 December 1997.

57 The husband has an obligation to financially support his wife for the entire duration of marriage even if she has personal resources. Failure to provide maintenance is considered as a special ground for divorce by art 4 of Decree-Law No 25 of 1920: if the husband proves his insolvency, the judge shall grant him a delay not exceeding one month after which, if he fails to pay maintenance, divorce shall be granted. The husband then retains the right to reinstate his wife during the waiting period if he pays the arrears of maintenance (art 6).

58 South Cairo First Instance Court No 1193/1919, 31 December 1992.

59 Tanta Appeal Court No 233/26, 7 February 1994, as confirmed by Court of Cassation No 175/64, 21 April 1998.

60 Mansoura First Instance Court No 1115/1983, 31 March 1985.

61 For example in the Family Court of al-Badrashin No 806/2006, 28 June 2007, the husband had beaten and insulted his wife and accused her of being a liar and a thief.

62 For example the First Instance Court of Giza divorced a wife who was beaten and insulted by her polygamous husband, who also had stopped spending money on her, Giza Court of First Instance No 561/97, 25 August 1997. The decision was upheld by the Cairo Appeal Court.

63 The wife can also get a divorce if her husband has been condemned to jail for more than three years, even if he has property from which she could secure maintenance. She can ask for divorce after at least one year of separation (art 14 Decree-Law No 25 of 1929).

64 The Court of Cassation decided that the list of defects enumerated in art 9 was not exhaustive, Court of Cassation No 13/44, 11 February 1976.

65 Art 9 Decree-Law No 25 of 1920.
66 Court of Cassation No 665/68, 9 March 2002; see also Court of Cassation No 135/63, 17 March 1997.
67 Court of Cassation No 96/56, 24 January 1989.
68 Court of Cassation No 19/44, 24 March 1976; further the Court of Cassation upheld the assessment of the lower court judge who – in consideration of the milieu to which the couple belonged – had characterized as harmful the behaviour of a husband who had assaulted his wife in the street, broken her necklace, and soiled her clothes while passers-by congregated to watch what was going on, Court of Cassation No 5/46, 9 November 1977.
69 Sayyida Court No 355/33, quoted in Aḥmad Naṣr al-Guinḍī, *Judicial Principles in Personal Status Affairs* (al-Ḥadītha li-l-Ṭabāᶜa 1992) 446.
70 Court of First Instance of South Cairo, 1973.
71 Court of Cassation No 133/64, 13 April 1998.
72 Court of Cassation No 15/47, 2 April 1980; in their decisions, lower court judges regularly refer to decisions of the Court of Cassation establishing this principle, see Giza Court of First Instance No 3322/2000, 29 January 2011 with reference to Court of Cassation No 62/63, 24 February 1997.
73 Court of Cassation No 15/47, 2 April 1980; see also Family Court of Badrashin No 1070/2006, 31 January 2008, where the court refused to grant divorce because only two women had been present when the husband was beating and insulting his wife.
74 Court of Cassation No 16/38, 5 June 1974, where the request for divorce was rejected because the witnesses were non-Muslim Austrians.
75 Court of Cassation No 16/38, 5 June 1974.
76 Court of Cassation No 11/47, 25 April 1979; in Court of Cassation No 509/65, 26 June 2000, the court refused to grant divorce because the two witnesses had described actions that the wife claimed had taken place but which they had not seen and heard by themselves; see also Family Court of Shubra No 196/2008, 2 August 2008, where the testimonies were not corroborating.
77 See Family Court of Shubra No 162/2008, where the wife could not bring witnesses to testify that her husband had abandoned her for five years.
78 In Court of Cassation No 202/62, 25 March 1996, a letter of a father to his son where he accuses his wife of having betrayed him and of having lost her morals was accepted as sufficient evidence.
79 Court of Cassation No 11/47, 25 April 1979.
80 Giza First Instance Court No 3322/2000, 29 January 2001.
81 Court of Cassation No 101/64, 28 December 1998 or Court of Cassation No 60/8, 14 December 1939.
82 Explanatory Memorandum to Law No 44 of 1979.
83 SCC No 28/2, 4 May 1985.
84 Spouses can agree on stipulations to add to their marriage contract at the time of marriage, in particular the right of the wife to repudiate herself (*ᶜiṣma*) at will or in a specific case, for instance if her husband engages in polygamy. She will in these cases retain her financial rights.
85 Art 11bis 1 Decree-Law No 25 of 1929 as added by Law No 100 of 1985.
86 Since any new marriage must be registered and the previous wife must be notified by the public notary, she should be informed of her husband's second marriage. If the husband is already married, he must state the name of his wife and her place of

domicile. If the new wife was ignorant of the fact that her husband was already married, she may also apply for divorce.

87 SCC No 35/9, 14 August 1994.

88 SCC No 7/8e, 15 May 1993. This stance was systematically repeated in all the Court's subsequent decisions dealing with the conformity of laws with art 2 of the Constitution.

89 Nathan Brown and Clark Lombardi, 'Do Constitutions Requiring Adherence to Shari`a Threaten Human Rights? How Egypt's Constitutional Court Reconciles Islamic Law with the Liberal Rule of Law' (2006) 21 American University International Law Review 379; Clark B Lombardi, 'Islamic Law as a Source of Constitutional Law in Egypt: The Constitutionalization of the Sharia in a Modern Arab State' (1998) 37 Columbia Journal of Transnational Law 81; Nathalie Bernard-Maugiron and Baudouin Dupret, 'Les principes de la *sharî'a* sont la source principale de la législation. La Haute Cour constitutionnelle et la référence à la loi islamique' (1999) 2 Égypte-Monde arabe 107.

90 SCC No 29/11, 26 March 1994.

91 See sura 4, verse 3.

92 SCC No 201/23, 15 December 2002, Official Gazette no 52 *tābi*[c] of 26 December 2002.

93 The Court of Cassation confirmed a judgement of a first instance court that had granted a wife divorce on the ground that, to the extent polygamy is allowed by the Sharia, the husband has to act fairly. In the case under review, the husband had abandoned his first wife for more than two years and had stopped providing for her financially, which the court considered to infringe upon the principle of equality between all wives, Court of Cassation No 34/48, 13 June 1979.

94 Courts have allowed wives to request both divorce for injury and divorce for polygamy; see Family Court of Badrashin No 1070/2006, 31 January 2008, where both grounds were included in the same claim.

95 Court of Cassation No 341/63, 27 October 1997. The Court allows wives to request divorce for injury if their request of divorce for polygamy failed (Court of Cassation No 553/65, 20 November 2000).

96 Court of Cassation No 256/61, 8 January 1996.

97 Court of Cassation No 225/59, 24 November 1992.

98 Court of Cassation No 465/68, 18 March 2002.

99 Court of Cassation No 256/61, 8 January 1996.

100 Court of Cassation No 129/59, 5 March 1991.

101 Court of Cassation No 504/65, 30 October 2000; Court of Cassation No 422/64, 29 September 1998.

102 Cairo Court of Appeal No 1133/110, 4 February 1999. The decision confirmed the decision of the First Instance Court of Giza, Giza First Instance Court No 281/1998, 20 September 1998.

103 Court of Cassation No 114/95, 24 March 1992.

104 Court of Cassation No 212/63, 5 January 1998.

105 Cairo Court of Appeal No 1133/110, 4 February 1999.

106 Art 3 of Law No 1 of 2000, which reasserted art 280 of the 1931 Sharia Courts Regulations, repealed by that same law.

107 For example, they referred to the Hanafi school to allow divorce for impotence of the husband, to fix the amount of the dower and the way it should be paid, to recognize the

right of a women of majority age to consent to her own marriage, to determine impediments to marriage, and to affirm the existence of a wife's obligation of obedience.

108 This lack of female representation in the courts has no legal basis. In fact, neither the Judicial Authority Law nor the State Council Law establish any discrimination based on gender in the recruitment of judges. In practice, however, no woman was allowed to sit for the recruitment examination. At the start of 2007, after years of struggle by feminist groups and due to international pressure, 30 women were finally appointed as judges in the ordinary judiciary.

109 For a praxeological study of those parliamentary debates see Jean-Noël Ferrié and Baudouin Dupret, 'Préférences et pertinences: analyse praxéologique des figures du compromis en contexte parlementaire. A propos d'un débat égyptien' (2004) 43 Information sur les Sciences Sociales 263.

110 See for instance Nathalie Bernard-Maugiron, 'The Judicial Construction of the Facts and the Law: The Egyptian Supreme Constitutional Court and the Constitutionality of the Law on the *Khul'* in Baudouin Dupret and others (eds), *Narratives of Truth in Islamic Law* (CEDEJ-IB Tauris 2007).

111 Only four women out of 444 members were elected at the 2005 parliamentary elections and five others were appointed by the President of the Republic.

112 For a sociological analysis of *khulᶜ* in Egypt see Nadia Sonneveld, *Khul' Divorce in Egypt: Public Debates, Judicial Practices and Everyday Life* (American University in Cairo Press 2012); from the same author 'Four Years of *Khul'* in Egypt: the Practice of the Courts and Daily Life' in M Badran (ed), *Gender and Islam in Africa* (Stanford University Press 2011).

113 ᶜĀliyya Shukrī, *The Egyptian Woman. Between Inheritance and Reality* (Cairo University, Faculty of Literature, Center for Research and Social Studies 2003) 181 (in Arabic).

114 Interview with OZ (Cairo, 2 November 2007).

115 Interview with WH (Cairo, 24 October 2007).

116 Interview with FA, lawyer (Cairo, 3 October 2007).

117 Shukrī (n 114).

118 Art 3 of Law No 1 of 2000 does not require assigning a lawyer for alimony claims.

119 Art 3 para 2 Law No 1 of 2000.

120 This is for instance the case of the Egyptian Center for Women's Rights and the Center for Egyptian Women Legal Assistance (CEWLA).

121 Art 18bis 2–18bis 3 Decree-Law No 25 of 1929 as amended by Law No 100 of 1985.

122 Art 18bis 3 Decree-Law No 25 of 1929 as amended by Law No 100 of 1985: the ex-husband has to furnish a home for his children and their custodian-mother during the entire period of legal custody.

123 Interview with FA, lawyer (Cairo, 3 October 2007).

124 Aḥmad al-Sāwī, *The Harvest: Two Years after Khul'* (CEWLA 2003) (in Arabic); Nādiyya Ḥalīm, *Social Effects of Khul'* (CEWLA 2006) (in Arabic).

125 Interview with HM (Cairo, 4 November 2007).

126 Baudouin Dupret, 'What is Islamic Law? A Praxiological Answer and an Egyptian Case Study' (2007) 24(2) Theory, Culture & Society 79.

9 Personal status law in Israel

Disputes between religious and secular courts

Imen Gallala-Arndt

Introduction

Israel and the Arab states have for many decades been in a state of war, sometimes openly and at other times implicitly. The two blocks share, however, the problem of the place of religion in the legal order.[1] They could learn from each other's experience.

On 28 October 2013 the Israeli parliament (the Knesset) voted in a law allowing couples who want to marry to choose the rabbi who will perform their marriage. This law does not end the monopoly of the orthodox rabbis over Jewish marriage and divorce but allows the marrying couple to choose a rabbinate who is more likely to accept to marry them. In fact, the Israeli rabbinates embrace different policies in accepting Jewish converts and immigrants.[2] When Israel was founded two socio-legal streams were opposed as to the place the religion should have in the political, social, and legal life of the new country. The result reached was a kind of compromise between these two positions. A monopoly was given to the religious tribunals over the adherents to their faiths, on matters of marriage and divorce. Nevertheless, the secular state law and the secular state tribunals also regulate and adjudicate matters of personal status. This coexistence has led to conflicts between the two orders, the secular and the religious. Some authors even speak of a 'battle between irreconcilable viewpoints as to the source of legal authority – divine or secular – a battle that is far from over'.[3] In fact, the application of Jewish law in personal status law has led to manifold violations of human rights in Israel. The Israeli judiciary plays a fundamental role in confronting this dilemma between the dominance of religion in the field of personal status and the necessity of avoiding the violation of individual rights. This chapter seeks to examine the features of the contribution of the judiciary in this problematic area.

This chapter traces first the history of the conflict between secular and religious forces in Israel. It presents afterwards the main features of the personal status law in Israel and then shows through some thematic points the way the secular tribunals attempted to overcome the opposition between religious laws and human rights. It later presents the characteristics of the impact of the secular judiciary on the personal status system in Israel.

History

Israel is a relatively young country. It was established on 14 May 1948 following the UN partition resolution of 1947. The history of the Jewish people is, however, much older. It can be traced back two millennia. The law has always played a central role in the Jewish faith. The pact concluded between God and the Jewish people was based on their obedience towards him and the observance of the Torah. The salvation of the Jews depended on the grade of their faithfulness to the norms of conduct God has put on them. The *Halakha* (Jewish Law) aspired to give guidance to the human life in all its manifestations without distinction between sacred and profane matters.[4] Thus, religious law is a central factor in the identity of the people. Even Jewish people who do not consider themselves to be religious do not ignore the tradition of their nation.[5] In addition, after the exodus of the Jewish people in the wake of the second destruction of the Temple in 70 AD the observance of the Torah has been the cement for the identity of the Jewish communities scattered throughout the world.

Israel does not have a written constitution.[6] The main reason for avoiding such a document was the status of religion within the state and within the legal order. Many attempts were made, even after the establishment of the state of Israel, to draft a constitution, but they all failed. This was probably because they could not tackle, in a suitable manner, the question of the relationship of religion and the state. More precisely, the most difficult and sensitive issue in this debate was the question of the applicable law to personal status matters. The drafters of one of the recent constitution proposals posited that there was a consensus that the issues of personal status do not belong to a constitution.[7] This is an erroneous conclusion, especially for a society that remains totally divided on that issue. This shows that the topic is still unresolved and is the main obstacle for finalizing a written Israeli constitution. The definition of the Jewishness of the state is a constant issue and still leads to vivid arguments, as did the law proposal of November 2014.[8]

The *millet* system, as it is regulated in Israel nowadays, is to a large extent due to the Ottoman and British Mandate period. The Ottomans ruled the territory of what is today called Israel from 1517 to 1917. After the First World War, Great Britain received the mandate on Palestine from 1918 until the establishment of the state of Israel. Under the Muslim Ottoman rule the *millet* system was applied. This means that different, recognized religious communities were granted a certain legal autonomy. These were subject, in matters of personal status, to their own religious law administered by their own religious tribunals. Historical studies assume that this autonomy was not granted to the same extent everywhere in the Ottoman Empire. They argue that the autonomy changed over time and depended on local arrangements.[9] There were three main communities: the Greek orthodox, the Armenians, and the Jews. As under the Ottoman rule the sovereign ruler and the state were Muslim, the Sharia tribunals were the tribunals of the ruler whereas the tribunals of the recognized religious communities were tribunals of tolerated minorities. They were not organically part of the state.[10] Foreigners were subject to the law designated by the treaties their countries concluded with the Ottoman ruler.[11]

Under the British Mandate the status quo was maintained. The religious communities were granted judicial and legal autonomy in the field of personal status. And so were the Muslim inhabitants of Palestine. Only religious communities recognized under the Ottoman rule were granted that privilege. The Druses and the evangelical church remained unrecognized. This, of course, corresponds to the classic attitude of Britain in its colonies. Britain had engaged itself, however, according to the terms of the mandate, to safeguard civil and the religious rights and to guarantee the respect of personal status in accordance with the religious law of the inhabitants of Palestine.[12] The Muslim tribunals were no longer state tribunals but they still could enjoy some privileges inherited from their Ottoman status. They had, under the British Mandate, the widest scope of jurisdiction. Article 52 of the Palestine Order-in-Council (POC) 1922 1947 granted the Muslim tribunals exclusive jurisdiction on all matters of personal status, whereas the other religious tribunals, Jewish and Christian, had exclusive jurisdiction only on matters of divorce, marriage, and confirmation of wills. For other matters, they had concurrent jurisdiction. The standing of the Muslim tribunals was larger as far as the individuals were concerned. Contrary to the religious tribunals of the Christian and Jewish communities, the sharia tribunals had exclusive jurisdiction on the personal status of Muslims (not only nationals but also foreigners).[13]

There were nevertheless some important jurisdictional changes. The matters of personal status opposing Muslims to Non-Muslims no longer belonged to the jurisdiction of the Muslim tribunals. They were referred to the Chief Justice for designation to the competent tribunal.[14] With the assistance of members from the communities concerned he designated the tribunal to adjudicate the matter. Conflicts of jurisdiction were resolved by a special tribunal.[15]

For non-Muslim foreigners their personal status matters were mainly subject to their national law (Art 64 POC).[16] These matters were also submitted to the jurisdiction of the civil tribunals.

The Mandate authorities refrained normally from interfering in the content of the religious law administered. They, however, introduced some institutional arrangements, such as the establishment of a rabbinical Court of Appeal in Jerusalem in spite of opposition to it. In fact, the double degree of jurisdiction lacked any foundation in *Halakha*.[17]

With the establishment of the state of Israel the political situation of the religious minorities changed dramatically. From that point, the rulers were Jewish who had to define their relationship to Judaism and to other recognized religious communities living under their rule. Interestingly the Zionist elite were secular.

A so-called status quo agreement determined the position of Judaism in the new state. As soon as a year before the establishment of Israel in 1948, an agreement was made between the future government and the religious leaders: Ben-Gurion, Rabbi Maimon Fishman (the Religious Zionist Movement), and Izhak Greenberg (centre-right).[18] According to the status quo agreements, the Orthodox communities supported the new state. In return, the state gave the orthodox authorities a monopoly on personal status issues, and control over kosher dietary sabbatical observance and Jewish religious education.[19] It should clearly be borne in mind that only Orthodox Judaism was recognized in Israel.[20] Other streams, such as the conservative, liberal, and Reform Judaism, do not enjoy such a privilege. Only the Orthodox authorities are considered to be legitimate and the real representatives of Judaism.

Some scholars explain the retention of the personal nature of family law with reference to the urgency of the situation (war) at that time and the failure of the commission entrusted with reforming the Mandate's legal regulations to achieve its goals. For them the personal choice was in fact a non-choice.[21] I do not agree. This system seems to be unavoidable given the circumstances of the birth of Israel.

One may ask why the secular governing elite decided to keep the personal status law regulation in the Ottoman mould. They wanted to build a modern state. Why did they then not enact a territorial law applicable to all residents or all nationals?

To answer this question one must distinguish between the new Jewish majority and the other recognized religious minorities. Keeping the status quo in personal status matters was easy in respect of the latter. In fact, the non-Jewish communities already under the British Mandate wanted to preserve their legal and judicial autonomy on personal status matters. After the establishment of Israel, they claimed, even more vehemently, their autonomy in the field of personal status. That was considered as part of their right to protect their identity.[22] It was a very difficult issue concerning the Jewish majority, since they were divided on secular and religious lines.

It seems two reasons led to the retention of Jewish Israelis' religious personal status: the need to guarantee the unity of the young Jewish nation of Israel, and to distinguish them from the other non-Jewish communities. This process, nevertheless, was not meditated over for long. The secular elite discovered, in the wake of the independence, in the status quo an effective tool for the priority that was nation building.[23] The secular founding leaders of Israel incorporated the religious authorities in the secular, civil and socialist state in order to avoid the beginning of a kind of 'Kulturkampf'.[24] In fact, although the elite in the Zionist movement was clearly secular, they knew that the religious tradition 'provided the affective ties of unity needed by the modern nation-builders'.[25] The Orthodox authorities wanted to monopolize the issues of marriage and divorce in order to determine the boundaries of the Jewish community.[26] They accepted compromises on the issues of Sabbath observance and kosher observance, but fiercely defended their jurisdiction in matters of marriage and divorce.[27]

In spite of that early status quo agreement, the regulation of personal status for Jews required long and heated debates. It was not before the early 1950s that the compromise could be concretized in legal statutes. The Rabbinical Court jurisdiction law recognized the Orthodox religious realm's monopoly on matters of marriage and divorce for Jews.[28]

Nevertheless, the compromise could be reached at that time because it reflected, to a large extent, the social realities. In fact, Jews mainly did not marry beyond outside their communities. The history will show that that the compromise was fragile, especially as it no longer reflects the social reality of Israel.[29]

The Israeli tribunals with jurisdiction in personal status matters

The Law and Government Ordinance provided that most of the regulations in force during the Mandate period would continue to be in force in Israel.[30] That is why after the independence of Israel the jurisdiction and the legal rules in personal status matters continued to be split between civil and religious tribunals.[31] However, the regulation of the judicial authorities in the field of personal status has continuously evolved since the establishment of the state of Israel.

Religious tribunals

Overview

The jurisdiction of religious tribunals is determined by Article 51 (1) of the POC and by subsequent Israeli statues. Only the recognized religious communities have been granted legislative and judicial autonomy in matters of personal status. Alongside the Jewish majority these communities are Muslim, different Christian denominations, and the Druzes.[32] After its independence, Israel recognized three more communities: the Druzes were recognized as a religious community in 1954, the Anglican Episcopalian Church in 1970, and the Baha'i faith in 1971.[33] However, the recognition of a religious community does not necessarily imply the establishment of its own tribunals in matters of personal status. Recognized communities need therefore special enactments of the state establishing their religious tribunals and determining their jurisdiction.[34] The Anglican Episcopalian Church was granted judicial and legislative autonomy on the basis of Section 54 of the POC concerning all the recognized Christian denominations. Special Israeli legislation established the Druze tribunals and determined their jurisdiction.[35] The Baha'i faith is still lacking the benefit of such legislation.

The jurisdiction of the religious tribunals has changed over the decades. In addition, the scope of jurisdiction depends on the religious community concerned. However, all of the religious tribunals in Israel have three types of jurisdiction: exclusive, concurrent, or parallel jurisdiction. The religious tribunals share concurrent jurisdiction with the civil tribunals. In that realm, the religious tribunals are competent to deal with a given matter only if it is brought before them first. In the matters over which the civil tribunals have parallel jurisdiction the religious tribunals are competent as far as the all the parties agree to submit the issue to them, such as with respect to succession matters. The religious courts apply their respective religious laws and the state laws applicable to them. For instance, the Women's Equal Rights Law addresses all courts, including the religious courts. Nevertheless, in respect of this law, the parties can agree to apply their religious law in place of this state law (§ 7).[36]

The religious courts are subject also to the supervision of the Israeli High Court of Justice (HCJ). According to Section 15(d) (4) of the Basic Law (Judicature), the judicial oversight exercised by the HCJ over the religious tribunals is more limited than that in relation to the civil tribunals. The HCJ ensures that they adjudicate in the limits of their jurisdiction. Nevertheless, in practice the control is more extensive. It includes the respect of the rules of natural justice and of the civil laws considered by the HCJ as also applicable in the religious tribunals.[37]

Rabbinical tribunals

The rabbinical tribunals have exclusive jurisdiction on matters concerning the marriage and divorce of Jewish residents or nationals of Israel (the Rabbinical Courts Jurisdiction Law (RCJL) (Section 1). In that regard, the personal jurisdiction of the rabbinical tribunals has been extended since the end of the Mandate period. This trend continued, as in 2008 an amendment of the RCJL granted the rabbinical tribunal jurisdiction over divorce suits of Jewish spouses married in a Jewish ceremony, regardless of the place where it was conducted.[38]

The rabbinical tribunals also have exclusive jurisdiction on 'connected matters' to divorce if they are presented in the divorce filing, including maintenance for the woman and the couple's children (Section 3 RCJL). The connected matters are matters naturally linked to divorce or those that the plaintiff inserts additionally in his divorce suit. Given that in Israel jurisdiction determines the applicable law and the interpretation of that law, litigants are always tempted to choose the tribunal that is likely to decide in their favour. It is generally assumed that Jewish men wish their cases to be adjudicated by the rabbinical tribunals, whereas women prefer to submit the matter to the civil tribunals.[39]

The rabbinical tribunals have concurrent jurisdiction with the civil tribunals on matters such as child custody and property claims of spouses. On matters of succession and adoption, the rabbinical tribunals have jurisdiction if all the parties agree to submit the case to them.[40]

The statute law does not determine the law to be applied by the rabbinical courts but they traditionally adjudicate according to their religious law.[41] The rabbinical tribunals almost never cite Knesset legislation or precedents of the Supreme Court in their decisions, although they are part of the state judiciary system.[42] In fact, the rabbinical judges, *dayyanim*, are considered state officials.[43]

Sharia courts

The Sharia courts are regulated by the Shari'a Courts Law (December 1953) and the 1961 *Qadi* Law.[44] They apply mainly the Ottoman family law code.[45] The *Qadis* are salaried state officials required to take the pledge of allegiance to the state of Israel;[46] they must be nominated by the President of the state of Israel. Because many of them are nominated for political reasons, there has been significant popular discontent about their position. As a consequence, an amendment of the *Qadi* Law in 2002 required that nominees have a significant religious education in Sharia or Islamic studies, or have considerable experience in a legal profession.[47]

The scope of the exclusive jurisdiction of the sharia tribunals has been progressively reduced. First, the Israeli Succession Law conferred jurisdiction on the sharia tribunals only if all the parties agree to submit the matter to them.[48] Second, an important reduction of the Sharia tribunals' exclusive reduction occurred through the 2001 amendment of the Court of Family Affairs Law.[49] Accordingly, the Sharia tribunals lost their exclusive jurisdiction on matters of child custody and maintenance. These matters are now shared with the civil family tribunals. The parties can decide which tribunal to attend.[50] This reduction of the scope of jurisdiction of the Sharia tribunals happened as a reaction to the demands of liberal groups within the Arab communities to offer women an alternative to the approach taken by the Sharia tribunals, which was deemed profoundly patriarchal.[51] In spite of this, a legal anthropological study has shown that many Arabs are not even conscious of the choice they now have. Moreover, Muslim women and their families are likely to avoid the civil courts for maintenance claims if they do not seek the divorce.[52]

Ecclesiastical courts

In addition, these tribunals saw their exclusive jurisdiction reduced through the amendment of 2001, in order to protect the interests of women considered disadvantaged before the ecclesiastical tribunals.[53] Their exclusive jurisdiction is strictly limited to matters of marriage and divorce.[54]

The tribunals of the Christian denominations lack a specific legal instrument regulating their activities.[55] This absence is especially notable in respect of their organization and rules of procedure.[56] They are part of the legal system but they enjoy a much wider autonomy than the Sharia tribunals. Their judges are appointed, trained, and paid by their communities.[57]

Not all the recognized Christian denominations have their own tribunals. In fact, some Eastern Catholic churches (Greek Catholics, Armenian Catholics, and Syrian Catholics) delegated their right to establish their own tribunals to the Roman Catholic churches.[58]

In addition, some of the appellate ecclesiastical tribunals are established outside Israel. Whether the Israeli Supreme Court has jurisdiction to review the decisions of those tribunals established outside of the scope of its territorial jurisdiction is thus problematic.[59]

The civil tribunals

The civil courts adjudicating personal status matters are called family law courts. They were established by the Family Court Law 5795–1995 and their decisions can be appealed to the district courts. The latter's decisions can exceptionally be appealed to the Supreme Court. This can lead to a lack of harmony in the decisions.[60]

The family courts share with the religious courts the adjudication of personal status matters. They have a residual jurisprudence if no religious court has jurisdiction. They also have an exclusive and a concurrent jurisdiction in personal status matters. They have, for instance, exclusive jurisdiction on personal status matters of persons who are not religiously affiliated to a religious community, on interreligious marriages, and on matters concerning a couple of which one is a foreigner.[61]

Within the framework of the concurrent jurisdiction, the civil tribunals also apply the religious law of the parties, if no civil law is available on the matter. They apply it, however, according to their evidence and procedural rules, which are different from those of the religious tribunals. As a consequence, the religious tribunals and the civil tribunals can come to different conclusions even when they apply the same religious law.[62]

The civil courts in Israel treat religious law as law and not as fact. This is due to the amendment of the Interpretation Ordinance in 1945.[63] This implies that they are supposed to know the content of the law and the parties do not bear the burden of proof. Nevertheless, this does not prevent the judges from relying on the experts' opinions and authoritative opinions of religious authorities. This is particularly necessary for the non-Jewish religious laws.

The HCJ does not review the application of religious law by the religious tribunals. It considers whether they acted in the framework of or beyond their jurisdiction (Section 7 of the Courts Law, 5717–1957). The doctrine of *stare decisis* is not applied in the case of religious law.[64] The rabbinical courts are not bound by the HCJ's interpretation of *Halakha*. This leads us to the conclusion that what the rabbinical tribunals really have is a complex status or ambivalent status.[65] On the one hand they are part of the state and integrated in the state judicial system, and on the other the rabbinical judges are 'autonomous institutions of the normative religious system'.[66] It seems even that the Supreme Court interpretations of religious law do not bind the lower courts. [67]

Issues of conflict between civil courts and religious courts

The split of personal status matters between religious laws and religious tribunals on the one hand and the civil statutes and civil courts on the other has led in Israel to tensions between these two systems, as the following cases illustrate.

Opposition between the civil tribunals and the religious tribunals of the Arab Palestinian religious communities

In spite of the traditional reserve of the Israeli Supreme Court towards the rulings of religious tribunals other than the rabbinical tribunals, its case law, however, offers examples illustrating a deeper interference in the religious laws for the sake of the individual constitutional rights.[68]

After a Sharia court summarily rejected a combined paternity and maintenance action as the presumed parents were not married, the Supreme Court held that the Sharia court lacked jurisdiction over claims of paternity or child support for a child born out of wedlock. The main argument of the court was the welfare of the child.[69]

The Sharia court sought to extend its jurisdiction on cases of custody although the parents were adherents of different religions. The father being a Muslim and the mother Christian, the Sharia Court of Appeals concluded that the child was thus Muslim and, as a consequence, custody must be granted to the Muslim parent. Nevertheless, the Supreme Court considered that, concerning custody matters of parents adhering to different religions, the Sharia courts lack jurisdiction and that an application should be made to the President of the Supreme Court to determine the competent tribunal.[70]

The Supreme Court also limited the jurisdiction of the Druze courts, arguing that the term 'divorce' in the Druze Religious Courts Law (1962), for which the Druze tribunals have exclusive jurisdiction, means only the termination of the marriage and not matters such as matrimonial property and custody of the children. In doing so, the Supreme Court reduced the jurisdiction of a religious tribunal. This is done in a context where the religious tribunals and their laws are generally deemed less favourable to women. Judge Cheshin from the Supreme Court once again asserted that the paramount goal is the wellbeing of the individual members of the society, regardless of their religious belonging.[71] Cases in which the Israeli Supreme Court (SC) has opposed the position of non-Jewish religious courts with the aim of protecting the individual constitutional rights of their members are, however, less numerous than the cases in which the court opposed the rabbinical tribunals.[72]

Tension between civil tribunals and rabbinical tribunals

The cases presented here show how the Israeli SC and civil courts could reduce the negative impact of Jewish religious law, and of the case law of the rabbinical tribunals on individual rights. The intervention of the SC has mainly addressed the monopoly of religious marriage in Israel. This happened through the institution of reputed spouses and the recognition of marriages conducted abroad. Moreover, the SC has sought to reduce the scope of application of religious law and the extension of the application of state law, especially constitutional individual rights.

The restrictive nature of religious marriage and divorce law in Israel

The monopoly of religious authorities on marriage and divorce leads to complex problems for the persons concerned. Israeli citizens may not be able to marry the spouse of their choice, because of his or her religious affiliation, or because he or she has no religious affiliation at all.[73] As a consequence, they cannot marry in Israel.[74] The religious laws applicable in Israel contain significant marriage impediments based on the religious affiliation of the future spouses. Interreligious marriages are generally not allowed. It is also not possible under Jewish law for a Cohen, a descendant of Aaron, to marry a divorcee. It is also forbidden for a Jew to marry a *mamzer* (the child of a married Jewish woman and of a Jewish man who is not her husband).[75] It is considered unthinkable that non-religious Israelis are obliged to undergo religious ceremonies that may infringe upon their right to privacy. For instance, women should before their marriage immerse themselves naked in a bath (*miqveh*) in order to purify themselves of their menstruation.

The *miqveh* must take place before an Orthodox woman to make sure that it happens according to the halakhic standards.[76]

The difficulties also arise from the strict regulation of divorce in Jewish law. Under this law, divorce is only valid if the husband delivers to his wife the *get* (a letter of divorce, to which both agree). Unless he does so, the woman remains chained to him (*agunah*) and is not allowed to marry again.[77] In some extreme cases the rabbinical tribunals have retroactively revoked a divorce granted two years before. By doing so they made the child of the divorcee, born out of a relationship with another man, a *mamzer*. It is also not possible for Catholic marriages to be dissolved in Israel.[78]

Independently of the content of religious laws, the principle of religious monopoly on marriage and divorce is in contradiction with the liberal character of the state of Israel.[79]

Reputed spouses

'Reputed spouses' indicates the situation of two persons cohabiting as husband and wife without being formally married. The legislature granted some rights to the cohabiting couples. These rights have been significantly extended by the Supreme Court.[80] It seems that currently Israel's approach to non-marital cohabitation is one of the most liberal in the world.[81] According to the case law one can claim the existence of a non-marital cohabitation even if the cohabitation was short (even three months).[82]

The Israeli SC has insisted on the idea that this cohabitation of couples as wife and husband does not confer on them a status. However, it considers non-marital cohabitation as an institution worthy of protection as this type of relationship has become deeply rooted in Israeli society.[83] They generally have all the rights and obligations of spouses,[84] including maintenance rights, succession rights, child adoption rights, and so on.[85]

The institution of reputed spouses is an internal solution for the flaws of the religious Orthodox monopoly on marriage law in Israel. The Israeli civil courts also imported support from outside Israel through the recognition of the validity of marriages conducted abroad.

Marriage conducted abroad

Some Israelis travel abroad in order to get married and circumvent the barriers imposed on them by the applicable religious laws or any infringements on their right to marry.[86] In the landmark decision in *Funk-Schlesinger* the SC asserted that the civil registrar was obliged to register marriages performed abroad. It added, however, that registering these marriages did not amount to recognition of their validity, emphasizing that the register collects statistical data.[87] Nevertheless, registered marriages enjoy the state's economic benefits. They have succession rights.[88] The SC justified the recognition of marital rights in respect of these marriages by considering them an implied agreement.[89] The SC, however, recently recognized the validity of a civil marriage concluded abroad between two Jewish Israeli citizens and residents in Israel. Interestingly, this important step was made possible by the position of a rabbinical court in the 'Noahide' case in 2003 and the justification made by the Grand Rabbinical Court (GRC). [90] In this clarification, the GRC held that a rabbinical court has jurisdiction to sever a marriage between Jews conducted in a civil ceremony abroad. The GRC confirmed the decision of the regional rabbinical tribunal, which divorced the couple without requiring, as is the norm for a Jewish marriage, the deliverance of the separation letter called the *get*. The GRC founded its reasoning on the Noahide Laws. These laws are provided in *Halakhah* for non-Jews. Jewish law recognizes marriages and divorces of non-Jews as long as they fulfil the conditions of validity in civilized societies. According to the religious court, the civil marriage of Jews is also to be recognized by the rabbinical tribunals. In fact, Jews can marry in two different ways: as Jews and as human beings. This rabbinical decision gave the SC the opportunity to recognize marriages between Israeli Jews conducted in civil ceremonies abroad.[91] The status of interreligious civil marriages performed abroad is, however, not yet clear, although they are granted some rights by the SC.[92]

Applicability of constitutional rights and state law in the religious tribunals

The SC sought on many occasions to reduce the scope of application of religious laws by instructing the religious tribunals to apply state law if available and to take into consideration individual constitutional rights. In this context, two landmark cases are often cited by Israeli scholars: *Bavli* and *Yemini*. In *Bavli* (1994), the SC ruled that the property should be divided equally among the divorced spouses. The Court justified its position by holding the Women's Equal Rights Law applicable in both secular and religious courts. [93] In addition, the Court asserted that the rabbinical courts are obliged to respect the general principles and norms of constitutional law. In a conference, the rabbinical court judges rejected the reasoning in *Bavli* on the basis that the equal division of spouse property does not exist in *Halakha* and that they consider themselves bound only by the religious law and not by state law or by precedents set by the SC.[94]

In *Yemini* (2003), the SC also instructed the rabbinical court to apply the Spouses (Property Relations) Law (1973) and not the *Halakha*. The SC held that state law is to be applied unless all the parties involved agree to apply religious law regardless of the forum before which the case is submitted.[95] The SC rejected, in this case, the position of the rabbinical court that the agreement of the parties to submit their dispute to the rabbinical court implicitly entailed their will to be adjudicated according to *Halakha*.

The impact of the civil tribunals on the personal status system

The secular tribunals reduce the flaws of the personal law system in Israel. That is why one could characterize their impact on the system as corrective. Nevertheless by following a case law that intends to limit the infringement of the religious tribunals on the constitutional individual rights, the secular courts make this system more liveable. However, as a consequence, they allow the system to persist.

A corrective impact

Clearly, the religious laws applied to family matters contain discriminatory rules prejudicing women and non-believers.[96] Moreover, the monopoly that religious communities enjoy on marriage and divorce issues undoubtedly represents a clear infringement upon freedom of religion.[97] The Israeli SC has taken positions in favour of secularism and sought to limit the negative effect of religious laws on the lives of members of religious communities.[98] The personal status system has been defended in the name of freedom of religion and the protection of the identity of the religious groups by allowing them to regulate the lives of their families and members according to their cultures and traditions. Serving these collective interests, however, often has detrimental consequences for individual rights.[99] The interventions of the Israeli SC represent an attempt to reduce the infringement on the individual rights without ignoring the constitutional and legal foundations of the personal law system in Israel.[100] In fact, the Supreme Court is not entitled to exercise judicial review over legislation enacted before the 'constitutional revolution' of 1992 (Israel Basic Law on Human Dignity and Liberty).[101] The statutes in which the religiously dominated personal status system of Israel is embedded were enacted before 1992.

But it uses other techniques (interpretations) to ensure that the rulings of the religious tribunals are respectful of constitutional human rights.[102] It should be added that the judicial activism of the Supreme Court goes further, as it instructs the religious tribunals to hand down their rulings in accordance with gender equality, although this principle has not been expressly enshrined in the Basic Laws.[103]

At this level of analysis one should ask why the SC has been playing this corrective role. According to dominant constitutionalist theories, constitutional courts assume, inside a liberal democracy, a counter-majoritarian function in order to protect the rights of minorities.[104] This does not seem the case for the Israeli SC. In fact, because of the peculiarities of the political system in Israel, the major political parties need the support of the smaller religious parties to build and maintain coalitions.[105] Thus, the non-religious elite must take into account the priorities of the religious parties, even if they do not reflect the wishes and preferences of the majority of Israelis. The monopoly of religious regulations over marriage and divorce are a main part of the political deal in Israel. The Supreme Court seems, through its case law, to reflect the aspirations of the majority of the Israelis to lessen the grasp of religious orthodox law on their lives, and especially family life.[106] The important role of the religious parties in the Knesset has led to a stalemate in respect of the enactment of civil and secular regulations on family issues, instead of religious regulations.[107] The wide interpretation of the Basic Laws, given in order to reduce the infringement of the religious tribunals on individual rights, is the unique instrument of the moment. International human rights instruments ratified by Israel do not assist as they become obligatory only after their incorporation into Israeli law.[108]

A perpetuating impact

Through the correction of some flaws of the religion-dominated personal status system, the SC has contributed to its survival. The SC made the system viable as it showed that the state institutions are not fully helpless in respect of the discrimination that the religious hegemony has brought in this field. The SC supports to a certain extent the status quo agreement between the religious and the secular forces by adjusting it to the new circumstances of social and political life.[109] The religious norms on marriage and divorce are still enforced by the state. The solutions offered by the Supreme Court are partial and have a piecemeal character. These 'subterfuge mechanisms' really only postpone real relief for the victims of religious discrimination, such as (and in particular) the introduction of the institution of the civil marriage.[110]

In addition, the corrective approach of the SC mainly seems to concern the Jewish religious establishment but not non-Jewish communities. The cases in which the Israeli SC intervened in the rulings of non-Jewish religious tribunals to safeguard the rights and the welfare of members of these communities represents a recent evolution.[111] The Israeli SC still avoids intervening in matters of the Arab-Palestinian religious tribunals. For instance, the SC seems to show greater deference when dealing with decisions of the Sharia courts.[112]

The Israeli state justified the monopoly of non-Jewish religious communities over matters of marriage and divorce as a sign of respect of the autonomy of these groups and a means of protecting their religious freedom. The policy of non-intervention was intended to avoid international critiques against Israel about the way it treats its minorities.[113] Another argument concerning more directly the attitude of the judge is that the civil judge (normally Jewish, at least culturally) is supposed to know *Halakha* well, or surely better, than the other religious laws. He would be more at ease when dealing with Jewish religious norms and allow himself more freedom in interpreting them without necessarily being bound by authoritative opinions. Being a foreigner to other religious cultures, the civil judge would avoid interfering in the interpretation and application of their religious laws.

Although understandable from a political and cultural point of view, legally this attitude is problematic. The legislature puts all the religious laws of the recognized religious communities on the same footing.[114]

Summary and outlook

The secular Israeli elite had no other choice at the eve of the declaration of independence than to make, with the Orthodox religious forces, a so-called status quo agreement. This agreement granted the Orthodox religious stream a monopoly over marriage and divorce. The same judicial and legal autonomy was recognized for non-Jewish religious minorities. This autonomy was inherited from the Ottoman *millet* system and from the British Mandate period. The non-Jewish communities wanted to keep the religiously dominant personal status system in order to preserve their identities and religious freedom. As far as the Jewish religious elite is concerned, the secular forces needed their support in that delicate phase of the establishment of Israel. It was also clear that the religious monopoly over matters of marriage and divorce would allow the definition of the barriers and frontiers of the religious communities.[115] The religious laws, with their marriage impediments, do not permit mixing between the religious communities. As a result, one can determine with some certainty who is a Jew. The Jewishness of the new state was the raison d'être for the establishment of the state of Israel. This religious monopoly on marriage and divorce was supposed to guarantee the unity of the Israeli people around one identity – their Jewishness – but it failed to hit its target. In fact, this personal system divided the Israeli people into those who accept the system and those who criticize the human rights infringements it inevitably brings.[116] This tension between secular and religious forces is also reflected at the level of the judiciary. The civil tribunals, and at their head the SC, seek to reduce the restrictions that the personal status system has imposed on individuals. They attempted, through a wide interpretation of the Basic Law, to make the religious tribunals render their decisions also according to constitutional principles, such as gender equality. The SC also took a huge step by allowing the registration of civil marriages conducted abroad and, by doing so, gave those married couples the opportunity to enjoy advantages similar to those of couples married religiously in Israel. The same has also happened in respect of the institution of reputed spouses. These non-married people can enjoy the rights of married couples, although they are simply just cohabiting as husband and wife without being bound by a formal marriage. The Israeli civil courts have been able to overcome the stalemate in the Knesset on these issues. The religious parties play an important role there, and guarantee coalitions. The Knesset does not have the ability to overcome religious dominance on the field of marriage and divorce. The Court could play that role as it is protected from partisan quarrels and strategies and because of the public acceptance of these positions. In fact, the secular positions are strongly represented throughout the public. One cannot imagine judges in an Islamic country considering two cohabiting spouses without a religious or civil marriage as eligible to enjoy marital rights and benefits. The social recognition of the institution in Israel makes the judge recognize it legally. The judge in the realm of his judicial activism remains dependent on the society in which he fulfils his functions.

The attempts of the SC remain partial and do not radically resolve the problem. On the contrary, in trying to make the system more viable the SC has allowed it to survive. There is in Israel a clash between the religious and the secular judicial authorities. This clash is set to remain for a long time.[117] I would even suggest that this tension is quite natural. In fact, the two orders, secular and religious, obey different rationales. The religious order extracts its legitimacy from God and his law. The state authorities, meanwhile, reason that the religious tribunals derive their legitimacy from state law, which delegates to them the authority to regulate certain aspects of social life. They conclude that religious tribunals must exercise their jurisdiction within the limits defined for them by state law.[118] They add also that by doing so they must subject themselves to state law. The rabbinical tribunals, however, refuse to apply state law when it contradicts Jewish religious law. The only viable solution is to submit personal status matters to civil laws and civil tribunals.

Notes

1 Patricia Woods, *Judicial Power and National Politics: Courts and Gender in the Religious-Secular Conflict in Israel* (SUNY Press 2008) 33.
2 Nathan Jeffay, 'Israel Jewish Marriage Relaxes Orthodox Grip a Bit – Allows Couples to Shop for More Liberal Rabbis' Forward, (31 October 2013) <http://forward.com/news/israel/186590/israel-jewish-marriage-law-relaxes-orthodox-grip-a/> accessed 27 July 2015.
3 Anat Sclonicov, 'Religious Law, Religious Courts and Human Rights within Israeli Constitutional Structure' (2004) 4 Int'l J. Const. L. 732, 734.
4 Izhak Englard, *Religious Law in the Israel Legal System* (Hebrew University 1975) 26.
5 Natan Lerner, 'Religious Liberty in the State of Israel' (2007) 21 Emory International Law Review 239, 241.
6 Lerner (n 5) 249.
7 Lerner (n 5) 250.
8 Binyamin Netanyahu submitted to the Knesset a law approved in the cabinet. The law is controversial because it proclaims Israel as the national state of the Jewish people and enhances the role of religious law in the legal order, for more on that see: 'How Jewish a State?' *The Economist* (29 November 2014) <www.economist.com/news/middle-east-and-africa/21635064-government-wants-controversial-law-would-deny-equality-arabs-how> accessed 27 July 2015.
9 Aharon Layish, 'The Heritage of Ottoman Rule in the Israeli Legal System – The concept of Umma and Millet' in Peri Bearman and Frank Vogel (eds), *The Law Applied – Contextualizing the Islamic Shari'a* (Tauris 2008), 128f; Talia Einhorn, *Private International Law in Israel* (Wolters Kluwer 2012) 193.
10 Layish (n 9) 145.
11 Einhorn, 'Private International Law' (n 9) 193.
12 Layish (n 9) 130.
13 Layish (n 9) 131f.
14 Layish (n 9) 134.
15 Einhorn, 'Private International Law' (n 9) 196.
16 Einhorn, 'Private International Law' (n 9) 195.
17 Eliash Ben Zion, 'Ethnic Pluralism or Melting Pot? The Dilemma of Rabbinical Adjudication in Israeli Family Law' (1983) 18 Israel Law Review 248, 349.
18 Woods (n 1) 36.
19 Woods (n 1) 36; Martin Edelman, *Courts, Politics and Culture in Israel* (University Press of Virginia 1994) 51.
20 Edelman (n 19) 51.
21 Adam Hofri-Winogradow, 'The Muslim-Majority Character of Israeli Constitutional Law' (2010) 2 Middle East Law and Governance 43, 55.

22 Avishalon Westreich and Pinhas Shifman, *A Civil Legal Framework for Marriage and Divorce in Israel* (Metzilah 2013) 22f.
23 Yüksel, Sezgin, 'The Israeli Millet System: Examining Legal Pluralism through the Lenses of Nation-Building and Human Rights' (2010) 43 Israel Law Review 631, 639.
24 Woods (n 1) 60.
25 Edelman (n 19) 49.
26 Woods (n 1) 61.
27 Woods (n 1) 73.
28 Westreich and Shifman (n 22) 23.
29 Westreich and Shifman (n 22) 23.
30 Law and Government Ordinance, 2 Official Gazette, Appendix A, P1, 19 May 1948.
31 Ruth Halperin-Kaddari, Women in Israel: A State of their Own (University of Pennsylvania Press 2004) 233.
32 The Jewish establishment is, however, no longer considered as a religious community like the others. It represents the majority and enjoys a particular status, see also Michael Karayanni, 'Living in A Group of One's Own: Normative Implications Related to the Private Nature of the Religious Accommodations for the Palestinian-Arab Minority in Israel' (2007) 6 UCLA Journal of Islamic and Near Eastern Law 1, 4.
33 Marcia Gelpe, The Israeli Legal System (Carolina Academy Press 2013) 287.
34 Ariel Rosen-Zvi, 'Forum Shopping Between Religious and Secular Courts and its Impact on the Legal System' (1989) 9 Tel Aviv University Studies in Law 347, 348.
35 Druze Religious Courts Law, 5723–1962, 17 LSI 27 (1962–63) (Isr); Halperin-Kaddari (n 31) 124.
36 Einhorn, 'Private International Law' (n 9) 190, fn 515.
37 Ariel Rosen-Zvi, 'Family and Inheritance Law', in Amos Shapira and Keren DeWitt-Arar (eds), *Introduction to the Law of Israel* (Kluwer Law International 1995) 90.
38 Rabbinical Courts jurisdiction (Marriage and Divorce) Law, 5713–1953, 134 LSI. Einhorn, 'Private International Law' (n 9).
39 Rosen-Zvi, 'Forum Shopping' (n 34) 350f.
40 Daphna Hacker, 'Religious Tribunals in Democratic States: Lessons from the Israeli Rabbinical Courts' (2011–2012) 27 Journal of Law & Religion 59, 63.
41 Menashe Shava, 'The Rabbinical Courts in Israel: Jurisdiction over Non-Jews?' (1985) 27 Journal of Church and State 99, 102.
42 Menachem Mautner, *Law and the Culture of Israel* (Oxford University Press 2011) 192f.
43 Edelman (n 19) 53.
44 Shari'a Courts Law, 5714–1953, 8 LSI 42 (1953–54) (Isr.); Qadis Law, 5721–1961, 15 LSI 123 (1960–61) (Isr).
45 Yitzhak Reiter, 'Judge Reform: facilitating Divorce by Shari'a courts in Israel' (2009) 11 Journal of Islamic Law and Culture 13, 14.
46 Yüksel Sezgin, *Human Rights and State-enforced Religious Family Laws in Israel, Egypt and India* (Cambridge University Press 2013) 85.
47 Sezgin, Human Rights (n 46) 86.
48 Succession Law, 5725–1965, 19 LSI 215 (1964–65) (Isr).
49 Court of Family Affairs Law 5755–1995 as amended in 2001 SH 1810, 6; Karayanni (n 32) 39.
50 Sezgin, Human Rights (n 46) 89f.

51 Ido Shahar, 'Forum Shopping Between Civil and Sharia Courts – Maintenance suits in Contemporary Jerusalem', in Franz von Benda-Beckmann et al (eds), *Religion in Disputes, Pervasiveness of Religious Normativity in Disputing Processes* (Palgrave Macmillan 2013) 147, 151.
52 Shahar (n 51) 158; see also Reiter (n 45) 19.
53 Karayanni (n 32) 40.
54 Sezgin, Human Rights (n 46) 91.
55 Einhorn, 'Private International Law' (n 9) fn 533.
56 Einhorn, 'Private International Law' (n 9) 197.
57 Sezgin, Human Rights (n 46) 91.
58 Sezgin, Human Rights (n 46) 90.
59 Einhorn, 'Private International Law' (n 9) 197.
60 Einhorn, 'Private International Law' (n 9) 199.
61 Rosen-Zvi, 'Family and Inheritance Law' (n 37) 79.
62 Einhorn, 'Private International Law' (n 9) 191.
63 Under Section 33 of the Interpretation Ordinance: Judicial notice shall be taken of every law, unless the contrary is expressed by law. After the amendment the term 'Law' was extended to cover also religious law. For more development on this, see Englard (n 4) 88 ff.
64 Englard (n 4) 134.
65 Englard (n 4) 111.
66 Englard (n 4) 111.
67 Englard (n 4) 115.
68 Karayanni (n 32) 40; Alisa Rubin Peled, 'Sharia under Challenge: The History of Islamic Legal Institutions in Israel' (2009) 63 Middle East Journal 241, 252–259.
69 Moussa Abou Ramadan, 'Judicial Activism of the Shari'ah Appeals Court in Israel (1994–2001): Rise and Crisis' (2003) 27 Fordham International Law Journal 254, 265.
70 Ibid. 267.
71 Karayanni (n 32) 42.
72 Karayanni (n 32) 39–44.
73 Westreich and Shifman (n 22) 25–26.
74 Talia Einhorn, 'Family Unions in Israel – The Tensions between Religious Law and Secular Law and the Quest for Coherent Law' in Giersten Frantzen and Moss Cordero (eds), Ret tog tolerance – Festskrift til Helge Johan Thue 70 Ar (Gyldendal Akademisk 2007) 697, 699.
75 Einhorn, 'Family Unions in Israel' (n 74) 699.
76 Gideon Sapir and Daniel Statman, 'Religious Marriage in a Liberal State' in Susanna Mancini and Michel Rosenfeld (eds), *Constitutional Secularism in an Age of Religious Revival* (OUP 2014) 269, 277.
77 The *get* is sometimes used as a pressure instrument to obtain economic advantages. See more on that Pascale Fournier, Pascal McDougall, and Melissa Lichtsztral, 'Secular Rights and Religious Wrongs? Family Law, Religion and Women in Israel' (2012) 18 William & Marry Journal of Women and the Law 333, 345.
78 Einhorn, 'Family Unions in Israel' (n 74) 700.
79 See Sapir and Statman (n 76) 282.
80 Einhorn, 'Family Unions in Israel' (n 74) 698.
81 Sapir and Statman (n 76) 280.

82 Einhorn, 'Family Unions in Israel' (n 74) 702.
83 Einhorn, 'Family Unions in Israel' (n 74) 702.
84 Westeich and Shifman (n 22) 98.
85 For more details about the legal effects of non-marital cohabitation, see Einhorn, 'Family Unions in Israel' (n 74) 702–706.
86 Yoav Dotan, 'Judicial Review and Political Accountability: the Case of the High Court of Justice in Israel' (1998) 32 Islamic Law Review 448, 460.
87 Einhorn, 'Family Unions in Israel' (n 74) 706; Sapir and Statman (n 76) 277.
88 Halperin-Kaddari (n 31) 244.
89 Halperin-Kaddari (n 31) 245.
90 Sapir and Statman (n 76) 278.
91 Sapir and Statman (n 76) 278–279.
92 Westreich and Shifman (n 22) 30.
93 Dotan (n 86) 460–461; Josh Goodman, 'Divine Judgement: Judicial Review of Religious Legal Systems in India and Israel' (2009) 32 Hastings International & Comparative Law Review 477–510.
94 Anat Scolnicov, 'Religious Law, Religious Courts and Human Rights within Israeli Constitutional Structure' (2006) 4 International Journal of Constitutional Law 732, 733.
95 Goodman (n 93) 511.
96 Hadas Tagari, 'Personal Family Law Systems: A Comparative and International Human Rights Analysis' (2012) 8 International Journal of Law in Context 231, 239–240; for a comprehensive survey of the discriminatory rules of religious laws against women see Halperin-Kaddari (n 31) 227f.
97 Sapir and Statman (n 76) 267.
98 Goodman (n 93) 509.
99 Ayelet Shachar, 'Group Identity and Women's Rights in Family Law: The Perils of Multicultural Accommodation' (1998) 6 The Journal of Political Philosophy 285, 293.
100 See Yoav Dotan, 'The Spillover Effect of Bills of Rights: A Comparative Assessment of the Impact of Bills of Rights in Canada and Israel' (2005) 53 The American Journal of Comparative Law 293, 316.
101 Basic Law: Human Dignity and Liberty, 1992, SH 1391, Section 10.
102 Goodman (n 93) 509.
103 Scolnicov (n 94) 739; Dotan, 'The Spillover Effect' (n 100) 316.
104 Dotan, 'Judicial Review' (n 86) 448.
105 Dotan, 'Judicial Review' (n 86) 455.
106 Dotan, 'Judicial Review' (n 86) 455–456; see also Edelman (n 19) 11.
107 See Woods (n 1) 53–54.
108 Scolnicov (n 94) 739.
109 Daphne Barak-Erez, 'Law and Religion under the Status Quo Model: Between Past Compromises and Constant Change', 30 Cardozo Law Review (2009), 2495, 2506.
110 Halperin-Kaddari (n 31) 228.
111 Karayanni (n 32) 43; also Tagari (n 96) 242.
112 Goodman (n 93) 514–515.
113 Karayanni (n 32) 26.
114 Englard (n 4) 86.
115 Woods, Judicial Power, 81: 'Marriage and divorce determine who is a Jew, who is inside and who is outside the social community. Marriage and divorce laws determine

who can marry whom, who can have children with whom, and whose children will be considered as part of the community'.

116 Yüksel Sezgin, 'The Israeli Millet System: Examining Legal Pluralism through the Lenses of Nation-Building and Human Rights' (2010) 43 Israel Law Review 631, 654.

117 Scolnicov (n 94) 734.

118 Scolnicov (n 94) 735.

Part IV

Party autonomy

10 Marriage contracts in Islamic history

Amira Sonbol

Introduction

Since the nineteenth century and the introduction of nation state hegemony as the dominant structure through which Islamic peoples would be ruled, the modern family has became a bulwark for that hegemony. Any laws or differences that touch on the nature and structure of the modern family are immediately attacked as a threat to Islam, to society, and to morality. It seems ironic that even though the modern family owes much to non-Islamic traditions, it is still vehemently held on to and fought for by social forces in the name of holding on to Islam.

In this chapter, the modern family that predominates in the Islamic world is labelled the *qiwama* (male guardianship) family because *qiwama* remains a central pillar upon which the prototype of the modern family in the Islamic world stands, giving the male power over adult females and minor children.[1] The family may be monogamous or polygamous, the household may shelter a nuclear or extended group, the mother may be the breadwinner or the father may be deceased, but it is always the father who is given the legal and social recognition as head of the family with almost absolute power over the womenfolk and children. It is only when there is no male alive or willing to take on the responsibility of the family that a woman becomes the recognized *qayyim* (guardian); even then it is seen as an exception or aberration allowed only because of circumstances. Whereas the father is automatically recognized by law as the *'a'il*, i.e. the financial supporter with the responsibilities and powers implicit in such a designation, a woman would first have to prove that she does not have a male supporting her or her children or minor siblings before she is recognized as having some form of *qiwama* over herself and them.

Efforts to change these conditions, to allow women equal rights, have met with opposition on the basis that such innovations would be adopted from foreign traditions and contradict the Sharia.[2] Focusing on marriage contracts, this chapter traces the origins of the modern family and its institutionalization by legal process through state structures. As the state developed and changed over time, experiencing socioeconomic transformations, so did the shape of the family and marital relations. These transformations, forming what can be described as a history of family, are reflected in the laws applied, the legal system that has enforced them, and the discourse representing the juridical and social outlook towards marriage and marital relations. Marriage contracts are an important source of social history, together with marital disputes brought to court to contest unfulfilled marriage contracts and demand financial rights included in them, as they give evidence of lived realities, gender relations, the laws, and the legal system that interpreted and applied these laws. Altogether, the information contracts contain or lack provides keys to opening up a wider understanding of women's history and the shift and turns this history has taken. It is important to indicate at this point that use of the word 'family' as a legal designation is a modern concept; whereas pre-modern literature speaks about *'asha'ir* (clans) and *qaba'il* (tribes), *usra* (family) was not a centre of social discourse or legal and state interest until the coming of the modern state. This fact is directly related to laws regulating marriage from various periods, with family becoming central to modern laws.

Roots of the Islamic marriage contract

One of the significant changes that Islam brought about in marriage is the institution of a prototype or what has been described as only one form of marriage based on a contractual agreement. Before Islam, various forms of marriage existed depending on the particular town or location in Arabia. Islam made a legally witnessed contract the only form of marriage acceptable and instituted rules to guide its formation and punish its breach. If advocates of the idea that Islam honoured women are right about Islam having saved women from a life of destitution, female infanticide, and near slavery, then this new uniform marriage can be seen as a great achievement for women of Arabia or at least in those parts of Arabia where onerous forms of marriage – like *mudaba'a* – existed. In *mudaba'a*, a man could ask his wife to copulate with another man who possessed particular sought-after qualities, such as a reputation for bearing sons or strength of body, in the hope of her becoming pregnant and giving him strong or talented sons. In another form of marriage, the woman co-habited with up to ten men; when she became pregnant and delivered a child, she designated the father and the man recognized it and became its financial supporter. These and other forms of marriage that existed in pre-Islamic Arabia give a glimpse of different types of relations and what has been described as disregard for women. The research is not conclusive on this issue; Leila Ahmed has shown that perhaps the contrary was true, namely that women were actually better off before Islam, that it was the women's sexual freedom which allowed them to be in relations with more than one man and that this was closed with the institution of uniform marriage and control of sexuality.[3] Perhaps the situation was more complicated; after all, women enjoyed power as *kahinat* (religious leaders) before Islam, and they wielded authority and handled property. At the same time, there was widespread poverty among women and abusive forms of marriage at the historical point when Islam appeared.[4] Given the diversity of Arabia's different parts and tribes, some being quite urban like Mecca and Medina, with others being nomadic as was the case in Eastern Arabia, a diversity of marriage patterns should have been expected, and the period before and after the appearance of the Islamic message can be seen as transitional as far as social relations are concerned.

Diversity in the forms of marriage continued throughout history, even with Islam's introduction of a uniform form. Transitionality can be seen in various ways during the formative period of Islam, although research is still needed to reach concrete conclusions. In the Islamic prototype, a man could take more than one wife but a woman had to be married to only one man at any one time.[5] This meant that she could have no sexual activities outside of marriage; at least that is how the law became established later in Islamic history. If the Quran is to be followed, it institutes equal punishments for wife and husband, 100 lashes for *zinā'* (sex outside of marriage); medieval *fiqh* (Islamic jurisprudence), however, extended the function of contracting to include copulation with slave women and formulated laws regarding the master's right to his slave woman and establishing paternity of children issuing from them. Yet the Quran clearly calls for taking wives from '*ma malakat aymanakum*' (of those you hold captive), described as slave women or prisoners of war; the Quran does not, by contrast, indicate that they are to become sexual partners outside of marriage. Extending contractual agreements to include slave women must be seen as (i) bringing in pre-Islamic traditions from both Arabia and the provinces into which Islam expanded, and (ii) making pre-existing sexual traditions Islamically legitimate through theological exegesis, this occurring as social fabrics evolved and structural transformations pushed for a recognition of new elites and class divisions. Hence, even though a relationship with a slave woman did not constitute a marriage, it was nevertheless greatly detailed by law and discussed by *fiqh* and *fatawa* (juridical opinions) and handled as legitimate in Sharia courts. The children of such relationships were recognized and their mother given the status of *umm walad* (slave mother of a child from a free man), not to be sold once she has provided her master with a son; however, such a child was never recognized as a full son or daughter and thus had no right of inheritance even if the father married the slave woman following the child's birth.

Narratives of early Islamic marriages show a move towards marriage on a contractual basis, confining sexuality, and establishing new gender relations. This does not mean that pre-Islamic marriages were not contracted, i.e. negotiated with conditions agreed upon between parties. We do not have enough details to show how marriages were actually arranged, but it is clear that the *mahr* was paid by a husband to his wife as part of the marriage agreement, so there must have been some negotiations. In the transitionality of the Prophetic period, there was a move towards new gender relations in which the woman's sexuality was confined to the marital bed and establishing paternity became an important issue, perhaps due to the appearance of a merchant economy, which was transforming social relations in Arabia.[6]

There is evidence of this transitional space in the Quran, like the verses on *li'an*[7] in which a man could dispute the paternity of a child by exchanging oaths of eternal damnation with his wife, declaring that the child was not his while she insisted that it was. They would take the oath five times, after which the couple would be permanently divorced and the child would become named after the mother. The verses on *li'an* give a glimpse into the hegemonic role medieval *fiqh* played in establishing what became known as Islamic marriage. Rules reflecting primarily their age and traditional laws diffused through *'urf* (customs and traditions) and *qiyas* (analogy) became established as an Islamic legal framework, disregarding the logic postulated by *li'an* or orders regarding slave-women, while legitimizing patriarchal practices and extending them in the name of Islam.

The historical disjuncture here is important. *Fiqh* is understood to be based on early Islamic practices and the Prophet's sunna, yet the material evidence we have from that period is very limited, and we do not have marriage contracts surviving from that timeframe. However, we do have written contracts surviving from other parts of the world from very early historical periods. Given the predominance of orality in early Islam, one must assume that contracts were not written down, and in fact written records of Arabian marriages continue to be rare into the modern period. In places where it was usual for marriage to be documented and where records and documents from various historical epochs are extensive, like in Egypt, recording marriage was actually a matter of choice until the Ottoman period, when recording marriage became an obligation required by law. The Ottomans, like other empires, were interested in taxation, and they passed laws that allowed for raising such taxes; fees on court registrations was one important source of income and this included the registration of marriage.

Textualization is therefore a point worth considering when studying marriage contracts and social institutions in general; the process of textualization involves the selection and identification of what to write down, what to leave out, specific interests and requirements of the process, and the authorities with a stake in it. It is important not to see only continuities from one period into the other but to appreciate the disjuncture between them. Here, for example, one should note the continued existence of orality in contracting marriage during the Ottoman period, notwithstanding the rules requiring that a marriage be registered. For example, a form of informal marriage called *al-sifah* was practised and accepted. In this marriage, there was no written/official document and the wife had no recognized financial rights.[8] In a case brought to court involving a marital dispute between a couple married according to this practice, the husband was asked whether a contract of marriage had taken place between him and his wife; the husband responded that he had shaken her brother's hand on it, hence the word *al-sifah* (from *musafaha*, shaking hands).

In another case, dated 958 H (1551 AD), the couple indicated they had married while away by declaration and celebration:

> At the court of Sheikh Shams al-Din al-Kitami al-Malki arrived Sheikh Abulfath b. al-Sheikh . . . resident of the port and with him 'Abdalnabi b. Khidr al-'Issawi and a woman . . . who said her name was Wag'a Abta 'Uthman . . . he [meaning Sheikh 'Abdulfath] explained that they [meaning 'Abdalnabi and Wag'a] were living together in sin, about which they were questioned. They responded that they were out west and a goat was slaughtered on the

> announcement [of their nuptials] and the marriage was consummated almost a year earlier . . .[9]

Today, informal marriages continue in various parts of the Islamic world: *'urfi* in Egypt and *mut'a* in Iran, as well as *misyar* in countries of the Arabian Gulf. Here marriages may be written as a document but are not usually registered in court.

To study early Arab marriages we have to turn to the narratives and *siyar* (biographies) that were popular subjects in Arabic literature, on into the medieval and modern periods. So even though we do not have actual marriage contracts, through these narratives we do have a good grasp of how marriage was transacted and what was involved in marital contracts. Here, however, we must be cautious since narratives and *siyar* date from long time after the death of the Prophet, a period during which Islam spread and interacted with large areas of the ancient world and with their diverse peoples, cultures and laws.

Siyar and narratives offer expansive stories of the Prophet's family. The Prophet's marriage to his first wife Khadija is described in *Sirat Rasul Allah* of Ibn Hisham in the following way:

> When the Prophet was twenty-five years old he married Khadija bint Khuwaylid . . . [she] was a merchant, of honorable descent and rich, for whom men worked or with whom she shared a portion of the profit . . .

First she hired the Prophet Muhammad to carry her goods and trade for her in Syria, and after his return and evidence of his success and honesty, she approached him asking that they marry. The Prophet took the matter up with his uncles, who approached her uncles and betrothed her to him. According to Ibn Hisham:

> The Prophet dowered her with forty *bikra* (young female camel) and she was the first woman the Prophet of God married and he never took another wife until she died *radiyya allahu 'anha*.[10]

Information regarding the amount of the *mahr* is also given in stories of the marriage of the Prophet's granddaughter Umm Kulthum to 'Umar bin al-Khattab: '. . . and he dowered her with forty thousand dirham'.[11] As with the Prophet's marriage, a betrothal took place, an agreed upon *mahr* was paid, and the marriage was consummated, all of which was brokered by male elders of the families of the bride and bridegroom. The same pattern is repeated in narratives of other members of the Prophet's family and the wider community of his Companions.

In all these stories, it is the bridegroom who paid the *mahr* to the bride; yet there are indications that the opposite also took place. 'Abdallah bin 'Abdalmuttalib, the Prophet Muhammad's father, was stopped by a woman as he crossed the marketplace in Mecca on his way to ask for the Prophet's mother's (Amna) hand in marriage. The woman asked 'Abdallah to marry her and offered him a *mahr* of camels equal in number to that with which his father had ransomed him from being sacrificed earlier following a dream in which God had asked 'Abdalmuttalib to sacrifice ‘Abdallah’s life. The latter refused the woman’s offer of marriage and went on to marry Amna. The importance of this story, narrated by Ibn Ishaq, Ibn Hisham, and others is that it tells of the centrality of the *mahr* in marriage, but it also shows that the *mahr* could be expected to be paid by women as well as by men and that women offered marriage as did the men. Although it is not clear how this worked, it may have been expected from the party seeking the marriage and the *mahr* was a matter of open negotiation.

Narratives of early Islamic marriages also tell us that witnesses were expected to be present when the marriage was concluded and that the families were directly involved. These details, however, could have been later additions to the original form of marriage at the time of the Prophet, and families may have been present in early Islamic marriages, too, without this necessarily having been a requirement. This would make the choice or consensus of bride or bridegroom the basis of the contract, at least when the marriage involved an adult woman. Given the fact that Khadija was married twice before the Prophet and that the woman who asked ‘Abdallah to marry her was an adult woman described as a person who could read, things may have been different depending on the age of the bride. That families were not necessarily involved in transacting marriages of adult women gains credibility given the story of the woman who offered marriage directly to ‘Abdallah. For one thing, he did not seem surprised when she asked him to marry her, but rather apologized since he had a previous obligation. Later, after his marriage to Amna, he sought the woman out and asked her why she was no longer seeking his marriage. No uncles or male relatives were involved in this aborted negotiation.

The age of the bride and her authority over her marriage are reflected in marriage contracts all the way to the modern period; during the Ottoman period we begin to see a differentiation made according to schools of law (*madhahib*), which distinguished between a previously married woman (*thayb*) and a virgin (*bikr*) girl. This movement towards patriarchy by state authority developed further under the modern state and the modernization of law when the presence of a male guardian (*wali*) was made a requirement by law in many Islamic countries, Jordan being one example, a central indicator of the construction of the modern *qiwama* family.[12]

One last detail can be deduced from the story of ‘Abdallah and Amna; after their marriage, ‘Abdallah travelled on trade and she remained with her people. He died on the trip, and it seems that betrothal and marriage had actually taken place at the same time and the marriage had been consummated in her home. Later, after his marriage to Khadija, the Prophet moved to live in her house in Mecca. However, after the Hijra, the Prophet’s wives moved in with him, and it is related that he built each one of them her own room. One can conclude that flexibility existed in regards to domicile and that the system was pragmatic rather than matrilocal or patrilocal.

By the eighth century marriage contracts were regularly written and documented by *qadis* (judges) in various parts of the Islamic empire. Basic principles of these contracts seem to fit with Quranic requirements of marriage such as limiting women to marrying one man at any one time, observing the waiting period (*'idda*), i.e. a three-month period following divorce or the husband's death during which the wife is not allowed to take another husband, the payment of the *mahr*, and the presence of witnesses. Many other details, as will be discussed in the following section of this paper, seem to have been the result of cultural and legal diffusions resulting from Islamic expansion into neighbouring territories; it can be argued that cultural and legal diffusion continue into the present with the interaction of Islam and other traditions.

Information about marriage is quite rich for the ancient world, whether we are talking about Ancient Egyptians, Akkadians, Persians, Greeks, Romans, or other peoples with whom Arabs came into contact after the expansions out of Arabia. Information is also rich in particular areas of the Islamic Empire, like Egypt, Andalusia, and Palestine. A look at early Muslim contracts may help illustrate the evolution of Islamic marriage traditions or what became established and endorsed by medieval *fuqaha'* and *qadis* as forms acceptable to Islam.

Early marriage contracts

A marriage contract from Egypt dated 252 H (866 AD) gives basic information regarding marital expectations during the third century after the Prophet's time.

> In the name of God the Merciful, Zakariyya . . . dowered his wife Muhamadiyya . . . six dinars he paid [before the marriage was consummated], two of which he paid at the time of the contract, two were delayed till Rabi' al-Awwal, year 252 . . . so four dinars advanced *mahr* and two delayed. Ja'far bin Ahmad b. al-Ma'mun acted on behalf of Muhamadiyya after her witness to him in front of two witnesses . . . and Zakariyya accepted this marriage for himself . . . and indicated that the advanced *mahr* was two dinars. Witnessed by . . .[13]

The *mahr*, then, continued to be central to the marriage contract; but here we see a difference in the form in which it is paid: part is paid in advance (*mahr muqaddam*) and part is paid later (*mahr mu'akhkhar*). In the Arabian contracts discussed above, the *mahr* was paid in the form of animal stock or cash money and was received by the bride at the time the marriage took place. In the Egyptian contracts from the third century, the *mahr* was divided, with one part to be paid at a later date. Another contract dated 259 H (872 AD) from the Upper Egyptian town of Ashmun also provides for advanced and delayed *mahr*, half paid in advance and half delayed for five years. The contract also elaborates on marital expectations, specifically what the wife and husband promised each other as conditions for their life together. 'Pre-nup' conditions, differing from place to place, appeared often in marriage contracts recorded in Egyptian Sharia courts; class and wealth, whether the bride was a minor or an adult woman, and the particular work of the bridegroom, all seemed to have played a role. The prompt and the deferred *mahr* and how they are dealt with in marriage contracts give us a sense of change during the Ottoman period. These terms do not appear in early contracts from

Arabia before Islam or during the Prophetic period; however, they parallel terms and divisions of the *mahr* that were normative to marriage contracts in territories outside Arabia in the ancient world and are still frequently found in contracts from Iraq and Egypt, for example.

Historians of Ancient Egypt have called marriage contracts 'financial settlements' and distinguished between the celebration of marriage, which took place as oral ceremony, and the contract, in which the parties concerned set down conditions for the continuation and dissolution of a marriage.

> . . . I joined myself to Your Propriety by a giving in legal marriage, based on sound expectations, if God should think best, also for the procreation of legitimate children; and, having found your sacred and secure virginity, I have proclaimed it. Wherefore I have come to this guarantee in writing by which I agree that I owe and am indebted for your wedding gifts or gifts before marriage . . . for 6 good-quality imperial solidi, less 36 carats . . . And I agree no less in addition to support you legitimately and to clothe you in likeness to all my family members of like status and in proportion to the wealth available to me, as far as my modest means will allow; and not to show contempt for you in any way or to cast you out from marriage with me except by reason of unchastity or shameful behavior or physical misbehavior established through three or more trustworthy free men . . . and never to leave your marriage bed or to run to disorder or wickedness provided however that Your Propriety is obedient to me and preserves all benevolence towards me and sincere affection all fine and useful deeds and words . . . and, having been asked the formal question, I have willingly and voluntarily agreed, not overcome by duress or fraud or violence or deceit or compulsion, and I have issued to you for security that which is written below . . . And I the aforementioned husband Horouonchis agree in addition that I cannot at any occasion or time introduce other wives above my lawful wife, and if I do so I shall pay the same penalty.[14]

This contract dating from the Greco-Roman period of Ancient Egypt is itself transitional in nature given earlier contracts, which are usually shorter and contain religious terminology. It is however a good example to use here because it contains the marital expectations that existed early on before the Islamic period. The contract documents obligations already agreed upon and textualized in court after the marriage had already taken place, and it represents the type of financial and marital relations and obligations that became normative for early marriage contracts in Islamic Egypt.

Not all contracts were registered in pre-Islamic Egypt, neither were they in early Islamic Egypt; rather, marriage was widely celebrated without a written contract, but marriages were documented and registered in courts when the couple wished and particularly when there were conditions and financial settlements involved. As indicated earlier, it was not until the sixteenth century that registration of marriage became compulsory, but even then oral forms of marriage continued in practice, as is exemplified by *'urfi* forms of marriage, which continue in practice till today.

Early Muslim marriages, like the one quoted above, almost always contain a prompt and a deferred *mahr*. As contracted in early Islamic marriages, these seem to reflect the actual payment of an advanced *mahr*, part of which was paid before or during the marriage ceremony and the other part at a later date. Compulsory registration of marriage under the Ottomans meant a wider, if by no means universal registration of marriages, and thereby also the textualization of already existing social norms and marital expectations, often beyond what *fiqh* presents or what is normatively understood about marriage and gender relations. For example, the following contracts show the evolution of the delayed *mahr* and other practices that appear in marriage contracts during the Ottoman period:

> The *hurma* [previously married adult] woman Zainab daughter of 'Abdallah b. 'Abdallah al-Zabidiya married her betrothed L'di al-Maghribi al-Nabili, the *sadaq* of four gold Maghribi, of which [she] admitted receiving one dinar and the rest delayed until death or divorce. She married herself and the mentioned husband accepted for himself, a legal acceptance (*qubul shar'i*). He determined four silver *nisfs* as clothing allowance and she gave her legal acceptance to that, and he took upon himself (*wa 'allaq laha 'alayhi*) with his acknowledgment that if ever he took another wife or took a concubine or moved her [meaning Zainab] from where she lives at present which is located in the Gura at the Suwaiqi market without her permission and she proves all this or part of it and she exempted him from one dinar of the rest of her *mahr* then she would be divorced one divorce with which she owned herself. With this I, the mentioned husband, permitted my mentioned wife to live in the mentioned place as long as she remained married to me (*fi 'ismati*) . . .[15]

Here the delayed *mahr* takes on another meaning by becoming a debt due to the wife at the time of the husband's death or in case they divorce. Earlier contracts saw the delayed *mahr* as part of the advanced *mahr*, part of which was paid ahead and the rest at a specific date. A further nuance occurs in contracts where the *mahr* as a whole is divided into parts to be paid out on instalments over time, a bit every year, or over periods agreed upon by the couple. Such contracts are an indication of the financial abilities of the people involved in the marriage.

> Mamay b. 'Abdullah, the freed-slave of Sinan Bek, *amir alliwa' sultani*, married his betrothed Amna, the virgin, daughter of Farag . . . freed-slave of Hajj Hussain . . . following God's good book and the Sunna of his esteemed Prophet, and a *mahr* totaling twenty gold Sultani dinars, of which she received ten dinars that Khadija, [Amna's] mother confirmed receiving . . . for *tashwirha* (trousseau) and the rest to be paid by instalments over twenty years' time, one payment each year half a dinar until the amount is paid . . . her brother contracted the marriage with her approval, due to her father's

absence over the previous nine years without any information of his whereabouts which was confirmed to the Maliki judge officiating with testimonies of witnesses . . .[16]

> . . . against a *mahr* of eight gold dinars and three hundred new silver *nisf* . . . The husband pawned in her power two silver bracelets and a silver crescent pin in a legal transaction, which she received and the rest of what is left of the silver due to be divided and paid over twenty yearly instalments . . .[17]

From the above we see that the marriage contract was used to set up conditions that the couple agreed upon and that appear mostly in the form of obligations of the husband towards the wife. As in the case of the Ancient Egyptian marriage from the Greco-Roman period quoted above, the husband gave a commitment to his wife to observe these conditions, which in themselves reflect an agreement and suggest that negotiations probably occurred between the two parties. The contracts also tell us that contractual discussions took the financial conditions of the couple into consideration, and the diversity of the contracts give a glimpse into class structure and social relations. In richer towns, the *mahr* was usually paid in its entirety in advance, with a delayed part held on to until divorce separated the couple or the husband died, at which time the delayed *mahr* was due for payment to the wife by the husband or his estate. The delayed *mahr* could also be divided into two parts, one part delayed to be paid at a later date and the other when the husband died or divorce took place. For contracts among poorer classes, in contrast, the *mahr* was often paid in instalments, like the previous contracts quoted above, over the long years of marriage. This was problematic because when a wife asked to be repudiated, she quite often lost all her financial rights, including what was left of her advanced *mahr*. The following illustrates disputes over unpaid *mahrs*. Such disputes are very valuable because they present even more details regarding marital agreement than may have appeared in the marriage document itself and could also be about marriages that were not recorded in the first place.

> [At the court of] the honored Shafi'i *hakim shar'i* (judge) . . . the respectable Ahmad al-Sayyid. . . . legal representative of the woman Safiyya, daughter of . . . sued her husband the respectable 'Ali ibn Ghanim . . . that he owes her seven riyals, the remainder of her advanced *mahr*; nine riyals, price of cotton; one riyal price of cinnamon block; six riyals, the price of a quarter share of a shop that he took from her . . . and her clothing allowance for two years since he married her. He asked that the husband be asked about this and that he pay her what is owed. The defendant was asked and agreed that he was married to her since the date mentioned, that he clothed her with a dress and three shirts and that he agreed to an eight riyal *mahr* of which he paid seven less ten *nisfs*, so he owed her one riyal and ten *nisfs*, and that he has already settled the price of the cotton with her . . . the mentioned 'Ali disagreed with him indicating that the advanced *mahr* was determined at twelve riyals of which only three were paid . . . the woman

> and her witness took the oath and asked the defendant to bring his evidence to court. He was not able to and asked that the woman give him her legal oath, which she did . . . the named *hakim* then ordered the man to pay her seven riyals advanced *mahr* and ten *nisfs* of silver which he had confessed to and to pay her two years clothing allowance, each year two seasons, each season one shirt and head cover, belt and underwear and shoes.[18]

Marriage contracts also illustrate the fact that women could marry themselves off and that the *fiqhi* requirement of 'no marriage without a guardian' ('*la zawaj bidun wali*') may have applied to minors but was not observed as a religious or marital requirement. A tenth-century Hijri (sixteenth-century AD) contract from Palestine shows that this was also the case for other parts of the Islamic world during the same period. In the contract quoted below a woman came to court with her fiancé and informed the *qadi* that she had been widowed for eight years and now wished to marry the man present with her in court, whom she described as her betrothed. She had no proxy (*wakil*) or anyone else with her and the marriage was completed 'according to the offer (*ijab*) and acceptance (*qubul*) of the named wife and the named husband'.[19]

We also see women acting as guardian quite regularly, sometimes using *wilayat al-ijbar* (the power to compel) to marry a daughter, a son, or a brother. This is illustrated by the following contract which is particularly interesting in light of its being from Upper Egypt, where the Maliki *madhhab* dominated. Yet here the application of the *madhhab* was applied according to *'urf* rather than to the normative understanding of the *madhhab* in both *fiqh* and Islamic discourse today, which makes it a requirement for a male guardian to officiate at a marriage.

> In the presence of the honorable (*al-fadil*) Mayor (*'umda*) the sheikh Mustafa Ragab Murad, and Ibrahim Hussain 'Abdin, and the Sheikh Sa'd 'Ali Marfa and 'Ali al-Qasabgi al-Misri, *al-mukaram* [*distinctive title like honorable*] 'Abdal-Wahid son of *al-mukaram* Mustafa 'Abdin married the minor virgin (*qasir*, *bikr*) Saluma daughter of the deceased 'Abdallah Khalaf in accordance to God's Book and the Sunna of His Prophet, the total *mahr* being 2,000 piasters, 1,500 advanced received by the hand of *al-mukaram* Mustafa son of the deceased Mahmud 'Abdin representing (*tawkil*) her mother the woman Khadija daughter of the deceased Amin al-Basrabi and whose *tawkil* from her has been proven through the witness of al-Hajj Hassan al-Tobgi al-Sabagh, Sulaiman b. Ginaina who knows the two of them. The delayed *mahr* is 500 piasters [to be paid] at time of death or divorce. He took as condition upon himself (*wa sharat laha 'alayhi*) as a central part of the contract (*fi silb al-'aqd*) eighteen *dhira'* (a measure about a meter) *banafsig* (type of fabric?) and two gold rings worth fifty piasters which was also received by the hand of the mother's deputy. She was thus married by her mother according to *wilayat al-ijbar* (the legal guardian's right to compel a minor when the guardian is the father, mother or grandfather), and the husband accepted for himself.[20]

> *Mawlana al-Hakim al-Shar'i* (the honorable shar'i judge), on behalf of her minor brother 'Abdalhamid after she gave him her permission witnessed by al-Sheikh 'Abdalgawad Taqildin and Mu'awwad Muhammad al-Radi *al-hati* (kebab vendor) married her to [the bridegroom] whose father was his legal deputy (*tawkilah anhu*) witnessed by Hussain Abdelgawad and 'Abdalrahman Muhammad al-Rashidi, a legal shar'i marriage on the second of Gamadi Awwal 1193.[21]

These last two contracts confirm that the position of women was quite different from what it is in the *qiwama* family today. While sisters and mothers were regularly given custody over their younger siblings and sons by pre-modern Sharia courts, the modern state almost never cedes this right to women except when there is no male relative of even second or third degree to be given this responsibility. The usual explanation used for this is that the Sharia requires a male relative as guardian and that no marriage can take place without the presence of a male relative. '*La zawaj bidun wali*' (no marriage without a male guardian) is a phrase repeated over and over in *fiqh* manuals and literature on marriage. In fact, in modern Jordanian law, women could not until recently ask the court for *khul*[c] divorce unless their *wali* was present.[22] Even though the minimum age of marriage in Jordan was raised from 15 to 18,[23] the same 2010 code makes it possible to lower the marriage age to 15;[24] and even though a woman above the age of 18 may conclude her own marriage, articles 14 to 19 (regarding the *wali*) limit this ability, requiring either the approval of a male *wali* of some degree or that the judge act as *wali*. Most interesting, the 2010 code continues to use *kafa'a* (parity) as a means of continuing the *qiwama* of the father or his male replacement by making it the right of the *wali* or the bride to nullify the marriage if the bridegroom proves not to be the *kuf'* of the bride. The law also limits the bride's ability to ask for the dissolution of a marriage if the husband proves not to be *kuf'* if she had children from him. In response to efforts demanding reforms regarding abuses in previous codes, the Jordanian Code of Personal Status, passed in 2010, introduced some changes, the most important of which was raising the minimum age of marriage from 15 to 18; however, the codes were reworded so as to keep the same *qiwama* system intact.[25] That the Sharia is today interpreted as forbidding a woman's right of *wilaya* over her children while pre-modern Sharia courts regularly allowed women *wilayat al-ijbar* when the father was dead raises questions regarding *'urf* and Sharia interpretations. Here the regular appearance of terms of *wilayat al-ijbar* in relation to women in courts of the Maliki judges in Upper Egypt illustrates the importance of marriage contracts in filling in disjunctures that have been bypassed so as to construct a more streamlined history confirming patriarchal *fiqhi* discourse.

One last question about these contracts has to deal with how 'religious' these contracts were. This is important since in today's discourse – even though marriage is described as a contract, i.e. an agreement between two parties – the laws defining and controlling it are seen as God's law and thus divine. The religious description of marriage is actually a modern construct brought about by reforms that (i) organized courts along religious lines, as is illustrated by the establishment of Sharia courts for Muslims and Milla courts for non-Muslims of different denominations in the Ottoman Empire, for example, and (ii) ordered the application of so-called religious codes formulated by government committees. This restructuring was at the heart of the establishment of a state-sponsored *qiwama* family, in which the father held legal authority. Legal codes selected by government committees codified selections of laws to be applied directly by judges. The codes themselves were based on a selective understanding of *fiqh* by the state and its organs during a process of modernization and centralization. Thus selection of laws became a new form of textualization, leading to a disjuncture with the past, as the new codes were considered as being equivalent to Sharia since God willed it.

As has been shown in previous research, Christians and Jews often came to court to register polygamous marriages, and non-Muslim women came to Sharia courts to be divorced.[26] Today, the marriage of a Christian outside his/her faith is not recognized by his/her church. For Christian men, this is not a problem, since in opposition to the church the state recognizes his marriage to a non-Muslim. He can thus take a Christian wife and his marriage will be recognized by both church and state. At the same time he can take a non-Christian wife and this second marriage will be recognized and legal in the eyes of the state according to polygamy laws. A woman can only have one husband and is only allowed to marry someone from her own faith and sect if her marriage is to be legitimated by church and state. Furthermore, divorce is not allowed among Christians, which again is a problem for women, since they cannot take another husband; conversely, a man can take another wife from another faith or sect whether his Christian wife approves or not and she would have to remain 'hanging' in a state of marriage-no-marriage.

The following marriage contracts from the pre-modern period show that society and social traditions were not entirely different for Muslims and non-Muslims, but that in fact marital expectations had little to do with religious divisions. This does not mean that marriages were not celebrated by the particular church or synagogue and then registered in Sharia court as the court of law of the state. What it means is that lived realities reflected in the registered contracts show little differences between marital expectations and marital relations. The following contracts, Muslim and Christian, illustrate this point.

> *Bism illah al-rahman al-rahim*
>
> This is what Isma'il, the *mawla* of Ahmed b. Marwan, resident of Ashmun, dowered 'Aisha, daughter of Yusuf [who was residing when he betrothed her at . . .] and she is an adult *ayyim* (adult), after delegating her grandfather Ya'qub b. Ishaq . . . with witnesses to her delegation and he accepted and undertook completion of her marriage contract. Isma'il, *mawla* of Ahmad . . . dowered her with four dinars . . . two dinars in advance and two delayed owed by him to 'Aisha . . . delayed for five years . . . and Isma'il . . . took upon

himself a stipulation of good companionship and treatment as God *'az wa jall* ordered, and the Sunna of His Prophet Muhammad, *salla Allah 'alayhi wa salam*, to hold with kindness or to let go [meaning divorce] with compassion. And Isma'il, *mawla* of Ahmad, stipulated that the fate of every other woman that he marries would be in the hands of 'Aisha, to divorce her however she willed . . .[27]

The contract begins with '*bism illah al-rahman al-rahim*' (in the name of God the Compassionate the Merciful), with which Quranic recitations and other important actions by Muslims begin. The contract also presents the Quranic line 'to hold with kindness or to let go [meaning divorce] with compassion', as expected in a marriage and a condition which is the basis for its continuance or dissolution. The inclusion of words of reverence following God's name or the Prophet's name is further indication of the effort to extend religious legitimacy to marriage. How much of the contract is Islamic and how much is actually due to traditions and marital expectations is answered by a look at other contracts from the same period. The following is a Coptic marriage dating from 336 H (947 AD):

Bism illahi al-rahman al-rahim,

This is what Taydur bin Isma'il . . . *al-shamas* (apprentice priest) dowered, Dabla Aday daughter of Yuhannis . . . son of Yuhannis the priest . . . and married her with it. He dowered her ninety gold dinars . . . [of which] he advanced fifteen dinars received by her father from him . . . and seventy-five dinars remained as debt to Dabla Aday from Taydur . . . and Yuhannis b. Buqtor officiated his daughter's marriage and transacting this contract for her (*iktitab hadha al-kitab 'alayha*), and she is *bikr* (not previously married, virgin) in her home, after he consulted her . . . and he [the bridegroom] swears to God to provide good companionship and happy marriage (*husn al-suhba wa gamil al-'ishra*) . . . witnessed by . . .[28]

What identifies this marriage contract as involving Christians rather than Muslims is the mention of the titles of the bridegroom, a *shamas*, and the bride's father, a priest; otherwise the stipulations in the contract differ little from the one of Muslims quoted earlier and others like them from this time period. In fact, the inclusion of Quranic words like '*bism illahi al-rahman al-rahim*' or such statements as '*husn al-suhba wa gamil al-'ishra*', which is similar to '*mu'amala bi ma'ruf*', is normative for contracts registered in Egypt before the modern period, including Christian ones. Similarities in marriage and divorce documents of different religious groups were not unique to Egypt but can be found in other parts of the Islamic world, too.

In Majlis al-Shari' . . . in front of *mawlana* . . . the Christian woman named Maryam bin 'Adbel-Ahhad al-Siryani, vouched for by her father, asked her

> husband 'Ibriyan Wild Habiyan, the Copt, who is present with her in court, to divorce her (*an yakhla'aha*) from his '*isma* and marriage knot (*'uqdat nikahih*) in return for her relinquishing her *mu'akhkhar sadaq* (delayed *mahr*) amounting to ten qurush and her *nafaqat al-'idda* (alimony for period of *'idda*) and housing expenses [during the '*idda*] and fifteen qurush remaining from her previous *nafaqa* according to this earlier document . . . He accepted and *khala'ha* (gave her *khul'* divorce) so she is divorced from him and cannot go back to him except with a new marriage contract and new *mahr* . . .[29]

The Christian marriage as well as the divorce case quoted just above give a glimpse into the nature of social relations before the modern period. The marriage is from the third century Hijra (tenth century AD) while the divorce dates from the Ottoman period (fifteenth to nineteenth century); together they illustrate the importance of *'urf* in legal and social practices. The form of the contract, the place where it was registered, the expected conditions and marital relations, and the terminology used are similar for Muslim and Christian marriages. It could be concluded that these were strictly Muslim rules and Christians were subjected to Islamic rules brought to Egypt and Syria following the Arab Islamic invasions of the seventh century. Here contractual details help in shedding light on these issues by tracing the production of law as part of the historical process as it unfolded. Structural changes brought with them changes in the law, combining traditions, social practices, and Islamic principles in response to the lived realities and social relations which were evolving.

In conclusion, I would like to present two documents from the modern period: the first transitional, showing the beginning of the impact of modern-state centralization on marriage, and the second a modern standardized contract in a fill-in-the-blank format with little space for individual needs.

> On Friday, first of Muharram 1311, at the hands of *ma'dhun 'aqd al-zawaj* (notary for the registration of marriage) in Suq al-Rib' alley (*hara*), subdivision of the port of Dumyat, and the names recorded here, a marriage was contracted between Zubaida, the adult woman (*thayb baligh*) daughter of Ahmad al-Ghigla b. al-Sayyid Ahmad, who was divorced by a triple divorce from al-Mutwalli al-Hamami on 28 Shawwal 1310, number 2, according to a certificate. She is from the people of al-Sinaniyya, Gharbiyya, and lives in Dumyat. The husband is Muhammad al-Haqq b. 'Abdu son of the late 'Abdalnabi al-Hag, from Dumyat. She was married to him by her brother Sayyid Ahmad al-Ghigli, with her permission and her proxy (*tawkilaha*) verified by the witness of those mentioned below. The *mahr* is thirty piasters advanced and delayed, all received by her brother in his hands at the marriage meeting (*majlis*), a legal contract without any legal problems. This took place by hands (*was handed over in persons*) after ascertaining that the two had nothing to stop them (*mawani'*) according to the witness of, etc . . .
>
> Names and seals of witnesses . . .

> On Saturday, 2 Muharam, 1311, Zubaida, mentioned above, was divorced from her husband Muhammad al-Haqq, mentioned above, [divorced] a triple divorce, [transacted] by me according to the witness of . . . .
>
> Names and seals of witnesses
>
> This divorce is made after the marriage was consummated (*ba'd al-dukhul*), according to the named witnesses . . .[30]

In this marriage/divorce document of a woman by the name of Zubaida who lived in late nineteenth-century Dumyat, a town on the Mediterranean in Egypt, the power of the modern state is represented in the authority of a *ma'dhun*, the notary for the registration of marriage, who is a state employee empowered to register marriages, divorces, childbirths, deaths, and other matters related to social relations that the state needs to keep track of and use to compile records. *Ma'dhuns* were assigned to different quarters of cities, villages, and towns, and marriages had to be registered with them. This did not mean that marriages were celebrated in their office; actually *ma'dhuns* went to the homes and weddings to celebrate the marriages. They were usually graduates of religious colleges and wore the usual clerical attire. Today that has changed, and *ma'dhuns* in cities appear in suit and tie and quite often weddings are transacted in mosques or in Dar al-Ifta' al-Misriyya (official authority for *fatwas*/religious opinions) and other places provided to couples for their celebrations, an indication of the heavy financial burden of such events on an increasingly struggling society.

It should be noted that the first such notaries actually appeared in France and that the creation of this institution in Egypt was part of the reform of Egyptian laws and courts by the French Code Napoleon. The leading Egyptian reformers were themselves graduates of Western, particularly French law schools. It is thus understandable that they re-conceptualized structures into what they saw as more efficient frameworks. Given the transformations of all other aspects of state institutions following Western models, from shape and structure of urban areas, to schools, to arts and culture, to fashion and the greater use of foreign languages, it was natural that new systems and personnel would appear. Thus as regards issues of family and marriage, hybridity became a way of holding on to what was considered Islamic while at the same time presenting it in a codified positivist form with clear codes, uniformly applied through government personnel and government-educated judges in courts modelled after European patterns.

The contract of marriage itself also had a transitional nature, showing the efforts to standardize marriage. Today a printed form headed by the title 'Registration of a Marriage Contract' (*qayd wathiqat 'aqd zawaj*) has to be filled in by the spouses. It has a blank space for a serial number and the official stamp of the *ma'dhun*. The two top lines of the form require filling in the date, the address of the particular *ma'dhun*, and the names of husband and wife. The rest of the certificate is devoted to other parties involved and information as presented in the translated marriage document above.

In pre-modern contracts, registration in so-called *sijills* was done in court, without a given order. Thus all sorts of transactions were recorded, one following the other, so that a marriage may be followed by a sale contract or a manumission. The *ma'dhun*, however, only records marriages and divorces. Registration is thus specialized. Most significantly, it is the same *ma'dhun* who records the marriage and the divorce, since he is the *ma'dhun* of the area in which the marriage and divorce took place. No differences are made according to the *madhhab* of the spouses; the language used and expectations are uniform. This is evidence of the standardization and more efficient record keeping that came into place with the modern central state.

One last point is worthy of noting, the above-mentioned marriage lasted for only one day and the *mahr* was quite hefty. One wonders why, but that is the type of mystery that contracts entail without giving a real answer, although a further search into records involving the bride and her mentioned brother may give some indication of what is at play here.

The final format that marriage contracts take in almost all contemporary Muslim countries is a fill-in-the-blank certificate, which can be purchased publicly or even be downloaded on the internet today. In fact, a look on the internet shows a large array and various types of marriage contracts, some regular, others innovative, such as *misyar* marriage and *zawaj siyaha*, which have appeared during the last few years and are increasingly gaining in popularity. One should look at *misyar* and *zawaj siyaha* as new forms of marriage in response to new social conditions. In *misyar* marriages the wife stays in her home and the husband visits her. This allows for sexual co-habitation without financial obligations. It happens when the wife is rich and does not wish to leave her home and the husband may already have a wife or may not be able to afford an official polygamous marriage. It also allows rich men to marry girls of lesser social classes without having to provide a home for them. This is particularly beneficial to men since the marriage remains secret and his already existing family need not know. For the girl and her family, the financial assistance that the man gives them compensates for an otherwise official marriage that she could have expected. As for a *zawaj siyahi* (tourist marriage), it is exactly as the expression describes, a transaction permitting sexual relations between a tourist, almost always a male, and a woman who is staying for a prescribed period of time. This form of marriage is in fact a source of abuse, particularly of younger girls whose families 'sell' them to rich old men for a few months. As long as the marriage is religiously valid and made official through a written contract by the presence of a *ma'dhun*, those who practice it see nothing wrong with it even though they break the laws requiring a minimum age for marriage and abuse young girls.

'Urfi marriage is also widespread, in particular in Egypt, where it has been made even more popular by regarding the children of such marriages as legitimate through the father's recognition. In *'urfi* marriage, the couple signs a paper together indicating that they are married and two adults sign as witnesses. Such a paper can be produced for families, neighbours, or authorities when sexual co-habitation is questioned. The husband often provides the wife with a domicile

and financial support. Today, however, with women holding an important sector of the job market, very often the two live in separate homes and meet in a third place at their convenience. The marriage is documented on a simple piece of paper and, quite often, paternity disputes in such marriages hinge on the existence or lack of such a document. The power of the male in such a relationship is clearly stronger as he has an absolute right to acknowledge paternity just by stating that he is the father. The woman on the other side has to prove the marriage, which is not easy given the refusal of courts to accept DNA evidence. This is, however, changing today as the celebrated Ahmad 'Izz and Zaina's oral/*'urfi* marriage case and the birth of twin boys led the Egyptian courts to require that DNA examination be undertaken.[31] The potential father has refused to do so, and it remains to be seen whether he will be forced to comply i.e. whether the state will take a step in the direction of conclusively accepting DNA as evidence made possible by changes in child law (*qanun al-tifl*) giving a child 'the right to prove his relationship to [his parents] in all ways including legitimate scientific ones'.[32] One would think that a modern state making efforts to standardize and regularize its laws and systems would use DNA tests, but that would provide a way of limiting patriarchal authority and that is against the basic philosophy of the modern state in the Muslim world. It should be added that filiation cannot be in respect of a woman alone and it is not recognized by state law – this being besides the fact that such situations open the door to social scandal and possible persecution on the basis of *zinā'* (fornication). In May 2008 the Egyptian Majlis Al-Shura, one of the two legislative parliamentary bodies at the time, passed a preliminary law recognizing the registration of a child with the mother's name only and without the need to identify the father. This very important step was meant to comply with international human rights agreements and came as a result of pressure by women's groups. The Azhar saw nothing against this, yet the outcry that followed – and that focused on the welfare of society and the damage this would cause – meant that the law was rescinded soon after. The above-mentioned child law requires the names of both father and mother for a birth certificate to be issued.[33] This is a far cry from what the Quran had to say in regards to *li'an*.

Finally, the fill-in-the-blank official contracts distributed by the *ma'dhun* are themselves an instrument of state control. The information contained includes the names, the birth dates, the names of the parents, the jobs of husband and wife if they have any, the witnesses, and the *wakil* acting for either husband or wife. The *mahr* is presented as advanced and delayed – the delayed *mahr* is normally due on divorce or the death of the husband. Most interesting, information on whether the wife receives a government pension of any type, such as a pension due to a deceased father, mother, or sibling, is required. This information is important for the state, as pensions will be cut off when the wife marries, as her maintenance becomes the financial responsibility of her husband. As for the additional conditions commonly found in contracts from the pre-modern period, there is hardly any place for them in modern contracts. If couples include them as 'notes' (*mulahazat*) or in some other format, courts dismiss them on the basis that they conflict with Islam. This is particularly so with regard to conditions wives insist on regarding husbands taking second wives;[34] state courts have been known to rule that since polygamy is sanctioned by God, then no one has the right to limit the husband's right to it. This is a far cry from a contractual agreement in which couples lay down the basis of a marriage, moving instead to one in which the state, using religious discourse and the extension of a religious umbrella over contractual agreements, has constructed and supports a patriarchal system.

Notes

1 See on the issue of *qiwama* Chapter 2 in this volume.

2 There have, however, been efforts to change this in some Muslim countries. In Jordan, for example, the law of guardianship was altered to make the mother the guardian in the event the father is deceased: Art 57 of the Jordanian Civil Status Law, Law No 9 of 2001, Official Gazette no 4480 of 18 March 2001 reads: 'For the purposes of this law, "head of family" (*rabb al-usra*) designates: 1. The father, and in case of his death or where he has lost or dropped the Jordanian nationality, the wife becomes head of the family. If he has more than one wife, each of the wives is issued, by a separate civil register, a family ID card. 2. The wife, for the purpose of the civil register, in case of a lack of a head of the family or in case of his continued absence from the Kingdom. 3. The oldest of the unmarried children in the event of the death of the head of the family and his wife.' (All translations in this chapter are by the author, unless stated otherwise).

3 Leila Ahmed, *Women and Gender in Islam: Historical Roots of a Modern Debate* (Yale University Press 1993).

4 See the articles by Hatoon Ajwad al-Fassi, Allen Fromherz, and Barbara Freyer Stowasser in Amira Sonbol (ed), *Gulf Women* (Syracuse University Press 2012) 25–47; 48–68; 69–103.

5 For an expanded description of forms of marriages in pre-Islamic Arabia see 'Abdalsalam al-Tarmanini, *Al-Zawaj 'ind al-'Arab fi al-Jahiliyya wa-l-Islam: Dirasa Muqarina* ('Alam al-Ma'rifa 1984) 18–22.

6 Mahmood Ibrahim, 'Social and Economic Conditions in Pre-Islamic Mecca' (1982) 14 International Journal of Middle East Studies 343–58, analyses the changes brought to Mecca by merchant capitalism and its impact on the rise of Islam and the social transformations involved.

7 Quran 24:6–8.

8 The references to the archival records are cited in the following manner: location, archival record, place, date, *sijill* number: page-case number. Government of Egypt, National Archives, Alexandria, 958 H (1551 AD), 1:483–1983.

9 Government of Egypt, National Archives, Mahakim Shar'iyya (religious courts), Alexandria, 958 H (1551 AD), 1:341–1443.

10 Ibn Hisham, *Sirat Rasul Allah*, vol 1, 183–85.

11 Shams al-Din al-Dhahabi, *Siyar A'lam al-Nubala': Siyar al-Khulafa' al-Rashidin* (Mu'assassat al-Risala 1996) 87; Shams al-Din al-Dhahabi, *Tarikh al-Islam wa Wafayat al-Mashahir wa-l-A'lam*, vol 2 (Dar al-Kitab al-'Arabi 1991).

12 See Amira Sonbol, *Women of Jordan: Islam, Labor, and the Law* (Syracuse University Press 2003) for a discussion of *wali* under Jordanian personal status law.

13 Jasir Khalil Abu Safiyya, *Huquq al-Mar'a fi al-Bardiyyat al-'Arabiyya 'ala Daw' al-Kitab wa-l-Sunna* (Markaz al-Malik Faysal li-l-Buhuth wa-l-Dirasat al-Islamiyya 2007) 79.

14 Marriage contract from Egypt dated 566–73 AD published in Jane Rowlandson, *Women and Society in Greek and Roman Egypt: A Sourcebook* (CUP 1998) 210–11.
15 Government of Egypt, Egyptian National Archives, Mahakim Shar'iyya, Jami' al-Hakim, 966–967 H (1558–1559 AD), 540:200–898.
16 Alexandria, Ishadat, 957 H (1550 AD), 1:71–330.
17 Alexandria, Ishadat, 957 H (1550 AD), 1:14–66.
18 Dumyat, 1215 H (1800 AD), 9:180–3821.
19 University of Jordan, Al-Salt Shari'a Court, 943 H (1536 AD), 27:98–4.
20 Alexandria, Ishadat, 1273 H (1857 AD), 1:6–40.
21 Isna, 1193 H (1779 AD), 30:26–54.
22 Sharia Court case no 24624 (dated during the 1990s) published in 'Abdel-Fattah 'Ayish 'Umar, *Al-Qararat al-Qada'iyya fi al-Ahwal al-Shakhsiyya hatta 'Am 1990* (Dar Yamman 1990) 5.
23 Art 10(a) Jordanian Law of Personal Status, Law No 36 of 2010, Official Gazette no 5061 of 17 October 2010.
24 Art 10(b) Jordanian Law of Personal Status 2010.
25 Arts 21–23 Jordanian Law of Personal Status 2010.
26 Mohamad Afifi, 'Reflections on the Personal Laws of Egyptian Copts' in Amira Sonbol (ed), *Women, the Family and Divorce Laws in Islamic History* (Syracuse University Press 1996) 202–19.
27 Egyptian Government, National Archives, 'Uqud Zawaj, 259 H (872 AD), no 159. Marriage contract edited and published by Adolf Grohman in Grohman, *Awraq al-Bardi al-'Arabiyya bi-Dar al-Kutub al-Misriyya*, vol 1 (Matba'at Dar al-Kutub al-Misriyya 1994), Glossary II, 'Uqud Zawaj, no 159, 259 H (872 AD), 73–74.
28 Coptic marriage contract edited by Nabiyya Abbot, translated and published by Jasir Khalil Abu Safiyya, *Huquq al-Mar'a fi al-Bardiyyat al-'Arabiyya 'ala Daw' al-Kitab wa-l-Sunna* (Markaz al-Malik Faysal li-l-Buhuth wa-l-Dirasat al-Islamiyya 2007) 10.
29 Al-Quds Sharia Court, 1054 H (1604 AD), 27–134, in al-Ya'qubi, *Nahiyat al-Quds*, vol 1, 127.
30 Government of Egypt, Egyptian National Archives, Dumyat, 1311 H (1894 AD), Ma'dhun of Harat Suq al-Riba, no 17.
31 *Al-Yawm al-Sabi'* (23 October 2014) <http://m.youm7.com/story/2014/10/23/اليوم_خامس_جلسات_دعوى_زينة_لإثبات_نسب_ضد_أحمد_عز/1918354#.VI7SV97Gefc> accessed 1 December 2014.
32 Art 6 Child Law, Law No 12 of 1996, Official Gazette no 13 (*tabi'*) of 28 March 1996 as amended by Law No 126 of 2008, Official Gazette no 24 (*mukarrar*) of 15 June 2008.
33 Art 16 Child Law.
34 In Jordan, marriage contracts do allow the wife to include a condition against polygamy in the written contract.

11 Our marriage, your property?

Renegotiating Islamic matrimonial property regimes

M. Siraj Sait

Introduction

In contrast to the relatively well-developed Islamic assertions of a Muslim woman's rights to personal property[1] and historical evidence of propertied Muslim women,[2] Islamic legal sources appear thin on her claims to matrimonial property. The emphasis on protecting women's personal property through marriage and possible dissolution offers the common but debatable corollary that Islamic law does not recognize the concept of matrimonial property. Thus, a Muslim wife supposedly has no independent stake in marital assets and retains no ownership interest in the marital home. Each spouse simply walks away from the marriage with his or her individual property, or that in their names. Without significant pre-marital assets, gifts, income, or savings of their own, the denial of matrimonial property renders many poor divorcees effectively destitute or reliant on natal family or the State. This is compounded in contexts of swift divorces (*talaq*), inadequate dower (*mahr*), and limited maintenance (*nafaqa*).[3] The perceived incompatibility of classical Islamic law with concepts of marital property and the supposed inability of Muslim societies to recognize the contributions of both spouses are now under challenge. This chapter discusses ongoing legal reform pointing to evolving equitable matrimonial property regimes and increased choices for spouses on how to manage and distribute their matrimonial property in the Muslim world.

Diversity of marital property regimes

Matrimonial property (or marital property) regimes define the legal ownership of assets brought to and acquired during the marriage. They exclude non-marital property that is owned individually by a spouse prior to the marriage or acquired as an individual inheritance, income, or gift during marriage. Matrimonial regimes differ radically across, and sometimes within, countries, and are broadly divided into separate property and community property regimes. Under separation of property, each spouse owns the property, including land, which is usually registered in his or her name prior to and throughout the course of the marriage. It does not create any legal presumption of co-ownership of assets acquired by the other spouse. Separate property rules are a regular feature in a majority of

Muslim societies. In most Middle East countries, such as Egypt, Jordan, Kuwait, Lebanon, Oman, Saudi Arabia, Syria, United Arab Emirates, and Yemen, the separate property system prevails. This is equally true of South Asia's Bangladesh, India, Pakistan, and Sri Lanka. In Africa a number of countries follow the separate property system, including Mali, Mauritania, Nigeria, Senegal, and Sudan.

Under the Community of Property regime, property acquired or owned during a marriage belongs to both spouses as a partnership and as tenants in common (hence 'community'), equally and subject to division on that basis in the event of separation or divorce. Community property regimes are further distinguished as 'partial' or 'full' community based on what happens to the ownership of property acquired prior to the marriage, as well as to inheritances received during the marriage. Several countries with significant Muslim populations (including those in this study, such as Indonesia, Iran, Kazakhstan, Morocco, Malaysia, Maldives, Tunisia, Turkey, Indonesia, and Malaysia) have adopted community property systems or offer a choice, often at the time of marriage. Muslim couples in a number of pluralist societies – as the case studies of South Africa, Tanzania, Kenya and Israel show – have a choice between different marital property regimes (Islamic, customary, or secular) at the time of marriage. If they do not choose, the default regime prevails and this varies by country.

However, even in the separate property marriages, courts in several countries routinely determine the financial and non-financial contributions of the spouses to family welfare in equitable terms (or equal division of marital property), including numerous cases involving Muslims. Muslims living, for example, in common law jurisdictions such as Australia, Canada, New Zealand, United Kingdom,[4] the United States of America, and much of the Commonwealth can expect courts to play an important role. As Muslim families are increasingly mobile, marital property regimes often involve multiple jurisdictions. In the US case of *Farah v Farah*,[5] a Muslim wedding was conducted in three stages – a *nikah* agreement in Virginia, United States, a proxy ceremony in London, and then a wedding reception and celebration in Pakistan. The US court was persuaded not to recognize the marriage because the process of formalization did not meet the requirements of the official law in Virginia, England, or Pakistan, which affected the matrimonial property claims. As such, European courts have experimented with Islamic law and property issues, including marriages between Muslims and non-Muslims, which are contentious and unclear. There are also issues arising from the marital property of unmarried, same sex, polygamous, and inter-religious marriage[6] that have not yet been adequately addressed but are beyond the scope of this chapter.

Diverse matrimonial property regimes are derived from distinct legal traditions and systems. Generally, community regimes are more likely in civil law systems than in common law or Islamic law systems. Thus, civil law systems in continental Europe and, generally, South American countries have some form of community of property regimes.[7] For example, nine of the 50 states in the United States of America that adopted the community property regime are primarily located in the West and South, and inherited them from civil law traditions of Mexico community system. Yet there are variations in the practice of community property systems. Norway, Denmark, Sweden, Germany, Austria, and Greece have 'deferred' community of property where spouses have separate property during marriage, but an equal division takes place upon divorce. Under the 'limited' community of property model in France, Italy, Spain, and Croatia, marital property is administered by both spouses in equal terms.[8] Netherlands distinctively follows, by the operation of law, 'complete' community of property from the moment of the solemnization of the marriage. Other countries, such as Burundi, Namibia, the Philippines, Rwanda, and South Africa, have full community property regimes.

The dominance of the separation of property regimes across the Muslim world is owed in part to the jurisprudential equation of Islamic personal property guarantees to separation of property regimes, but more broadly the social structure of the Muslim marriage.

This chapter has two parts. The first engages briefly with the Islamic legal framework of marriage and property to explore whether Islamic law in itself does not inhibit equitable, if not equal, marital property distribution among spouses. The second part offers an exploration of practice in over a dozen countries where Muslims reside as a majority or in multi-religious countries,[9] demonstrating that community property regimes are far more widespread among Muslims than assumed.

These case studies of Turkey, Kazakhstan, Indonesia, Malaysia, Morocco, Tunisia, Iran, Maldives, Tanzania, Kenya, South Africa, and Israel underscore the complex but often accommodative relationship between marital property doctrines and Islamic principles. Several themes emerge from the analysis. A Muslim marital property regime is negotiated not merely from religious conceptions, but through its intersection with custom, family, kinship, and the construction of property itself. In Muslim societies, legal pluralism prompts choices over marital property regimes between remnants of colonial law, modern constitutional, and human rights provisions, Islamic, customary, and secular laws. The varied legal reform methodologies of Muslim matrimonial property regimes include secularization, Islamic re-interpretation, cohabitation of custom and Islamic law, and legal pluralism.

Marital property laws as contested zones

Like marriage itself, marital property relations are socially constructed and politically mediated.[10] An individual's perceptions of property ownership within marriage and social norms may not conform to legal norms[11] and legal sanctions may lack legitimacy. Marital property assumptions, for example, vary between customary/religious and civil unions in many Muslim and pluralist societies. Separate marital property regimes are not to be dismissed as simply traditional, patriarchal, or obscurantist resistance to gender equality. Many argue that the community property regime places marriage on the moral foundations of an 'equal co-operative partnership of different efforts', recognizing material and non-financial contributions.[12] It allows women to upgrade their user rights during marriage into independent land rights in case of divorce or further marriage. It helps women who do not hold a paying job and/or significant assets as, once they divorce, they cannot have a claim on the husband's property even if acquired during the marriage. A wider effect is that the husband and the wife have equal responsibilities in respect of the management of the land and running of the matrimonial household. Yet there are scenarios where a community property arrangement may disadvantage the wealthy or employed wife. The advantages and disadvantages of joint marital property are vigorously debated, though beyond the scope of this chapter.

Disentangling complex issues to determine who is entitled to or owns different assets within the household prompt debates over legitimate expectations, fairness, efficiency, and socially acceptable outcomes. Marital property divisions are often among the toughest court cases, particularly in addressing claims of non-material contributions. Avoiding these moral and cultural variables, policy makers, lawyers, and economists tend to favour the oversimplified notion that all marital assets are jointly owned.

The role of religious law in a modern world with secular marriages is often challenged. Some argue that all marriages in a pluralistic society should be 'privatized' to let communities develop their norms and dispute mechanisms, with minimal state interference.[13] The general principles of contract, property, and tort law would ensure legality and equity.[14] For example, in the United Kingdom, Sharia and Jewish *Beth Din* 'courts' – recognized as Arbitration Tribunals under the Arbitration Act 1996 – resolve marital cases, including marital property disputes. Islamic law, in fact, provides a wide range of mediation, conciliation, and arbitration mechanisms.[15] However, deference to religious law is often considered a threat to gender equality and human rights. For example, more than a dozen states in the United States of America have had proposals to ban Sharia law in state legislatures and on ballot initiatives. Yet, for a vast majority of Muslims across the world, the sanctity of marriage and legitimacy of family law is often derived from their religious law. Marital property is not merely a battleground for gender equality but a contest between tradition and modernity over the evolving image of the family and the interpretation of women's roles under Islamic law itself. Marital property rights are hardly a settled matter and conjure diverse interpretations of Islamic law in many Muslim societies.

This research examines the legal frameworks – inevitably pluralist – for marital property in select Muslim majority and pluralistic countries. However, the mere existence of provisions for women's property rights and equitable distribution of marital property are not enough. Even in countries where marital property laws have been enacted, they are 'very difficult to enforce because they go against the grain of cultural practice'.[16] Equally, codification of rights has run the risk of rendering informal property rights unstable.[17] This research therefore explores the legal framework in its socio-cultural and political context. One of the limitations of this chapter is that it focuses on marital property almost exclusively, without being able to address other dynamics of Muslim women's status and role in marriage, marriageable age, guardianship (*wali*), the right to divorce (*talaq*) and the notion of fault,[18] polygamy,[19] other property rights (such as inheritance and maintenance), and other dimensions (such as child custody).

The objective of this research is not to promote community property regimes over separate property principles, but to support Muslim couples' freedom to select from various marital property systems that allow for spouses to best protect their interests in case of divorce. It has been argued that making the *community* of *property* regime the default, as *Turkey* did in 2001, will result in higher uptake than if couples have to choose to opt in. Even in community property states, Muslim couples can opt out by executing a valid pre-nuptial agreement to that effect, but few have the knowledge or opportunity to choose the arrangement they prefer. The research does not contest the reality that the regular regime in Islamic law is separate property, but explores the theory and practice among Muslim communities that demonstrates that Islamic law can accommodate community property arrangements.

Marital property in Islamic law

Concept of marital property under Islamic law

While the Holy Quran specifically prescribes personal property rights and sets out inheritance rights for women,[20] it does not explicitly refer to women's marital property. Classical Islamic jurisprudence (*fiqh*) in turn appears to be content with emphasizing a separate property regime to protect women's property by ensuring neither spouse usurps the property of the other.[21] As a result, throughout history, most Muslim marriages were enacted under the separation of property regime, where neither spouse had a legal claim to or interest in the property of the other.[22] Some scholars have deduced that, since both partners maintain an independent financial status throughout the marriage, Muslim marriages do not create community property.[23] Property acquired during the marriage belongs to either the husband or the wife, not jointly to the couple. As such it is argued that there is no equivalent to marital property or community property under the classical Islamic jurisprudence (*fiqh*), and that under Islamic law there is no such thing as marital property to distribute.

Under a common interpretation, since there exists no concept of marital property, there can be no Islamic premarital agreements for the division of marital property upon divorce. Upon divorce, a wife cannot have a claim to her husband's assets under the theory that their acquisitions constitute marital property. Women have no independent right to marital assets and retain no ownership interest in the marital home. Each spouse is entitled to individual property acquired before marriage, or property acquired during marriage in their individual names. If marital property is in the husband's name, as is mostly the case, a Muslim wife has no proprietary interest in matrimonial property, only access to the use of such property during marriage. However, a global review among Muslim communities finds that this is not how Muslims inevitably construct marital property. A significant proportion of Muslims view joint marital property regimes as an option and this Muslim practice is significantly observed in diverse Islamic legal systems.

Islamic jurisprudential constraints to community property principles

There are no jurisprudential constraints under Islamic law for incorporating joint marital property. Considerable osmosis between the three major legal systems – civil law, common law, and Islamic law – has resulted in legal pluralism and hybridity in Muslim countries. The community property that emerged from civil law in continental Europe and pollinated in the French and Spanish colonies were also accepted in common law and Islamic systems. In fact, Islamic marriage concepts have several features that make Islamic law more receptive than common law systems to community property doctrine. To start with, traditional common law property systems (particularly separate property) are based on title, while civil and Islamic are not. The common law system is based upon title; neither spouse has an interest in the property of the other, unless property is jointly owned.[24] The rights of a wife in a community property system are not based on title, but derived from undivided shared ownership interest in the couple's family estate. Thus, in Indonesia, only a small proportion of joint-owned marital property had both spouses as co-owners,[25] since the marital property rights of both spouses are recognized and respected, regardless of how the land is registered.[26]

Community property arises as an operation of law that can only be facilitated in a developed legal system and a mature socio-legal culture. First, the community property regime is predicated on the recognition of property rights of women and a degree of independent legal status for married women.[27] The Holy Quran comprehensively established Muslim women's independent property rights in the seventh century. In contrast, such recognition came to most common law countries relatively recently. For example, married women in Britain were granted the right to hold separate property only through the 1870 Married Women's Property Act. The legal disabilities with regard to married women's property rights, which were a feature of past Anglo-American jurisprudence, were never a feature of Islamic law.

The relationship between husband and wife under civil law is based on a contract, similar to Islamic law. In traditional common law systems, the principle of covenant was sometimes relied upon to characterize the relationship between husband and wife. Despite the religious character of Islamic law, the marriage contract is a civil agreement without sacramental associations.[28] This is in contrast to the traditional common law reliance on the principle of covenant or divine institution, though most common law systems have since secularized. It is not possible to enter into a Muslim marriage without signing a contract, *'aqd*, or *nikah* contract. As seen in the case studies from Morocco to Iran, community of property clauses or separate agreements are simply added onto the main Islamic marriage contract.

Another pre-requisite of civil law community property regimes is the notion of partnership – where each spouse is regarded as a contributor (material or non-material) to the acquisition of marital property and is entitled to its distribution.

Early common law commentators, including William Blackstone, saw marriage as uniting husband and wife into 'one person in law'.[29] Islamic law, with its recognition of women's independent property rights, has never included any device equivalent to the common law doctrine of coverture, or other restrictions on married women holding property. The common law existence of the wife was traditionally merged with that of the husband during coverture (marriage). Islamic law, on the other hand, always deemed the marriage to be a partnership – though the parameters of equality were contested.

A common but flawed argument is that the existence of a dower (*mahr*) amount negates or compensates for a woman's right to her marital property. Dower, paid by the husband to the wife at the time of marriage (or deferred), is potentially an important source of financial security for the wife. The *mahr* is exclusively the wife's personal property, which she is not expected to offer to the family. The *mahr* amount, however, is not fixed and could vary but is often much smaller than the marital property. However, the marriage (*nikah*) contract does not constitute a comprehensive premarital agreement because the wife has not agreed to a quantified *mahr*, in lieu of any claims on marital property. In short, by agreeing to *mahr*, the wife has not waived her rights to marital property. In several cases, such as *Chaudry v Chaudry* (1978)[30] and *Re Marriage of Shaban* (2001),[31] courts in Canada and United States have sometimes linked the existence of a dower contract to the wife's claim for equitable allocation of marital property. In other cases, such as *Ahmad v Ahmad* (2001),[32] the US courts rejected the husband's claim that the *mahr* provision barred the court from awarding an equitable distribution of marital assets.

The dower (*mahr*) is a different category of property largely unrelated to the distribution of marital assets on divorce. Most jurists consider *mahr* to be a debt owed by the husband to the wife, as a promise arising out of a marriage contract.[33] It is owed as a debt to the wife even if there is no marital property. Thus, most Muslim countries consider *mahr* and marital property as largely unconnected matters. In Iran, this leads to two different contracts, and a refusal to pay dower could lead to imprisonment. Oman – referring to Muslim marital property court disputes in the United States of America – rightly points out that 'treating *mahr* contracts as pre-marital agreements is not simply a misunderstanding; it can also have perverse results. Most seriously, courts may use the contract to limit a spouse's claims to equitable distribution of marital assets when those rights have not been bargained away'.[34] Where marital property is blocked, *mahr* is often the only asset the Muslim divorcees can access. However the availability of marital property diminishes the importance of dower.

Muslim women's marital status and contributions

Under classical Islamic law, the wife's contributions to the family are invisible and unaccounted for simply because she is not under any obligation to contribute anything materially. Muslim conservatives argue that women chose to provide services or contributions *gratis* because they have no obligations. They can seek gifts (*hiba*) or compensation (*'iwad*)[35] in return, but have no entitlements to marital property. However, Hibri points out that the Islamic marriage contract is 'a contract for companionship and not as a service contract', citing classical theorists from major Islamic jurisprudential schools.[36] Thus, article 4 of the Moroccan family code (*Mudawwana*) refers to the purpose of marriage as 'fidelity, virtue and the creation of a stable family, under the supervision of both spouses'. Muslim wives who perform household chores are entitled to financial compensation from their husbands for this work.

The husband bears the entire responsibility for the maintenance of his wife and family, and thus attaches his name to anything acquired – though on behalf of the family. This designation of the husband as the sole breadwinner, however fictitious, also disrupts the gender equality in marriage. The oft-quoted Quran verse (4:34) says men are to spend their property in the support of women. Furthermore, this exclusive responsibility of the husband to provide also creates a higher status for the male. The implications of this verse for gender equality have been vigorously debated, with a modernist interpretation that this hierarchy does not apply where a wife works or contributes financially. Muslim women undertaking family tasks that were previously in the male domain are challenging both notions of male superiority, as well as their stakes in marital property.

The objections to community property regimes do not come from within Islamic law itself, but from conceptions of the wife's role and the model of marriage itself. One anxiety is that community property undermines the extended family and kinship relationships by individualizing property and undermining inheritance assets. In atomizing the marriage, it is feared that women would lose broader family and community support. However, the Muslim marriage contract between spouses, and community property principles, do coexist with Islamic inheritance laws and resilient social codes. Community property principles, based on the idea of monogamist marriage (see article 181 of the Swiss Civil Code), are seen as unworkable in polygamous societies, as they could allow men to use the property of their primary wives to support the new wives. Most Muslim countries have regulated polygamy but have not seen it as an obstacle to community property. The 2004 Moroccan *Mudawwana*, which introduces community property, does not abolish polygamy, but requires prior court authorization to safeguard the rights of the first wife and her children.[37]

Both promoters and opponents of community property rule recognize the likely profound implications for Muslim societies generally, and gender equality within marriage more specifically. Marriage is set up as an institution of partnership of equals; rather than complementarily situated spouses. The first casualty would be the notion of the husband as the 'head' of the conjugal union, as both spouses would be equal partners. Instead of the husband representing the union, either spouse may represent in matters as may be agreed, or is practical, to meet the requirements of the family during their matrimonial life. During the marriage the husband's views do not automatically prevail but would have to be exercized jointly and negotiated where necessary. For example, rather than the husband choosing the conjugal home, the spouses would jointly determine the conjugal home under the new model. While the traditional roles gave the husband exclusive responsibility for maintenance of wife and family, and the wife supreme in the management of household affairs, the new approach would foster joint care and maintenance of the family, each according to his or her capacity, with interdependent and overlapping roles. Significantly, the propriety interest in family property would offer wives a greater incentive to participate and an increased role in management of property.

Case studies

This research is based on an examination of the marital property laws and practice of a dozen selected countries. They have been chosen as representatives of different geographical areas and Islamic schools that exhibit innovation and propensity towards implementing marital property rights. There are classified according to the four broad methods through which Muslim communities have come to recognize community property. The first group are those experiencing 'secularization' whereby modern Western civil codes were adopted, as in our case study of Turkey, at the threshold of Europe. Another process is the secularization through the influence of Soviet communist ideology, as in Albania, Bosnia, and Kosovo in the Balkans, and the Central Asian republics of Azerbaijan, the Kyrgyz Republic, Tajikistan, and Uzbekistan, as explored through a case study of Kazakhstan.

The second process was through Islamic law's accommodation of the pre-existing customary community of property system, as in our case studies of Indonesia and Malaysia in South East Asia. While custom often is seen as an impediment to gender justice, these examples show how customary rights can sometimes enhance women's property rights.

The third set of Muslim countries are those consciously adopting community property principles as part of Islamic law reform, as our case studies of Morocco and Tunisia from North Africa explore. Another strand of marital property reform within conservative Islamic legal structures can be seen in Iran in West Asia and Maldives in South Asia.

The fourth category is Muslim minorities living in multicultural societies under legal pluralist societies with a choice of marital property regimes. Our case studies are Tanzania and Kenya in East Africa, the Republic of South Africa, and Israel in the Middle East.

There are several other categories of Muslim communities that are not studied in this chapter. The practice in the remainder of countries with Muslim majorities, from Jordan and Egypt[38] to Pakistan and Sudan, is mostly separation of property. In some countries, Muslim women do not have access to property at all owing to restrictive customs or patriarchal norms. Another significant country, India, with the second largest Muslim population in the world, needs a closer examination of limited marital property options for Muslim women.[39] The practice of marital property distribution of substantial Muslim populations in Europe, North America,[40] Australasia,[41] and other regimes also need further study elsewhere.

'Secular' introduction of community property in Muslim countries

Turkey

In Turkey, efforts to enhance property rights for women had begun during the Ottoman Islamic rule, during which time the property rights of Muslim married women were ahead of European practice. The *Tanzimat* Reforms (1839–76) extended the property and land rights of women through classical Islamic law, which governed the separation of property regime. After the official abolition of the Caliphate, the Turks adopted the 1926 Civil Code, which, *inter alia*, emulated the Swiss model of a joint approach for inter-marital property gains, based on the German earnings partnership approach *(Zugewinngemeinschaft)*. Under articles 186–237 of the Turkish Civil Code 1926, in force until 2001, a couple could choose between three different property regimes upon marriage: separation of property, union of property, or an aggregation of property through a pre-nuptial agreement. Under article 170, in the absence of a property regime being specified by the couple, they were automatically considered to have accepted the separation of goods property regime.

Some commentators referred to the 1926 reforms as a 'revolution' with 'the adoption of codes of European origin – virtually lock, stock and barrel'.[42] However, others noted that it was the inevitable outcome of changes in Ottoman laws, which received Western ideas. Hamson argues that the adoption of the Swiss Civil Code model was not a dramatic upheaval, but simply the next step in a century-long process of legal reform initiated by the Ottomans.[43] The most significant change brought about by the reform was the introduction of civil marriage, which needed to be registered, and that both spouses could initiate divorce based on the enumerated grounds. However, the 1926 Code retained the husband as the head of the family who represented the union. The wife's right to work outside the home was subject to the husband's permission. Alternatively, the wife could seek such permission from the courts. While the wife did retain control of her individual property rights, all types of property entering the family unit came under the control and management of the husband, who was under a general duty to protect his wife's interests.

The new marital regime was constructed out of a fusion of Western and Islamic legal principles. To begin with, article 1 of the 1926 Code allowed the judge to consult custom and tradition where there was no written law on point. Many articles used Islamic Arabic terms and concepts. Moreover, the role of the civil judge in the Turkish Republic was no different from that in Islamic courts in the Ottoman Empire. Yildirim notes that 'the 1926 Code set up an ownership system within the marriage very similar to Islamic law'.[44] He points out:

> Even though the Swiss Civil Code recognized a system of shared property, the 1926 Code changed this to recognize a property regime whereby each spouse retained what he or she brought into the marriage. Under Article 146, upon divorce, both parties keep what they bring into the marriage. The rest of the property was shared as specified in the marriage contract.

Marital property changes were among the 'most popular' because society was prepared to accept the 'huge change in social life' through European ideas.[45] While the reforms transformed the lives of Muslim women,[46] they were contingent on the support of local and unofficial Islamic legal practices and customs.[47] However, in practice, women lost out as most property tended to be registered under the husband's name, thus depriving women of much of the marital property upon dissolution.[48] The new system struggled to take hold in Turkish small towns and villages, where the vast majority of the population resides.[49] The debate over the extent to which Ataturk's civil code reforms have taken hold in Turkey continues. More generally, conjugal relationships are more joint in nature with wives participating more in important familial decisions and public roles.[50]

For 70 years, proposed revisions to the 1926 Code were rejected in parliament – in 1951, 1971, 1974, 1976, and 1984. In 1998, a new draft finally received approval and the proposed law replaced the 1926 Code in 2002. The new Civil Code 2001 (*Turk Medeni Kanunu*) brought about a greater level of gender equality in marriage, with the husband no longer the leader or the representative of the family (articles 185–86, 189), in contrast to the 1926 Code (article 152). The married couple is contractually free to choose a form of marital property ownership as provided by the law, where joint ownership is among the forms provided by the new code. Significantly, the community property regime with equal shares between spouses became the default.

The 'participation in acquisitions' is the regular regime while 'separate estates', 'allocable separate estates', and 'community of property' are other arrangements which can be adopted through a marriage covenant.[51] This is largely modelled on the Swiss default regime, which consists of acquisitions and of each spouse's own property (article 218). Where there is co-ownership of property and a spouse provides evidence of a preponderant interest in this property, he or she can, besides the legal measures, demand that the undivided property be allotted to him or her against compensation. Each spouse retains individual ownership rights over his or her personal property, or that acquired prior to the marriage or received as personal gifts during the marriage. More specifically, both spouses have equal rights over acquired property and the marital home.

Turkey's political will to become the first Muslim-majority country to have community of property as the default can be attributed to the accommodation between Islamic and modernist ideas. European directives and policies are filtered through distinctive social, political, and cultural attitudes towards gender, property, and women's place in society.[52] The quest for greater gender equality in Turkey takes place during the period of increasing Islamization of 'secular' Turkey, and as the country balances its concept of secularism (*laiklik*) with the reality of Islamic consciousness.[53] The success of Turkey's experiment with the Swiss code lies in balancing the progressive changes 'while actually maintaining much of Muslim law and custom'.[54] The 2001 Civil Code retains Islamic law features, for example replacing Arabic words, for Islamic terms, with Turkish words. The Turkish community marital property system has been hailed as a model for allowing religious customs alongside civil registration, and promoting marital property choices while making community property the default.[55]

Kazakhstan

A variation in the theme of secular introduction of community property principles occurs through communist ideology in the Central Asian Republics. The Republic of Kazakhstan was the largest republic in the former Soviet Union outside Russia, and still comprises an area larger than all of Western Europe.[56] Over 70 per cent of its population is Muslim, according to its 2009 census, with the majority of the population comprising ethnic Kazakhs, Uzbeks, Uighurs, and Tatars belonging to the Hanafi Sunni school. The much smaller Chechen population are from the Shafi'i Sunni school. Despite the current increasing post-Soviet religiosity, the once largely nomadic Kazakhs are often seen to be not as religiously conservative as the neighbouring Uzbeks, Tajiks, or Uighurs (in China).[57] Kazakh women are rarely veiled, unlike in the neighbouring countries. Since the eleventh century, Sufism – the mystical Islamic doctrine – has been an influential order in Kazakhstan and the Central Asian Republics.[58] Local Sufi brotherhoods have become national symbols of Kazakhstan, and 1993 was declared the year of Ahmad Yasawi, the founder of the Sufi brotherhood Yasawiyya, who was born in Kazhakstan.[59] Despite Soviet efforts to snuff out Islamic influences, Sufism played a pivotal role – through clandestine and parallel processes – to retain a liberal Islamic version of family law.

Both customary and Islamic law exerted influence over Kazakh family law in the seventeenth century.[60] Even after Central Asia became part of the Russian Empire and the Governorate General of Turkistan was established in 1867, the Russian authorities allowed Sharia law and *adat* (custom) rules to apply to marriage and property matters.[61] Shortly after the establishment of the Soviet Union, however, the campaign to abolish the perceived 'backwardness' in Central Asia led to fierce battles over the fate of Muslim women,[62] particularly by the women's wing of the Communist Party (*Zhenotdel*). The Sharia and *adat* laws and courts were soon replaced by secular, uniform, and centralized Soviet laws and courts.[63] Around the same time, private ownership of goods was terminated, and land was declared to be the property of all people. All means of production and assets – except for some personnel dwellings, cattle, and poultry – were forcibly pooled into collective farms (*kolkhoz*) and state farms (*sovkhoz*).

The role of Islamic law and Kazakh customs, in the face of communist propaganda and purges, were debated among Kazakh people from the very beginning, between the traditionalists (*kadimists*) and the reformists (*jadidists*). Kendirbaeva provides a fascinating account of the debate through reviews of the Islamic oriented magazine *Aiqap* and the pro-Western newspaper *Qazaq* between 1911 and 1916.[64] In addition to implications of the increasing settlement of the nomadic Kazakh and the seizure of grazing lands by Russian immigrants (*muzhiks*), the main concerns were the preservation of Kazakh customs and identity (*qazaqtyq*), and Islamic law. The reformist *Alash* movement, which was influential until it was purged in 1938, gained the upper hand, advocating that Islam be open to modern ideas and not be the dominant force. Another reason why Kazakh Muslims were receptive to communist ideas were the perceived 'common directions as the priority of the collective over individual, subordination of man to a community, authoritarianism of State power as a norm of political culture, and the orientation of the people not towards economic effectiveness but towards social justice'.[65] Even the collectivization of property (*kolkhoz*) was seen as a form of family community (*avlod*), and not contrary to Islam.

The Soviets were the first in Europe to introduce a limited form of the community property regime in 1926, which spread to other parts of the Union and Europe.[66] In Kazakhstan, marital property became the common property of both spouses though there was not much to own, except livestock.[67] From the pre-Soviet times to the present, Kazakh families have followed religious customary norms in relation to marital property,[68] which provided a strong basis for marital property. Writing in 1886, Makoveckii notes:

> [while the role of the Kazakh wife] is restricted to the boundary of *aul* [i.e. nomadic village], all of the domestic economy and property lies in her hands. Whereas a Kazakh man spends most of the year on the horseback, in continuous moves, taking care of social affairs of the kin, district, and village, his wife remains the real head of the household and manages all of it, thus reducing her husband to the role of the nominal head.[69]

The amount of dower payable by the husband to the wife was regulated at a high level of 47 livestock heads for wealthy families and 17 heads for poorer families. The community property system was seen as an improvement on the existing ethos, despite some patriarchal features in society.

Kazakhstan declared itself an independent country in 1991, adopted a secular constitution, and acknowledged a liberal version of Islam. It embarked on a process of privatization of land and property and family law reforms. Article 14 of the 1995 Constitution emphasizes non-discrimination, including on the grounds of sex. There are no restrictions on women's rights to own, use, or inherit property. The Civil Code 1999 makes no distinction on the basis of gender on inheritance and property rights, similar to the relevant legal provisions before 1991. Under the current Marriage and Family Code, community of property has been established, following the standard civil law clauses on marital property. Under article 29, joint spousal ownership applies to property acquired during the marriage, but does not apply to inheritance or to property brought to the marriage, unless the property has undergone significant improvement with the help of marital funds.[70] Spouses can change the standard marital contract through an alternate marital property arrangement. Unless the parties agree upon their respective shares, the shares shall be considered equal.

The law requires the marriage to be registered (article 2) and identifies marital property broadly as including the incomes of each spouse, incomes from common and separately owned properties, together with movable and immovable belongings, securities, shares, deposits, and shares in capital investments made in loan institutions or any other commercial organization.[71] It also includes any other property acquired by spouses regardless of who has legal title and who paid to acquire the property. It also factors in non-financial contributions including child-care and household work, where the spouse has no income for valid reasons.[72] The division of common property by a court may be made both during marriage and after divorce by the application of either spouse, or on a creditor's complaint. However, there are no provisions on the management of marital property, apart from the (male) head of household. The Land Code 1995, adopted by Presidential Decree, does not establish co-management of the marital property nor does it provide for registration of that property in both owners' names. Without defined conventions for ownership titles, this law may be 'relatively incomplete'.[73]

When the new family law was debated in the Parliament (*majlis*), some deputies raised Islamic issues such as the legalization of polygamy.[74] Issues of gender equality in inheritance or marital property were not challenged as being un-Islamic. There has been an increase in Islamic consciousness and practice in Kazakhstan since the fall of the Soviet Union. Islamic arguments are often raised in gender debates,[75] even though the role of Islamic parties in politics is strictly regulated. In Kazakhstan, as in other traditional societies, land tenure refers to 'the legal principles, written or oral laws, or (more broadly) culturally accepted rights and privileges with respect to property in natural resources'.[76] A 2002 World Bank review of land reform and farm restructuring in Kazakhstan found, despite the gender neutrality of land legislation, 'that many women felt their inferior bargaining power relative to men had caused them to receive more remote or poorer quality land plots'.[77] The recommendation was that women needed better information and support in pursuing their land and property rights, beyond legislation. The implementation of a community property regime also needs to be supported by customary and religious norms.[78]

Community property regimes through fusion of Islamic and customary law

Indonesia

Indonesia, the country with the largest number of Muslims in the world, has a number of gender equality features in its marital property regime. Among them is concept of jointly owned marital property or the community of marital property (*harta bersama*) under Indonesian Islamic law. While community property regimes found in other Muslim countries were brought about by exogenous or secular pressures, the Indonesian experience emerged from within.[79] Emanating from custom, *adat*, the concept is legitimized within the legal system as an Islamic institution.[80] Thus, the indigenous customary concept of marital property has encountered relatively little resistance from Islamic authorities. Though community property is 'not regulated by the *Qur'ân* or *hadîth*, nor in the jurists' books, but is to be found in the *adat* of Muslim Indonesians and lives in the legal consciousness' of Indonesia as an Islamic principle.[81] The 1974 Indonesian Marriage Law formally adopted the concept of co-ownership by husband and wife of property purchased during marriage. The binding Indonesian Islamic Compilation (*Kompilasi Hukum Islam*), which outlines the applicable family law for courts, also spells out the innovative doctrine of equal matrimonial property division.[82]

The Indonesian system bears resemblance to community of property regimes in other parts of the world, including California in the United States.[83] Communal or marital property acquired by a couple during a marriage (*harta bersama*) is distinguished from separate property or 'brought property' (*harta bawaan*) which is pre-existing wealth brought to the marriage by either spouse or acquired by gift or inheritance thereafter. The marital estate consists of property acquired during the marriage through the contribution of either of the spouses. It may consist of land, tangible assets, or entitlements. Such property cannot be sold, transferred, or used as collateral without the consent of both husband and wife under Indonesian law and custom. Unless there is a pre-nuptial agreement, the *harta bersama* will be divided equally between husband and wife, at divorce or death. The law also allows married couples to execute a pre-marital agreement to create their own property regime, such as maintaining separate property, but these agreements are not common in rural Indonesia.

The Indonesian community of property system, read alongside other statutes, directly empowers Indonesian women and strengthens their land rights. The 1960 land law (Basic Regulations on Agrarian Principles) broadly recognizes the importance of women's ownership of property.[84] So does Indonesia's Marriage Law, which provides important protection for women's land and other property rights, during marriage and at the time of widowhood or divorce. The single marriage law, the 1974 Marriage Act, governs all Indonesians, regardless of religion or ethnicity, and the concept of co-ownership of property purchased during marriage is clearly stated (article 35).[85] Where one spouse dies half of the joint matrimonial property will be transferred to the surviving spouse, and the remaining half will be added to the deceased's *harta bawaan* and distributed among that spouse's heirs (including the surviving spouse).[86]

Indonesian women traditionally had the choice of taking property disputes either to the Sharia or secular courts (*pengadilan umum*), as seen in the 1989 Law on Religious Courts, whereby Indonesians could rely on national law, *adat* law, or Islamic law. However, a 2006 amendment of the 1989 law appears to have reduced this and in practice most inheritance and marital property suits involving Muslims go to the Islamic court. Bowen shows that studies confirm that women are more likely to use courts for division of marital property and, generally, 'they won more frequently than did male plaintiffs'. He notes that 'women often perceive Islamic courts to work in their interest, not because the substantive rules constitute an improvement over traditional rules, but because the courts can offer property divisions relatively quickly'.[87] The Islamic courts have also been creative, for example by protecting the putative spouse's marital property rights. Through the institution of *isbat nikah*, women are able to have their marriage recognized retroactively by the courts if they were unable to register it owing to exceptional circumstances. Thus, 'the Islamic courts have demonstrated the kind of pragmatism necessary to deal with such a situation in the interest of the weakest party instead of sticking to their doctrinal guns'.[88]

There is nothing in Islamic law or custom to frustrate titling of land. However, while marital property laws recognized equal ownership rights by both spouses, Indonesian Registration Law and its accompanying regulations are silent on the question of how marital property should be titled. Indonesia is one of the countries where joint titling projects have been implemented. However, a 2003 study finds that less than 5 per cent of property is in both spouses' names – marital property is almost always titled in the name of the male head of household only.[89] In Java, Brown finds only a third of these properties are registered in the name of women, raising concerns that women's land rights may be vulnerable.[90] However, this lack of correlation between women's co-ownership of property rights and joint titling is not surprising. Though the lack of awareness of titling is a contributing factor, the real reason is that women and men will continue to deal with property rights in accordance with their own customary norms, regardless of what title documents and registration records say. What is relevant, as Brown emphasizes, is that marital property norms are 'reinforced by custom and supported by Islamic law'. Community property regimes have been accommodated into Islamic law through custom (*adat*) norms, based on the Islamic jurisprudential (*fiqh*) principle of '*al-'adatu muhakkamat*, adat that is good can be made into (Islamic) law – for community property'.[91]

Malaysia

In neighbouring Malaysia, customary *adat* also forms the basis of the joint matrimonial property regime, which is referred to as *harta sepencarian.*[92] The regime, however, is not based on automatic gender equality, with a homemaker wife entitled to claim a substantial share of matrimonial assets upon divorce, but more if she has contributed. Generally, where a woman has helped to cultivate the land, she is entitled to one half of the property. If there is no contribution to the land, the entitlement is to one third of the jointly acquired property. Some authors have looked at the *adat* rule as a 'particularly awkward example of conflict between Islamic law and custom',[93] but is also remarkable for the convergence of the two.[94] The acceptance of the joint property doctrine in Malaysia has been hailed as the 'substantive and procedural dynamism of Islamic law itself, and the uniqueness and applicability of Malay customary laws, which transcend temporal and spatial differences'.[95]

A significant protection is that, in most cases, a divorcee's share in matrimonial property would not be lost based on initiation of divorce or fault such as adultery, unless giving up the share was part of the divorce agreement.[96] Under customary law, if the husband wants a divorce without any fault accruing to the wife, then the joint property is divided into three: two parts to the woman and one part to the man.[97] In the case of divorce by stipulation, the wife retains the whole of the property, whether the husband's own property or joint property. Upon the death of the husband, all property acquired during marriage goes back to the woman's family under the matrilineal system. Property obtained before marriage goes back to either parties' relatives. In practice, in the case of small estates, the widow could be granted all the land.[98]

Courts are often called upon to determine what constitutes matrimonial property *harta sepencarian* and the proportion in which it should be divided. This has been legislated for in Section 58 of the Islamic Family Law (Federal Territories) Act (Hukum Syarak) 1984[99] Crown 1988[100] – once regarded as among the most progressive in the Muslim world. Under Section 58(2), the court must seek an equitable division, based on the contributions made by each party in terms of money, labour, or property towards the acquisition of the assets; debts incurred by either party for their joint benefit; and the needs of any minor children of the marriage. Under Section 58(3) and (4), assets acquired by the sole effort of one party to the marriage may also be divided, taking into account the extent of the contribution to the welfare of the family made by the party who did not acquire the assets and the needs of any minor children of the family. However, the division must be reasonable, and the party by whose efforts assets were acquired must receive a greater proportion. Under Section 58(5) assets to be divided can include assets owned before the marriage by one party but which have been substantially improved during the marriage by either the other party or by the parties' joint effort.

The application of the customary matrimonial property law in an urban setting can be explored through the landmark case of *Roberts alias Kamarulzaman v Ummi Kalthom* (1966).[101] Chan[102] considers this case to be one of Singapore's five most influential. A husband and wife bought a house in Kuala Lumpur for RM 50,000, with the husband contributing RM 40,000 and the wife RM 10,000. The house was registered in the name of the wife only as the husband was at the time not a Malayan citizen and needed permission to own property. When the parties divorced after 12 years of marriage, the husband brought an action in the High Court to determine how the joint matrimonial property *harta sepencarian* was to be divided. Even though the financial contribution of the husband was far greater than that of the wife, the Court decided to divide the shares of the property equally among the parties. In other cases, for example in Sarawak, even assets acquired by the sole effort of one spouse may be shared with the other spouse having regard to the latter's contributions made to the welfare of the family by looking after the home or caring for the family.[103]

Malaysian Courts, as noted above, are required to under Section 58(4) of the Islamic Family Law 1984 to consider 'the extent of the contributions made by the party who did not acquire the assets, to the welfare of the family by looking after the home or caring for the family' in dividing assets acquired during the marriage by the sole efforts of one party to the marriage. The Malaysian National Islamic Fatwa Council declared that Employees Provident Fund (EPF) savings for Muslims are not a joint matrimonial property liable to be divided in the event of divorce, but an individual asset. Hence, being a sole effort property, the EPF savings could be attached for the purpose of satisfying the claims for financial support after divorce. In some Malaysian states, the Sharia courts recognize the husband's EPF as *harta sepencarian*. In another leading case, *Rokiah bte Haji Abdul Jalil v Mohamed Idris bin Shamsudin* [1989],[104] the court awarded the housewife one third of the matrimonial home and other assets that had been acquired by the husband's money, based on the wife's indirect contribution to their acquisition by looking after the house and the family. The Malaysian Court of Appeal in 2003[105] referred to Singaporean cases and the pioneering Singaporean Women's Charter 1961, noting the common origin of their matrimonial law,[106] even though it does not directly apply to Muslims.

The joint marital property regime, however, is becoming more Islamic and also less women specific.[107] As the 2006 constitutional amendment (article 121) provides that the civil courts shall not have jurisdiction over designated Islamic matters, claims relating to marital property by Muslims can now only be brought to the Sharia court now. At the same time, the Islamic Family Law (FT) (Amendment) Act 2005 made the *harta sepencarian* (matrimonial property) regime gender-neutral. Thus, a court has the power to order the division of matrimonial property (*harta sepencarian*) upon the application of either husband or wife. Organizations such as Sisters in Islam are concerned that husbands could seek to freeze wives' bank accounts and assets to claim their share of *harta sepencarian* for a variety of reasons, including contracting a polygamous marriage.[108] They are also fighting for an equal division of matrimonial assets, instead of the present one third award to the wife.[109]

Community property regimes through Islamic law reform

Morocco

The 2004 *Moudawana* Family Code in Morocco – which introduced an optional community property regime – has been hailed as a breakthrough for women's rights and an examplar of modernist interpretations of Islamic law. In contrast to modernist codes in other Muslim countries derived from secular, civil, or customary codes, the Moroccan Code is derived from Islamic law, specifically the Maliki school of jurisprudence. It has brought about significant changes to matters relating to marriage, divorce, parentage, child custody and guardianship, inheritance, and family property matters, thereby considerably affecting women's rights. The new marital property regime was thus located within a broader framework of gender equality, which grants husbands and wives joint responsibility for the family and grants adult women the right to exercize self-guardianship freely and independently. Since the reforms, the husband is no longer the legal head of the household. However, given the high expectations it generated, the Moroccan responses have been complex and implementation full of challenges.[110]

The earlier code, the 1957–58 *Mudawwana*, completely separated estates in terms of both land and money brought into the marriage, and property and wealth acquired during the marriage. Numerous judgements rejected women's petitions on the grounds that they had not proved their participation in acquiring the assets. Without explicit legal recognition, divorcees struggled to acquire their share in marital property. The 2004 *Mudawwana* grants spouses the choice of full or partial community regimes to govern their property relationships. Though this provision has been controversial, it has been legitimized as an Islamic legal principle. The significance of the 2004 Code is that it elevates broad Islamic principles into mandatory rules, which mandate the intervention of the public prosecutor's office, public authorities, and the courts.[111]

Significant as the introduction of the community property concept was, the new law contained only one article addressing the division of marital property upon divorce. Article 49 of the new *Mudawwana* authorizes spouses, with respect to the administration of property that is acquired during the marriage, to agree on the way these will be managed and divided. A separate property regime is the norm but the law permits the spouses to make a written agreement on the investment and distribution of assets acquired during the marriage. The optional community of the marital property regime works through spouses developing a written agreement for the management of assets acquired during the marriage. This agreement must be recorded in a document that is separate from the marriage contract. This feature was meant to facilitate the enforcement of such contracts under the various legal orders concerned.

However, the success of the marital property scheme depends on the attitudes of the public notaries, who are marriage registrars with a religious character (*adouls*), as well as the courts. The *adouls* are central to the marital property choice and play an important role as community legal experts in family matters. However, the very religious notaries who had expressed their opposition to the new *Mudawwana* – as it took away their considerable powers and were contrary to their conservative interpretations – have resisted its implementation.[112] Though they are required to inform spouses of the option of equal marital property provisions as part of their oversight of the marriage, they rarely do so.[113] Many *adouls* point out to inappropriate timing of any marital property discussion, which could lead to the wedding falling apart. More often, the *adouls* often express a lack of confidence in the ability of the young partners to decide future property matters. Though the *Mudawwana* expressly states that adult women may now sign their marriage contract themselves, many *adouls* refuse to form such contracts or discuss marital property matters without a guardian (*wali*).[114]

In the absence of a pre-nuptial agreement, courts have considerable leeway in determining property division upon divorce. Therefore, there is considerable inconsistency, with some individual judges arbitrarily applying their own interpretations of religious law. They sift through the evidence, taking into account the contribution of each spouse, any efforts made, and the responsibilities assumed in the development of the family assets. There are 66 specialist Family Courts located in large cities and medium-sized towns dealing with marital property disputes. The courts, however, are dependent on the 4,500 *adouls* across the country, and particularly in the rural areas where the courts do not have much reach. For example, Global Rights reports that of the 289,821 marriages that took place in 2006, only 424 had additional marital property contracts concluded, while in 2007 there were 900 marital property contracts for 316,411 marriages.[115] Awareness of the community property option is increasing among Moroccan women, and depends on how successfully the country negotiates the delicate phase in its drive for greater gender equality and justice.[116]

Tunisia

The 1956 Tunisian Personal Status Code (*Majalla*) (article 11) and the Algerian Family Code 1984 (article 19)[117] also allow spouses to negotiate and incorporate additional clauses relating to marital property into their marriage contract. The history of family law in Tunisia is interesting, as the French colonial officers changed property laws and contract laws but did not interfere with Islamic family law, as they did in Algeria.[118] However, it was the secular approach of President Habib Bourguiba that liberalized traditional Islamic laws governing women, abolishing polygamy, establishing a minimum age for marriage, and instituting formal legal procedures under which women could inherit property, obtain a divorce, and divide property. Tunisian women saw their legal status change significantly when the Code of Personal Status was promulgated in 1956 and supplemented by additional laws thereafter. For the marriage to be legally valid, the bride must now attend her own marriage ceremony and give her verbal consent, divorce can take place only in court, and husband and wife are equally entitled to file for divorce. Polygamy is abolished outright. The law also ends the legal guardianship of men over women and redefines the rights and obligations of husband and wife so as to make them more equal.[119]

Tunisia instituted an optional community property regime for married couples under Law 98–91 of 9 November 1998. The similarities between the Tunisian and Moroccan cases, both originally following the Maliki Sharia law, should be noted.[120] While separate marital property for assets acquired by the spouses during marriage is the regular regime, the Tunisian law created the legal possibility for spouses to draw up a framework for the joint management and investment of assets acquired during the marriage. This agreement must be written in a document separate from the marriage contract, and the *adoul* must notify the two parties of this possibility at the time of marriage. In the absence of a written agreement, recourse is made to general standards of evidence, while taking into consideration the work of each spouse, any efforts made, and the responsibilities assumed in the development of the family assets. Like in Morocco, Tunisian brides rarely have the real option of considering community property regimes as there is no opportunity to study the contract in marriages conducted by the registrar (*adoul*), which are mostly held either in the bride's parent's home or at the mosque. She is only given the completed document to sign. There is a gap between marital property law, and the reality, for Tunisian women.

Iran

The Islamic Republic of Iran is another country which recognizes the equal division of marital property, albeit by contractual agreement. Shortly after the 1979 Islamic revolution, the Parliament *(majles)* introduced a provision to the marriage contract that entitled the divorced wife to claim half of the wealth acquired during marriage, providing that the divorce is not her fault. Modern reforms in Iran go back to 1967 where the Shah regime attempted substantial reforms to the Sharia provisions through the Family Protection Act, restricting men's rights to unilateral divorce and polygamy, and giving women easier access to divorce and maintenance. The Family Protection Act 1967, as well as its successor the Family Protection Act of 1975, sought a fine balance between Sharia law and secular law aimed at modernizing Iran. The reforms also established family courts, which exercized wide discretion in respect of divorce matters, including, in some cases, marital property.

Among the first communiques from the Ayatollah Khomeini, in February 1979, was to declare the Family Protection Act non-Islamic, to be replaced by an Islamic system.[121] The post-revolutionary state set out to Islamicize family laws in Iran, intent on abrogating Western-inspired law. However, in the process of engagement, it actually revisited and reinstated several substantive and procedural Western gender equality innovations, found compatible with Islamic law, leading to Iran's 'hybridized Islamico-civil legal system'. The equitable marital property division is an outcome of this process.[122] Since 1982, the post-revolutionary marriage contracts stipulate that the husband pay his wife, upon divorce, up to half of the wealth he has acquired during that marriage, provided that the divorce has not been initiated or caused by any fault of the wife.[123] Parties can consent to this marriage contract clause by signing it.[124]

Before 1982, the only legally sanctioned recourse was to seek adequate maintenance (*nafaqa*) through the courts. However, Iranian women now could negotiate marital property rights through marriage contracts and enforce them through Islamic courts. In September 1979, the post-revolutionary government set up Special Civil Courts *(dadgahha-ye madani-ye khass)*, headed by an Islamic judge, to replace the earlier family courts. Yet, their designation as 'special' granted them the same degree of discretionary powers as the pre-revolutionary family courts. While there is no evidence as to the proportion of signed marital property clauses in marriage contracts, women are increasingly active in accessing the court systems. 'Women contest cases through well thought-out legal strategies based on Iran's own reformulated marriage and family codes. They prepare their legal documents, give evidence, and make statements in accordance with stated legal procedures'.[125] By using the marriage contract, based on the Quranic basis to rightful shares, Iranian women strive to assert their rights to marital property.

There are mixed reviews on how women have fared since the revolution. Since 1993, another Iranian reform requires husbands divorcing to pay 'wages for housework' in addition to the maintenance (*nafaqa*) and dower (*mahr*) due to wives according to the Islamic family law. A divorcee's rights to her own property are unaffected by the contract, while she also retains her right to the dower (*mahr*), the consideration given by the husband for performance of the contract: The amount the wife actually gets is determined by the court on the basis of the number of years of marriage and the status of the couple. The laws, irrespective of the extent of their implementation, have considerably strengthened women's bargaining power and in particular have effectively redressed some of the imbalances present in custody and divorce provisions for women.[126] There have been improvements in women's education but several Iranian activists, feminists, and external commentators argue that more needs to be done to challenge patriarchal trends.[127] Far from being passive victims, Iranian women are resisting, negotiating, and pressing for their economic rights within the Islamic law framework.[128]

Maldives

The island nation of Maldives offers what a recent World Bank report calls 'startling' information on matrimonial property rights. Maldives is ranked second in South Asia on both the UNDP's Human Development Index (HDI) and Gender Related Development Index (GDI), after Sri Lanka, and therefore above Bangladesh, Bhutan, India, Nepal, Pakistan, and other countries.[129] In part, this is owing to its high rates of female literacy of 93 per cent, which is almost the same as male literacy. Maldivian women have always kept their own name after marriage, sign pre-nuptial agreements to negotiate marital property terms, inherit property, and remarry.[130] On the other hand, there has been an increasing influence from orthodox Wahhabism – a conservative form of Islam originating from Saudi Arabia. The country's constitution specifically promotes Islamic Law and Maldives has entered a reservation to article 16 of CEDAW, which relates to the equality of men and women in all matters relating to marriage and family relations. At the same time, Maldives ratified the Optional Protocol in 2006, and was among the first Muslim majority states to do so.

Despite the CEDAW reservation, Maldives enacted a family law reform in 2001 that in several respects departs from traditional aspects of Islamic family law norms. One significant feature appears to be community of marital property. Byrnes and Freeman note that a Maldives report to the CEDAW Committee (in 1999, even before the 2001 reforms)[131] recorded that:

> in case of divorce, any property, which has been registered as joint property, is divided equally. Any property which is seen by the court to have been acquired by the couple during their joint partnership in marriage (the woman's domestic and child-care contributions are taken into account) is also divided between the two.[132]

Curiously, the CEDAW Committee did not take notice of this remarkable account in an otherwise conservative Islamic family system, nor did it follow up in its 2007 dialogue on ongoing family law reforms. There is a paucity of research on the proportion of women who benefit from the law which must be socially difficult, but the existence of equal division of marital property again underscores that it could co-exist within Islamic family law.

Community property options for Muslim minorities in pluralist countries

Tanzania

Tanzania, with an estimated 45 per cent of its population being Muslim, recognizes civil, customary, and Islamic marriages, but a common marriage law integrates the personal laws of different communities.[133] Thus Muslims adhere to aspects of their faith-based Islamic practices, including inheritance, but their marriages are covered by the 1971 Law of Marriage Act (LMA). Under Section 56 of LMA, married women are granted the same rights as men in acquiring, holding, and disposing of property. This has to be read alongside the Land and Village Land Act 1999, which reiterates 'the right of every woman to acquire, hold, use and deal with land . . . to the same extent and subject to the same restriction . . . as the right of any man.' Under Section 56 of LMA, parties to a marriage can sign an agreement for the division of joint matrimonial property; otherwise each spouse retains separate rights in their property. Importantly, under Section 59 of LMA, neither the husband nor the wife may unilaterally transfer rights in the matrimonial home without the other's consent. Where such a prohibited transaction occurs, the other spouse retains the right to reside in the house as long as the marriage remains intact.

In the absence of agreement between spouses, matrimonial property obtained by parties 'during the marriage by their joint efforts' is to be divided upon divorce by courts according to 'the extent of the contributions made by each party'.[134] Any property obtained in the name of one partner during the course of the marriage creates a rebuttable presumption that the property 'belongs absolutely to that person, to the exclusion of his or her spouse'. However, the 1999 Land Act protects the interests of married women in land by establishing a presumption that spouses hold land as occupiers in common:

> Where land held for a right of occupancy is held in the name of one spouse only but the other spouse or spouses contribute by their labour to the productivity, upkeep and improvement of the land, the spouse or those spouses shall be deemed by virtue of that labour to have acquired an interest in that land in the nature of an occupancy in common.

Rwezaura notes that there has been sustained efforts by the Tanzanian superior courts to 'create a new blend of family law out of a plural legal system'. These creative efforts have in turn further expanded the marital property rights of Muslim women.[135] The superior courts have limited the role of the Muslim Conciliation Board in conciliation efforts and the court has refused to entertain the Board's recommendations on how matrimonial property should be divided (*Njobeka v Mkogoro*). However, courts do exercize their post-divorce powers with regard to customary norms of the community.[136] A study of the courts' approach to matrimonial property in Tanzania demonstrates that the strength of religion is an influence.[137] In some cases, women themselves may be reluctant to assert their matrimonial property rights. In other cases, without clear a statutory prescription on division, lower courts tend to lean towards custom and traditions in allocating marital property. In fact, under Section 114(2)(a), courts are permitted to defer to customary or Islamic law in the distribution of marital property upon divorce.

In contrast to their helplessness in Islamic inheritance matters, the Tanzanian courts have greater teeth in securing equitable, if not equal, marital property distribution. Ezer points out to that this leads to the 'absurdity' of Tanzanian women being economically better off when their marriages are dissolved by divorce rather than by the deaths of their husbands.[138] The Court of Appeal, in the landmark decision in *Bi Hawa Mohamed v Ally Seifu* (1983),[139] recognized that women could claim housework and child care as contributions to jointly acquired marital assets. Thus, in *Mohamed v Makamo*,[140] the High Court ordered an equal division of matrimonial property thereby reversing a lower court decision that provided the divorced Muslim wife only five per cent of matrimonial properties without fully considering her material or non-material contributions. However, Section 114 of the LMA grants the court the power to order the division of any assets acquired during the marriage 'to the extent of the contributions made by each party in money, property or work towards the acquiring of the assets'. There are cases where the court may order a smaller or no share for the wife.[141]

Kenya

In neighbouring Kenya, which also has a substantial proportion of Muslims, the position is slightly different. The 1971 Tanzanian law came out of a joint Kenyan-Tanzanian study,[142] with Kenya hesitating to pass a comprehensive statute to cover marriages for all communities. As such, there is no single detailed law dealing with matrimonial property. Curiously, the division of matrimonial property in Kenya still takes place in accordance with an old English colonial statute, the Married Women's Property Act 1882 (MWPA).[143] This 1882 law was a major improvement on its 1870 predecessor, as it recognized the wife's separate legal interest in the property. While it overturned her incapacity to obtain marital property under common law, it offered a rigid doctrine of separate property. However, most women are unaware of this colonial law, and with most family property being registered only in the husband's name, women are disadvantaged.

Instead it has fallen on courts to address marital property rights, including those of Muslims. Even where there was no civil marriage but only an Islamic marriage, the Kenyan courts have tended to apply common law principles. In the landmark case of *Essa v Essa* (1996),[144] a couple married for ten years after an Islamic wedding brought their marital property dispute to the courts.

The court rejected the argument that MWPA did not apply to a Muslim marriage, noting that the statute of general application 'applies equally to Muslims as it does to non-Muslims in Kenya'. The court awarded the wife a half share in one of the properties, a rental commercial building, based upon evidence that she made payment from her business towards the purchase of the property. There are contentious legal issues for Muslim minorities in Kenya and Tanzania but reconciliation is taking place.[145] Kenya awaits new laws on matrimonial property, under which it is likely that Muslim couples will retain the option of marriage under community property regimes.

South Africa

South Africa is widely known for its default regime of 'in community of property', but this applies to most customary and Muslim marriages. In fact, Muslim marriages were technically not recognized under South African law[146] until 2014, though the post-apartheid 1996 Constitution acknowledges issues such as Muslim marriages among the growing community since the seventeenth century. The debate over Muslim marriages generally, and the marital property regime in particular, offers an absorbing narrative of how a constitutionally secular state responds to claims of distinctiveness from customary and religious groups.[147] This incorporation of Muslim personal law in the new democratic dispensation is the acid test of 'accommodation of religious diversity' within a rights-based framework.[148] The non-recognition of Muslim marriages seriously undermines the rights of Muslim women in several respects, including the inability to claim financial support during marriage, maintenance and custody on divorce, inheritance, or even financial compensation for an unlawfully killed husband.[149] In fact, for persons married in terms of the Islamic law only, there exist no legal grounds for obtaining a divorce in a South African court.[150]

South African courts refused to recognize a marriage under Islamic rites as a valid civil marriage under the Marriage Act 1961, and therefore Muslims have no legal redress to take the matter further. In *Ismail v Ismail* (1983),[151] it was explained that a potentially polygamous Muslim marriage is *contra bonos mores*, contrary to the accepted norms that are morally binding in society. However, since 1994, the South African judiciary has sought to provide some relief to Muslims married under Islamic law,[152] given the enhanced rights and public rights under the new constitutional dispensation.[153] In *Ryland v Edros* (1997)[154] the court, without having to recognize a de facto monogamous Muslim marriage, agreed to enforce a contract. After several such cases, in *Amod v Multilateral Motor Vehicle Accidents Fund* (1999)[155] the court allowed an insurance claim by a widow against the insurer of a driver who had negligently killed her husband. *Daniels v Campbell* (2004)[156] extended protection to parties to a monogamous Muslim marriage and considered inheritance claims. In *Khan v Khan* (2005) the court heard a maintenance case despite it being a polygamous Muslim marriage. In *Jamalodien v Moola* (2006)[157] the court made an award relating to maintenance, property and custody for a Muslim divorcee. In 2010, a court enforced the equal rights of Muslim women under the City of Cape Town's housing policy. The judge said Muslim women should be entitled to joint ownership of properties, even though this had been granted by the city solely to their husbands or partners.

However, such *ad hoc* court interventions being inadequate, the need for legislative recognition had long been on the cards but was difficult to achieve. In 1994, the African National Congress government established a Muslim Personal Law Board (MPLB) mandated to draft legislation to recognize Muslim personal law. When it became controversial, a more inclusive project committee comprising nine Muslims took the work forward. The South African Law Reform Commission worked on the draft from 1999 and submitted a report in 2003, but though the draft bill that emerged was discussed within government it did not gather momentum until 2009, and is presently before Parliament and imminent. The wide-ranging Muslim Marriages Bill deals with the proprietary consequences of the marriage. A marriage is automatically out of community of property, except if the spouses entered into a contractual arrangement in terms of which they mutually agree to another marriage regime – excluding the accrual system, unless the parties enter into an ante-nuptial contract.[158]

The draft bill, which recognizes Islamic marriages as valid and enforceable within the South African legal framework, also offers Muslims a unique opportunity to opt for the community of property arrangement.[159] For the diverse and substantial South African Muslim population (which doubled between 1994 and 2001 with Muslim migration from the rest of the continent), it represents an interesting synthesis between Islamic law and the related human rights and constitutional provisions of South African law.[160] Some Muslim women, such as the Women's Legal Centre, have objected to the proposed default regime of 'out of community of property', which differs from the default regime of 'in community of property' for all other marriages in South Africa, particularly because women may not be aware of their choices. Yet, with other conservative Muslim groups expressing anxiety over the departure from the conventional Islamic marital property separation, the bill offers a compromise.

Israel

Despite demographic changes, Muslims comprise about 16 per cent of the Israeli population, making them the second largest religious group after Israeli Jews.[161] Given the intense political sensitivities, Israel has continued the application of respective personal laws under the *millet* (religious community) system from the Ottoman period, which was retained throughout the British Mandatory rule. This autonomy applies to not only Jews and Muslims but also to all 11 recognized religions, including the significant Christian and Druze communities. Thus, an 'accommodationist family law policy' lets Muslims and other communities determine their own intra-group traditions and controls[162] – to an extent. Several aspects of family law, such as adoption, succession, maintenance, and matrimonial property, are regulated by secular, territorial legislation enacted by the Israeli Parliament, the Knesset, irrespective of religious affiliation.[163]

Marital property regimes are said to be a feature of ancient Palestinian culture – Jewish, Christian, and Muslim.[164] However, the dominant construction of *Halakha* (Jewish law), similar to Islamic law, promotes a separate property regime. In effect, the husband retains total rights over his spouse's property.[165] In 1974, the Spouses (Property) Relations Law came into force and established a 'community property rule' through which each spouse has an equal share in the marital property. This set aside the dominant construction of marital property under both the *halakhic* and the Sharia.[166] All couples married after 1 January 1974 are bound, when the marriage comes to an end, by a 'resources-balancing arrangement', applicable to all assets acquired during the marriage. As such, there is a separation of property with a division of surplus upon dissolution of the marriage, whether due to death or divorce. The spouses may opt out through written agreement to a different arrangement, which must be approved by the competent authority. The Property Relations between Spouses (Amendment No 4) Law, 5769–2008, obliges spouses to divide equally, at the time of divorce, all assets that they accumulated jointly, including savings accumulated during the marriage (the law replaced the discriminatory arrangement that had been in place since 1973).

Matters such as the division of marital property are often decided by religious courts under Israel's dual legal system. Israel has Sharia courts for Muslims which, alongside civil courts, exercize potential jurisdiction to decide on any ancillary matters to a divorce, such as division of property. The *Hanafi* Islamic school is dominant in the Sharia courts (owing to the Ottoman legacy) even though most of the population, especially in rural areas, belong to the *Shafi* school. Sharia courts apply several civil laws such as the Marriage Age Law of 1950 (which raised the marriage age for women to 17), the Women's Equal Rights Law of 1951 (which banned polygamy and unilateral divorce), and the Maintenance (Assurance of Payment) Law of 1972 (whereby women can attain their right to maintenance without delay).[167] Yet, the most significant legislation implemented by the Islamic courts, and the religious courts of other communities, is the Property Relations between Spouses Law 1973 (and the reforms of 1991) relating to marital property.

Layish points out that the 1973 law signified 'a far-reaching reform for Muslims whose religious law does not recognize community property of spouses'.[168] In cases of unilateral divorce by the husband, the wife was now entitled to half the spouses' combined property, while the husband becomes liable to penal sanctions if he does not comply. In practice, this rarely happens.[169] There were two initial Muslim responses to this law. On one hand, Muslim women who ordinarily had only dower as per marriage contract (*mahr*) and waiting-period maintenance benefited from these additional rights, which to many seemed compatible with Islamic norms. On the other, a deep distrust of the Israeli courts led to Arabs retreating to informal methods and custom (*urf*) to resolve personal and property conflicts.[170] However, the primary strategy has been to adopt an alternate agreement, which keeps the 1973 community property regime at bay, and to stick to the Sharia courts, which dispense justice closer to community norms – to the extent possible.

While the religious courts in general have been reluctant to enforce community property rules, the Israeli Supreme Court has ruled that rabbinical courts are bound to implement the principle of equal property rights in cases of divorce.[171] In *Bavli v Great Rabbinical Court* (1994),[172] Mrs Bavli's claim for an equal share of the couple's property was rejected by the Regional Rabbinical Court on the basis that such division of property contradicts Jewish religious law. The Great Rabbinical Court upheld the regional court's ruling, but the Israeli Supreme Court overturned this decision, arguing that religious courts must take account of the equality between men and women under Israeli Constitutional Law, and Jewish or other personal laws cannot derogate from such rights.[173] There are practical obstacles. The only form of marriage that is recognized under Israeli law is religious marriage. The community property arrangement will only be triggered by divorce or the end of marriage, not before. Under Jewish law, it is the husband who signs a writ of divorce (the *Get*), without which the wife cannot benefit from the resources-balancing arrangement under the statutory community property rule.

In *Yemini v Great Rabbinical Court* (2003),[174] the Supreme Court was again called upon to enforce the community property rule. In this divorce case, the rabbinical court rejected the application of the wife for an equitable division of the marital property in accordance with the Spouses (Property Relations) Law 1973. The religious courts were flouting the equal division of marital property under a creative theory of jurisdiction. The civil statute regarding equal division of marital property was to apply unless the parties consented to the application of religious law. The rabbinical courts postulated that once both the parties consented to the jurisdiction of the religious court it was implicit that they had both consented to the adjudication of the case based on religious principles, and community of property regimes did not apply. The Supreme Court overruled the religious court, declaring that the consent to the application of religious tenets must be explicit and clear, and could not be inferred merely because the parties had appeared before a rabbinical court.

Hacker's recent research shows that despite the secularist interventions of the Supreme Court, religious judges still follow religious laws that divide the property according to the notion of individual property.[175] Some Supreme Court judges such as Aharon Barak ventured to engage with Jewish law (*Halakha*) to seek legitimacy for principles such as marital property. Among judges in rabbinical courts (*dayans*) the debate over the compatibility of community property with Jewish law continues. Rabbi Shlomo Dichovski, for example, has interpreted *Halakha* to the effect that Jewish law does not stand in the way of marrying couples intending to own their property jointly, thus approximating the civil courts' presumption of community property.[176] Others such as Rabbi Sherman, currently a judge at the Great Rabbinical Court, argue that judges should not rule according to the communal property presumption, even if the parties agreed to it, as it stands in contradiction to religious law.[177]

The Sharia courts in Israel face a similar dilemma over the Islamic legitimacy of community property regimes. However, these have not been sufficiently debated owing to the tense relationship between the Israeli civil and Sharia courts.

Moreover, the 1973 law, and subsequent reforms, were top down and were perceived as an attack on Arab autonomy and culture, rather than a step towards gender equality.[178] Marital property is an arena of contest between the secular constitution and religious conceptions of marital property rights. The Sharia courts, as noted above, regularly implement civil law but interpret it in accordance with Islamic principles. As the Islamic courts negotiate custom and civil laws in an evolving Muslim community, its embrace of the community property rule will depend on how judges, and other stakeholders, interpret the relationship between Islamic law and marital property in a political context.

Conclusions

Islamic legal pluralism and marital property

The vast majority of Muslims live under separate property regimes but a significant and increasing number do have the choice to enter into community property arrangements. In addition to Muslim minority communities in European and American countries, marital community property regimes are available to Muslim communities in Europe (Turkey), South Asia (Maldives), West Asia (Iran), South East Asia (Indonesia, Malaysia), Central Asia (Kazakhstan), Middle East and North Africa (Morocco, Tunisia), East Africa (Kenya, Tanzania), and South Africa. In addition to the geographical spread, these countries are representative of both Islamic jurisprudential schools – Sunni and Shiite. The main Shiite country, Iran, with the *Ithna 'Ashari* school, recognizes community property principles. Among the Sunni schools, three out of the four – *Hanafi* (Turkey), *Shafi'i* (Malaysia, Indonesia, Maldives) and *Maliki* (Morocco) – demonstrate a capacity to embrace community property regimes. Marital property is also recognized in Kazakhstan, where *Sufism* – the mystical doctrine of Islam – is influential.

The findings of this research serve as an advocacy tool in Muslim countries for policy makers and civil society to promote marital property options for Muslim couples, compatible with Islamic law. There are also opportunities for comparative study and cross-fertilization among legal systems. The research indicates that there is a lack of both tools and capacity in implementing marital laws in several of the countries examined. In Muslim countries with non-existent, inadequate, or inequitable marital laws, there is need for urgent legal reform. Community property regimes have been introduced in Muslim countries through a variety of means – modern secular reforms, the accommodation of customary practices, internal Islamic reforms, and statutory measures affecting Muslims in legally pluralist societies. In contrast to inheritance laws, which are mostly considered to be part of personal law and beyond reform, marital property laws have been subject to changes.

Engaging with Islamic and customary dimensions

In each of the dozen countries studied in this chapter, the process through which community property regimes have been accommodated within Islamic law has varied. It has ranged from legislative change to gender rights campaigns, judicial activism, or jurisprudential debates. Perhaps the most important has been the development of community property doctrine in Indonesia through innovative interpretations of Islamic family law and gendered property law. Equally important has been the active role of Muslim women in shaping the religious culture and their rights in Indonesia,[179] as elsewhere in the world.[180] For example, in Indonesia, in the 1960s, Professor Hazairin, who was a scholar of Islamic and customary (*adat*) systems, argued that the well-established norms are that both men and women have property rights, but the detail depended upon culture. Since classical extrapolations were based on Arab culture, those in different times and places could adapt them to their context. Bowen recounts how Professor Muhammad Daud Ali in the 1990s rationalized the Indonesian law on equal property, drawing on the 'general Islamic principle of equity plus the social practices in Indonesia that underlie a local sense of justice'.[181]

Thus, the successful examples of incorporation of community property systems in Muslim countries (Indonesia and Malaysia, for example) are those underwritten by supporting Islamic and customary arguments. While Morocco, Iran, Maldives, and Tunisia base their marital property legislation on Islamic grounds, they are still in the process of addressing the Islamic dimensions or are developing institutions to implement them. As can be seen from the so-called 'secular' imports in Turkey and Kazakhstan, Islamic and customary dimensions are not far away and need to be addressed. Muslim minorities in diverse Western, African, Asian, and Arab countries also frequently query the compatibility of marital property with Islamic law. While customary and religious norms could undermine marital property rights, they could result in positive outcomes.

Developing a model marriage contract

Traditionally considered a status-based institution, marriage is now increasingly a matter of contract.[182] One of the positive features of Islamic law is the marriage contract, whereby marital property clauses or separate agreements can simply be added onto the main Islamic marriage contract.[183] It is not possible to enter into a Muslim marriage without signing a contract, called a *nikah* contract. Unlike other cultures, where marriage contracts or pre-nuptial agreements were the prerogative of the elite, this was the essential component of every Muslim marriage, as noted in all case studies above. Muslim women have historically used the marriage contract to negotiate their property rights,[184] and in many countries, including Iran, 'the underlying logic of marriage as a contract is used by women as an effective strategy to negotiate their marital terms'.[185]

However, in practice, women are unable to take advantage of the opportunity owing to several reasons. In Morocco and Tunisia, the religious minded registrars (*adouls*) rarely fulfil their obligation of informing the spouses of their marital property options. The Moroccan Family Code (articles 47 and 48), Algerian Family Code (article 19), and 1956 Tunisian Personal Status Code (article 11) allow spouses to negotiate and incorporate additional clauses into the marriage contract. Women can use these contracts to protect their rights in marriage and at its dissolution by stipulating clauses on property ownership and division, children, monogamy, her right to work, accounting of unpaid contributions to the household, and matters requiring her consent. For example, the Model Marriage Contract addresses property rights and financial relations, allowing spouses to stipulate ownership, administration, use, and disposition of property acquired prior to the marriage and during the marriage. Global Rights is campaigning for the development of a model contract with sample conditions in order to give women examples to draw upon.[186]

Recognizing Muslim marital property debates

Community property notions are often resisted on the assumption that foreign and Western imports could destabilize Muslim society and increase divorce rates. There are also conventional Muslims who see the community property rule as tinkering with the Islamic notion that Muslim wives have no obligation to spend out of their separate property or dower (*mahr*) for their family, but they often do. Another common position is that community property would put the wife in a more favourable position than the husband, as she retains both possession and management of whatever property she brings to or acquires during the marriage. However, this is equally true for men, though a woman often inherits half of what an equally positioned male would. At divorce, Muslim women, for example in Indonesia, may have a range of rights (such as maintenance (*nafaqa*), which includes financial support, clothing, and housing), but the husband is required to provide only during the obligatory waiting period of a few months (*idda*). Post-marital gifts (*mutat*) may be possible, but these are a 'matter of custom and goodwill'.[187] Dowers (*mahr*) are intended to provide some financial security, but they may be a nominal amount and bartered away during divorce. They do not justify or compensate for loss of marital property.

Muslim societies do accord a high status to women and recognize their roles as primarily wives and mothers; the key test, however, is whether those contributions, material and non-material, could be quantified in cases of divorce without undermining Muslim family structures. While marital property is important for women generally, it needs to be recognized that, as pointed out in the Indonesian context, these rights 'hardly play a role for the poor and neither do rights to maintenance, or even marital property – of which there is usually almost none'.[188] In Tanzania, rural poverty and the general economic insecurity of peasant families render certain legal provisions relating to matrimonial property rather nugatory.[189] Others stress that, rather than ownership itself, it is access to land and its management that is a priority. Marital property is a key pathway for land ownership for women. One commentator recognizes the domino effect of and importance of marital property law for every society:[190]

> The law of marital property is so intimately related to the social and economic life of a nation that, more than any other branch of private law, it affects the nation's character and sets the course for its legal development.

Despite the law, the distribution of marital property processes are fluid and, depending on the judge, could be used in combination to either the advantage or disadvantage to women. The courts in carrying out a 'just and equitable' division of property that constitutes the matrimonial assets do not always have a clear or consistent approach. In addition, gender-deprecating customs or patriarchal norms work against women when it comes to the division of marital property, even by the courts. In common law jurisdictions, for example in the landmark *Bi Hawa*[191] case granting marital property to the Muslim divorcee, the Tanzanian court applied the 'mischief rule', whereby it construed statutes according to the intention of the legislature to eliminate inequality. Courts routinely face questions as to whether Muslim women have 'bargained away' their rights, as they accepted dower (*mahr*), initiated divorce, agreed to fault, or were granted custody of their children. A sound basis of understanding of Islamic marital property is essential for secular courts.

Muslim families in the urban world at least are rapidly changing from extended families to nuclear families and further into non-traditional living arrangements. There is a need to re-examine:

> concepts of personhood, property, and the conjugal contract in the new evolving contexts, in which cultural ideas are reworked as women and men reposition themselves and attempt to secure their economic futures in the context of changing material conditions and shifting fields of power.[192]

The results of this comparative study certainly lend support to the view of Mashhour who argues that:

> the dynamic nature of Islamic teachings, the evolving character of Sharia, the spirit of Islam towards women's rights, the principles of justice and public welfare, and the essentiality of feminist Ijtihad leave no room for doubt that a common ground could be found between Islamic law and gender equality.[193]

Notes

1 Siraj Sait and Hilary Lim, *Land, Law and Islam: Property and Human Rights in the Muslim World* (Zed Books 2006) 134.

2 Annelies Moors, *Women, Property and Islam: Palestinian Experiences,* (CUP 1995); Maya Shatzmiller, 'Women and Property Rights in Al-Andalus and the Maghrib: Social Patterns and Legal Discourse' (1995) 2 Islamic Law and Society 219.

3 Yolanda Aixelà Cabré, 'The Mudawwana and Koranic Law from a Gender Perspective: The Substantial Changes in the Moroccan Family Code of 2004' (2007) 7 Language and Intercultural Communication 133; Safia M Safwat, 'What Happens to the Matrimonial Home on Divorce in Islamic Law' (1995) 20 International Legal Practitioner 76.

4 Royston J Lawson, 'A comparative study of domestic contribution and family property allocation in Australia, New Zealand and the United Kingdom' (1991) 15 Journal of Consumer Studies & Home Economics 367; see also PA Buttar, 'Muslim personal

law in western countries: the case of Australia' (1985) 6 Institute of Muslim Minority Affairs Journal 271.

5 *Farah v Farah,* 429 SE2d 626 (VA Ct App 1993).

6 Hilmar Krüger, 'Some Questions of the Law of Arab Countries in German Courts' (1977) 18 Die Welt des Islams 41.

7 Gert Steenhoff, 'A Matrimonial System for the EU?' (2005) 74 International Family Law; Walter Pintens, 'Europeanisation of Family Law' in Katharina Boele-Woelki (ed), *Perspectives for the Unification and Harmonisation of Family Law in Europe* (Intersentia 2003) 1, 9ff.

8 Veronique Chauveau and Alain Cornec, 'France' in C Hamilton and A Perry (eds), *Family Law in Europe* (Butterworths LexisNexis 2002) 253, 261.

9 As part of a UN-Habitat funded research.

10 Wayne Van Der Meide, 'Gender Equality v Right to Culture-Debunking the Perceived Conflicts Preventing the Reform of the Marital Property Regime of the Official Version of Customary Law' (1999) 116 South African Law Journal 100.

11 Carmen Diana Deere and Cheryl R Doss, *Gender and the Distribution of Wealth in Developing Countries* (UNU-WIDER 2006).

12 See, for example, Singaporean Women's Charter 1961, s 46 (not applicable to Muslims).

13 Daniel A Crane, 'A Judeo-Christian Argument for Privatizing Marriage' (2006) 27 Cardozo Law Review 1221; Elizabeth S Scott, 'A World Without Marriage' (2007) 41 Family Law Quarterly 537; Edward Stein, 'Symposium on Abolishing Civil Marriage: An Introduction' (2006) 27 Cardozo Law Review 1155.

14 Ann Laquer Estin, 'Unofficial Family Law' (2008) 94 Iowa Law Review 449.

15 Sait and Lim (n 2).

16 Sandra F Joireman, 'The Mystery of Capital Formation in Sub-Saharan Africa: Women, Property Rights and Customary Law' (2008) 36 World Development 1233.

17 Susana Lastarria-Cornhiel, 'Impact of privatization on gender and property rights in Africa' (1997) 25 World Development 1317.

18 M Brinig and F Buckley, 'No-Fault Laws and At-Fault People' (1998) 18 International Review of Law and Economics 325.

19 Javaid Rahman, 'The Sharia, Islamic family laws and international human rights law: Examining the theory and practice of polygamy and talaq' (2007) 21 International Journal of Law, Policy and the Family 108.

20 See, for example, Quran 4:7: 'From what is left by parents and those nearest related there is a share for men and a share for women, whether the property be small or large – a determinate share'.

21 John L Esposito, *Women in Muslim Family Law* (2nd edn, Syracuse University Press 2001) 12; M Abu Zahra, 'Family Law' in Majid Khadduri and Herbert J Liebesny (eds), *Law In The Middle East* (The Middle East Institute 1955) 132, 142f.

22 Mary Ann Fay, 'From Concubines to Capitalists: Women, Property, and Power in Eighteenth-century Cairo' (1998) 10 Journal of Women's History 118.

23 Wael Hallaq, *Sharia: Theory, Practice, Transformations* (CUP 2009) 279.

24 Thomas Oldham, 'Management of the Community Estate during an intact Marriage' (1993) 56 Law and Contemporary Problems 99.

25 Jennifer Brown, 'Rural Women's Land Rights in Java, Indonesia: Strengthened by Family Law, But Weakened by Land Registration' (2003) 12 Pacific Rim Law and Policy Journal 631.

26 Susana Lastarria-Cornhiel, 'Joint titling in Nicaragua, Indonesia and Honduras: Rapid appraisal synthesis' [2003] University of Wisconsin-Madison, Land Tenure

Center Research Paper, 51 <www.nelson.wisc.edu/ltc/docs/sl0301joi.pdf> accessed 29 July 2015.

27 Caroline Bermeo Newcombe, 'Origin and Civil Law Foundation of the Community Property System: Why California Adopted It and Why Community Property Principles Benefit Women (2011) 11 University of Maryland Law Journal of Race, Religion, Gender and Class 1.

28 Hallaq (n 24) 271.

29 William Blackstone, *Commentaries on the Laws of England* (John L Wendell (ed), Harper & Brothers 1850) 513.

30 *Chaudry v Chaudry*, 388 A2d *1006* (NJ Super Ct App Div 1978), finding that the *mahr* agreement in the case limited the wife's claim to the husband's assets to the specified $1,500.

31 *In re Marriage of Shaban v Sherifa Shaban*, 105 Cal Rptr 2d 863, 867ff (Ct App 2001) (holding that the statute of frauds prevented the court from enforcing the *mahr* as a premarital agreement).

32 *Ahmad v Ahmad* (2001) No L-00-1391, 2001 WL 1518116 (Ohio Ct App 2001).

33 See Jamal J Nasir, *The Islamic Law of Personal Status* (2nd edn, Graham & Trotman 1990) 89.

34 Nathan B Oman, 'Bargaining in the Shadow of God's Law: Islamic Mahr Contracts and the Perils of Legal Specialization' (2010) 45 Wake Forest Law Review 287, 334.

35 Lindsey E Blenkhorn, 'Notes, Islamic Marriage Contracts in American Courts: Interpreting Mahr Agreements as Prenuptuals and Their Effect on Muslim Women' (2002) 76 Southern California Law Review 189, 197f.

36 Azizah Yahia al-Hibri, 'Muslim women's rights in the global village: challenges and opportunities' (2000) 15 The Journal of Law and Religion 37.

37 Marie-Claire Foblets, 'Moroccan Women in Europe: Bargaining for Autonomy' (2007) 64 Washington & Lee Law Review 1385.

38 Farida Deif, 'Divorced from justice' (2005) 1 Journal of Middle East Women's Studies 108; Richard A Debs, *Islamic Law and Civil Code: The Law of Property in Egypt.* (Columbia University Press 2010); Maitre Attiat El-Kharboutly and Aziza Hussein, 'Law and the Status of Women in the Arab Republic of Egypt' (1976) 8 Columbia Human Rights Law Review 35.

39 B Sivaramayya, *Matrimonial Property Law in India* (OUP 1999); Siobhan Mullally, 'Feminism and multicultural dilemmas in India: Revisiting the Shah Bano case' (2004) 24 Oxford Journal of Legal 671.

40 Saminaz Zaman, 'Amrikan Shari'a, The Reconstruction of Islamic Family Law in the United States' (2008) 28 South Asia Research 185; Asifa Quraishi and Najeeba Syeed-Miller, 'No Altars: A Survey of Islamic Family Law in United States' in Lynn Welchman (ed), *Women's Rights and Islamic Family Law: perspectives on reform* (Zed Books 2004).

41 PA Buttar, 'Muslim personal law in western countries: the case of Australia' (1985) 6 Journal Institute of Muslim Minority Affairs, Journal 271.

42 JND Anderson, 'The Family Law of Turkish Cypriots' (1958) Die Welt des Islams 161, 161.

43 CJ Hamson, The Istanbul Conference of 1955, (1956) 5 International & Comparative Law Quarterly 26, 29; Paul Magnarella, 'East Meets West: The Reception of West European Law in the Ottoman Empire and the Modern Turkish Republic' (1993) 2 Journal of International Law and Practice 281.

44 Seval Yildirim, 'Aftermath of a Revolution: A Case Study of Turkish Family Law' (2005) 17 Pace International Law Review 347, 359.

45 Arzu Oguz, 'Role of Comparative Law in the Development of Turkish Civil Law' (2005) 17 Pace International Law Review 373, 386.

46 June Starr, 'Role of Turkish Secular Law in Changing the Lives of Rural Muslim Women 1950–1970' (1989) 23 Law & Society Review 497.

47 Ihsan Yilmaz, 'Secular law and the emergence of unofficial Turkish Islamic law' (2002) 56 Middle East Journal 113.

48 Nurhan Süral, 'Legal Framework for Gender Equality' in World Bank Poverty Reduction and Evonimic Management Unit (ed), Working Paper on *Bridging the Gender Gap in Turkey: A Milestone Towards Faster Socio-economic Development and Poverty Reduction* (2003) 10, 16 < http://siteresources.worldbank.org/INTECAREG TOPGENDER/Resources/TurkeyCGA.pdf> accessed 21 July 2015.

49 Paul Magnarella, 'The reception of Swiss family law in Turkey' (1973) Anthropological Quarterly 100.

50 Paul Magnarella, 'Conjugal Role-Relationships in a Modernizing Turkish Town' (1972) International Journal of Sociology of the Family 179.

51 Birte Scholz, 'In Search of Equality: A Survey of Law and Practice Related to Women's Inheritance rights in the Middle East and North Africa (MENA) Region' (Centre of Housing Rights and Evictions 2006) <www.gewamed.net/share/img_documents/41_in_search_of_equity-_a_survey_of_law_and_practice_related_to_women_inheritance_rigths.pdf> accessed 29 July 2015; Ela Anıl and others, *The New Legal Status of Women in Turkey* (Women for Women's Human Rights 2002).

52 Saniye Dedeoglu, 'Equality, Protection or Discrimination: Gender Equality Policies in Turkey' (2012) 19 Social Politics: International Studies in Gender, State & Society 269; Esin Orucu 'Judicial navigation as official law meets culture in Turkey' (2008) 4 International Journal of Law in Context 35.

53 Seval Yildirim, 'The Search for Shared Idioms: Contesting Views of Laiklik Before the Turkish Constitutional Court' in Gabriele Marranci (ed), *Muslim Societies and the Challenge of Secularization: An Interdisciplinary Approach* (Springer 2010), 235.

54 Seval Yildirim, 'Aftermath of a Revolution: A Case Study of Turkish Family Law' (2005) 17 Pace International Law Review 347, 357ff.

55 Brett Scharffs and Suzanne Disparte, 'Comparative Models for Transitioning from Religious to Civil Marriage Systems' (2010) 12 Journal of Law and Family Studies 409, 422.

56 Shirin Akiner, 'Post Soviet Central Asia: Past is Prologue', in Peter Ferdinand (ed) *The New States Of Central Asia And Their Neighbours* (4th edn, Royal Institute of International Affairs Council on Foreign Relations Press 1994) 5.

57 Uralic L Krader and Altaic Series, *Peoples of Central Asia* (Curzon Press 1997) 125.

58 Gregory Maskarinec, 'Muslim Turkistan: Kazak Religion and Collective Memory' (2002) 104 American Anthropologist 991; Ingvar Svanberg, 'In search of a Kazakhstani identity' (1994) 2 Journal of Area Studies 113.

59 B Pasilov and A Ashirov, 'Revival of Sufi traditions in modern Central Asia: jahri zikr' and its ethnological features' (2007) 87 Oriente Moderno 163.

60 Martha Olcott, *The Kazakhs* (Hoover Institution Press 1995); Allen J Frank, *Muslim Religious Institutions in Imperial Russia: The Islamic World of Novouzensk District and the Kazakh Inner Horde* (Brill 2001) 1780–1910.

61 OI Brusina, 'Sharia and Civil Law in Marital Relations of the Muslim Population in Central Asia' (2008) 47 Anthropology & Archaeology of Eurasia 53.

62 Adrienne Lynn Edgar, 'Emancipation of the Unveiled: Turkmen Women under Soviet Rule, 1924–29' (2003) 62 The Russian Review 132; A Bennigson *The Islamic Threat to the Soviet State* (Pap-Board Printers 1984).

63 GJ Massell, *The Surrogate Proletariat: Moslem Woman and Revolutionary Strategies in Soviet Central Asia, 1919–1929* (Princeton University Press 1974) 196.

64 Gulnar Kendirbaeva, '"We are children of Alash . . ." The Kazakh intelligentsia at the beginning of the 20th century in search of national identity and prospects of the cultural survival of the Kazakh people' (1999) 18 Central Asian Survey 5; See also Saulesh Yessenova 'Routes and Roots of Kazakh Identity: Urban Migration in Postsocialist Kazakhstan' (2005) 64 The Russian Review 661.

65 Laura Yerekesheva, 'Religious identity in Kazakhstan and Uzbekistan: Global-local interplay' (2004) 28 Strategic Analysis 577.

66 Branka Rešetar, 'Matrimonial Property in Europe: A Link between Sociology and Family Law' (2008) 12 Electronic Journal of Comparative Law 1.

67 Samuel Kucherov, 'Property in the Soviet Union' [1962] The American Journal of Comparative Law 376.

68 P Makoveckii, *Materials for the Study of Legal Custom of Kirghizs* [Kazakhs] (in Russian, Materialy k izucheniju juridicheskih obychaev kirghiz) (1886) 31, <www.lib.okno.ru/ebook/11100405.pdf> accessed 29 July 2015.

69 Gani Aldashev and Catherine Guirkinger, 'Deadly anchor: Gender bias under Russian colonization of Kazakhstan.' (2012) 49 Explorations in Economic History 399.

70 Steven Hendrix, 'Legislative Reform of Property Ownership in Kazakhstan' (1997) 15 Development Policy Review 159, 164.

71 Renee Giovarelli and Jennifer Duncan, 'Women and land in Eastern Europe and Central Asia' in Patrick Webb and Katinka Weinberger (eds), *Women Farmers: Enhancing Rights and Productivity* (Rural Development Institute 1999) 26f.

72 FM Abugaliyeva, 'Joint Spousal Entrepreneurship' [2012] Modern Scientific Research and Their Practical Application; Committee on Elimination of Discrimination against Women, Kazakhstan Report (Chamber A 757th & 758th Meetings, 16 January 2007).

73 Janet Hunt-McCool and Lisa Granik, 'The Legal Status of Women in the New Independent States of the Former Soviet Union' (1994) Report prepaired for the USAID NIS Programme <http://pdf.usaid.gov/pdf_docs/pnabw057.pdf> accessed 29 July 2015.

74 Emmanuel Karagiannis, 'The Rise of Political Islam in Kazakhstan: Hizb Ut-Tahrir Al Islami' (2007) 13 Nationalism and Ethnic Politics 297.

75 Edward Snajdr, 'Gender, power, and the performance of justice: Muslim women's responses to domestic violence in Kazakhstan' (2008) 32 American Ethnologist 294.

76 Illiya I Alimaev and Roy H Behnke Jr, 'Ideology, land tenure and livestock mobility in Kazakhstan' in KA Galvin and others (eds), *Fragmentation in Semi-Arid and Arid Landscapes* (Springer 2008) 151.

77 Nora Dudwick, Karin Fock, and David J Sedik, *Land Reform and Farm Restructuring in Transition Countries: the experience of Bulgaria, Moldova, Azerbaijan, and Kazakhstan* (No 104, World Bank Publications 2007).

78 Hendrix (n 71) 164.

79 Suprihatin Atin, 'Status Harta Bersama Menurut Perspektif Undang-undang No 1 tahun 1974 dan Hukum Islam' [2012] Jurnal FAI: Maslahah 1.

80 John Bowen, *Islam, Law, and Equality in Indonesia: An Anthropology of Public Reasoning* (CUP 2003).
81 John Bowen, 'Intellectual Pilgrimages and Local Norms in Fashioning Indonesian Islam' (2008) 123 Revue des mondes musulmans et de la Méditerranée 37.
82 Jan Michiel Otto, 'Sharia and national law in Indonesia' in Jan Michiel Otto (ed), Sharia Incorporated: A Comparative Overview of the Legal Systems in Twelve Muslim Countries in Past and Present (Leiden: Leiden University Press 2010) 469.
83 Mark Cammack, 'Marital Property in California and Indonesia: Community Property and Harta Bersama' (2007) 64 Washington & Lee Law Review 1417.
84 Brown (n 26) 642.
85 See Fitzpatrick Harper, *Land, Inheritance and Guardianship Law in Aceh* (International Development Law Organisation 2006) 55f.
86 Lastarria-Cornhiel (n 27).
87 John Bowen, 'Fairness and law in an Indonesian court' in R Michael Feener and Mark E Cammack (eds), *Islamic Law in Contemporary Indonesia: Ideas and Institutions* (Harvard University Press 2007) 170, 177.
88 Adriaan Bedner and Stijn Van Huis, 'Plurality of marriage law and marriage registration for Muslims in Indonesia: a plea for pragmatism' (2010) 6 Utrecht Law Review 175.
89 Lastarria-Cornhiel (n 27) 4.
90 Brown (n 26).
91 Bowen (n 82) 37–54.
92 Ahmad Ibrahim, *The Status of Muslim Women in Family Law in Malaysia, Singapore and Brunei* (Malayan Law Journal 1965).
93 Andrew Harding, 'Islamic law in Malaysia' in E Cotran and C Mallat (eds) *Yearbook of Islamic and Middle Eastern Law* (2nd Vol, Kluwer Law International 1995) 61.
94 David J Banks, 'Islam and inheritance in Malaya: culture conflict or Islamic revolution?' (1976) 3 American Ethnologist 573.
95 Raihanah Abdullah, Patricia Martinez, and Wirdati Mohd, 'Islam and Adat' (2010) 38 Indonesia and the Malay World 161.
96 MB Hooker, *Adat Laws In Modern Malaya: Land Tenure, Traditional Government And Religion* (OUP 1976) 40.
97 RO Winstead and JE Kempe, 'A Malay Legal Miscellany' (1952) 1 Journal of the Malaysian Branch of the Royal Asiatic Society 1, 6.
98 Ahmad Ibrahim, *Family Law in Malaysia* (3rd edn, Malayan Law Journal 1997).
99 Norliah Ibrahim and Abdul Hak, 'Division of matrimonial property in Malaysia: the legal historical perspective' (2007) 15 Jurnal Jabatan Sejarah Universiti Malaya 143.
100 BC Crown, 'Property Division on Dissolution of Marriage' (1988) 30 Malaya Law Review 34.
101 *Roberts alias Kamarulzaman v Ummi Kalthom* [1966] 1 MLJ 163 (High Court).
102 Wing Cheong Chan, 'Giving homemakers due recognition: Five landmark cases on the road to gender equality' [2011] Singapore Journal of Legal Studies 111.
103 Ahmad Ibrahim, 'The Law Reform (Marriage and Divorce) Bill, 1975 [1975] Journal of Malaysian and Comparative Law 354.
104 *Rokiah bte Haji Abdul Jalil v Mohamed Idris bin Shamsudin* [1989] 3 MLJ ix, xv (Malay. Fed. Terr. App. Comm.).
105 Abdul Hamid Mohamed JCA, '*Sivanes a/l Rajaratnam v Usha Rani a/p Subramaniam* (2003) 3 Malayan Law Journal 273.
106 Wai Kum Leong, 'Division of Matrimonial Assets upon Divorce — Lessons from Singapore for Malaysian Practice' in Alan Tan Khee Jin and Azmi Sharom (eds),

Developments in Singapore and Malaysian Law (Marshall Cavendish Academic 2006) 246.

107 Maznah Mohamad, 'Islam, the secular state and Muslim women in Malaysia' (1989) Dossier 5/6 of Women Living Under Muslim Laws.

108 Zanariah Noor and Tanjung Malim, 'Gender Justice and Islamic Family Law Reform in Malaysia' (2007) 25 Kajian Malaysia 145.

109 Zainah Anwar and Jana S Rumminger, 'Justice and Equity in Muslim Family Laws: Challenges, Possibilities, and Strategies for Reform' (2007) 64 Washington & Lee Law Review 1529, 1548.

110 Beth Malchiodi, 'Assessing the Impact of the 2004 Moudawana on Women's Rights in Morocco' (Fulbright-Hays Summer Seminars Abroad 2008).

111 Foblets (n 38).

112 Presentation by Stephanie Willman Bordat, Program Director, Global Rights Field Office (MACECE, Rabat, 2 July 2008).

113 Katja Zvan Elliot, 'Reforming the Moroccan Personal Status Code: A Revolution for Whom?' (2009) 14 Mediterranean Politics: 213.

114 Stephanie Willman Bordat, Susan Schaefer Davis, and Saida Kouzzi, 'Women as Agents of Grassroots Change: Illustrating Micro-Empowerment in Morocco' (2011) 7 Journal of Middle East Women's Studies 90.

115 Global Rights (ed) *Conditions, Not Conflict: Promoting Women's Human Rights in the Maghreb through Strategic Use of the Marriage Contract* (Global Rights 2008).

116 Elliott (n 114).

117 Zahia Salhi, 'Algerian women, citizenship, and the Family Code' (2003) 11 Gender & Development 27.

118 Mina Baliamoune, 'The Making of Gender Equality in Tunisia and Implications for Development' (2012) World Bank World Development Report Background Paper <http://siteresources.worldbank.org/INTWDR2012/Resources/7778105-1299699968583/7786210-1322671773271/baliamoune.pdf> accessed 29 July 2015.

119 MM Charrad, 'Tunisia at the Forefront of the Arab World: Two Waves of Gender Legislation' (2007) 64 Washington and Lee Law Review 1513.

120 MM Charrad, *States and Women's Rights: The Making of Postcolonial Tunisia, Algeria, and Morocco* (University of California Press 2001).

121 Ziba Mir-Hosseini, *Marriage on Trial: A Study of Islamic Family Law* (IB Tauris 1993) 11.

122 Arzoo Osanloo, 'Whence the Law: The Politics of Women's Rights, Regime Change, and the Vestiges of Reform in the Islamic Republic of Iran'(2008) 101 Radical History Review 42, 52; see also Osanloo 'Islamico-civil 'rights talk': Women, subjectivity, and law in Iranian family court' (2006) 33 American Ethnologist 191.

123 Louise Halper, 'Law and Women's Agency in Post-Revolutionary Iran' (2005) 28 Harvard Journal of Law & Gender 85, 95

124 Mehranguiz Kar and Homa Hoodfar, 'Personal Status Law as Defined by the Islamic Republic of Iran', in Homa Hoodfar (ed), *Shifting Boundaries in Marriage and Divorce in Muslim Communities, Special Dossier* (Woman Living Under Muslim Laws 1996).

125 Osanloo (n 123) 53.

126 Cassandra Balchin, 'Family Law in Contemporary Muslim Contexts: Triggers and Strategies for Change' in Zainah Anwar (ed) *Wanted: Equality and Justice in the Muslim Family* (Musawah/Sisters in Islam 2009) 209.

127 Alison Graves, 'Women in Iran: Obstacles to Human Rights and Possible Solutions' (1996) 5 American University Journal of Gender, Social Policy & the Law 57.

128 Roksana Bahramitash, 'Iranian women during the reform era (1994–2004): A focus on employment' (2007) 3 Journal of Middle East women's studies 86.

129 Shobana Nelasco, 'A Study on Women Empowerment in South-Asian Countries: A Contemporary Analysis' (2012) 3 (16) Mediterranean Journal of Social Sciences 37.

130 AM Shaljan, 'Population, Gender and Development in Maldives' (2004) 39 Economic and Political Weekly 1835.

131 Committee on the Elimination of Discrimination against Women, 'Consideration of reports submitted by States parties under articles 18 of the Convention on the Elimination of All Forms of Discrimination against Women, Initial reports of States parties: Maldives' (1999) CEDAW/C/MDV/1, para 169 < http://daccess-dds-ny.un.org/doc/UNDOC/GEN/N99/211/34/IMG/N9921134.pdf?OpenElement> accessed 29 July 2015.

132 Andrew Byrnes and Marsha Freeman, 'The Impact of the CEDAW Convention: Paths to Equality' (2012) World Bank World Development Report Background Paper < http://siteresources.worldbank.org/INTWDR2012/Resources/7778105-1299699968583/7786210-1322671773271/Byrnes-and-Freeman-FINAL-18-May-2011-with-acknowledgements.pdf> accessed 29 July 2015.

133 James Read, 'A milestone in the integration of personal laws: the new law of marriage and divorce in Tanzania' (1972) 16 Journal of African Law 19; see also Reform Commission of Tanzania, 'Report on the Law of Marriage Act 1971' (1994) 2.3.1–2.3.2.

134 Rose Mtengeti-Migiro, 'The division of matrimonial property in Tanzania' (1990) 28 Journal of Modern African Studies 521.

135 Bart Rwezaura, 'Tanzania: Building a New Family Law Out of a Plural Legal System' (1995) 33 University of Louisville Journal of Family Law 523.

136 Mark Calaguas, Cristina M Drost, and Edward R Fluet, 'Legal Pluralism And Women's Rights: A Study In Postcolonial Tanzania' (2007) 16 Columbia Journal of Gender & Law 471.

137 Barthazar Rwezaura and Ulrike Wanitzek, 'Family law reform in Tanzania: a socio-legal report.' (1988) 2 International Journal of Law, Policy and the Family 1.

138 Tamar Ezer, 'Inheritance Law in Tanzania: The Impoverishment of Widows and Daughters' (2006) 7 Georgetown Journal of Gender and the Law 599.

139 *Bi Hawa Mohamed v Ally Sefu* [1983] TLR 32, 35.

140 Civil Appeal No 45 (Tanz High Ct 2001).

141 Rachel Howland and Ashley Koenen, *Divorce and Polygamy in Tanzania* (BePress 2011).

142 The LMA was modelled largely on a Kenyan proposal to reform its own family laws that urged reform and integration of the disparate systems of religious, customary, and law. See Mapendekazo ya Serikali juu ya Sheria ya Ndoa (Government's Proposals on Uniform Law of Marriage) (1969) Government Paper No 1.

143 Presentation by Nancy Baraza, Kenya Law Reform Commission, 'Family Law Reforms in Kenya: An Overview' (Heinrich Böll Foundation's Gender Forum in Nairobi, 30 April 2009).

144 *Fathiya Essa v Mohammed Essa* (Unreported) Civil Appeal No 101 of 1995 (Nairobi).

145 Abdulkadir Hashim, 'Muslim personal law in Kenya and Tanzania: Tradition and innovation' (2005) 25 Journal of Muslim Minority Affairs 449.

146 Rashida Manjoo, 'The Recognition of Muslim Personal Laws in South Africa: Implications for Women's Rights' (2007) Human Rights Program at Harvard Law School Working Paper No 08–21 <www.brandeis.edu/hbi/gcrl/images/RashidaWP.pdf> accessed 29 July 2015.

147 Kirstin Henrard, 'The Accommodation of Religious Diversity in South Africa against the Background of the Centrality of the Equality Principle in the New Constitutional Dispensation' (2001) 45 Journal of African Law 51.

148 C Rautenbach, NMI Goolam and N Moosa, 'Constitutional Analysis' in JC Bekker, C Rautenbach, and NMI Goolam (eds), *Introduction to Legal Pluralism in South Africa*, (Butterworths LexisNexis 2006) 151.

149 Christa Rautenbach, 'Islamic marriages in South Africa: Quo vadimus?' (2012) 69 Koers - Bulletin for Christian Scholarship 121.

150 N Gabru, 'Dilemma of Muslim women regarding divorce in South Africa' (2009) 7 Potchefstroom Electronic Law Journal/Potchefstroomse Elektroniese Regsblad.

151 *Ismail v Ismail*, 1983 (1) SA 1006 (A).

152 Firoz Cachalia, 'Citizenship, Muslim Family Law and a Future South African Constitution: A Preliminary Enquiry' (1993) 56 Tydskrif vir Hedendaagse Romeins-Hollandse Reg 392.

153 Abdulkader Tayob, 'The Struggle Over Muslim Personal Law in a Rights-Based Constitution: A South African Case Study' (2005) 22 Recht Van De Islam.

154 *Ryland v Edros 1997* (2) SA 690 (C), 705C.

155 *Amod v Multilateral Motor Vehicle Accidents Fund*, 1999 (4) SA 1319 (SCA).

156 *Daniels v Campbell NO and others*, 2004 (5) SA 331 (CC).

157 *Jamalodien v Moola,* NPD, unreported case number 1836/06 (2006).

158 Waheeda Amien, 'Overcoming the conflict between the Right to Freedom of Religion and Women's Rights to Equality: a South African case study of Muslim marriages' (2006) 28 Human Rights Quarterly 729.

159 Goodsell Erin, 'Constitution, Custom, and Creed: Balancing Human Rights Concerns with Cultural and Religious Freedom on Today's South Africa' (2007) 21 Brigham Young University Journal of Public Law 109.

160 Rashida Manjoo, 'Legislative Recognition of Muslim Marriages in South Africa' (2004) 32 International Journal of Legal Information 271.

161 Reference to Israel as made in this chapter relates to the pre-1967 borders of the State of Israel. Consequently, the discussion does not relate to East Jerusalem, or to any other territory occupied by Israel during the Six-Day War.

162 Ayelet Shachar, 'Group identity and women's rights in family law: the perils of multicultural accommodation' (1998) 6 Journal of Political Philosophy 285.

163 Ruth Lapidoth and Ora Ahimeir (eds), *Freedom of Religion in Jerusalem* (Jerusalem Institute for Israel Studies 1999).

164 Brian Capper, 'The Palestinian Cultural Context of Earliest Christian Community of Goods' in Richard Bauckham (ed), *The Book of Acts in Its First Century Setting* (Eerdmans 1995).

165 Ruth Halperin-Kaddari, *Women in Israel: A state of their own* (University of Pennsylvania Press 2003) 249.

166 Pascale Fournier, Pascal McDougall, and Merissa Lichtsztral, 'Secular Rights and Religious Wrongs-Family Law, Religion and Women in Israel' (2011) 18 William and Mary Journal of Women and Law 333.

167 Hoda Rouhana, 'Practices in the Shari'a Court of Appeal in Israel: Gendered Reading of Arbitration Decisions' (2003) Dossier 25: Women Living Under Muslim Laws.

168 Aharon Layish, 'Reforms in the Law of Personal Status of The Muslims in Israel Legislation and Application' (1994) 12 Recht van de Islam, 45.
169 Alean Al-Krenawi and John R Graham, 'Divorce among Muslim Arab women in Israel' (1998) 29 Journal of Divorce & Remarriage 103.
170 Adrien Katherine Wing and Shobhana Ragunathan Kasturi, 'Palestinian Women: Beyond the Basic Law' (1995) 13 Third World Legal Studies 141.
171 Ariel Rosen-Zvi, 'Family and Inheritance Law' in Amos Shapira and Keren C DeWitt-Arar (eds), *Introduction to the Law of Israel* (Kluwer Law International 1995).
172 *Bavli v Great Rabbinical Court* (1994) HCJ 1000/92, 48(2) Israel Supreme Court C 221, 48(2) *PD.*
173 Ruth Halperin-Kaddari, 'Rethinking Legal Pluralism in Israel: The Interaction Between the High Court of Justice and Rabbinical Courts' (1997) 20 Tel Aviv University Law Review 683 (Hebrew).
174 *Yemini v Great Rabbinical Court*, HCJ 9734/03 (2003).
175 Daphna Hacker, 'Religious Tribunals in Democratic States: Lessons from the Israeli Rabbinical Courts' (2010) 27 Journal of Law and Religion 59.
176 Shlomo Dichovski, 'Partition of Spousal Homes' (1991) 16–17 *Hebrew Law Yearbook* 501, 508; Shlomo Dichovski, 'The Joint Ownership Doctrine – is it *dina d'malchuta*?' (1998) 18 Tchumin 18.
177 Avraham Sherman, 'The Communal Property Division' – Is Not Grounded in Jewish Law, 19 *Thomin* 295 (Hebrew); See also Adam Hofri-Winogradow, 'The Acceleration of Israeli Legal Pluralism: The Rise of the New Religious-Zionist Halachic Private Law Courts' (2011) 34 Tel Aviv Law Review 47 (Hebrew).
178 Adam Hofri-Winogradow, 'The Muslim-Majority Character of Israeli Constitutional Law' (2010) 2 Middle East Law and Governance 43.
179 Pieternella van Doorn-Harder, *Women Shaping Islam: Reading the Qu'ran in Indonesia* (University of Illinois Press 2006).
180 Amina Wadud, *Qur'an and Woman: Rereading the Sacred Text from a Woman's Perspective* (OUP 1999).
181 Bowen (n 82).
182 Gregory Alexander, 'New Marriage Contract and the Limits of Private Ordering' (1997) 73 Indiana Law Journal 503.
183 Kathleen Miller, 'Who Says Muslim Women Don't Have the Right To Divorce? A Comparison Between Anglo-American Law and Islamic Law' (2009) 22 New York International Law Review 201, 225f., discussing how marriage contracts may be used to enhance a woman's access to divorce.
184 Moors (n 3).
185 Mir-Hosseini (n 122).
186 Global Rights (n 116).
187 Hafiz Nazeem Goolam, 'Gender Equality in Islamic Family Law: Dispelling Common Misconceptions and Misunderstandings' in Hisham Ramadhan (ed), *Understanding Islamic Law: From classical to contemporary* (AltaMira Press 2006) 117, 122.
188 Adriaan Bedner and Stijn Van Huis, 'Plurality of marriage law and marriage registration for Muslims in Indonesia: a plea for pragmatism' (2010) 6 Utrecht Law Review 175.
189 Rwezaura and Wanitzek (n 138).
190 Joseph English, 'Married Women and Their Property Rights: A Comparative View' (1961) 10 Catholic University Law Review 75.
191 *Bi Hawa Mohamed v Ally Sefu* TLR 32 (1983) 35f.

192 Tania Murray Li, 'Working separately but eating together: personhood, property, and power in conjugal relations' (1998) 25 American Ethnologist 675.

193 Amira Mashhour, 'Islamic law and gender equality: Could there be a common ground? A study of divorce and polygamy in Sharia law and contemporary legislation in Tunisia and Egypt' (2005) Human Rights Quarterly 562.

Index

access to justice: Egypt 115–6, 119–20; Gulf states 89; Iran 265; Pakistan 42, 54
adat/*'urf* (custom/customary law) 39, 62 n. 55, 228, 236, 239, 246, 247, 253, 273–6; Egypt 187, 235; Gulf states 85; Indonesia 258–60, 274; Iran 133; Israel 271, 273; Kazakhstan 256–8; Malaysia 260–1; Pakistan 40–3, 44–5, 54, 62 n. 55; South Africa 269; Tanzania 267–8; Turkey 254–5
admissibility of litigation 6–7; Egypt 114–9, 121–2; Gulf states 88; South Africa 269; Tunisia 71, 75
adoption (*tabanni*) 7, 55; interreligious 70, 71, 73, 74, 154, 166, 174; Algeria 179 n. 69; Israel 209, 213, 270; Morocco 179 n. 69; Tunisia 68, 70–1, 73–4, 76, 154, 157, 165–6, 172, 174
adoul (notary) 263–65, 274
adultery/fornication/sex outside of marriage (*zina'*) 227; Egypt 182, 242; Nigeria 127 n. 65; Pakistan 53–4, 56–7, 67 n. 122; Tunisia 178 n. 53
Anglo-Muhammadan law/Anglicization of Islamic law 35, 39–42, 44

best interests/welfare of the child (*maslahat al-mahdun*/*al-tifl*) 7, 8; Gulf states 100–2, 103; Israel 211; Tunisia 68–9, 71, 74–6, 100–3, 154–5, 163–66, 169, 172–4, 211

Caliphate 17, 28, 33 n. 50, 254
CEDAW 86; Gulf states 86, 92–3, 106 n. 24; Maldives 266; Tunisia 74, 75, 175
centralisation (of the state) 116, 120–1
citizen/-ship 20, 23, 24, 29; Egypt 21, 130 n. 97; Libya 31 n. 27 and 31; Tunisia 73–4; Gulf states 107 n. 41
codification 3–9, 18–9, 35, 37–8, 46, 54, 84–5, 93, 113, 237; Egypt 113–15, 181, 197, 240; Gulf states 83–4, 85–7, 89–93, 102–3; Iran 132; Iraq 92, 109 n. 67; Pakistan 35, 41–47, 54; selectivity 39, 46, 55, 93, 101, 237; Sudan 18; Tunisia 68, 69, 156
colonization 39–44, 50–2, 54, 57, 84
common law 246, 250–1, 276; Kenya 268; Pakistan 35, 39–41, 44, 50–1, 57–8, 62 n. 43; Tanzania 276
contribution to family income 245, 246, 247, 248, 250, 251–3, 275; Indonesia 259–60; Iran 137, 143; Malaysia 260–2; Morocco 263; Tanzania 267–8
conversion: Tunisia 154–5, 159–61, 165–7, 174; Israel 204
courts/tribunals 2; *adat* 256; colonial 39–40, 156; Druze 208, 212; ecclesiastical 210; Egypt 114–15, 120, 125 n. 36, 186, 199 n. 39 and 40, 240; family 86–7, 89, 186, 199 n. 40, 210, 263–5; Federal Shariat Court 48, 50, 58; Gulf states 86–7, 89–90; Islamic/Muslim 206, 254, 259–60; Indonesia 259–60; Iran 265; Israel 204–22; Jewish Beth Din 248; Kazakhstan 256; Malaysia 261–2; *milla* courts 237; Morocco 263–4; Pakistan 39–40, 48, 50, 58; rabbinical 68, 156, 206–7, 209, 211–14, 218; religious 68, 70, 153, 204–6, 208–12, 214–18, 237, 259; secular/civil 68, 86, 156, 204, 206, 208–9, 210–12, 214–18, 259; Sharia 68, 114–15, 120, 125 n. 36, 156, 199 n. 39 , 205–6, 209–10, 211–12, 216, 237, 256, 259, 262; Tunisia 68, 70, 153, 156, 264
custody (*hidana*) 4, 6, 13 n. 22, 21, 100–1, 236; Egypt 195, 196, 199 n. 33, 203 n. 122; Gulf states 89, 100–2, 103, 112 n.

120; interreligious 6, 70, 71, 100–2, 154–5, 164, 172, 211–2; Iran 266; Israel 209, 210, 211–2, 236; Morocco 262; South Africa 269; Tunisia 68, 70, 71, 74–5, 154–5, 164, 172–4, 178 n. 58

customary law *see adat*

difference of religion: Gulf states 101–2; Israel 211–2; Tunisia 71–2, 154–5, 157–61, 166–7, 169–71, 174, 177 n. 36

divorce 5, 6–7, 21–2, 47, 51, 55, 64 n. 78 and 83, 95–6, 98, 181–2, 184, 237–40; compensation for (*mut'a/mut'at al-talaq*) 96, 98–9, 103, 137–8, 143, 185, 195–6, 199 n. 31; Egypt 5, 75, 83, 96, 104 n. 2, 123, 130 n. 100, 181–203; *get* (letter of divorce) 213, 214, 220 n. 77; on grounds of harm/damage (*darar/zarar*) 18, 21–2, 43–4, 132, 137–8, 154, 167–9, 181–4, 186–94, 197; Gulf states 88–9, 95–9, 103, 110 n. 94 and 96, 111 n. 102; Iran 131–2, 136–40, 148 n. 64; Israel 204, 213, 214; Jordan 104 n. 4, 236; by *khul'/ mukhala'* (consensual/by compensation) 6, 13 n. 16, 36, 47, 51–2, 56, 64 n. 85, 75, 83, 95–8, 103, 104 n. 2 and 4, 110 n. 94 and 96, 111 n. 102, 123, 130 n. 100, 148 n. 64, 181, 184–6, 192, 194–6, 198 n. 27, 236, 239; by *li'an* (oath of damnation) 8, 227–8, 242; Morocco 6; by *mubara'a/ mubarat* (mutual consent) 51, 148 n. 64; Pakistan 43–4, 46–7, 51–7, 59 n. 4, 63 n. 61, 64 n. 78 and 83; registration of 53–4; Sudan 18; by *talaq* (unilateral divorce by husband/repudiation) 6, 18, 47, 51, 53, 55–6, 58, 59 n. 4, 64 n. 83, 68–9, 73–6, 78 n. 23, 88, 95–6, 98–9, 111 n. 102, 136–7, 139, 156, 193, 195, 196; Tunisia 6, 68–9, 73–6, 78 n. 23, 98, 154, 156, 167–9, 176 n. 14

empowerment of women 42, 62 n. 55, 103, 259, 266

equality, gender 3, 17–9, 21–4, 35–8, 95, 247–8, 252–3, 276; Egypt 20, 32 n. 39; Gulf states 95; Indonesia 258; Iran 265; Iraq 22; Israel 215, 217, 273; Kazakhstan 258; Malaysia 260; Morocco 262; Tunisia 69, 70, 72–6, 78 n. 23, 153, 155–6, 171–2, 264; Turkey 22, 255

erroneous cohabitation/sexual relations entered into in error (*wat' bi-shubha*) 7, 132, 144 n. 11; Iran 132; Tunisia 7

evidence/proof 116–8, 122, 190; Egypt 115–20, 122, 183–4, 187, 190–1, 201 n. 73, 74, and 78; Pakistan 42; Tunisia 161–3, 172–3, 264

fault, principle of 6–7, 132, 137, 143, 249, 276; Egypt 83, 183, 199 n. 31; Gulf states 96, 98–9, 103; Iran 132, 136–7, 139, 143, 265; Malaysia 260; Tunisia 98, 103

filiation *see nasab*; *see also* paternity

firash (presumption of paternity) 13 n. 20, 117; Egypt 116–8, 122; Tunisia 162–3, 177 n. 41

freedom of conscience/religion: Israel 215, 216, 217; Tunisia 10, 69–71, 73–4, 155, 170–1

gender roles 4, 20–1, 34, 64 n. 70, 100, 131, 142–3, 225, 252; Gulf states 100; Indonesia 260; Iran 131, 142–3; Kazakhstan 257–8; Morocco 262; Tunisia 168; Turkey 254

guardianship (*wilaya*): for children 4–7, 38, 68, 74, 100, 146 n. 42, 236; in marriage 38, 88, 93–4, 230, 235–6; Gulf states 88, 93–4, 100; Iran 146 n. 42; Jordan 230, 236; Morocco 94; Tunisia 68, 74, 156, 163, 165–6

Halakha (Jewish law) 1, 204–6, 211, 213–14, 216, 218

halala/tahlil (marriage to a third party) 55–58

human/fundamental rights 7–8, 10, 19–20, 30 n. 17, 34, 36, 59 n. 2, 247, 248; Egypt 186, 242; Israel 204, 215–17; South Africa 270; Tunisia 68–70, 74–6, 155, 169–70, 172, 174–5

'idda (waiting period) 230–1, 239, 275; Egypt 195, 200 n. 57; Gulf states 99, 111 n. 113; Indonesia 275; Pakistan 53, 56

ijtihad (interpretative reasoning) 3, 10, 14 n. 23, 50–2, 58, 191, 276

ikhtilaf al-fuqaha' (diversity of opinions) 36, 38, 40, 52–5, 58

imprisonment: Pakistan 47, 53; Egypt 114–5, 188–9; Iran 134–5, 251

indigenous legal norms: Pakistan 40, 42; Indonesia 258

inheritance 21–2, 35, 37, 57, 68, 71, 141–3, 227, 245–6, 249, 252, 273; interreligious

70–1, 74, 154–5, 157–61, 169–71; Iran 141–3; Iraq 22; Pakistan 43, 48; Tunisia 68, 70–1, 74, 154–5, 157–61, 163, 165, 169–72, 178 n. 53; Egypt 113, 115–16, 118–19, 128 n. 73; Kazakhstan 257–8; Indonesia 259; Morocco 262; Tanzania 267–8; testamentary dispositions 113, 115–16, 118–19, 128 n. 73; Tunesia 154; Turkey 22; South Africa 269
interreligious law: adoption 70–1, 73–4, 154, 166, 174; custody 6, 70–1, 100–2, 154–5, 164, 172, 211–2; Egypt 119; Gulf states 100–2; inheritance 70, 71, 74, 154–5, 157–61, 169–72; Israel 211–2, 214; marriage 5, 70, 71–2, 74, 102, 154–5, 157–61, 167, 169–71, 177 n. 36, 212, 214, 237; Tunisia 70, 71, 73–4, 153–5, 157–61, 164, 166–7, 169–72, 177 n. 36
ISIS/SIC 28, 33 n. 50
Islamic law, interpretation of 11, 35–8, 44, 52, 236, 247–49, 252; Egypt 113, 186; Gulf states 83, 85, 102; Indonesia 274; Morocco 262–3; Pakistan 40, 48, 49, 50, 52–5, 57
Islamization: Iran 22; Pakistan 43, 45–7, 50–8, 59 n. 5; Sudan 59 n. 5; Tunisia 71, 160, 166; Turkey 255

judges, discretionary powers of 6, 9–11, 12 n. 3; Egypt 181, 183–4, 187, 189–93; Gulf states 98, 100–1, 103; Iran 265; Malaysia 262; Morocco 12 n. 6; Pakistan 49–51, 98; Tanzania 268; Tunisia 153–5, 157, 158, 163–9

khul'/mukhala' (divorce by compensation/consensual) 13 n. 16, 36, 47, 51, 56, 64 n. 85, 75, 83, 96–7, 104 n. 2, 184, 192, 239; Egypt 75, 83, 96, 123, 130 n. 100, 181, 184–6, 192, 194–6, 198 n. 27; Gulf states 95–8, 103, 110 n. 94 and 96, 111 n. 102; Iran 148 n. 64; Jordan 96, 104 n. 4, 236; Morocco 6; Pakistan 47, 51–2, 56; Tunisia 75

li'an (oath of damnation) 8, 227–8, 242

ma'dhun (marriage registrar/notary): Gulf states 88; Egypt 114–5, 130 n. 100, 184, 195, 239–42, 239–41, 242
mahr/sadaq (dower) 131, 132, 227, 229–35, 237–9, 242, 245, 251, 275–6; Egypt 75, 96, 185, 188, 195–6, 199 n. 32; Gulf states 87–8, 96–8; Iran 131–5, 137–8, 144 n. 13 and 14, 251, 265–6; Israel 271; Kazakhstan 257; Tunisia 75
maintenance/alimony (*nafaqa/nafaqih*) 21, 131–2, 138, 143, 182, 242, 245, 252–53; Egypt 115, 117, 120, 182–3, 185, 195–6, 198 n. 13, 200 n. 57; Indonesia 275; Iran 131–2, 136, 138, 143, 265; Israel 270–1; South Africa 269; Tunisia 163, 167–8
marriage 5–6, 7, 21, 39, 136–7, 143, 188, 226–7, 229–30, 236; age 5, 65 n. 90, 72, 88, 104 n. 8, 143, 150 n. 111, 153, 156, 236, 241, 264, 271; certificates 95, 132–3, 136–9, 143, 240, 241; civil 213–14, 216–17, 268–9; conclusion of 72, 93–4, 133, 230, 236; contracts/pre-nuptial agreements 8–9, 36, 95, 132, 136, 191, 201 n. 84, 225–44, 244 n. 34, 249–52, 254, 259, 263–6, 271, 274–5; costs of 87–8; Egypt 117, 119, 120–2, 181, 183–4, 188, 190–3, 241–2; Gulf states 87–8, 93–5, 102–3; impediments to 5, 72, 154–5, 157–61, 167, 169–70, 177 n. 36, 212, 217; informal 72–3, 116–17, 119, 120–2, 228–9, 241–2; interreligious 5, 70, 71–2, 74, 102, 154–5, 157–61, 167, 169–71, 177 n. 36, 212, 214, 237; Iran 117, 136–7, 143, 150 n. 111, 265; Israel 204, 207, 212–14, 216–17, 271; Jordan 236, 244 n. 34; Morocco 5, 7, 117, 252; temporary (*mut'a*) 111 n. 107; nature/purpose of 39, 136–137, 143, 188; Pakistan 39, 47, 49–50, 61 n. 24, 65 n. 90, 117; as a partnership 38, 137, 153, 157, 246–7, 250–1, 254, 266; registration of 47, 88, 116–17, 213, 217, 228–9, 232–3, 239–41; religious 212, 217; Saudi Arabia 104 n. 8; South Africa 269; Tunisia 5, 7, 21, 68–76, 117, 121–3, 124 n. 5, 153, 154–5, 157–61, 167, 169–72, 177 n. 36, 264; Turkey 124 n. 5; validity of 71–2, 93, 132, 159–60, 162, 213–14
matrimonial property regimes 5, 133, 135, 249; acquisition of 250, 255; Algeria 5; community of property 5, 68, 131, 246–7, 249–50, 253, 255, 257, 259, 269–70; contractual regimes 255, 265, 270; default regime 246, 249, 255–6, 269–70; distribution of 249–51; Gulf states 96; Indonesia 5, 246–7, 250, 253, 258–60, 273–75; Iran 131, 133, 135–7, 246–47, 250–51, 253, 265–266; Kazakhstan 246–7, 253, 256–8, 273–4; Malaysia 246–47, 253, 260–2, 273–4; Maldives, 246–7, 253,

266–7, 273–4; Morocco 5, 246–7, 250, 253, 262–4, 273–4, separation of property 5, 96, 135, 245, 247, 249, 253–4, 271; Tunisia 5, 68, 246–47, 253, 264, 273–74; Turkey 246–7, 249, 253, 254–6, 273–4
millet system 237; Israel 205, 217

name law: Egypt 130 n. 95, 242; Maledives 266; Tunisia 165, 179 n. 73
nasab (filiation) 162, 242; Egypt 117–8; Gulf states 110 n. 74; Tunisia 154–5, 157–8, 161–3, 172–3
nationality: Egypt 29 n. 13, 122; Gulf states 107 n. 41; Jordan 243 n. 2; Tunisia 68, 70, 72, 156
nikah 246, 250–1, 259, 274

obedience of the wife (*tamkin*) 37–8, 131–2, 136, 139, 157, 168, 182

paternity 7–8, 117, 226–7, 241–2; Egypt 113, 115–18, 120, 122, 241–2; Morocco 7–8, 13 n. 21; Tunisia 7, 154–5, 162, 163
patriarchy/patriarchal society 2, 27, 34, 37, 39, 55, 58, 68, 175, 228, 230, 236, 242–3, 253, 276; Egypt 186; Gulf states 92; Israel 210
piecemeal reform: 19, 59; Egypt 108 n. 47, 114; Gulf states 87; Pakistan 35, 45, 49
plurality/hybridity of law 250; Egypt 240; Pakistan 35–6, 41–2, 54; Tunisia 155, 156
polygamy 5, 21, 49–50, 65 n. 102, 124 n. 5, 191–2, 227, 237, 241, 243, 244 n. 34, 252; Egypt 181, 183–4, 190–3; Gulf states 93, 94–5, 103; Iran 265; Israel 271; Morocco 252; Pakistan 47, 49–50, 61 n. 24; Tunisia 5, 21, 68–9, 73–6, 124 n. 5, 153, 156, 264; Turkey 124 n. 5
post-marital claims 131, 133, 137–8; Egypt 185, 195–6, 198 n. 30; Gulf states 96; Iran 136–41, 148 n. 74; *mut'at al-talaq* 96, 98–9, 103, 137–8, 143, 185, 195–6, 199 n. 31; *nihlih* 148 n. 74; reimbursement of expenses incurred by the wife 141; *ujrat ul-misl* (compensation for household work) 131, 138–41
private international law: Tunisia 72, 75, 164, 173–4; Egypt 119–20
procedural law 21; Egypt 108 n. 47, 113–17, 119–22, 124 n. 8, 184, 186, 190; Gulf states 87–9, 106 n. 19; Iran 135, 265; Pakistan 40, 53
property rights 5, 248–51, 253, 274–5; Indonesia 259–60, 274; Iran 265–6; Israel 272–3; Kazakhstan 257–8; Kenya 268; Maldives 266; Tanzania 267–8; Turkey 254

qiwama/qayyim 34, 36–9, 57, 225, 230, 236–7

Rashid Commission (Pakistan) 46–7, 50
reception of Western laws 10, 253, 275; Egypt 114–15, 240; Iran 265; Turkey 254
recognition of foreign judicial decisions 70–1, 74, 154, 164–6
repudiation *see talaq*
reputed spouses (Israel) 7, 212, 213, 217
revolutions 17–33; Bahrain 20; Egypt 20–1, 26–7, 32 n. 40; Iran 18, 22, 27; Islamist movements 19–20, 27–8; Lebanon 27; Libya 28; nonviolence 17–8, 25, 28–9, 32 n. 40; Syria 20, 27–8, 32 n. 40; Tunisia 20, 26; violence against women 26–9; women 17–8, 20, 26–9, 32 n. 40; Yemen 25, 32 n. 40

siyasa shar'iyya 115
status quo agreement 206, 207, 216
succession *see* inheritance
Sufism 256, 273

takhayyur (eclecticism) 18, 23, 185
talaq (unilateral divorce by husband/repudiation) 47, 51, 55–6, 59 n. 4, 64 n. 83, 95, 98; Egypt 193, 195, 196; Gulf states 8, 95–6, 98–9, 111 n. 102; Iran 136–7, 139; Libya 78 n. 23; Morocco 6; Pakistan 47, 51, 53, 55–6, 58; Sudan 18; Tunisia 6, 68–9, 73–6, 78 n. 23, 156
talfiq (law-shopping) 23, 185–6
Taliban 54

ujrat ul-misl (compensation for household work) 131, 138–41
'*urf see adat*

wali/vali see guardianship
women, participation in the public sphere 20, 23–4; Egypt 26, 32 n. 39, 194, 203 n. 108 and 111; Iraq 24; Libya 24–5, 31 n. 31; Tunisia 24, 26
women's rights groups 19, 86; Egypt 186, 203 n. 108, 242; Gulf states 86, 87, 89–93; Iran 266; Libya 24; Morocco 19; Pakistan 46, 61 n. 24

zina' see adultery